FOR LOVE & MONEY

FOR LOVE & MONEY

A Writing Life

1969–1989

JONATHAN RABAN

1817

An Edward Burlingame Book

HARPER & ROW, PUBLISHERS, New York
Grand Rapids, Philadelphia, St. Louis, San Francisco
London, Singapore, Sydney, Tokyo

FIRST U.S. EDITION

LIBRARY OF CONGRESS CATALOG CARD NUMBER 89-45058

ISBN 0-06-016166-3

89 90 91 92 93 HC 10 9 8 7 6 5 4 3 2 1

To my parents,
Peter and Monica Raban

CONTENTS

FOR LOVE & MONEY

I

This is partly a collection, partly a case-history. I've clocked up nearly twenty years as a professional writer, and in that time I've made the intimate acquaintance of all of Cyril Connolly's enemies of promise, with the sole exception of the pram in the hall. I've written out of compulsion, for love, and I've needed the money. It is a curious occupation, this business of short-distance commuting between the bedroom and the study, and a subject in its own right. It puzzles people. Strangers at parties, striking up a "literary" conversation, don't (usually) want to haggle over the contents of your review of Martin Amis in last week's *Observer*, let alone whether your most recent book got off to a bad start in the first chapter. They have quite probably read neither, but they're still interested. They want to know whether you use a pen or a typewriter, what time you get up in the morning, whether you keep regular working hours, whether you can really make a living from it and – the big clincher – exactly what and how you get paid. Average-adjusters, lecturers in economics, shoe salesmen, property developers, don't wince, shuffle and gaze distractedly at the ceiling when someone politely asks "And what do *you* do?" For the professional writer that question (which is quickly followed by "Oh, should I know your name?") is the prelude to a searching catechism of a kind more appropriate to a VAT inspector than to a fellow-guest in a drawing room. The safest response to it, if you can summon the requisite bottle, is to say "I'm a steeplejack" and beam ferociously.

Alternatively, you might answer the catechism by hauling your surprised questioner off for a weekend to give them the works – the hours, the commissions, the block, the aborted beginnings, the continuous themes that slip from fiction to non-fiction and back to fiction again, the double-spacing, the advances, expenses, public lending right, royalties, and the editorial advantages of using wide margins. Part of this book consists of blue-pencilled scenes from that weekend, because the questions *are* worth answering. Conditions on New Grub Street change with every generation. The world originally described by Gissing in the 1880s connects with, but is significantly different from, the world described by Cyril Connolly in the 1930s and '40s. Mine, in turn, is different from Connolly's; and someone now in their twenties, setting out as a professional writer in the late 1980s, would encounter a working world much changed since I first knew it in 1969. This is a particular story, of someone born in 1942 who wanted to be a writer and found himself working in a very specific set of industrial and economic circumstances. How did he come to get the job, and what sort of a job is it?

I was eight or nine when I knew that I was – in the merely occupational sense of the word – a writer. It was a knowledge founded on no evidence at all of any special verbal or imaginative talent. Yet it was a fact, just like the fact that I was asthmatic. I was a writer. More precisely, I was an author. For writers, or so I supposed, actually did quite a bit of writing, moving fast from one piece of paper to the next. Authors were as immobile as waxworks. They sat at desks in photographs. The paraphernalia of their trade – expensive fountain pens, gilt-edged blotting pads, silver inkwells, marbled notebooks – were arranged in tasteful still-lives in front of them. They had the glossy hair and jutting chins of matinée idols. They were – oh, A. E. Coppard, Edgar Wallace, Michael Gilbert, Nevil Shute, H. E. Bates – and I could feel the glow of their fame radiating out from their pictures to include me.

It was what I was going to be: a personage in a photograph by Karsh of Ottawa. It seemed a reasonable ambition, not because anyone had yet suspected that I could write, but because I enjoyed a secret intimacy with authors, all authors, that was conspicuously lacking from my relations with any other human beings. They might not know it yet, but I was one of them; and this perverse conviction was the tranquillizing drug on which I dosed myself, several times a day, through ten years of childhood and adolescence.

Outside these daydreams of literary celebrity, I cut a fairly sorry figure. It was the old, too-often-written story of the "delicate child", packed off at eleven to a school of daunting military and athletic traditions, where milksops were not suffered gladly. Fusewire-thin from several years of a wasting disease called coeliac, the boy wheezed when he moved, and sounded as if he'd trapped a flight of herring gulls inside his chest: he was no asset as anyone's friend. So (and this is how the story always goes) the child made friends with books instead.

Books admitted me to their world open-handedly, as people, for the most part, did not. The life I lived in books was one of ease and freedom, worldly wisdom, glitter, dash and style. I loved its intimacy, too – the way in which I could expose to books all the private feelings that I had to shield from the frosty and contemptuous outside world. In books you could hope beyond hope, be heartbroken, love, pity, admire, even cry, all without shame.

No author ever despised me. They made me welcome in their books, never joked about my asthma and generally behaved as if I was the best company in the world. For this I worshipped them. I read and read and read – under the bedclothes with an illegal torch, surreptitiously in lessons with an open book on my knees, through long cathedral sermons, prep, and on the muddy touchlines ("*Kill him, Owen!*") of rugby pitches, to which I was drafted as a supporter. I did not then see any logical hiatus in the proposition that since I was happy only when I was with authors, I must therefore by definition be an author myself.

I had long ago discovered the trick of switching the world off like a light and entering fictions of my own. First, you had to let the room full of boys drift out of focus and wait for their voices to dissolve into a blur of white noise. Then – *Jim turned on his heel. The smoke from the cigarette in his ivory holder rose in slow coils. "Let's go," he said, picking his way, agile as a mountain buck, through the huge boulders of the tinder-dry watercourse* . . . Jim was my heroic alter ego. His chronicles were never written, but they lay in my head as accessible and as palpable as memories. He began as the natural leader of a band of men called The Marines, whom he conducted round the world on adventures that were a distillation of all the best bits of Buchan, Edgar Wallace, W. W. Jacobs and Conan Doyle. Jim, who was sometimes called The Captain, smoked a lot, drank Green Chartreuse, solved crimes, found things for people, did a great deal of camping out, spent whole days fishing, and every so often led his men off to wars fought with épées and sabres.

The story was continuous and I could slip into it at will, anywhere. Jim lasted me for several years; he had as much stamina as a character in Anthony Powell's *Music of Time*. Like Widmerpool, Jim altered with the years. When I was thirteen he hung up his sword, changed his tipple to malt whisky and fell head over heels for a girl called

Clarissa, whom he rescued from burning houses, runaway stallions, a cad with a Bentley and a Chinaman in the white slave trade. Clarissa was a clinging, lissom, wispy girl who cried easily. She and Jim went in for bouts of tender kissing but never, as I remember, got beyond Number 3.

But I grew ashamed of him. It was painful to see so transparently through the artifice of one's own fiction and recognize the facts it was meant to palliate and disguise; and I began to suffer from daydreamer's block. I hit on a more naked and modern form of autobiographical fiction. The new trick was to turn whatever was happening in the present into the past tense and the third person. Walking from School House to the library building, I thought: *He walked to the library. A cold smile played round his lips. The avenue of trees, heavy and dusty with summer, closed round his head. He was thinking of death.* This sort of thing could go on for hours at a time, an epic plotless melodrama into which I absentmindedly withdrew and from which I sometimes needed to be roused by brute force.

I suppose it happens to almost everyone, or at least to almost every adolescent, this urge to constantly rewrite one's experience in terms more glamorous and significant than those in which it's actually happening. But when the urge is hopelessly muddled up with dreams of authorship, and one hears the words falling in one's skull in complete, plagiarized sentences, the symptoms of *scribendi cacoethes* are probably incurable.

In any case, I was now on a serious training scheme for authorship. I sent away to all the postal schools whose ads claimed that your pen could pay for your holiday. From the Regent College of Successful Writing I got a free copy of a booklet called *101 Infallible Plot Situations*. The situations weren't much in themselves. They went something like:

> 17. X contrives system of perfect murder. Confides it to Y. Y puts it into practice, but knows that X alone will know he's guilty.

> 18. Girl's dog goes missing. Found by stranger. Subsequent relationship between girl and stranger.

> 19. Eccentric conditions of wills.

> 20. Tribulations of lovers from widely differing social backgrounds. Resolution of same by third party.

As the introduction explained, all 101 situations were everyday occurrences, not plots in themselves. Yet when you combined three (or, if you were suitably experienced, even more), you had a unique plot, never before used by any of the world's top novelists and masters of the short story, involving dog, girl, stranger, perfect murder, eccentric will, class conflict and third party, with fire and theft to boot. With *101 Infallible Plot Situations*, you could evolve narratives of such dazzling originality that in half an hour the merest tyro could out-Dickens Dickens.

I kept a notebook of plots. I also bought a little orange monthly magazine called *The Writer*, whose articles were calculated to flatter and feed the ambitions of 14-year-old authors. There were articles about how to write a successful Letter to the Editor, about how to choose your *nom-de-plume* (Nosmo King was thought a particularly apt and witty example), about margins, spacing, return postage and the absolute necessity of the twist-*dénouement*. The contributors all affected an airy sophistication about their trade that I found toxic ("Writing the *short* short story, I prefer to take one bite at the cherry, at most two . . . ").

I was almost there. I had a stock of plots, I knew how to lay out the title page of a manuscript, I knew it was pure folly to try using foolscap paper (*always* stick to quarto), I knew about swift, vivid characterization, how to cut down on description and when to introduce the Surprise Revelation. The profession of authorship lay wide open, and beyond the doors stood Karsh of Ottawa ready with his camera. I could see my stories already printed in *Lilliput, Men Only, Wide World, Tit-Bits* and all the other "outlets", as I'd learned to call them, where the literature of the twentieth century was being forged.

It took a little while to discover that I'd fallen for a sad, shabby, sub-literate version both of writing and of being a writer. It was shattered, and not before time, by the experience of reading. Drawn to the book by its title (I'd never heard of its author), I read Joyce's *Portrait of the Artist as a Young Man*. I hadn't realized. I'd thought that novels were cleverly contrived escapes from the world, and that writing them must be something a bit like fretwork. *Portrait of the Artist* made the reader live in its language, and made him live more arduously, more unhappily, more intelligently in the book than he had ever lived in the world. It made some obscure but fundamental change to the essential grammar of things. I read it with excitement and shock, three times over in quick succession, dazed to find myself simultaneously so deep in a book and so deep in the world. Every work of literature turns the successful collaborative reader of it into its co-author. In an important sense, we write what we read. My *Portrait of the Artist* defined my brimstone relations with my father and my family, with my boarding school and with my shamed sense of sexuality. Reading it, I stole it from Joyce and wrote it for myself; and as I went on reading I saw that if *this* was writing, it disenfranchised every book I'd read up to this moment. It turned *The Writer* and *101 Infallible Plot Situations* into facetious piffle.

That sense of literature as an astounding private discovery is hard to bring back without sounding either superior or over-flushed with romance. The books themselves now have the ring of items on a syllabus: Joyce, Hemingway's short stories, Salinger's *Catcher in the Rye*, Iris Murdoch's *Under The Net* . . . nothing much that is out of the way there, yet in 1958 each one happened for me like an accident on a wet road, sending the world into a spin.

I was academically backward, and a more sophisticated 16-year-old would probably have taken these novels more casually in his stride. But the boys I was at school with were not sophisticated either: they went in for *Motor Sport*, Leslie Charteris and Hank Janson, and thought that Hemingway's *In Our Time* was lousy value as a swap. We did our Goon Show imitations, listened to Radio Luxemburg, the Station of the Stars, and tried to set light to each other's farts. It was not like Cyril Connolly's Eton at all.

I left the school with a handful of mediocre O-levels and was transferred to the sixth form of a very civilized co-educational grammar school, where the girls read D. H. Lawrence and the boys read John Betjeman and Evelyn Waugh. Hadn't I read *Scoop*? *Women In Love*? *Black Mischief*? *The Waste Land*? *Summoned by Bells*? Actually, no. It took me at least a fortnight of whirlwinding round between the Lymington public library and the vicarage just outside the town to catch up with the literary circle in which I now moved. My target was to gut ten books a week – one a day from Mondays to Fridays, and five in the course of each weekend. I was paying little more attention to my formal lessons than I had done at boarding school, but I was reading Eliot, Beckett, Pound, Lawrence, Amis's *Lucky Jim*, Wain's *Hurry on Down*, Olivia Manning, Sartre's *La Nausée*, Kerouac's *On The Road*, Ginsberg's *Howl*, all of Christopher Isherwood, Mailer's *The Naked and the Dead*, Anouilh, O'Neill, John Osborne, Wodehouse, Waugh. Racing through to catch the flavour, I worked like a reviewer with a deadline.

I'd found serious competition. Iris, who sat across the aisle from me in English classes, was also going to be a writer. In the second week of term she announced in a deep, actressy voice that she wanted nothing to do with babies and that it was woman's higher calling to give birth to books. I was torn between craven infatuation and affronted pride. Like Hitler and Mussolini settling their differences over the Austrian border, Iris and I became allies, then friends.

Iris was a Lawrentian. She'd discovered *Women In Love* in the same spirit as I'd come across *Portrait of the Artist*. She organized Lawrentian walks through the New Forest, where she opened her arms to the sun and sighed as if she was coming to a slow climax. She challenged me to roll with her in wet grass, not for the usual reasons, but so that we could both experience a mystical communion with the earth. When I made the mistake of trying to put my arms round her, Iris reminded me, a shade coolly, that not only was she a Lawrentian, she was a Platonist as well. I thought this disingenuous: it was well known that Iris was up to something unplatonic with a bus conductor called Jim – my own lost *doppelgänger*. She sometimes told me about the muscles on Jim's back and his strong thighs as if she was describing a landscape that she'd seen in Scotland or the Lake District. Jim was her Mellors – a legitimate object of physical passion because it said so in the book. I was afraid that Iris saw in me a convenient stand-in for Clifford Chatterley.

In 1959 the magazine *John O'London's Weekly* announced a short story competition for young writers aged between 16 and 23. Iris and I both rather despised *John O'London's*; it was middlebrow and suburban, new words of abuse for both of us. It went in for cosy chat about authors (how Caryl Brahms couldn't bear to face the day without first brushing her teeth with a certain brand of toothpaste), neo-Georgian poems, well-turned Coppardian stories and kid-glove reviews. Yet even Iris admitted that publication in *John O'London's* (with a suitably large photograph) would constitute a recognizable "start".

"If I win the first prize and you win the second . . ." she said generously.

For a month Iris worked on her story in secret, occasionally giving out hints as to what it was about. It was "tonal". It was to be dominated by images of darkness and blood. *Blood and the moon, didn't I see?* I did, and guessed that Iris's masterpiece was going to be way over the heads of the people at *John O'London's*. Then I heard that she was having to cut it down, because it had turned into a novel.

My own effort was written between lunch and suppertime up in my room in the vicarage, and was posted off to *John O'London's* the next morning, without revision. I didn't admit to Iris that I'd written it. I knew that if I did, she'd plague me about the "images" in it, and I'd have to invent all sorts of symbols and ironies in the piece that I knew were not there.

When, three months later, it was announced that my story had won joint first prize in the competition, I was first thrilled, then embarrassed. On publication (for which I got eleven guineas and a scholarship to the Writers Summer School at Swanwick), "Demobbed" was posted up on the school noticeboard among the football and hockey results. The headmaster's praise at school prayers was fine, but I was alarmed about Iris and the intelligentsia of the sixth form – for the story was culpably innocent of all my adventuring among the classics of modernism. It read like a story written by someone addicted to *The Writer, 101 Infallible Plot Situations* and *John O'London's Weekly*.

> I had wandered in the garden, among the marigolds and around the tall, sour-smelling hollyhocks. The flowering cherry flung gaunt arms towards me, while at the bottom of the fence the stone toad glared at my fingers as they explored the grain of the creosoted wood. The great grey bird bath erupted from a patch of grass and stood like the pillar of a desert temple. I could reach its gritty top and see my face in the hollow of green water . . .

"Well," Iris said, "I suppose that's what they *would* have wanted, isn't it?"

Had a course in English Literature at university not been a few months away, "Demobbed" might, as Iris put it, have been a start. It wasn't, though it did prove that the 17-year-old could now manage what he'd been dying to do three years before. So maybe in three years' time . . .

Iris went to Oxford. I went to Hull (the only university in England which then accepted candidates for an honours degree in English without requiring a G.C.E. pass in Latin), and found there a more elevated literary vocation than that of authorship. Authors were inspired innocents, barely conscious of their real intentions, half-witting creators of texts whose ultimate glory lay in their transfiguration by the critic. Just as my head had been turned at sixteen by *Portrait of the Artist*, at eighteen it was almost wrenched clean off my shoulders by William Empson's *Seven Types of Ambiguity*. In my first term at Hull, I heard someone in his final year say that *Seven Types* was the most famously difficult book in the pantheon. I bought it that afternoon, and went through a course of instruction with Empson that closely resembled the process of conversion at the hands of Ronald Knox or Father D'Arcy. It was tough. I read, and thought I understood, then thought I didn't. The revelation that Shakespeare's "bare ruined choirs, where late the sweet birds sang" was alluding importantly to the dissolution of the monasteries (and its brutal recency, at the time when Shakespeare was writing), to the homoerotic charm of choirboys, and to much, much else, made me realize, for a second time, that I'd never really read a book before.

Empson's dizzying ambiguities were phrased in a language of exuberant common sense, of as-any-chump-can-see. He didn't stand on ceremony, was interested in all kinds of distinctions of writing, from poems in *Punch*, newspaper headlines and 1930s proletarian novels to Chaucer and Spenser and Shakespeare. He was impertinently funny. After a chapter devoted to the deep reading of Shakespearian puns, Empson could remark:

> It shows lack of decision and will-power, a feminine pleasure in yielding to the mesmerism of language, in getting one's way, if at all, by deceit and flattery, for a poet to be so fearfully susceptible to puns. Many of us could wish the Bard had been more manly in his literary habits, and I am afraid the Sitwells are just as bad.

Empson's taste in literature was wonderfully broad, and there wasn't a milligram of cant in his writing.

The dominant tone of the English department at Hull was palely Leavisite, and the leader of the movement was always referred to in lectures as "Doctor Leavis" as if he was the visiting consultant surgeon, a specialist in amputations, at the cottage hospital. "As Dr Leavis observes . . ." was a favourite tag of C. B. Cox, Hull's most notable critic in residence and co-editor of the *Critical Quarterly*. I took against Leavis. His voice came clearly through his books, *The Great Tradition* and *Revaluations in English Poetry*, and it was a narrow, rancorous voice – a voice that I recognized as belonging to the moralizing evangelists from whom I was on the lam. Where Empson was a no-bones atheist, Leavis's books had the smell of the chapel on them. He was obsessed with false gods, like Swift, like Dickens (dismissed as a mere entertainer). His authorized canon of masterpieces were books that were good for you, or, in Leavis's phrase, "culturally sanative". I had enjoyed reading Conrad and Lawrence until I read Leavis extolling them for their powers of cultural sanativeness, when their work suddenly seemed to go stale under the weight of Leavis's praise.

The more I read of Leavis, the more I hero-worshipped Empson for his playfulness, his generosity, his extraordinary cleverness, his literary hedonism. If I imagined Leavis taking a book down from a shelf, I saw a man either reverently handling a gospel or fastidiously rejecting a heretical tract. If I imagined Empson doing the same thing, I saw him carting it off to a comfortable chair for an hour or two of delight. Empson would laugh aloud. You couldn't ever imagine Leavis laughing. Leavis would read what you had just read, and castigate you for your bad taste in liking it. Empson would read what you had just read, and read it twenty times better, finding jokes you'd never seen, sly allusions that you'd missed, richnesses and contradictions that made you want to kick yourself for having skimmed too fast over. He wasn't "difficult" at all, I discovered. He just took his reading more slowly, and relished it in more detail, than any other critic.

When I sat down to write my fortnightly essay, I asked myself, "What would Empson see in this?", and turned in pages of earnest Empson-pastiche, complete with attempts at Empson's inimitable style of slangy, low-falutin', *this is the line to try on the dog* talk. In photographs of that time, Empson always appeared in a straggling Fu Manchu moustache, with flying sidewhiskers; for three weeks I tried to cultivate something similar, but all I managed to grow was an unappealing crop of pubic down.

In the early and middling 1960s, there was a lot of higher education about. The new universities were being built at Sussex, Essex, Warwick, East Anglia, Lancaster and York. Kingsley Amis (then a lecturer at Cambridge) announced his political apostasy with the slogan More Means Worse. More certainly meant people like me. The drift from being a student to research to an appointment as a university lecturer was an easy one, even if one started from an unfashionable place like Hull. I joined the drift. In my last year as an undergraduate I'd been reading the novels of Henry Roth, Nathanael West, Malamud, Bellow and the young Philip Roth, and thought I'd found in them a suitably grave doctoral topic with a solemn-sounding title to match. *Variations on the Theme of Immigration and Assimilation in the Jewish American Novel from 1870 to the Present Day.* In fact this ugly threat of a title was only a cover, designed to throw the professors off my scent. I saw it as licensing a three-year wallow in the most exciting contemporary fiction that was being written in English. Saul Bellow had just published *Herzog*, a book so redolent of its period, so lavish in its style, so rich in metaphor (and irony, and ambiguity, and wit), that it seemed as if the English novel in the late twentieth century had at last found its masterpiece; a work to set beside Dickens's *Our Mutual Friend* or James's *Portrait of a Lady* without feeling that the art of fiction had seriously diminished since its great Victorian maturity. To spend whole weeks reading Bellow, and to try to read him with the alertness and the subtlety of Empson, seemed an improbably lucky fate, and I was paid £450 a year for keeping the best possible company in the living literary world.

By 1965, the drift had quickened to the speed of an avalanche. The advertisement pages at the back of the *New Statesman* were clogged with Academic Appointments, and almost anyone with a good honours degree and a reasonably plausible line in academic talk could land a salaried job as an assistant lecturer at £1050 a year. The University College of Wales at Aberystwyth employed me to teach English and American Literature at their converted railway hotel, a magnificent piece of high gothic that fortuitously resembled an inferior Oxford college. Though the flood of job advertisements might have suggested that our services were urgently needed, and that we'd be worked flat out, the actual duties involved were still gentlemanly and donnish – seven or eight teaching hours a week, with an ocean of leftover time in which to read and write.

I scrapped my thesis and wrote a textbook called *The Technique of Modern Fiction*, which was based on the "practical criticism" classes that I was taking with first-year students. It should probably have been called something like *The Technique of Chatting about Fiction in First-Year Seminars*, but it was accepted, with a £50 advance, by Edward Arnold, the educational publishers, who went on to commission a 22,000-word essay on Huckleberry Finn (£100 more) for their "Studies in English Literature" series. Between books, I wrote a handful of articles with footnotes for journals that paid with parcels of offprints.

For someone in love with the idea of writing, the joy of writing something hasty, derivative and bad goes as deep as the joy of writing something genuinely original. The play of the words on the page, the illusion of forming a fresh pattern, crisply phrased, the heady sense of having nailed a fragment of the world with a telling metaphor, come more easily, if anything, to the bad writer than to the good one. Sitting at the kitchen table in the first-floor rented flat in Moreb (Welsh for Sea-View, though the sea was obscured by a bingo hall) on Bath Street in Aberystwyth, I was intently happy as I tapped away at very threadbare sentences. It was what I had daydreamed of doing for as long as I could remember. When the first galley proofs arrived, they gave off a faint whiff of old clothes, as if the rags from which their paper had been manufactured had been stripped from the backs of tramps. It was the authentic smell of writing as a trade, a trade secret. So was the page of proofreaders' marks that I sellotaped to the wall – columns of arcane squiggles and cross-hatchings and underlinings and code letters. I enjoyed the daily wrangles in the classroom with my students, who were so nearly my own age that it was like arguing about books with a ready-made party of friends, but they couldn't compare with the glamorous musk of the writing stuff on the kitchen table and its promise of another, riskier career.

After five terms of teaching at Aberystwyth I applied for a lectureship at the University of East Anglia. The novelist Malcolm Bradbury held a senior lectureship in American literature there, and I was appointed as his junior. Angus Wilson also had a part-time chair at Norwich, teaching in the summer term and starring at parties during the rest of the year. Wilson gave the university a generously disproportionate amount of his time. He was its Public Orator, he entertained students and staff at elaborate, lantern-lit evenings in the garden of his Suffolk cottage, he was a continuous waterfall of talk – about literature, writers and the business of writing. Between them, Wilson and Bradbury kept the students, at least, reminded that there was a fundamental marital relationship, however tricky, however punctuated by resentful arguments and riddled with mutual incomprehension, between the activity of writing and academic reading and criticism. Wanting to write – and wanting to write something looser than the strangulated exercises in lit. crit. that I'd managed so far – was made into a perfectly ordinary and reasonable ambition by their presence. During the time that I was at East Anglia, Bradbury and Wilson's students included Rose Tremain, Clive Sinclair, Ian McEwan and the playwright Snoo Wilson; the university was, unusually among universities, a place that had a place for writers, whether they were teachers or students.

I saw the university as a springboard from which to dive into Grub

Street. London was 100 minutes away by train, an inky city of editors, publishers, agents and producers. It was where writers lived – the city where *you* would write, if only you could live there.

Working in vacations in an attic room in Norwich, I wrote fast and sloppily, trying to gain a ticket of entrance to the city at the far end of the line. A long play for television, set on the campus of a university somewhere in the north of England where the smell of the fishdocks got into the lecture theatres. An interval talk for Radio 3 about Browning and Pound (accepted and broadcast, £30). Another, about Jewish American novels (ditto). An unkind piece of reportage about the filming of a political T.V. programme at the University of East Anglia which had ended prematurely in a small riot (*New Society*, £15, and an angry wigging from the Professor of Fine Arts). Another *New Society* piece about fruit machines in pubs. A book review (about 19th-century poetry) for the *New Statesman*. A piece, which wasn't exactly a short story, or a slice of autobiography, or a satire, about the sort of people I'd been meeting on the New Left. A short story, in thrall to the early stories of Angus Wilson, about a modish lecturer at a new university, rather too full of the brand names of the moment.

Malcolm Bradbury and I had talked of the difficulty of freelancing for a living, and he'd used the word "diversification". It was like working in any other industry, he said; you had to learn to diversify, cutting and running from fiction to journalism, broadcasting to print. I took him more literally than I think he had intended, and tried to set myself up on so many fronts that I deserved to fail on every one of them.

I sent the television play to Curtis Brown, the agency which handled Bradbury's work. The T.V. man there, Stephen Durbridge, read it, asked me to lunch (the lunch alone would actually have been enough to sustain my fantasy life for several months), and sent the script to a producer who said it was unproducible but liked it enough to commission another play from me, for £500, nearly a third of my annual salary as a lecturer.

A radio producer, Russell Harty, who'd listened to the talks on Radio 3, invited me to join the weekly programme "The World of Books" as a regular contributor. One programme a month, £18 a programme.

Anthony Thwaite, the literary editor of the *New Statesman*, wrote to say that there was a space on the "fiction roster" – another monthly job (£25 a throw), which involved sifting through all the novels published in a particular week and choosing three or four of them for review. The books (and there were often more than twenty of them) would remain the property of the reviewer, and he could sell them at half price to the library supplier, or knacker's yard, off Chancery Lane. This turned the original £25 into something nearer £50.

I sent the stories – or, rather, the story that wasn't and the story that was – to Alan Ross, the editor of the *London Magazine*, enclosing a quarto stamped addressed envelope. Ten days later, I spotted the magazine's printed letterhead on a much smaller envelope and knew, with a whoop of relief, that Ross hadn't sent me a rejection slip.

A SENIOR LECTURESHIP

Anthony Freeman's first marriage had ended somewhere around the back of Baker Street, in the consulting room of a psychoanalyst who had something to do with the Tavistock Clinic. On the third joint visit he'd come back alone to the Volkswagen, just in time to watch the Excess Charge plate click into place on the parking meter. Two months later he took up a temporary lectureship at the University of St Andrews, where he "recovered". He dined out a good deal ("We must have Anthony round; introduce him to Agnes/Fiona/poor Mrs Taggart"), took to birdwatching with a huge, military-looking pair of Zeiss binoculars, and wrote four drafts of an article on Chartism for the English Historical Association *Bulletin*. He wore his divorce like a campaign ribbon. The psychoanalyst became a major character in his rather good after-dinner stories: "Curious chap, actually. Jewish, of course. Had a chest-expander on his desk . . ." He swapped the Volkswagen for an M.G. and took a quite pretty Ph.D. student on a walking tour of the Highlands.

Two universities later he was splendidly remarried. At Leeds he slept with a beautiful third-year girl in his Foreign Policy course. She had a chiselled face and body that looked as if they'd been assembled by a master craftsman from the best available materials. She had all the Rolling Stones records and occasionally smoked pot for social reasons, but she was perfectly adapted to Vice-Chancellorial dinners and everyone thought Julia was marvellously right for Anthony. In the past, lecturer-student affairs had been subjects of scandal and concern, but this one was in a class apart. Julia would have been incapable of anything vulgar. Anthony was such a young 38, and Julia would be so good for him. She became a favourite of professors' wives, the expert on hemlines and pop and interior decoration. She bought David Levine ceramics and the latest Liberty prints; she made the Pink Floyd sound wholesome and taught the wife of the Professor of Constitutional History to say things were "draggy" or "super". Anthony changed the M.G. for a Rover 2000 and was offered a senior lectureship at the University of Warwick. In the summer vacation after Julia's graduation (she got an average upper second; Anthony had a "good" one), they were married.

For their first year at Warwick, things were perfect. Their life looked like the product of some extremely sophisticated piece of electrical circuitry. The Great Programmer had done a fine job with Julia's beauty and Anthony's after-dinner stories. "There's rather a good one going round about L.B.J.," Anthony would say, and Julia's exquisite face would signal, *this is a super story, you must listen to this*, like a puppet on *Thunderbirds*. Each of them expressed their opinions with the marital "we". "We don't really care for Godard, he is rather overrated"; "We rather liked that book by Marcuse, what's its name?"; "We thought the David Mercer play was absolutely super . . ." When someone brought up a new film, one would ask the other, "Did we see that, darling?" Then they would glaze simultaneously and the nervous junior lecturer (curiously he always was junior to Anthony) would be left awkwardly sketching the plot. Somebody once suggested that they both must have had an identical, vital part of their brains removed by surgery in their infancies. But that was not in the professorial circle, where they were oddly popular.

When they entertained Anthony's junior colleagues, the evenings tended to dissolve into unrecognized disaster. With Assistant Lec-turers, they developed a technique for encouraging intimacy by sitting intertwined on their sofa. Julia would nuzzle Anthony and stroke the neat fur on the back of his neck, while Anthony, with his arm around her, was saying things like, "I think that's only one side of the story. You see, the Vietnamese . . ." or "We thought it was rather a good novel. The plot and the dialogue —". The Assistant Lecturers would meet in one another's offices and rehearse favourite well-worn scenes from the private life of the Freemans over coffee or beer. The couple were made to lie in bed tenderly grappling with one another like delicate, copulative robots, and discuss the merits of Ayn Rand, Leon Uris, the Wolverhampton Problem and Marshall

McLuhan, arriving at their perfectly timed climax with an ecstatic "We think – we think – we think!"

But the jokes wore thin and gave way to new fictions. It was decided – quite why nobody knew – that Julia was more "intelligent" than Anthony, that she was bored with robot sex and robot intellectuality in their pastel coloured period house. If she was bored, perhaps she was seducible. She could turn on, have an affair, storm into Anthony's office, crash the Rover, take an overdose, cover the floor and walls of the drawing room with scraps of paper, notes, newspaper cuttings. She could be found alone in pubs in the early evening, develop a bronchitic cough, take courses in sociology, disappear for days to London. But nothing. She failed to transmit signals of any kind. At half-past five every evening she collected Anthony from the university. She moved into the passenger seat; they kissed through the window; Anthony moved round the front of the car, sat in the driving seat. Pause. Kiss. Anthony drove off. Every bloody evening.

Then she got pregnant. Or rather, "Julia is – ah – having a baby." In Anthony's terms, only neurotic, undisciplined, unmarried students got pregnant. Anthony bought Doctor Spock in the university bookshop and the professorial wives closed round Julia in a tight knot of coffee mornings and communal trips to the baby boutique. Julia made a tiny dent in the offside wing of the Rover after taking a corner on the campus (limit 20 m.p.h.) at 35. The Assistant Lecturers put this down, in their ignorance, to her pregnancy. The following week, Anthony drove himself in and out of the university, and Julia stayed deep in among the pastel colours, listening to the gurgle of the central heating, or playing the Fugs records that a friend had brought back that summer from the States. From the outside you might have forgotten she existed, if it hadn't been for the sudden and incongruous blooming of Anthony.

It started with a leather jacket. He'd always gone around in lightweight summer suits before, and the glistening new leather made him look like some sort of hatching chrysalis. Almost immediately he started the beard. It grew in scattered patches of fuzz, as if unwilling to take root on the unlikely surface of that smooth face. An Assistant Lecturer found some excuse to visit the pastel Freeman house one evening. "Don't you think Anthony will look super in a beard?" Julia had said over the top of a Fugs record. "We decided he ought to grow one."

"Very nice," said the Assistant Lecturer, marvelling at the extraordinary effect of Julia's very unpregnant two-months-gone body in a maternity smock.

"It'll have to grow before the V.C.'s Thanksgiving Day party," said Anthony, "otherwise it'll have to come off."

Julia picked up Doctor Spock and held Anthony's hand as she read.

The beard grew, first lame and untidy, then darkening into a magnificent fierce wedge. Anthony arrived one morning to take a tutorial in a fez. "Going abroad?" someone inquired at the door of his office. Anthony shrugged uncomprehendingly and walked on. His ties widened to kipper width; the collars of his shirts began to grow down his chest. His trousers, like creatures participating in an evolutionary cycle, first narrowed, then swelled and flared around and over his new yellow moccasins. His vocabulary took a sudden uncertain lurch towards the West Coast; at a department meeting Anthony remarked that the preliminary examination results were "a pretty rough sort of scene". Someone sniggered and asked, *sotto voce*, for a translation.

In the fourth month of Julia's pregnancy Anthony exchanged the Rover for a Renault 4L. They gave a party, sending out invitations under plain Anthony and Julia, and leaving out the Freeman. These invitations came, not on deckle-edge cards as before, but on slips of duplicating paper, processed by the department secretaries in the lunch hour. For the first time the pastel house was opened to students, a promiscuous research assistant, and a huge fat man who was believed to write for *International Times*. All these besides the cadaverous professors and their wives, the business neighbours, and the junior faculty arriving in their beat-up Minis. "Hi," said Anthony to each new guest, while Julia stood placidly behind him, all inwardness and maternity wear.

"I think Julia's already had her baby," said an Assistant Lecturer, looking at the unused spaces of Julia's smock as she stood beside the resplendent Anthony. In fact all the clichés about fulfilled motherhood seemed true of Julia then; it was hard to imagine how a real child could possibly compete with the brand new Anthony in his flared trousers and lace fronted shirt.

"Let's get high," Anthony said at large. He was carrying a gallon jar of cheap burgundy.

"Got any beer?" said the professor of Medieval History who was president of the Wine Committee.

"Is that the Beatles, dear?" his wife asked Julia, by the stereo equipment.

"No, the Fugs."

"Oh, how nice," said the professor's wife doubtfully.

Someone from the group of students asked Anthony if he wanted to smoke, and Anthony said to wait till later, but was evidently flattered to be asked. The man who wrote for *International Times* was talking about R. D. Laing who he called Ronnie, and a girl was sick in the downstairs lavatory. The professorial circle established itself in the dining room, all apart from a sociologist who'd once been on *Late Night Line-Up* and was under the impression that it was a student party anyway. Anthony got a research student to help him roll up the carpet.

"I've never actually seen a carpet rolled up before," said the student. "I thought it was just an expression."

Anthony shrugged, and tucked an exposed tail of his lace fronted shirt into the waistband of his hipsters.

The professors took their wives away early. Anthony and Julia stood at the front door while the wives gazed at Julia and glanced puzzledly at Anthony.

"Thank you so much, dear," they said to her. "You must come round for coffee again this week."

In the cars with their husbands, the wives said, "I do want to see Julia by herself. I'm quite worried about her. Anthony is so strange nowadays . . . those dreadful clothes —"

"I expect it's just a phase," said the professors, changing gear. Pregnancy was such an odd affair anyway; some men sat it out in the Senior Common Room bar, or took to visiting the flats of their girl students. Leather jackets and flared trousers seemed, by comparison, quite a harmless survival strategy. And that shirt rather suited him, really.

The students sat around like rabbits on the bare floor of the Freemans' drawing room drinking beer out of cans. Four of them passed a cigarette from hand to hand and stared, preoccupied, at the dusty floorboards. Julia reigned above them, curled into a corner of the sofa, as an earnest fragile boy talked to her about babies. Anthony's shirt rippled uneasily above his waistband. "Ah . . . yes . . . ah . . . rather . . . yes . . . ah," he said teetering from one foot to the other. "Like the . . . ah . . . whole political history scene is . . . ah . . . kind of shaking up —"

In the pale mauve hall the fat man who wrote for *I.T.* had found a tiny student in a white dress and was feeding her with whisky from a flask. "Man," he said, "what a bloody zombie. Did you see those books in there? It's the first time I ever met someone who had the complete works of Herman Wouk."

"I did a history seminar with him once," said the student. There was a long pause. The man tugged at the tufts of the thick pile carpet. "It was rather boring," she said.

In the week after the party Anthony cancelled his survey lectures because, as he explained, lectures were non-participatory. Instead, he parcelled out "projects" – the theme of Betrayal in psychology and history, the theory of Apocalypse, the Charismatic Leader. He shelved his old Ph.D. thesis which he'd been turning into a book for the last eight years because, he said, like it wasn't the sort of history that mattered; like, it wasn't Relevant. The students though, unsurprisable, put up with his Projects as they'd put up with his lectures. They took incomprehensible notes; their pens ran out of ink; they stared out of the window of his room at the neat university lake with its expensive collection of eider ducks. Anthony would lean forward and raise his hand like a priest. "Like, ah . . . John Cage . . ." he would say, blinking at the girl who fingered her indian beads.

In the sixth month of Julia's pregnancy he slept with a third-year student. This was, in fact, rumoured long before it happened. Anne was taking his modern politics course in the irregular intervals between experimenting with hand-held shots of the campus with a baby Bolex. "Like, all this academic work is, like, categories," she said. "Like it's all mixed media kind of things now." She recognized Anthony's new life as a miraculous conversion, and began to gaze at him during seminars with pot distended pupils. For her class essay she handed in a poem (a Black Mountain collage of places, dates, fragments of news and vague intimacies). Anthony gave it a $\beta-$. Anne whipped out her Bolex and snapped him in his office. "Picture of a fink," she said. Anthony slept with her that afternoon in the double bed in her untidy flatlet with damp patches on the ceiling. Julia waited for him for 15 minutes in the Renault; went to his room, found it was locked, drove home, and started a *ragout* from Elizabeth David.

No one was certain if Julia knew. Perhaps she'd planned it this way. Perhaps Anthony described every detail to her, starting with the scene in the pub when Anne kicked off her shoes and wiggled her toes in front of Anthony's astonished face. He'd coughed, grinned, and gone on drinking beer. At any rate Julia grew, if anything, even more placid. She sat (reported the Assistant Lecturers) at the plain deal kitchen table surrounded by books on baby care.

Chills . . . Colic . . . Colitis . . . Colds . . . Croup . . . Cuddling. Methodically, like a student revising for finals, she plodded alphabetically through every infant ailment known to Spock. She practised folding nappies and stood in front of the bedroom mirror with her arms cupped around an imaginary child. For an hour each day she stretched and swung and bent her body until it was supply ready to spring forth her baby like an oiled trap.

Anthony, though, woke with beery headaches and pains in his abdomen. He muttered in his sleep (Julia would slowly run her forefinger down his spine and he would quieten), and started ordering newspapers which he spread round the drawing room floor, reading into the small hours. "Do you think it's good for your eyes, darling?" Julia asked. "I just read a poem," said Anthony. "There was this line in it, 'We are *all* in the da-nang.' It sort of *means* – you know?"

"Would you like some cocoa before we go to bed?" said Julia.

Anthony crawled over the newspapers on the floor on hands and knees towards a day-old copy of the *Morning Star*. "No thanks," he said, hunting for the Foreign News page.

His seminars began to hum with words like "class" and "justice" and "control". He prescribed Eldridge Cleaver as a set book and talked slowly, in a low sad voice, of revolution. In bed with Anne, he confessed. Holding his head in his hands he said, "Like, she's so bloody . . . middle class." Anne narrowed her eyes, composing Anthony into a shot in an underground movie.

"Leave her," she said.

"I couldn't . . . hurt her that much," said Anthony.

"Well, that's that then, isn't it!"

Anthony looked round at her. "She's so dependent on me . . . she's almost like a child —"

Anne shrugged.

"Anne, Anne . . . ? Do you want me to stay with you?"

"Okay – like, I don't want to make you go one way or the other —"

"You need someone to look after you. I'll take care of you, Anne —" Anthony said, sorrowfully.

He drove the Renault back to the pastel house, only just missing a milkvan in a sidestreet. Julia was doing her exercises. "Julia," said Anthony, "I've *got* to be honest – with you – and with myself." Julia straightened up slowly, rising on the balls of her feet. "I've just got one more exercise to do," she said. "For the tummy muscles."

"You're so bloody middle class," Anthony said, tremulously.

"There, that's it," said Julia.

"We're not being honest with each other," said Anthony.

Like ballet dancers in rehearsal, they began to row.

At the beginning of the eighth month of Julia's pregnancy she parked the Renault off Baker Street and spent two and a half hours with Anthony's ex-psychoanalyst. When she returned to the car the Excess Charge sector showed on the meter. She fed another sixpence into the slot and sat tranquilly in the driving seat, touching the stretched skin of her stomach with wonder.

At the same time, Anthony lay stretched naked on the crumpled sheet of Anne's enormous double bed. His beard flared around his mouth. He leaned over, touched the damp line of Anne's stomach. Between them lay a copy of R. D. Laing, *The Politics of Experience and the Bird of Paradise*. Anthony reached for his glasses from his trousers pocket, hung untidily over the back of a chair. He put on his spectacles and began to read.

1969

Ross added in his letter, "Are you interested in criticism? Do you want to review books for us?" I gave in my notice to the dean of the School of English and American Studies, who told me I was probably doing the silliest thing in my life. He was 25 years older than I was and could remember a world where jobs were not so easily got nor so lightly thrown away. But in 1969 I'd had a six-month run of lucky flukes, and times were flush. The idea of living in London and writing for a living – writing *anything* for a living – possessed me completely. Every morning was distinctly brighter because of the idea. I had Larkin's lines running in my head:

Ah, were I courageous enough to shout *Stuff your pension!*
But I know, all too well, that's the stuff that dreams are made
    on . . .

But it's not, and it wasn't.

II

Inflation and decimalization have made 1969 prices look antique and the time more remote than it really is. A lecturer's salary, with a handful of increments, was £1750. A hardback novel cost from 21s to 25s. To turn those figures into today's values, one would have to multiply by a factor of between eight and ten.

In 1969 it was still – just – possible for a newcomer to scrape by on literary journalism, writing book reviews for the weeklies and for magazines like *Encounter* and the *London Magazine* at anything from £15 to £30 a piece. In 1987 terms, say £125 to £250. Taking part in arts and books programmes on the radio (another standby of the freelance) brought in very similar fees. Here are some actual comparisons from 1986/7 (three of them are mine, two are someone else's):

> Book review (1000 words) for the *Listener*, £90; for *The Times Literary Supplement*, £75; for the *Spectator*, £70. For reviewing a book on the radio programme *Kaleidoscope*, £78.75. For appearing on a half-hour T.V. programme (*Cover to Cover*) and discussing four books, £125.

The rates haven't kept up. Although some national newspapers like the *Observer* and the *Sunday Times* do pay their reviewers a good deal more than this (on a base-rate of about £200 a go), book reviewing has effectively ceased to be a means of serious subsistence. It may pay for itself, by a knifeblade margin, but it won't buy time for other, more speculative literary work. You'd be so busy writing reviews that you wouldn't have a spare minute in which to get on with a book.

It had not quite reached that stage in 1969. For £7 a week (or about 300 words), I rented a large and comfortable room in a flat in Highgate and set up in business as a professional writer. The floor was littered with the jiffybags in which review copies arrived and with the wreckage of the commissioned play for television, which had stalled on me.

To write was still an intransitive verb. There was no story which insisted on being told – no object, except the act of writing itself. All the pleasure and interest lay in simply playing with words. Write! – but write what? If nothing else came to mind, you could write about not writing in a room in Highgate.

LIVING IN LONDON

The best place to commit suicide in north London is from the top of the Archway Bridge, a magnificently vulgar piece of Victorian ironwork that carries Hornsey Lane high over the top of Archway Road. Your death leap will cast you from the precarious gentility of N.6 into the characterless squalor of N.19. All Highgate trembles on the edge of that abyss, perched, like a gentlewoman of rapidly reducing means, above the "vapid plains" of that "hot and sickly odour of the human race which makes up London". Highgate was firmly behind the 19th-century rector of Hornsey, Canon Harvey, who declared (in a letter to *The Times*): "I have tried to keep Hornsey a village but circumstances have beaten me." It was always a place for prospects and dreams of the city lying below it: Dick Whittington turned again on Highgate Hill; Guy Fawkes's cronies gathered in Parliament Hill Fields to watch the Houses of Parliament blaze. Then it became an escape hatch, as the middle classes built their purple brick villas like castles on the northern heights, in defence against the cholera and typhoid germs of William Booth's Darkest London. N.6 is an embattled vantage point; it overlooks the city with a chronic mixture of anticipation and fear.

Highgate Village still has the air of a tiny community of local gentry huffing and puffing about the encroaching council estates, the new commuters and the decline of churchgoing. The gentry have their Literary and Scientific Institute (whose president is a knight), their Highgate Society, their self-consciously "local" pubs and tea-shop. Forget the Renault 2 C.V.'s, the Volkswagens and the Citroëns, and Pond Square could be in Wiltshire. A querulous, female upper-class voice braying "Colonel . . ." through the elms; a Red Setter vainly pointing towards Kentish Town, scenting, perhaps, some dim racial memory of pheasants ker-rumphing up from where only sparrows now cough bronchially on the washing lines of Albion Villas. But the huddled old ladies have had their day: the awfulness of N.19 has got a stranglehold on Highgate Village and it won't let go. Already there are signs. In the evenings a gang of skinheads congregates at the bus turnaround in Pond Square, scuffling their heels proprietorially. I don't know where they come from, but their soft jeers mark them, like a crew of seedy dealers moving in on the dissolution of the Big House. They know that history's on their side.

For the rest of us, Highgate is a kind of sidestep from the main current of things, an uneasy and ambiguous transit camp, a compromise. Jews who have fallen out somewhere on the great migration from the East End to Golders Green to Cricklewood just manage to maintain their synagogue and ailing delicatessens. The Irish live in a tatty group of streets off the Archway Road; their Islington from home, as it were, is a huge, fusty gin-palace of a pub called the Winchester Hall Tavern, practically next door to the synagogue. Behind the engraved glass-nouveau they do a great trade in stout and reminiscences. On Archway Road, there are moody West Indians in fluorescent shirts and mittel-Europeans in brown raincoats embarking on complicated bus rides to Swiss Cottage. The pompous villas of the 1880s and '90s have been split up into flats, full of admen and T.V. technicians with white Ford Cortinas. An interior landscape of bulrushes and green bottle glass, of stained Penguins by Elizabeth David, of stripped pine and Parker Knoll, of dinner parties that sag on the stroke of ten, of cheerless bedrooms rarely used for fun. N.6 is too nervous and unconfident to have flair; dolly girls hardly ever venture further north than N.W.1, unless to Hampstead or the suburban dottiness of Muswell Hill. My brother, an art student, lives only a mile away in Kentish Town, N.W.5. There people keep broken-down Bond three-wheelers under flapping tarpaulins in their front gardens. William and his friends play penny whistles and chant mantras; they drink pale coffee out of mugs that have lost their handles. The students get high on cough mixture in Lady Margaret Road and beat their gas meters with broomsticks. You can't imagine that sort of thing going on in N.6.

For my part of Highgate is anxious, isolated, hopeful, frightened. Hornsey Lane Gardens, where I live, is on the ragged fringe dividing Highgate-proper from Crouch End. Along the road at Saint Augustine's they teach karate on Thursdays ("Fast . . . Safe . . . Sensible"), and stringy men in kimonos lean on the railings outside, shrivelled

Oddjobs who could deal you a death chop if they cared. They gaze mournfully down Archway Road. Or the man with the ratty moustache who runs the used-car lot; he twitches at customers on the pavement like a decayed colonel trying to interest a trout with the wrong fly on a hot day. Just after midnight once I listened to a conversation between two Irish girls outside my ground floor window. One was crying. The other said, "He's only a man, for godsake, Bridie. He's only a man." And last Sunday I was walking up Archway Road to the pub at half-past seven; a man stopped me, holding out a glistening cellophane package. "Would you . . . by any chance . . ." his voice fled, then came back in an enthusiastic rush ". . . be interested in buying a shirt, sir?" All gestures that have the resonance of impossibility about them; in vain, but still believing.

I'm so new to London that – I suppose inevitably – my response to it is strident. For years I've been circulating around distant provincial perimeters – Lymington, Hull, Aberystwyth, Norwich – growing more and more infatuated with a starry notion of London life. In Aberystwyth I read Margaret Drabble's *Jerusalem The Golden* and identified completely with the marvellously naive aspirations of Clara the heroine: . . . "What social joys are there . . ." In Norwich, more knowingly, but still in love with a dream of a faraway city, I taught courses on literature and society in 19th-century London. The deep swirling fog, the crowded tenements, the clerks streaming over London Bridge, the tramways and the endless alleys, each ready with a coincidence to turn the plot, in Dickens, Gissing, Wells. The "London" series of prints by Gustave Doré; W. E. Henley's resounding, mock-epic *London Voluntaries*. Visiting London, you can impose almost any fictional identity you want upon it, and at weekends I stayed in a city which might easily have turned up Edwin Reardon or George Ponderevo in the subway at the top of Charing Cross Road.

Coming to N.6 last June, with the urban equipment of a reader of *Tono Bungay* and *The Nether World*, was the kind of appropriate accident that makes one really believe one is a character in the hands of the Great Fiction Writer. For Highgate is sufficiently far above, and far away from, the involving complexities of Central London, Kensington, Chelsea, to enable one to see the city itself as a sequence of perfect images. Soho is a squalid nightmare, full of men in raincoats on their way up to Françoise, 3rd Floor; South Kensington is foreign girls working at the Swiss Centre and eating huge cakes in patisseries; Belgravia is bored girls with white M.G.B.'s waiting for sugar daddies

. . . It's so easy to acquire a kind of pseudo-knowledge, to feel that, from the top of Highgate Hill, the whole of London is within one's conceptual grasp. It's all height, distance, dreams. The best literary analogy I can think of is Fitzgerald's *The Great Gatsby*: the islands of East and West Egg, places for ever-hopeful westerners like Gatsby and Carraway to gaze across towards the sparkling possibilities of New York City. The Valley of Ashes, that symbolic wasteland presided over by the rotting eyes of Dr T. J. Eckleburg on the giant hoarding, finds its exact correlative in the grisly acres that stretch from Archway to the northern (and so far unreclaimed) half of Camden Town.

And dreaming is a lonely, private occupation. Gatsby and Carraway subsisted mysteriously; they might, from all we see of their actual work in the novel, have been freelance writers. In some sense the isolation of my own routine seems perfectly to match the landscape I'm trying to identify as N.6. It's dependent on, yet distant from, the activity of Central London; it looks hopefully out towards Great Turnstile, Thurloe Place, Broadcasting House, Wood Lane; it hangs on the end of a telephone. There are days when I can feel the telegraph wires crossing the north London escarpment, homing in a dense net to the centre; sometime in the day it's got to be my line buzzing – a message, like in a bottle, from *down there*. One day I'll pick up the phone and there'll just be the faint sound of Bow Bells. Perhaps.

I don't belong. My clock is odd; I get up late and my curtains stay publicly pulled-to. I'm not a student, nor on the Assistance, nor exactly a housewife. At lunchtimes I sometimes play snooker at the Winchester Hall Tavern. There old men, Irish mostly, talk very slowly. When they go to the billiard table their cues seem to move with a lugubrious deliberation. The man I play snooker with, an old friend, currently works part-time as a laundry delivery driver, and somehow his job shows; you can see he's employed. But the old men watch me curiously; I'm displaced, have no badge of office. I work in the bay of an enormous five-sided window at home, a sort of announcement that I work therefore I am. Stray kids, tightroping on the low wall outside, occasionally grimace at me, but other people don't take much notice. My work is socially unestablished, placeless; beside it, N.6 becomes a tangle of contingencies that seem always to be slyly forming themselves into a sinister logic.

On days like this my room feels like a tethered ship, somehow afloat from the tall villas and straggly trees of the road outside. It's cold and windy; a dog is barking in someone's distant garden, and smoke from a chimney is flattened into a thin, transverse line across a colourless sky. Work is bits and pieces: reviews, written in single sentences and stray paragraphs on separate sheets of paper; a pile of novels to read, crisp from the publishers but mostly soggy inside; this piece, written disjunctively over the last ten days; the messed-about script of a T.V. play; notes to prompt me at a radio recording tomorrow. Nothing in my room relates to the street beyond the window; to work is to disconnect oneself from N.6, to untie the mooring rope and drift into a geography mercifully free from postal districts.

Going out, for food, cigarettes or papers, can induce a kind of culture-shock. I know the people in the newsagents and the Irish couple who run the off-licence: talking to them is suddenly awkward, spluttering, full of helplessly grinning silences. One has to retrieve one's identity as local resident, unsheathe and dust it, before speaking. I suppose this sudden inability with words is merely an occupational hazard for those who don't live in the constant chafe of an institution; in a day you can almost forget how to talk. But for me, it's a sensation rooted in place. Like most suburbanites, I live in one place and work in another, but both places mysteriously have the same address. It's like leaving home in the morning to arrive knocking on your own front door.

Perhaps this is why it's so reassuring when, on a good day, work includes some appointment in London – seeing an editor, going down to the B.B.C., having tea with my agent. Then, living in N.6 pays off. I get up early and drive euphorically down to the centre; everywhere south of Camden Town takes on the air of a party to which one is lucky enough to have received an invitation. The girl at the reception desk is suddenly beautiful, the liftman friendly, the corridors welcoming. It'd be awful if it were possible just to drop in from round the corner; the distance of N.6 sustains all the best illusions of W.1 and W.C.2.

But on the bad days, when the telephone's dead and the post dull, N.6 feels like a debtors' spunging house. If nothing will go, I walk round Waterlow Park, a few hundred yards away, on the far side of Highgate Hill. There girls mind people's children, calling, "Johnnie, where's your other gumboot?" across the ornamental lake whose bank is carpeted with duckshit. Serious-looking men read the *Radio Times* on benches, and retired ladies read Ruby M. Ayres up by the tennis courts. Tramps in raggy overcoats talk to the squirrels – an amazingly insolent and unafraid lot – and demented women carry religious literature across the grass in string bags. Below us all, London falls away behind the cemetery, a promise that didn't quite work out.

One is one's own projectionist, making one's environment amenable to metaphor, screening it with the complete fictional shape of a movie. A dinner party: with some fact and a measure of nightmare. It's by candlelight; a precarious, anxious gesture, typical of my N.6. The people are proud, uncertain, but above all, innocent. They're bunched around that slippery-sided peak of partial success, and they talk overloudly, as if deliberately to be overheard.

– Oh, he's making it in the art world –
– Still hard edges? –
– Not *made it* yet, mind you, but he's going to be a big name soon –
– I've heard that *disposables* are the latest thing –
– Darling! –
– You won't know him. He's just got his divorce –
– Do you *know* Ronnie Laing? –
– I find New York so *stimulating* –
– He's got this marvellous *idea* –
– Madness is a kind of . . . spiritual necessity –
– Of course, in my job, you have to keep up with the trends –
– The art world does sound fascinating –
– The first time I turned on, nothing happened. Then –
– Have you read Timothy Leary? –
– Trends –
– Richard Hamilton –
– Fabulous idea –
– My lovers are always finding out that they knew the one-before –
– He's so frightfully well-informed –
– God, Alison, you are *lucky* –
– It's really because of my contacts, you see. I know all these showbiz people . . . and The Church –
– Really the most brilliant man I know –
– The latest thing. He burns them when he's finished –
– Leonard Cohen –
– Do you think it's *valid*, though? –
– What I don't *quite* understand –
– But what do you think the *psychology* of it all is? –
If this sounds too like a crude *Trendy Ape* parody, it is, I think,

because my N.6 is so much more naked and yearning than the Gloucester Crescent of the Stringalongs. So many of the people I've met here in the last few months live on the fine blade of their aspirations, tempered on the one side by their sense of how far they have already come, and on the other by their untarnished vision of the Jerusalem of London life. They suffer from the immigrant's classic pains of assimilation. Their habitual tone, of slightly dated knowingness, is a mark of their good faith. They're earnest believers, dreamers, innocents; hill people. A favourite phrase is "in London": someone will talk breathlessly of "one of the top writers/analysts/reporters/photographers *in London*". Behind the expression lurks the plea that the speaker has lost all his old, clinging connections to the provinces; he's in the know, his only world is London, he's unmarked by the humiliating stigmata of Northampton or Weston super Mare.

So, guiltily, I identify with N.6. At its worst it provides a kind of parodic theatre in which my own notions of coming to London, making my living by writing, sharing in an idealized metropolitan community, are played out in cruelly accurate caricature. The wording may be vulgar (Mark Boxer in *Life and Times in N.W.1* would never have allowed his characters to be quite so direct), but the dream is real enough. So is the anxiety, the fear that there's no further to go, that the provincial town lies in wait with its Cadena, its three cinemas, its endless talk of mortgages and gardening. Or, worse still, perhaps, we'll stay in London; festering, unknowing and unknown, in a room without a view in N.19.

1969

With a weekly circulation of close to 90,000 copies, the *New Statesman* was the parish magazine of the English liberal intelligentsia (if such an entity can ever be said to have really existed). It was then edited by Paul Johnson, though with its political front half and literary back half it had always been famous as an unwieldy pantomime horse, with its two sets of legs tending to walk off in quite different directions. The back legs were being worked by Anthony Thwaite, who edited the literary pages from a pair of attic rooms in the *Statesman* building at Great Turnstile. The chief glory of the paper

lay in V. S. Pritchett's regular review-essays, which I sometimes saw
Thwaite preparing for the printer when I went to his office.

There was no mistaking a manuscript by Pritchett – it was overlaid
with small embellishments in longhand, many of them crossed out
and recorrected, to the point where the sheet of paper was in places
blackened. Revisions on revisions on revisions. Pritchett (so Thwaite
told me) first wrote his review in longhand, then gave it to his wife
Dorothy, who typed it up, then Pritchett added the final highlights,
erasions and qualifications. From a distance of several yards off, you
could see that a review by Pritchett was a serious and intricate piece
of work.

It's thought vaguely smart to denigrate "mere" book reviews as
writing done with the left hand, and it's true that most people's book
reviews do read as if they'd been jotted down in the taxi on the
way to an overrun deadline. But Pritchett's reviews, even his most
seemingly casual and brief ones, have never read like that. They are
small, exquisitely paced narratives. The subtlety of their tone, their
brilliant characterization of the book in hand, their air of talking their
way carefully through their own arguments, make them closely akin
to Pritchett's fiction.

His presence in the back pages of the *New Statesman* set an
intimidating, encouraging and unfollowable example. It left one in
no doubt that writing a review was worth doing for its own sake and
that a well-written book review might be a more estimable thing
than a poorly written story. It made one work harder, and sharpened
one's pride in working for the *Statesman*'s literary pages.

A reviewing job carries with it a licence to read more freely and
widely than any academic, whose set books crop up year after year
on the same courses and for whom keeping up with one's field tends
to mean reading the same words, or minor variations of them, a
hundred or a thousand times over. I once knew a man who staked
an entire academic career on his reading of two novels – *The Golden
Bowl* and *Giles Goat Boy*. Scavenging freelances, sorting through the
piles and shelves in the office (a more productive arrangement than
the one in which the literary editor commissions a review of a
particular book over the phone), can go off on sprees, immersing
themselves in Trollope one month, Ted Hughes the next, the architecture of cities the month after, Philip Roth the month after that. The
literary framework in which they live is necessarily provisional and
in a state of continuous expansion and alteration. *No depth to it*, says
the academic; yet the reviewer, working like a bowerbird to spin a

web of connections between the different bits and pieces of his reading, is in a position to gain a sense of the broad proportions of things that few academics can rival. So long as he's not exclusively confined to sampling last week's second-best novel (the literary editor's version of a furlough in quarantine), but can cart off volumes of letters, diaries, biographies, books of criticism, he's being maintained in full-time education, a perpetual graduate student. A happy fate.

He is as much a writer as a reader. After the chimes, the amiable Dr Jekyll emerges as the malevolent Mr Hyde. For a review, though it must of course be a report and an appraisal, is also a literary entertainment in its own right, and its first duty is to be a "good piece" – which, from the point of view of the author of the book, is quite often synonymous with a "bad review".

W. H. Auden once wrote that every reviewer ought sometimes to be able to confess that "this book is more important than anything I can say about it", but it's not as easy as that. Most books, even rather bad ones, are more important than what their reviewers say of them: their sheer length and longevity, compared with the sparrow-flight of a review across a single page in a newspaper, guarantees them their pre-eminence, and Auden's remark sounds a useful warning note about the chronic vanity of book reviewers in general. Yet it's a lousy prescription for actually writing a review. It has the authentic alloy ring of a puff written by someone commending a friend's book that he hasn't yet had time to read. The reviewer is there to write, not to melt away from the book in tongue-tied wonder.

As a writer, then, and not just as a penner of notices, the reviewer has a form in which to work that closely resembles that of the cartoon. He has to capture a good likeness in as few strokes as possible, with the stamp of his own style in every line, to be vivid, intelligent and impossibly concise. A tall order, and one which is rarely if ever executed in full.

It's as hard to bring a book convincingly to life on the page as it is a landscape or a character. You have to tweak it into being from a handful of scattered details and build a story round it to dramatize its particular worth in the world. At least, that's the idea, and the blank page of the unwritten review is a promising space to be approached by the writer in the same apprehensive way, fearing failure and hoping for unexpected shafts of light and luck, as that in which he sits down to his more obviously ambitious productions. When reviews are written with the left hand, it shows.

As with cartoons, there's a congenital streak of cruelty in the form of the review: it's easier to tell good stories about bad books than it is about good ones, easy to seize on small deformities and make much of them, easy to fall back on the big red nose and the tombstone teeth as the handiest method of conveying personality. The reviewer, especially if he's new to the job and trying to make his name, finds a style of pert mockery ready and waiting for him like an off-the-peg suit.

The style is boisterously smartyboots in tone and fake-Augustan in its grammar. The surest way to sound as if your vast learning is tempered by sturdy common sense is to go in for showy latinisms; a mastery of sarcastic inversion, circumlocution and the ironic negative is the official mark of a superior intelligence at work. Here is Clive James reviewing a book about T. S. Eliot by Donald Bush:

> Eugenio Montale once said that there is a danger that scholarship and criticism will act together to shed "too much light" on a work of art. Only the captious would accuse Donald Bush of having shed too much light here . . . Deafness to tone is not among Mr Bush's drawbacks . . . Too appreciative of his subject to be completely fooled by his own theories about it . . .

This (though you wouldn't guess it) is from a broadly "favourable" review, and James here comes nowhere near the heights of condescension that he used to scale in his T.V. columns – but the tricks, or tics, of style keep on nudging the reader to remember that the reviewer is a sight more clever than the man he's reviewing. He's also one of the boys. The fake-Augustan is carefully offset, at least once a paragraph, by touches of jocular saloon-bar:

> The poetic moments are the real McCoy, but the overall pattern is a put-up job . . . It is lucky that the body of the book contains nothing to match a lulu in the notes at the back: "My gesture towards *Finnegans Wake* is deliberate". My own gesture, upon reading this, was equally deliberate: a hand pointing toward the door. Get out, sir, and come back when your tongue is clean . . .

The dialect in which James is writing here is as recognizable as Mummerset; at once donnish high-falutin' and come-off-it-mate low slang, it is the received standard accent of the smart English book review.

There's no doubt that the ruck of reviews do belittle books. At one level, they have to. Large and complicated books are miniaturized to fit the available space of 1000 words or so, and much of the reviewer's craft goes into reducing their description to a deft and pretty paragraph; and it is this paragraph, this genius of abridgement, which is subsequently argued with, praised, derided; even, sometimes, cravenly admired. What actually gets reviewed is not the book itself, but the reviewer's fiction, based on the book he or she has read. No wonder, then, that the terms of the prep-school master, or the nanny, or the disappointed parent ("Get out, sir, and come back when your tongue is clean") come so readily to hand, for the books themselves have shrunk to pint-size in the process of transfiguration inside the reviews.

Given the verbal equivalent of an oval sliver of ivory on which to work, the miniaturist reviewer often finds that he must paint not just one, but four or five likenesses on it. Though almost any political memoir, however dull, is accorded two columns, most fiction and most poetry gets lumped together in rag-bag reviews, whose chief interest lies in the shaky Bailey-bridges constructed by the reviewer to enable him to scramble across from one book to the next.

> The past which haunts Jakov Lind's *The Inventor* is partly this same dark modern history. But . . .
> China, on the other hand, has more history than most of us can grasp, something which Bei Dao presents, in one of the stories from his collection *Waves* . . .
> John Mole inhabits, in a more lyrical manner, territory contiguous with Brownjohn's . . .

There's a plangency in that last quote which bespeaks the small-hours desperation of the reviewer, faced with a river as wide as the Amazon and equipped only with a coil of rope, six planks and a pogo stick. The one sure thing about the far side of the river is that it is contiguous territory, though always more lyrical/mountainous/boggy/fever-ridden/snake-infested than the bank one is standing on.

Yet it is in the reviews, more than in seminar-rooms or in Foundation-funded colloquia, that the main dialogue about modern literature is sustained, that new writers are discovered, old ones revalued, that standards of comparison are established and the essential small-talk of a literary culture goes on, often at a much more sophisticated level than was the case 50 years ago. Then, books of formal criticism like those by Empson and Leavis had a far wider currency than they do now, while book reviewers were drawn from a rather narrower spectrum of the writing world. The senior reviewer on the *Sunday Times* today is the Merton Professor of English at Oxford; his counterpart on the *Observer* is the most prolific, and probably the best-read, of all living English novelists. The reviewing professors (Carey, Kermode, Ricks, Davie, Donoghue) and the reviewing novelists (Burgess, the two Amises, Angela Carter, William Golding, Peter Ackroyd), together with the reviewing poets (James Fenton, Peter Porter, Tom Paulin, Douglas Dunn), keep up a level of discourse about writing which is pitched far higher – at least on its good days – than the journalistic commentary which passes for criticism of the other arts. Lucian Freud and Francis Bacon don't write reviews of new exhibitions; Harold Pinter doesn't review new plays, and Harrison Birtwhistle doesn't review concerts. Yet book reviewing is a craft dominated by book-writing practitioners. That's no guarantee of fairness but it does mean that book reviews in general are more interesting as pieces of writing than other kinds of reviews.

In 1938, Cyril Connolly saw book reviewing as the first stage of the downfall of promising young Walter Shelleyblake:

> The most Shelleyblake can expect is that, by reading two books a day and writing for three papers, he may make about four hundred a year. During this time he will incur the hostility of authors, the envy of other reviewers, and the distrust of his friends against whose books he will seem invariably prejudiced; the public will view him with indifference or accept him as an eccentric on whom they will launch their views and their manuscripts while old friends will greet him with, "Are you writing anything now?" – "Apart of course from your articles," they will add.

Connolly ended up by writing nothing else except reviews (though he wasn't half as hard-worked, or as ill-paid, as Shelleyblake), and *Enemies of Promise* is an accurately prophetic book about Connolly's own disappointed future; but his black picture of the hack in harness has dated badly (if it was ever a fair portrait in fact).

First, Shelleyblake now would have to be an ass to consider reviewing as a possible career. If he were extravagantly famous, he might be paid £20,000 a year to contribute a dozen or so reviews to one of the Sunday papers, on condition that he wrote for them exclusively; but such a price could only be justified by the continuing

appearances of Shelleyblake books, Shelleyblake television programmes and Shelleyblake opinion pieces on the state of the nation.
Most of the £20,000 would be a bribe to persuade Shelleyblake not
to write reviews while he added lustre to his name in other ways.
But Shelleyblake is supposed to be a young and relatively unknown
writer, and the cheques he'll get for his first half-dozen reviews will
be enough to shake him out of any illusions about making reviewing
his full-time job.

His reviews will necessarily be more infrequent than they might
have been in 1938, and he'll almost certainly write them more for love
than for money. (It's hard to corrupt anyone now with £70.) The
worst that's likely to happen to him is the discovery that he very
much enjoys writing book reviews for their own sake. Waking to the
flop of the jiffybag on the mat, he knows it as the sound of the
beginning of a good day. This morning, he can read in bed and tell
himself he's working. The fact that the book in the typewriter is stuck
fast at page 59 (the same page that Shelleyblake was on this time last
week) can be forgotten for a spell. He tears the book out of the bag
and settles down to hog it. The first reading (unless the book is
maddeningly bad) is for pleasure only. No notes in the margins. No
prudish exclamation marks and squiggles. Thus Shelleyblake in his
Dr Jekyll phase, curled up with a good read.

Hyde emerges on the second reading, which may happen on the
same afternoon, or may (preferably) be delayed for a week or ten
days. This time Shelleyblake has one eye for the book and the other
for his review of it. The questions of "what does it do?" and "what
can I write?" jostle for precedence in his head. He scribbles in the
margins, on the review slip and in the endpapers (though, if he wants
to sell it for half its cover price to the knacker's yard, he has to make
these marks in pencil and rub them out afterwards). He looks at
other books by the same author, and tries to see where this one fits
in to the sequence of the writer's work.

The problem of his piece, its approaching deadline, its slyly combative opening sentence, its running allusion to an idea culled from one
of Henry James's prefaces, looms larger now than the book itself
does, which is why Shelleyblake has taught himself to read every
book twice. As he writes he can keep on testing what he writes
against the memory of his first, innocent reading. If it rings true to
his enjoyment, or irritation, or disbelief then, it's probably on the
right lines; but his main concern is with his own words on his own
page.

The review is delivered. The proofs arrive two days later. On Friday, or Sunday, Shelleyblake is back in print, boosted by the reassurance that he can still write something that's worth publishing, even if the review has set him five days back on his sluggishly moving novel. Two friends call to say how much better his piece reads than Gissingwaugh's effort in the *Sunday Times* does. On Monday, the novel suddenly begins to move less sluggishly, and Shelleyblake feels better than he's done for a month.

Shelleyblake counts reading, and being able to write about his reading, as one of the major joys of his various occupations as a freelance. His reviews earn less, proportionately, than anything else he does, but give him a disproportionate private satisfaction. They come as heaven-sent distractions (mostly). They make him learn and think about writers and topics that are new to him. They get him writing when he seems to have run clean out of words. His last book came out two years ago (and it looks as if his next won't be out for eighteen months at least), and the magically rapid passage of his reviews from the typewriter to the printed page cheers him through the dog-days. During this between-books period the name of Walter Shelleyblake can seem as dusty as that of his progenitor, Walter Savage Landor; and his occasional reviews at least prove his survival, tap-tapping away somewhere up in the garrets of the literary world. To finish something, however short, to post it off and see it printed, all in the space of a few days, is balm.

The literary editor in *Enemies of Promise* was called Mr Vampire, because he sucked Shelleyblake's young blood and diverted his talents to the manufacture of ephemera. Today Shelleyblake prefers to think of him as an Uncle Bill or an Auntie Flo – one of those cherished courtesy aunts and uncles who breeze in out of the blue with surprise dispensations and excursions.

However fair-minded the literary editor is, however capable and assiduous the reviewer, the complaint stands. The newspapers don't review enough books, and they don't review them at sufficient length or with sufficient seriousness. (How can anyone write a proper review of someone's novel in 300 words?) Vampire and Shelleyblake may be reasonably happy about things as they are, but publishers, authors and readers aren't.

Publishers effectively subsidize the book pages with their advertisements – the fewer the ads, the fewer the reviews. If new books, by writers whom the publishers believe to be important, are repeatedly ignored, or dismissed in a few lines, why bother with reviews at all? In the world of *Enemies of Promise*, books sank or swam on the basis of their critical reception, and the publishers were, on the whole, content to be spectators of the process. Books that were seen to swim led to offers of lunch, larger advances and bigger advertisements; books that sank led to apologetic rejection slips.

We have now reached the point where most of the books published never get wet because there's no room for them in the dwindling critical pool. The publisher can no longer afford to be a spectator, because there's no process to spectate. So he turns his back on critical discourse as a waste of his firm's money, and looks elsewhere for space in which the books he publishes will be discussed – in gossip columns, chat shows and the rest of the promotion and publicity circuit. "The reviews don't matter – she's going on Wogan." Or, "There's a feature about her in *Vogue*."

This building frustration with the review pages is accompanied by the power to make them shrivel even further. So we get less close-reading, less critical comparison, less reassessment – less and less of the kind of writing about writing by which a literary community is sustained. So, too, we get more routine disparagement of the reviewer as a man who never reads the books he reviews, who copies out the blurbs, who's too ill-read to formulate a worthwhile judgment, whose only genius is for missing the point, etc., etc. The irony of this particular *de haut en bas* tactic is that the abused reviewer also happens to be the same Walter Shelleyblake whose magnificent last novel was so incompetently mangled last year by "the reviewers". Reviewers have never been very popular in society; they've always been seen to be stupider than they should be and always been seen to be living parasitically on other people's talents. But they have had their place – and their space. They've kept up the debate.

Now, with reviewing space diminishing and publishers failing to support the literary pages, the language of reviewing has become noticeably more telegraphic. The 400 or 600 word notice is taking over from the 1500 or 1800 word essay, with a corresponding loss of argument, qualification and definition. More and more reviews only have time to say "Hooray!" or "Boo!" before they're gone; and British publishers, authors, reviewers, literary editors and readers must look equally wistfully across to the United States, with their

New York Times Book Review and *Washington Post Book World*, where reviews are far longer and more detailed, and there are more of them.

Anthony Thwaite on the *Statesman* made me an addict of the book review as a happy form to work in. He was generous with space, with books and with the time he took to vet my efforts when I brought them in. He was good at chuckling aloud when he got to the jokes, and I spent three years trying to write reviews that would make Thwaite laugh. He encouraged me to rummage freely, to ride my own literary hobbyhorses and to return books that, once read, didn't promise to be fun to write about. There was no question that writing reviews should be fun. The dutiful review, the review written more in sorrow than in anger, was not worth writing. I took the lesson to heart, and returned roughly half the books given to me. It wasn't until several years later, when another literary editor wrote, on the verge of his retirement, to say that I was the most troublesome reviewer he'd ever dealt with, that I learned that Thwaite's precept was not universally accepted. Sending the review copies back, I'd thought I was doing the literary editor a favour by sparing him a dull and nit-picking piece. I still think Thwaite was right and J. W. Lambert quite wrong. Reviewers ought to return books unless the reviews they write of them are going to give them pleasure. You should be able to read the book at leisure, come to the end and know it's not for you without risking the wrath of an editor too busy to reassign it elsewhere.

The pieces that follow were all written as book reviews, though some do more reviewing than others.

BYRON

I

In 1813 Byron was twenty-five. *Childe Harold* had been published the year before and at last it seemed as if the albatross of Newstead Abbey had been transferred to Thomas Claughton. Bar a few formalities, Claughton's £140,000 was almost in Byron's pocket. Annabella Milbanke had said no; Caroline Lamb had been more or less satisfactorily ditched; the obliging Lord Oxford had rented him a dower house on his estate, from which convenient distance Byron could make love to his landlord's wife. Lady Melbourne – an engaging, sophisticated, powdered bitch of sixty-two – had become Byron's adopted aunt and confidante, and was playing banker for him with her younger female relations . . . withdrawing Caroline, and setting up Annabella. As Byron's affairs went, things had never been in better order. By the end of the year, however, he had managed to turn all this into a turmoil of proportions unprecedented even for him – a situation which causes more genuine distress to his biographers than it ever really did to Byron. He had a genius for making the outside world conform to the state he imagined his own mind to be in: anything he touched he could turn into chaos.

Doris Langley Moore's book on Byron's finances is not laundry-bill scholarship.* For Byron was, in the fullest, most richly metaphorical sense of the word, a spender. To follow the amazing sweeps and tidal movements of his income and outgoing is to see the Byron who spent himself and his great fortune of language just as he spent his money. The rhymes in *Don Juan*, like his love affairs and his grandiose projects abroad, are extravagant and conspicuous: they offer up a heroic, doomed challenge to the parsimony of the world. Money was a way of making life real by turning feelings into things. In the February of 1813, his obscure entanglement with Lady Oxford became a little less so when he went to Love & Kelty, the crown jewellers, and bought her 160 guineas' worth of baubles. In March, aching to be abroad, but with no real prospect of going, he bought enough uniforms and underwear to clothe an as yet quite imaginary expeditionary force. By July, furiously frustrated at the delays caused him by Claughton's failure to pay up for Newstead, he was buying camping equipment on a scale that makes William Boot's spree at Harrods in *Scoop* look cheeseparing. Beds, trunks, camp kettles, canteens, came to £400. Nine days later he added telescopes, field glasses, a sextant, compasses and a thermometer to his pile of gear. Everything was on account. The more surely the £140,000 evaporated away into a legal hassle over a broken promise, the more Byron bought. The mere purchase of these expensive toys, and the spiral of debt in which they enmeshed him, were action enough for the time being.

I think Mrs Langley Moore is wrong to come down as hard as she

* Doris Langley Moore, *Lord Byron: Accounts Rendered* (London: John Murray).

does on the friends and hangers-on at whom Byron capriciously flung his cheque book and by whom he was very rarely paid back – especially on poor Leigh Hunt. Anyone who came into contact with Byron's economy – hardly the best word for the financial operations of this one-man banana republic – was bound to be infected by its mad prodigality. He had elevated accounting to the realm of heroic fiction, and who keeps a proper reckoning with a Corsair or a Giaour? That he was in fact often wriggling on the pins of the money-lenders while he distributed his largesse can only have added to its air of unreality.

In September, Byron went to stay at Aston Hall, the home of a silly man of his own age called James Wedderburn Webster. Webster had recently married and, between bouts of unsuccessfully pursuing one of Byron's girl servants at Newstead, was fond of comparing his wife's forbearing temperament with that of Jesus Christ. Within a couple of days of arriving at Aston, Byron wrote to Lady Melbourne, "I shall have some comic Iagoism with our little Othello". Lady Frances Webster – "She is pretty but not surpassing – too thin – & not very animated – but good tempered" – was duly propositioned over a game of billiards. Byron passed her a *billet-doux* "in tender and tolerably turned *prose*" which she had just hidden "not very far from the heart which I wished it to reach", when her husband walked in. "It was a risk – & *all* had been lost by failure." But then comes the real excitement:

> My billet prospered – it did more – it even (I am this moment interrupted by the *Marito* – & write this before him – he has brought me a political pamphlet in M.S. to decypher and applaud – I shall content myself with the last – Oh – he is gone again) – my billet produced an *answer* . . .

The action has shifted to the writing of the letter itself. Byron's hectic, hiccuppy epistolary style, with dashes scattered like peppercorns between the phrases (was he parodying *Clarissa?*), comes into its own and quite takes over from whatever lingering interest we may have in the bloodless Lady Frances. The symmetries are surely deliberately over-refined: the twin entrances of the husband, the pairing of the tender prose of the *billet-doux* and Webster's bilious pamphlet, the two anticipated answers to the documents. When Byron says "Oh – he is gone again", the *again* must mean "again in my letter", as if all life was happening here where the ink is still wet on the page. This is *spending*, too; a cascade of brilliant tokens, a substitute for real events and actions which outdoes them in splendour at the same time as it robs them of all moral and emotional depth.

But Byron wasn't content with just fleshing out these delicious complications in letters to Lady Melbourne. Two days after his letter about the *billet-doux*, he authorized a loan of £1000 to Webster – another thread in Byron's devious, sticky web. A month later, by which time Byron had all but forgotten Lady Frances and was busy selling himself to Annabella again, Webster was beginning to sweat. He wrote to Byron about repaying the loan, and Byron noted in his journal:

> Mem. I must write tomorrow to "Master Shallow, ∗∗, who owes me a thousand pounds," and seems, in his letter, afraid I should ask him for it; – as if I would!

To Webster, Byron was grandly dismissive: "even if my exigencies were pressing – I should not trouble you on the subject – and you know me well enough not to doubt me on such *worldly* matters —". The underlining of "worldly" suggests a sniggering private pun, particularly when set beside three phrases a little further on: "I suppose you will at least prefer me to a *Jew*. – I meant to write you a long letter on lighter topics – but talking of money materialises ones thoughts . . ." It is a sustained flight of malicious *double-entendre*, gloating over Webster's ignorance of Byron's intrigue with his wife. Byron was getting his money's worth; and it seems churlish to chide the cuckold – as Mrs Langley Moore does – for not honouring his bond. In fact, Byron did not even need to sleep with Lady Frances; "a few kisses" was all he claimed he had from her. Her confession of love for him (it was, he reported to Lady Melbourne, "a little too much about virtue – & indulgence of attachment in some sort of etherial process in which the soul is principally concerned") and the snares and deceptions which he was able to set for Webster were quite enough for him.

For Byron, romantically in love with the idea of action as he was, the tokens were more than sufficient. Through the year, he piled "scrape" on top of "scrape", debt on debt, jollying himself along, like Feste, with frequent "Heigh-ho's" in his journal. In the mornings he boxed; in the small hours, scribbled furiously.

> Who would write, who had anything better to do? "Action
> – action – action" – said Demosthenes: "Actions – actions,"
> I say, and not writing, – least of all, rhyme.

But the bills, the *billets*, the letters and the poems constituted a hysterical tumult of activity. Deprived of the Near East as a theatre on which to strut, Byron turned his private life, and private writing, into a battlefield. His "pagod" Napoleon, exhausted by his campaigns and attacked by his political enemies, was heading for a dramatic downfall. Byron was giving himself every chance of going down too. In the spring of 1814, he wrote in the journal:

> The more violent the fatigue, the better my spirits for the rest of the day; and then, my evenings have that calm nothingness of languor, which I most delight in.

He ached for stillness, for an end to spending. But it could only come about through exhaustion in action. His self-created chaos, his fanatical improvidence, his determination to live his life as a series of climactic scenes out of a Restoration comedy, were courted and cultivated because of the languorous nothingness which he believed might succeed them. He was trying to outstrip his own life-span.

There is an odd remark in the journal:

> To be popular in a rising and far country has a kind of *posthumous feel*, very different from the ephemeral *éclat* and fêteing, buzzing and party-ing compliments of the well-dressed multitude.

He was talking about his American reviews, but that phrase haunts his whole life. Pathologically committed to tokens, the nearest he could come to being posthumous was to get married. "One must end in marriage," he wrote to Thomas Moore, and the best he could say of matrimony was "I should like to have somebody now and then to yawn with one." Late in 1813, feeling that he had reached an appropriate degree of withered senility, he approached Annabella with the solemn decorum of a man inviting someone to join him in a double burial in the family vault.

He had never behaved in a more cool and businesslike fashion. His letters to her are inventories of himself, phrased in a language of legal deadness and precision. His bids are hedged and cautious. Had he only managed to put Newstead on the market in the same efficient way, he might have been happily living it up in Turkey. At the end of November, just as he was preparing the customer for the final offer, he wrote in his journal:

> What an odd situation and friendship is ours! – without one spark of love on either side, and produced by circumstances which in general lead to coldness on one side, and aversion on the other.

Cold and clever, Annabella was to be the conclusion of Byron's life. Thinking of marriage as a termination, he does not seem to have speculated on what might happen beyond the altar – all he saw was the calm and silence of a life beyond the grave. On 1 December he asked himself with an uneasy mixture of mockery and heroism: "Is there anything in the future that can possibly console us for not being always *twenty-five*?"

The last words of Byron's first journal are "O fool! I shall go mad." At twenty-six, Byron was trying on Lear's wrinkles, and finding that they fitted him perfectly. Then he tore the rest of the pages out of the book, as if – tokens again – he could thus tear out the remaining years of his life. That gesture was in character: absurd, vainglorious and, to Annabella if to no one else, unspeakably cruel. It was also tentative and experimental in a way that only Byron knew how to be. He would buy all the fripperies and accessories first, then see whether the reality of the expedition would follow in their wake. We of course have the posthumous view he craved for: he didn't know what was going to happen – we do. Annabella Milbanke got the living grave he wanted for himself, while for Byron the whole crazy mouse-wheel was to start up again almost as soon as it had seemed to stop. One wishes that Leslie Marchand and John Murray could bring the forthcoming volumes out a little faster: at the current rate, we shall be dead before he is.

1974

II

Byron would have enjoyed seeing his life on exhibition at the Victoria & Albert Museum. An avid collector of old letters, lockets and sentimental keepsakes, he liked to preside as the curator over the museum of his own immediate past. At 15, in a premature valedictory to Newstead Abbey, he was mooning indulgently over the bits of armour which hung in the draughty hall of his family seat:

> Of the mail-cover'd Barons, who, proudly, to battle,
> Led their vassals from Europe to Palestine's plain,
> The escutcheon and shield, which with every blast rattle,
> Are the only sad vestiges now that remain.

Now it is the sad vestiges of Byron himself which are on show – a pair of rotting surgical boots under glass, a shirt with a faint rime of Byronic sweat still shadowing its collar and armpits; letters from various ladies, set among pink wax roses. Coiled snips of their hair are numbered and catalogued. A Spanish girl appears to have scalped herself for Byron; he parcelled up the switch and sent it to his mother for safe-keeping.

Lady Frances Webster, whom Byron casually seduced for the amusement of his friend Lady Melbourne, is here – a shabby trophy. "Oh! My Byron I am dead between hope & fear – What can I imagine when I said when I candidly confessed how much depended upon my hearing from you what can I imagine from your silence!" Her syntax sobs and heaves; her handwriting is a characterless, finishing-school copperplate. At the top, some anonymous 20th-century penciller has labelled it "Despairing Letter" to distinguish it from "Letter enclosing verses". Her hair, one notes as one passes on to the next victim, was mousy.

Even the smell of the exhibition seems right: a whiff of must, brocade and camphor, like an unused room in the house of an elderly aunt. Alan Tagg has designed it as a series of peepshows; as one follows the arrows through the labyrinth one is turned into a trespasser, made to feel both the pleasure and the heartlessness of peeking at these long-dead intimacies. Tagg has mounted two brilliant, confidently vulgar set-pieces. One is the gloomy interior of a Venetian palazzo, full of chandeliers, folio volumes, and stuffed cats and dogs. Beside it there's a back-lit bright blue window from which you can hear the simulated gurgle of a canal swilling around the piles of South Kensington.

Further on, passing through the corridor to "Byron's Death", you find yourself peering through a mosquito net at an empty bed whose occupant has apparently just been removed, leaving only a bloody bandage behind him, along with a trunkful of ineffective medicines. A clever piece of circuitry produces a candlelight so dim and sputtering that one expects it to go out as one watches. That stroke of ravishingly bad taste sets the tone of the whole exhibition.

The immensely interesting collection of portraits, letters, manuscript drafts and personal curios and memorabilia is coloured throughout by a sturdy sentimentality, alternately gushing and cruel, which brings us closer to Byron himself than most of his biographers have succeeded in doing.

For Alan Tagg and the V. & A. have completed an enterprise which Byron started in his own adolescence. Almost as soon as he had lived through a moment, he got busy turning it into something from a legendary Past; it was as if nothing were real for him until it was over, marked by a new sad memento in his collection. At 21, he commissioned a group of miniatures of his friends from the painter George Sanders. Quite aside from the fact that he was flat broke at the time, it was an odd thing to do, and one wonders how the sitters must have felt, being asked to pose, in the first flush of their friendship, for the keepsakes by which Byron would remember them when they were gone.

At 26, when his new interest in the theatre was blazing, he had a screen made to go in his bachelor rooms at Albany: one side of it is decorated with pictures and newspaper-clippings of boxers; the other is a gallery of contemporary actors and actresses. Its lacquer has aged now, gone to an antique, verdigris-green; but even when it was first put together it must have seemed to commemorate a past which wasn't yet past.

There was a strong streak of aristocratic philistinism in Byron. Music stopped for him beyond what could be hummed or whistled; painting was there to provide him with snapshots for his album. More powerful than any cultivated taste for art was his jackdaw passion for souvenirs. In 1817, he trudged over the battlefield of Waterloo, picking up trinkets for his collection. They are here, housed in the sort of glass case which ought to contain a stuffed auk: a ball of grapeshot, three regimental badges, and a mouldy tricolour. He was an insatiable and indiscriminate collector of gew-gaws, animals, experiences and people.

The trouble was that the people, especially the women, weren't content to play possum, tastefully framed behind glass. In the hysterical aftermath of his affair with Caroline Lamb, Byron wrote to Lady Melbourne, Caroline's aunt, "I beseech her for her own sake to remain quiet". For Byron a week in love was a very long time, and a week out of love was as good as an eternity: he simply could not understand why these plaguey women should continue to bother him when as far as he was concerned they were as dead and gone as his mail-covered barons. He could wax sentimental over the lock of hair and casket of letters which they'd left behind, but he was self-righteously appalled by their fury and disappointment at his desertion. They were part of a past he wanted to gloom over, and it baffled him when they refused to take up their appointed positions in his museum.

So it's not surprising that the exhibition should contain so many casualties. There they lie, these women, in faded letters, struggling for life, struggling against their dismissal by Byron into an omnivorous past. His mother, a vast tub of luxuriant fattiness in her portrait by Stewardson, writes to Hanson the family solicitor complaining that her boy will be the ruin of her. Claire Clairmont begs for another assignation in an English which combines flowery literary pretensions with some awful grammar. Caroline Lamb embellishes a nice conceit about a dead rose for Byron's entertainment. Annabella, in a letter of frozen gravity to Augusta Leigh, explains why she and Byron have had to separate. Ironically, we see them now, as Byron saw them then, as glass-case cases – touching curiosities at best, with their brown ink and pretty notepaper.

They were all woven long ago into Byron's own Byronic legend. He was 33 when he wrote in his "Detached Thoughts":

> If I could explain at length the *real* causes which have contributed to increase this perhaps *natural* temperament of mine, this Melancholy which hath made me a byword, nobody would wonder; but this is impossible without doing much mischief. I do not know what other men's lives have been, but I cannot conceive anything more strange than some of the earlier parts of mine.

Even when he was addressing himself, Byron could not help hinting at the unspeakable gothic secrets hidden in his closet. He became a voyeur of his own past, twitching a curtain aside to reveal an old escapade, and hurriedly closing it again. He was his own most impressive exhibit. Grimly dieted down, white faced, clothed in black, his whole person spoke of sins and sufferings too ancient or shocking to be directly told. When Mrs Jarley conducted parties of schoolgirls round her waxwork show in *The Old Curiosity Shop*, she refurbished Mary Queen of Scots into "such a complete image of Lord Byron that the young ladies quite screamed when they saw it". In his lifetime, Byron did Mrs Jarley's work for her with a macabre artistry she might have envied.

He had a genius for turning his entire life into a grand retrospective exhibition – and the triumph of that same genius was his poetry. His early writing was straightforwardly gloomy and antique, a literary version of old suits of armour clanking in the hallway. The echoing romantic emptiness of "Childe Harold" provides a museum building which is just as gothic and imposing as the V. & A. itself, but there is precious little to see inside it. It was in the *ottava rima* stanza, which he borrowed from the Italian to write "Beppo" and "Don Juan", that he found the perfect vehicle for turning his collection of life into verse. He used it like his screen of pictures and cuttings, as a base on which to stick an encyclopedic rag-bag of past experiences, suitably cut out and framed by the order of regular rhyme. Old love affairs . . . political squabbles . . . things culled out of books . . . gossip . . . chance remarks . . . brief snapshots of his enemies and friends – there was nothing that could not be pasted on and preserved behind a coat of lacquer.

He foresaw no particular ending for "Don Juan". The poem was to last as long as he cared to write more cantos. Its function was to laugh at and memorialize the world he lived in. Looking at the manuscript in Byron's hasty, forward-leaning writing, one sees just how sternly he marshalled his experience behind his rhymes. There are, surprisingly, many crossings-out and second thoughts, but the rhyme-words stay almost completely untouched. Once Byron had fixed the sequence of chimes in his head, he pulled life about until it fitted in. Auden once observed of Byron's notorious gibe about Keats:

> 'Tis strange the mind, that very fiery Particle,
> Should let itself be snuffed out by an Article.

– that if Keats's mind "had been, let us say 'an organ made for thinking', then the *Edinburgh Review* could never have hurt his feelings, and he would have died, not of consumption, but of over-drinking." So often, the shadow of a giggling embalmer falls over Byron's rhymes, with their brilliant, cruel finality: every rhyme preserves and varnishes a fragment of life which it has had to kill. Perhaps it's not a proper question to ask, but one does find oneself wondering just how much of other people's pain went into the making of each of Byron's comic masterstrokes. Here are Annabella's mathematically cool letters, a scruple in every sentence; there is that ribald couplet from "Don Juan":

> But – oh ye lords of ladies intellectual!
> Inform us truly, have they not henpecked you all?

For a moment the varnish seems to crack, the witticism to be embarrassed by rather more of life than it can comfortably handle. Inevitably, his contemporaries were more bothered by such things than we are. In William Gifford's satire, "The Illiberal", "Lord B." is found "solus". He takes up his pen and writes . . .

LINES ON THE PAST

How have I spent the moments of my life?
I have deserted Home, Friends, Child and Wife,
(Oh! melancholy retrospective view,)
They've felt some pain, and I have felt some too.

Gifford's Byron, with his irrepressibly cheerful bathos, is a savage caricature, but there is at least a measure of justice in that sneer. Byron found mementos easier to deal with than life. This exhibition, in reminding us of the human causes and consequences of his poetry, doesn't at all lessen the poems, but it greatly darkens them.

1974

THACKERAY

John Carey is, in fact, Merton Professor of English Literature at Oxford, but he sits on his professorial chair so deftly and lightly that one suspects that there is a whoopee cushion on it. For Carey brings to academe all the virtues of Grub Street: cleverness, wit, concision, impertinence and an endearing readiness to sacrifice messy accuracy for a memorable and slashing phrase. He is a hatchet man's hatchet man – one of the very few hired killers in the business who can use 800 words as a lethal weapon. He is a thoroughly entertaining, unreliable maverick.

The coupling of Carey and Thackeray had to be productive. I can think of no other academic critic as well placed to appreciate Thackeray's hasty and offhand brilliance, his wild subversive irony, his malicious and insatiable appetite for trivia. Had television been invented in the 1840s Thackeray would undoubtedly have revelled in *The New Avengers*, just as he revelled in pantomime and pulp fiction. He would probably have been infuriated reading Carey's book about him; but (imagine Dickens reading Leavis) he would have accepted

the ground-rules, and answered back in kind. For Carey's *Thackeray**
is brisk, insolent, often very funny, in exactly the same way that
Thackeray himself was in his own criticism.

What Carey offers here is a vividly exaggerated cartoon – a Cruik-
shank sketch of Thackeray's career, full of bold colours, sweeping
lines and comic noses. The first chapter, called, simply, "Life", takes
Thackeray from the womb to fat, snobbish middle age in just 21
pages. There are elisions and simplifications, of course, but there is
not a word of excess fat.

Seven succeeding chapters – each with a title of combative simplicity: "Commodities", "Food and Drink", "Theatre", "What Went
Wrong" – pin Thackeray's work out on the table for inspection.
Carey's tone is as cool as a garage mechanic's: he has a racy, no-nonsense way with literature, and a gift for trenchant quotation. Indeed,
Thackeray reads like a breezy A.A. report on a rather ropey used car.
Carey's forthright conclusions are that the chassis and suspension are
first-rate, but he finds the engine clapped out and the respray job
shoddy.

According to the report, the rot set in in 1848 – the year after
Vanity Fair was published. Up till then, Thackeray had been cruel,
sceptical and quick as lightning, the most dazzling of all the Grub
Street wits who'd gathered around Douglas Jerrold's *Punch* and
Shilling Magazine. He had set out on the dandified margins of society,
sniping at its pretensions from the sidelines. Carey traces a clear line
of continuity from the early reviews, feuilletons and sketches to
Thackeray's one undisputed masterpiece, *Vanity Fair*. But the book
both made and ruined him. By giving him his entrée into clubs and
fashionable drawing rooms, it enabled him to be seduced by the very
world he should have satirized. Thackeray grew pious, moralistic,
snobbish and – in his later novels – profoundly boring. Before the
blandishments of Society, his scepticism departed from him like an
exorcized demon, leaving only a dull old clubman behind.

Carey's report is so spirited and sure of itself that it seems churlish
to quibble: and if only quibbles were at stake, it could be admired,
accepted, and kept well away from students in search of a good
quarrelsome "line" on Thackeray. In the interests of its own consistency, though, the report badly misrepresents its subject: Carey's
Thackeray is not just cartooned, he is a character of fiction.

Carey's basic quarrel with Thackeray is that in 1848 the novelist

* John Carey, *Thackeray, Prodigal Genius* (London: Faber & Faber).

changed sets. He stopped moving among Jerrold's irreverent young men, and started going for carriages and titles. That is surely right; but Carey seems to me to be quite wrong to claim that the first Thackeray, the radical sceptic, was the authentic one, while the second was a pompous fake. "Authenticity" was never Thackeray's strong point. As a writer, he was always dodging behind masks and pseudonyms – M. A. Titmarsh, Fitzboodle, Lancelot Wagstaff, F. Tudge, and others.

His strongest talent was for impersonation, and when he was narrating a story he could "do" a Covent Garden radical or a Grosvenor Square prig with equal ease: his best writing is always dramatic, in the sense that W. M. Thackeray is a creature of elusive quicksilver, disappearing in and out of the characters and types which he creates in order to be able to speak at all. When – in the last sentence of *Vanity Fair* – he talks of the "puppets" and the "puppet box", there is a gleeful irony in play: for no puppet master has ever danced more to the tunes of his own creations than Thackeray himself. He was someone of such provisional identity that he looked constantly to his novels to discover who he was.

For Carey, the republican sentiments at the end of *The Book of Snobs* reflect the real 24-carat, sceptical Thackeray. But dip into *Punch*, or the *Shilling Magazine*, or *Fraser's*, or the *National Standard*, and the same phrases, the same synthetic anger, the same rhetorical élan, jump from the page. Most of *The Book of Snobs* could just as easily have been written by one of the Mayhew brothers, or Mark Lemon, or Douglas Jerrold. The surprising thing is that it was written by the author of *Vanity Fair*. With hindsight, we can see that it is the preliminary notebook for Thackeray's masterpiece; but there is a world of difference between the crude, typecast sketches in *The Book of Snobs* and the full-colour portraits of *Vanity Fair*. Thackeray, a pathological actor, could bring off an exact mimicry of the style of the bohemian set, but he was not really one of them; and his egalitarian fury seems just as much of a pose as his later attempt to pass himself off as a comfortable old buffer.

Just as Carey exaggerates the continuity between the radical journalism and *Vanity Fair*, so he exaggerates the difference between the masterpiece and books like *Pendennis* and *The Newcomes*. Listen to the undercurrent of self-mockery in the narrator's voice in the last paragraph of *Pendennis* and one will not find it half as complacent a novel as Professor Carey does. The truth is that Thackeray's insecure art lay always in the realm of risk, luck and brilliance; it was an art of remarks and set pieces, and one book has better remarks and more fine set pieces than any other. Carey's chronological thesis, sparkling as it is, does explain Thackeray's wayward genius. But perhaps Thackeray's most lasting power is in his capacity to inconvenience and discomfit his critics. The cleverest (which is not to say the most intelligent, by any means) novelist in English, Thackeray won't be caught, even by a critic as clever as Professor Carey.

1977

HENRY MAYHEW

In *London Labour and the London Poor* Mayhew gave faces, voices and characters to people who had hitherto only existed as figures of rumour and nightmare. He made the invisible visible, lifted the metropolitan fog to reveal a sector of English society – the men and women who had fallen clean through the industrial system – which his contemporaries had been keeping deliberately dark. But Mayhew himself has disappeared; and his invisibility is not so much the tactful withdrawal of the reporter who leaves his reports to speak for themselves as a case of abduction – he has been spirited away into the same fog which he did so much to clear. Dickens and Mayhew knew each other, probably well; certainly they acted together at least twice in an amateur production of *Every Man in His Humour*, and Mayhew's young brother Horace wrote for *Household Words*. But nowhere in Dickens's papers is there a mention of Mayhew. Douglas Jerrold, the editor, socialite and man of letters, was Mayhew's father-in-law and he and Mayhew were among the contested founders of *Punch*; there are two biographies of Jerrold, and in both Mayhew is just an occasional name, more shadowy than the servant girl. He knew George Augustus Sala, but Sala's copious memoirs leave no record of Mayhew. In that chronically gossipy milieu of Victorian literary bohemia, Mayhew, who was as keen a drunken clubman as anyone, is an Enoch Soames in search of a Beerbohm.

He clearly didn't think of himself as anonymous and peripheral. He had his portrait engraved for *London Labour and the London Poor*, and it has a preternatural solidity, all girth, weight, and heavy black cross-hatching. It shows a great, flattened-oval slab of a head – tufty, balding, symmetrical – with the fleshy nose, sunken eyes and querulous mouth of a butler who has been too long at the port. It is a portrait of the author as Victorian busybody. All Mayhew's interviewees insistently call him "Sir"; and here, in waistcoat and wing-collar, is the substantial personage they were addressing. (It was a device with a double point. Mayhew's readers knew his characters only as a lewd-mouthed rabble with no respect for person or station. Mayhew makes his dog-dung collectors and mudlarks exaggeratedly genteel, simultaneously enhancing their status and his own.) Indeed, his anecdotal prose is studiedly stodgy, much given to elaborate circumlocutions and judicial parentheses; as a literary manner it is almost comically self-important. He presents himself as the ambassador of the genteel world, and the "I" of *London Labour* embodies the stuffiness, the pedantic curiosity, the moralism, and the crackpot theorizing of the Victorian gentleman at large. It is an artfully stage-managed posture.

For, until 1849 when the cholera epidemic broke loose in Bermondsey and Mayhew contributed his first piece on the wretched of London to the *Morning Chronicle*, Mayhew had kept steadily on the run from gentility. He was 37 when he began the London project; and for nearly twenty years he had lived in the nether world of the Victorian freelance, editing short-lived satirical magazines, writing squibs and articles, dashing off dreadful farces, and collaborating with his brother Augustus on a series of novels. In 1846, he went bankrupt, owing £2000, with an income of around £400. From his own memoirs, quoted – with a parsimonious note on their authorship – in Walter Jerrold's biography of his father Douglas, Mayhew seems to have spent an inordinate amount of time in the Garrick Tavern in Bow Street, where he and his friends got up a drinking club called The Rationalists. Writing afforded a congenially dissipated way of life; it took Mayhew out on to the rim of society, displaced him from the shabby bourgeoisie into which he had been born. But he had neither a subject nor a style of his own. He flirted with fashionable radicalism and educational theory, and attempted – in the novels, the plays and the pieces for *Punch* – to write brittle satiric comedies of manners. His one sure quality lay in his position as a professional outsider of society, and he became a railer, sniggering entertainingly at the mannerisms of both the wealthy, from whom he was cut off, and of the poor, whom he was precariously avoiding joining.

The novels he wrote with Augustus are displays of winking ventriloquism. The brothers' great party piece was female impersonation, and in *The Greatest Plague of Life: Or The Adventures of a Lady in Search of a Good Servant* and *Whom to Marry and How to Get Married: Or The Adventures of a Lady in Search of a Good Husband* they went cackling in drag, doing proficiently vulgar travesties of the Victorian nice young lady. They are sharp on genteel hypocrisy, religiosity and the rapacious greed with which their heroines treat money, but the real energy of the books springs from their naughtiness as they trespass on the secrets of the toilet, and creep, clad in heavy *double-entendres*, between the sheets of the marital bed.

> Charles and I thought that our happiness was never to end. Scarcely a pleasure but what we could join in it, and enjoy it together. We hunted, and shot, and fished together; and scarcely a sport that he indulged in that I didn't participate in the pleasure with equal joy . . .

Both novels are crammed with domestic details – prices, materials, bits of kitchenware, meals, lessons in etiquette, brand names, and London topography. They are bewitched, and clearly revolted, by the bric-à-brac of Victorian family life. They burst sporadically into a hopeless ironic savagery at the twittering awfulness of the mistress of the suburban villa, mixing her sentimental whimsies with her contemptuous treatment of her social inferiors in a style of shrill mockery. It is customary to detect at least a hint of serious social concern for the conditions in which servants worked in *The Greatest Plague of Life*, but the Mayhews are much more interested in ridiculing the mistress than in sympathizing with the servants; that she flings them one after another into the street is supposed to tell us more about her than about them.

The novels are shot through with an aimless, insouciant talent for observation. They are inexhaustibly curious, and they delight in simple mimicry – getting a voice down on paper, writing exaggeratedly "in character". But they stand in a complacent, cock-a-snook attitude to the society whose manners they catalogue; their satire is without control or direction and they fizzle out in bumptious foolery. Yet, between 1847, when *The Greatest Plague of Life* was published, and 1849, Henry Mayhew was able, somehow, to transform himself from the facetious bohemian outsider of the novels into the solemn, stolid enquirer represented in his portrait in *London Labour*.

His first *Morning Chronicle* assignment took him, in September 1849, to Jacob's Island, an unsavoury, overcrowded patch of land around St Saviour's Dock below Tower Bridge at the wrong end of Tooley Street, where the cholera epidemic was at its worst. Eleven years before, Dickens had used Jacob's Island as the setting for the death of Sikes in *Oliver Twist*; and in 1850, Charles Kingsley used it for the grotesque climax of *Alton Locke*. The place hardly needed writers to make it a crucial symbol of the state of the Victorian city: it was a line of mean cottages and broken-down warehouses perched over an open sewer. The Thames, still the main artery of London commercial life, pushed sluggishly past it. It was from near here that Gaffer Hexham practised his profession of fishing bodies out of the river; and even now – Jacob Street, Dockhead and Mill Lane stand, although Mr Seifert has posted notices of demolition on the warehouses – it is an eerie, empty, half-ruined quarter, smelling of turmeric and Thames sludge. There are tramp-fires on the floors of deserted buildings, and the dock water is gurgling and opaque. For Dickens, Mayhew and Kingsley, Jacob's Island was natural raw material; they each imprinted on it their vision of the city, and the three passages, so close in subject yet so different in details of execution, are exact measures of their authors' individual styles. Set beside his contemporaries, Mayhew's peculiar qualities of mind become immediately and dramatically apparent. I quote parallel paragraphs from each passage.

> It is a creek or inlet from the Thames, and can always be filled at high water by opening the sluices at the Lead Mills from which it took its old name. At such times, a stranger, looking from one of the wooden bridges thrown across it at Mill Lane, will see the inhabitants of the houses on either side lowering from their back doors and windows, buckets, pails, domestic utensils of all kinds, in which to haul the water up; and when the eye is turned from these operations to the houses themselves, his utmost astonishment will be excited by the scene before him. Crazy wooden galleries common to the backs of half-a-dozen houses, with holes from which to look upon the slime beneath; windows, broken and patched, with poles thrust out, on which to dry the linen that is never there; rooms so small, so filthy, so confined, that the air would seem too tainted even for the dirt and squalor in which they shelter; wooden chambers

thrusting themselves out above the mud, and threatening to fall into it – as some have done; dirt-besmeared walls and decaying foundations; every repulsive lineament of poverty, every loathsome indication of filth, rot, and garbage; all these ornament the banks of Folly Ditch.

[Dickens, *Oliver Twist*]

The striking peculiarity of Jacob's Island consisted in the wooden galleries and sleeping rooms at the back of the houses overhanging the turbid flood. These were built upon piles, so that the place had positively the air of a Flemish street, flanking a sewer instead of a canal; while the little rickety bridges that spanned the ditches, and connected court with court, gave it the appearance of the Venice of drains. At some parts of the stream whole rooms had been built out, so that the houses on opposite sides nearly touched one another; and there, with the very stench of death arising through the boards, human beings slept night after night, until the last sleep of all came upon them years before its time. Scarce a house but yellow linen was hanging to dry over its rude balustrade of staves, or else they were run out on a long oar where the sulphur-coloured clothes fluttered flag-fashion over the waters, and you were startled not to see their form and colour reflected in the putrid ditch beneath.

[Mayhew, "Pest-Nests"]

The light of the policeman's lantern glared over the ghastly scene – along the double row of miserable house-backs, which lined the sides of the open tidal ditch – over strange rambling jetties, and balconies, and sleeping sheds, which hung on rotting piles over the black waters, with phosphorescent scraps of rotten fish gleaming and twinkling out of the dark hollows, like devilish grave-lights – over bubbles of poisonous gas, and bloated carcases of dogs, and lumps of offal, floating on the stagnant olive-green hell-broth – over the slow sullen rows of oily ripple which were dying away into the darkness far beyond, sending up, as they stirred, hot breaths of miasma – the only sign that a spark of humanity, after years of foul life, had quenched itself at last in that foul death. I almost fancied that I could see the

haggard face staring up at me through the slimy water; but
no – it was as opaque as stone.

[Kingsley, *Alton Locke*]

One needs to add, perhaps, that in Kingsley a man has fallen into
the ditch; which may account for the hectic stew of dashes, hyphen-
ations and lurid adjectives. By contrast with both Dickens and
Kingsley, Mayhew is oddly detached and leisurely. He is not insensitive to the poverty and suffering of the cholera victims, but, even as
he describes their deaths, he can afford to be playful, curious, exact.
He notices that some washing is hung out on oars, some on staves;
another writer might have been content with the bizarre echo of
Venice, but Mayhew carefully qualifies the image by referring to the
Flemish streets as well; along with the oars, he introduces "flags",
and manages to suggest a quaint, picturesque armada. While Kingsley
diverts himself in an orgy of theatrical moral feeling, and Dickens
cunningly depopulates and recreates the place for his private fictional
purposes, Mayhew keeps his eyes open and keeps cool. He is wonderfully faithful to the irreverence and irrelevance of the eye as it enjoys
itself when it ought to be shocked and sees things from which it
ought to have averted its gaze. This spectator's lack of natural morality
– the habitual outsider's essential trick of the mind – paradoxically
enables Mayhew to be more, not less morally forceful. Later on,
Kingsley observes with horror how the inhabitants of Jacob's Island
draw buckets of polluted water from the sewer and make tea with
them. He is so shocked that he cannot bear to look further. Mayhew
does, and notices that the buckets are left to stand for a day or two
on the windowsills, then the fluid is skimmed "from the solid particles
of filth and pollution which constitute the sediment". Such details of
ordinary, common-sense practicality, like the single red dahlia which
Mayhew notices sprouting at the foot of the benighted Providence
Buildings, are totally submerged in the writing of conventional
moralists. But Mayhew is liberated from a concern with his own finer
feelings; he is, among Victorian writers, uniquely unsententious.

He understood very well what he was doing and cultivated this innate
oddity of vision. In a piece on "Getting Up a Pantomime", he remarks
on how the decline of the theatrical spectacular has led to the mass
unemployment of "supers":

There was a goodly show of fine old regulation "supers" at
Astley's while "Mazeppa" was being played some time ago;

and I confess that the sight of the curious old banner-bearers
in that extraordinary drama had more interest for me than
the developed charms of the "beauteous Menken".

The dreariest bohemian prides himself on standing outside the conventions of the middle class, but Mayhew was able to translate that
commonplace affectation into a deliberate blindness to all conventions. At the theatre, he didn't notice the star; in society at large, he
failed to observe any of the rules of the morality of perception. He
followed his eye, and it told quite a different story from the one
which the educated Victorian was supposed to listen to. Mayhew's
imagination was astonishingly and fruitfully uncontrolled: it carelessly and casually broke every law it encountered, and in 1874,
explaining why he had attended a public execution, Mayhew was
able to boast that he had "been everywhere – seen everything, which
maybe a gentleman should not".

Ungentlemanliness was his style. It started out as naughtiness and
thumb-nose satire, and developed into the magnificent disregard for
convention which enabled him to write his masterpiece. Yet when
he came to portray himself in *London Labour*, it was as *Sir*, Mr
Mayhew doubling as Mr Bumble, a travesty-gentleman. The phrasing
of the preface is interesting here. Mayhew proposed to investigate
London life as if the East End was a jungle of savages and he a
venturing anthropologist setting forth with canoe and native guides.
The tactic was a subtle one: it enabled him to see the poor not as a
class but as a caste. His street folk are outside the class system,
they are not members of the industrial proletariat; their status is
determined, as in a real Indian caste, less by their relationships with
each other than by their relationships with objects – the things they
can touch, or, in the case of London, the things they buy and sell,
from fresh eatables down to dog-dung. From anthropology Mayhew
borrowed the distinction between "settlers" and "wanderers". Settlers
had big heads; wanderers big jawbones. Civilized people (including
the industrialized working class) settled, uncivilized people wandered.
The street folk of London were uncivilized wanderers with large
jawbones. It was an alarmingly plausible statement of the sense of
profound difference and alienation which the metropolitan middle
class felt when they confronted their impoverished brethren. But
Mayhew took pains to underline it even further.

The nomad is distinguished from the civilized man by his
repugnance to regular and continuous labour – by his want

of providence in laying up a store for the future – by his inability to perceive consequences ever so slightly removed from immediate apprehension – by his passion for stupefying herbs and roots, and, when possible, for intoxicating fermented liquors – by his extraordinary powers of enduring privation – by his comparative insensibility to pain – by an immoderate love of gaming, frequently risking his own personal liberty upon a single cast – by his love of libidinous dances – by the pleasure he experiences in witnessing the suffering of sentient creatures – by his delight in warfare and all perilous sports – by his desire for vengeance – by the looseness of all his notions as to property – by the absence of chastity among his women, and his disregard of female honour – and lastly, by his vague sense of religion – his rude idea of a Creator, and utter absence of all appreciation of the mercy of the Divine Spirit.

This is Casaubon, or the gentleman in the engraving, speaking; not Mayhew. Yet the impersonation, as shrill in its way as the drag acts of the novels, is deeply mixed up with what is most serious and necessary in Mayhew's method. Henry Mayhew, ex-bankrupt, lover of fermented liquor, devoutly satiric, anti-clerical, reputedly bad husband, is dressing up in frock coat and gaiters for a dangerous expedition into the territory of the depraved. Disraeli's Two Nations are about to meet between the covers of the book.

Yet the people Mayhew finds, or creates (and in *London Labour* it is impossible to draw the line accurately between the two), turn out to be nature's gentlemen. The language they use, as they recite their lives of extreme poverty, illness and degradation, has a consistent poetic dignity. It is, undoubtedly, a literary language; highly organized, poised, often syntactically elaborate. Mayhew's most fully developed single character, Jack Black the Queen's Ratcatcher, illustrates this with a resonant, labyrinthine story:

One night in August – the night of a very heavy storm, which, maybe, you may remember, sir – I was sent for by a medical gent as lived opposite the Load of Hay, Hampstead, whose two children had been attacked by rats while they was sleeping in their little cots. I traced the blood, which had left lines from their tails, through the openings in the lath and plaster, which I follered to where my ferruts come

out of, and they must have come up from the bottom of the
house to the attics. The rats gnawed the hands and feet of
the little children. The lady heard them crying, and got out
of her bed and called to the servant to know what the child
was making such a noise for, when they struck a light, and
then they see the rats running away to the holes; their little
night-gownds was kivered with blood, as if their throats had
been cut. I asked the lady to give me one of the night-gownds
to keep as a cur'osity, for I considered it a *phee*nomenon,
and she gave it to me, but I never was so vexed in all my life
as when I was told the next day that a maid had washed it.
I went down the next morning and sterminated them rats.
I found they were of the specie of rat which we term the
blood-rat, which is a dreadful spiteful feller – a snake-headed
rat, and infests the dwellings. There may have been some
dozens of 'em altogether, but it's so long ago I a'most
forget how many I took in that house. The gent behaved
uncommon handsome, and said, "Mr Black, I can never pay
you for this"; and ever arterwards, when I used to pass by
that there house, the little dears when they see me used to
call out to their mamma, "O, here's Mr Ratty, ma!"

It is a condensed, highly coloured allegory of the English class system,
and it has the promiscuously suggestive symbolism of a dream. The
stormy night, the violation, the stained nightgown, the "snake-
headed" rat, and the saving presence of the proletarian in the
Hampstead house, a ratlike creature himself who turns by day into
the children's favourite, "Mr Ratty" – these are exactly the same
ingredients which we meet with in the most delirious and secret
passages of Kingsley's fiction. Sex and class are inextricably mixed
up, and the story is full of the illicit excitement of trespass and
invasion as a man from one class goes, literally, with all the trappings
of a gothic phantasmagoria, to the bed of the children of another.
Jack Black, of course, was real, and no doubt he did tell Mayhew
about a night call to the house of a Hampstead medical gent; but
the actual telling belongs to fiction not sociology. Pulsing just beneath
the surface of the language, one can feel Mayhew's own thrill at
tasting the forbidden fruit of class transvestism as he speaks in the
voice of the rat man.

In *London Labour*, Mayhew was able to let loose, at full power, the
passion for going about in the clothes of another sex, another class,

which he and Augustus had toyed with in the novels. But in the street life of the London poor, he hit on a rich seam of mythic gold – the great underground power source of the Victorian imagination. *London Labour* is Mayhew's *My Secret Life*. It is an infinitely greater book than that shoddy, ponderous sexual fantasy, because Mayhew's private imaginative drive was being constantly held in check by his remorselessly truthful eye. He buttressed himself by statistics (his love of figures verged on the self-parodic, as when he solemnly quantified, in grammes and pounds, the daily input and output of a horse), by prodigious and untiring research, and by a genuine sense of concern and outrage at the living conditions he found himself exposing. Yet the heart of the book is a personal drama. Mayhew was playing out a fantastic, guilt-ridden romance between the gentleman and the proletarian, and he lets us in, as no other Victorian writer dares, on its secrecy, its darkest, most sequestered pleasures.

It was, in fact, the secrecy of the city which aroused Mayhew most. He loved what was hidden, the foggy places, the areas into which he could go incognito, in disguise. He grasped the central paradox that a great city is one of the most truly private places on earth, where a single man by playing many parts may become invisible – one moment a gentleman, the next a coster girl, the next a rat catcher, the next an unclouded eye floating free over the urban profusion of detail. Looking over London from the gallery around the dome of St Paul's, Mayhew noticed that:

> The haze which hung like a curtain of shadow before and over everything, increased rather than diminished the giant sublimity of the city that lay stretched out beneath. It was utterly unlike London as seen every day below, in all its bricken and hard-featured reality; it was rather the phantasm – the spectral illusion, as it were, of the great metropolis – such as one might see in a dream, with here and there stately churches and palatial hospitals, shimmering like white marble, their windows glittering in the sunshine like plates of burnished gold – while the rest of the scene was all hazy and indefinite . . . It was impossible to tell where the sky ended and the city began . . . But as the vast city lay there beneath me, half hid in mist and with only glimpses of its greatness visible, it had a much more sublime and ideal effect from the very inability to grasp the whole of its literal reality.

This intrinsic illegibility and hiddenness of the city acted as a powerful liberating force on Mayhew's imagination. He set out, a professional nomad, to lose himself in the fog. He gave himself over to a sustained, wildly diverse, career of impersonation. Nowhere in his work can one put a finger on a style and say that *that* is Mayhew. Everything, except his extraordinary accuracy of observation which is so devastatingly truthful as to be impersonal, is disguise, imposture, dramatic monologue. He wanted, in a lifetime of what he modestly called "knocking about London", to be *the* man of the city, embodying in one frame all its classes, sexes, contradictions, secrets. No wonder his contemporaries seem to have conspired to exclude him from their memoirs. His whole work and existence mock at the conventions of order, degree and category by which society is customarily kept going. He was a dangerous figure whose Protean character reflected everything that the Victorians most feared in the Protean nature of the industrial megapolis. The bitchy remarks which were made about him by several of his fellows while he was working on *London Labour* – he was accused of indulgent invention and grotesque embroidery, and it was said that he was simply living it up on *Morning Chronicle* money, taking cabs everywhere and eating out lavishly – pinpoint the nagging mistrust which attended his progress through the city. People didn't quite believe in Mayhew. They sensed in him a basic lack of continuity, as if he had carried bad faith to the point of moral principle. So, in a sense, he had. He had been inside the £600-a-year mansion in Hyde Park Gardens, and the sempstress's garret at half-a-crown a week which the mansion concealed, and he could talk in the language of each with equal conviction.

But the passion for crossing class boundaries, for extreme impersonation coloured by guilt and sexual excitement – the side of Mayhew which inspired Gissing and Orwell – fizzled out as Mayhew grew older. He wrote a puzzling, under-read, late book called *London Characters*, which was published in 1874. The first part, a facetious charivari, with "thumb-nail sketches" of London legal, theatrical, and social life, can be skipped; and the final chapters are rejigged versions of his early *Morning Chronicle* articles. But three substantial essays, "Outsiders of Society and their Homes in London", "Life in London", and "Housekeeping in Belgravia", form the aborted beginnings of a study of genteel society which might have been comparable in scope and detail to *London Labour*. "Outsiders of Society" is a sad, exact and funny dissection of the personal columns of Victorian newspapers, and of the people who masquerade behind such titles as

"respectable elderly lady" and "City gentleman of convivial dispo-
sition". Mayhew's eye is still sharp and scathing, and he allows himself
a style of full-blown satire, a sarcastic orotundity which is new in
his work. On the lady housekeepers of Belgravia, he meticulously
documents their accounts, tells one exactly how to set about getting
a cut-price ostentatious carriage, goes fascinatingly into the details
of mistress–servant ritual relationships. The subject should have been
perfect for Mayhew, but something is drastically wrong. A quotation
from the general introductory section of "Housekeeping in Belgravia"
shows the shift in his tone:

> Oh railroads! much have ye to answer for. Twenty years
> hence we may look in vain for the social, kindly, hospitable
> country life now only to be met with in remote counties, in
> Cornwall, in Scotland. Already have you made the "Great
> Houses" independent of their neighbours. Their fish and
> their friends come down from town together. And the
> squire, the small proprietor despairing of husbands for his
> girls or his rubber for himself, where the doors around are
> closed nine months of the year, leaves his acres in the care
> of his bailiff and takes refuge in the nearest watering-place,
> or yields to his wife's solicitations, and launches also into
> the care and troubles of HOUSEKEEPING IN
> BELGRAVIA . . .

The trouble is that Mayhew here has no one to impersonate. He
aspires to the most dangerous of all satirist's tones, that of patrician
irony, the lordly aristocrat condescending to the lesser life beneath
him. Accuracy turns into mere knowingness; the alert eye, though
it still sees, is bored with the view. Mayhew made a good
travesty-gentleman because, in 1851, he had a thorough-going contempt for gentility. But the new, quasi-aristocratic Mayhew has
a plaintive earnestness; one feels him straining for the right to
condescend.

Perhaps the effort of holding all of London in his head had told on
him; perhaps he was searching for a secure identity – a dignity
commensurate with his sense of the importance of what he had
already achieved. It is a pity that such an intensely productive bohem-
ianism should have turned so easily – as it turns so often – into
snobbery. And there is a deep irony – which Mayhew himself might
have appreciated – in the fact that the invisible man, crossing and

recrossing the city in borrowed clothes, striving to become the soul of London, should have finally revealed himself as a parvenu.

1973

TROLLOPE

I

Trollope is the yeti of the English novel; a creature of rumour, footprints, blurred portraits, most of which are faked. He has left his biographers stumped: both Michael Sadleir and James Pope-Hennessy succeeded in producing books which appeared to be about no one in particular at all. Trollope criticism is, frankly, monstrous. Worst of all, the dedicated Trollopians have usually extolled him in terms that make him sound like some snobbish and gossipy granny. It is not really surprising that literary people, who would bite their tongues out rather than confess that they hadn't read *Middlemarch*, actually boast of not having read Trollope.

Trollope himself is responsible for much of this. He was a pathological ironist who, both in his life and in his work, loved to disappear behind an endless succession of elaborately raised smokescreens. In his *Autobiography*, he tried to pass himself off as a no-nonsense literary grocer. Elsewhere, he pretended to be a waggish old buffer, or a philistine hunting man, or a whey-faced public servant. Like many people haunted by a terror of their own unpopularity, Trollope liked to sneer at himself before anyone else got the chance to. There are few surviving anecdotes about him; and those that do exist – like the story about how he ragged his hosts at a Boston dinner party for their wine snobbery – show a man completely hidden behind a very English, very clubbish, very exasperating ironic cover. Around his marriage, he built a high wall which was so well laid that so far no one has been able to remove a single brick to spy on what was going on inside. Even his letters – and there are precious few of them – are masked.

The most revealing sentence in the *Autobiography* is a chance remark: "In our lives we are always weaving novels, and we manage to keep the different tales distinct." Trollope did manage his life like a novel, constantly switching from being one character into being another, changing from persona to persona without ever keeping to one voice for long enough to be recognized as a person. He is just as elusive in his novels: when Trollope appears to be most straightforward and bluff he is usually at his most untrustworthy. In his relationship with the reader, he is a chronic flirt, trading on with flattery, professions of intimacy, hints of secret collusion. Then the trap is sprung, and the reader finds himself left cruelly alone, with only brute paradoxes for company, in a world as morally icy as any in English fiction.

He is an engrossing, dangerous, maddening character; and people who write books about him usually end up wrecked on that huge, self-protective reef of Trollope's irony. C. P. Snow succeeds in avoiding being wrecked by employing the cautious but useful tactic of not trying very hard to land. *Trollope** is an amiable picture book, though some of its pictures have a press-ganged air of having been hauled into service on the slimmest of pretexts. It reads like an affectionate memoir of a somewhat distant acquaintance. Nevertheless, it is to be welcomed for the way in which it cleans a few patches and corners of the dreadfully oxidized portrait of one of the most misunderstood writers in the language.

Snow is especially good on Trollope's childhood and on his career as a civil servant. There is no beefy simplicity in this Trollope: there is, rightly, a very great deal of hurt and self-mistrust, a shaky pride and a saving, inner obstinacy. Trollope's parents made no secret of thinking him a stupid boy; his intelligence, like almost everything in his life, had to be his own secret. Even now, it remains a well kept one. His childhood was spectacularly awful: despised, neglected, bullied, carelessly shifted about from school to school, he learned of necessity how to play all his feelings very close to his chest. His later success in the Post Office, and in the Garrick Club too, were really triumphs of impersonation. Exactly the same exhaustive artifice which created the novels transformed the miserable runt of the family into a brisk, sociable, conventional pillar of middle-class society. It was a sweet revenge. It was also so seamless a performance that hardly anyone since has ever noticed that Trollope was acting at all. His ear and eye were perfect. He knew exactly what to say. Yet the very ease and perfection with which he carried through the role must have sharpened his already profound scepticism about the nature of social and moral behaviour.

* C. P. Snow, *Trollope* (London: Macmillan).

Snow rests his case for the novels on what he calls Trollope's "percipience", a term which he uses rather as Keats used the phrase "negative capability", to convey Trollope's natural inwardness and empathy with the lives of his characters. That is true as far as it goes; but it does not go far enough. For in his own life, Trollope had grasped one overwhelming, cold and relativistic truth: that the fundamental system of values upon which society was based, its measure of good and evil, failure and success, was, essentially, one of manners. What really counted in the world was a man's performance as an actor. In Trollope's fiction, it is very easy to be good if you are moderately stupid and have an income of more than £2000 a year. It is equally easy to be evil if you are intelligent and poor. (Foreign antecedents make you bad; so does coming from the wrong class. Women are generally good, so long as they obey all the instructions issued to them by their menfolk, and don't try to think for themselves.)

Trollope's view of the world often resembles Lewis Carroll's. Both saw it as a giant spider's web of arbitrary, cruel and silly rules and roles. Trollope, though, is an infinitely greater writer than Carroll because he understood the tragedy of the people who get caught in the web. On social failure, on the sheer difficulty of surviving in a world of pure convention, and on the terrible consequences that attend those who fail to obey the rules, Trollope is among the greatest of novelists. There is not a single major character in all his work who is not haunted by the continuous possibility of disgrace, humiliation, suicide or madness. All of them – Glencora, Lizzie Eustace, Phineas Finn, Augustus Melmotte and the rest – are poised dangerously on the web like tightrope walkers. Some, like Melmotte and Ferdinand Lopez, get stuck, struggling, in the gum. Others, like Crawley in the *Last Chronicle of Barset*, are saved, but their salvation is quite arbitrary. If Trollope usually manipulates the plot to bring about happy endings and good marriages, he does so with a kind of breezy wilfulness which is itself an expression of a moral cynicism so profound and conclusive that it has generally been mistaken for benignity. Trollope is no more benign than Kafka; and Trollope's exploration of social terror is in some ways very close to Kafka's exploration of psychological terror.

The trouble is that, in his books as in his life, his gift for mimicry, for being a chameleon, was perhaps too precise for his own good. Snow praises Trollope's "lucid and undecorated English" and calls it "perfectly adequate" – which is the conventional view of Trollope's style, that it merely has the merits of serviceable plainness. Yet

Trollope was chronically incapable of being plain. He always had to write "in character" – when he wrote the *Autobiography* he had to invent the plain-spoken hack who narrates it. Is the seeming plainness of the novels really more reliable?

The Trollope narrator is perhaps his most interesting, certainly his most neglected character. The tone is so definite, so instantly recognizable: liberal, uncensorious, anxious to believe the best of people, but prepared to face up squarely to the worst if need be, sentimental, charitable, a great lover of marriages, a bit of an old woman. It is the voice of a person so sympathetic that Trollope never leaves one room enough to speculate whether it might be another mask, a persona. Yet the narrator does behave like a character in his own right. His provisional judgments about people are always being disproved in the course of the action. His own morality – which is that of educated, conventional England – again and again turns out to be inadequate to the events he has to describe. When society really shows its claws, and some hapless social climber or careless debtor begins to suffer in earnest, we begin to see the outlines of a world so complicated and inherently nasty that even someone as knowing and civilized as Mr Narrator cannot survive in it intact.

He is simply not as plain a writer as Snow makes him out to be; and it is generally true that the great engines of literary criticism have failed abysmally to come to any serious terms with Trollope's genius. The New Criticism, with its emphasis on the single sentence, the local metaphor, the paragraph, makes no sense of his work at all. For Trollope seized on the length of the novel as its most important formal attribute. His books are masterpieces of literary architecture on a large scale; his metaphors are long-range ones; his greatest effects come from playing whole chapters against each other, from a subtle modulation of tone that may take hundreds of pages to achieve. Trying to write about Trollope, the first thing one discovers is that he offers very few brief quotations that are resonant; yet it is on the brief quotation that the critical reputations of writers like Dickens and George Eliot are founded. His irony is not an irony of remarks; it is an entire lifetime's strategy for surviving in an untenable world.

Oddly, for a writer who has left so little of his life on public view, his biography and his work are one. It is all there in the novels: the secretiveness, the refusal to be pinned down, the percipience, the ebullient laughter of the tragic visionary who has seen the world in which he lives to be a joke, the extraordinary histrionic energy of the actor whose greatest performances have been watched only by himself. Trollope is still up there among the glaciers, waiting to be coaxed down.

1975

II

In the upstairs billiards room of the Garrick Club there is a big, smoky, dun-coloured painting by H. O'Neil. It shows the billiards room in the club's old premises at King Street in 1869, with 12 members playing snooker and another 31 members looking on. Trollope is one of the onlookers. He stands at the far left of the painting, bald, tufty, tangle-bearded, peering rather dolefully at the action through wire-rimmed granny spectacles. He looks as if he's trying to work out the rules of the game, and even in the thick of the crowd Trollope has the grave, self-contained air of one of nature's outsiders.

That is exactly how he is in his novels. Readers who have just skimmed Trollope's books have often come away with the impression that he is a gossipy, maiden auntish writer. They have mistaken his meticulous dissection of the Victorian ruling class for mere social chitchat. He manages his black humour so craftily that careless readers sometimes fail to notice that he's joking – which, for an ironist like Trollope, is the best and blackest joke of all.

In the Palliser novels he studied the rules of success and failure in English society with the same appalled scepticism with which he regarded that snooker game at the Garrick. He was fascinated to the point of obsession with social gamesmanship, and followed each intricate gambit as it led from a lady's drawing room to a gentlemen's club to an obscure city lodging house to a moneylender's office and, finally and supremely, to the House of Commons. Failure at this game meant disgrace, sometimes suicide. Success meant the esteem and flattery of a whole nation.

Yet Trollope himself had the character of a born loser. From childhood, he had learned to think of himself as someone to be despised. He was shifted about from school to school by his parents, who both thought him stupid. At Winchester, he said, "I suffered horribly". He was beaten there daily by his elder brother, and when his feckless father failed to pay his bills, he was jeered at by half the school. "I was big, and awkward, and ugly, and skulked about in a most unattractive manner." He was removed to Harrow, where "I had not only no friends, but was despised by all my companions."

His father, an ineffectual barrister turned hopeless country farmer, went bankrupt and Trollope, then aged 19, had to help smuggle him on to the Ostend packet at the docks. When he returned to the house, the bailiffs were taking possession of the family furniture. Trollope knew exactly what it was to be a failure, knew how failure could so easily creep up on a man from behind and silently garrotte him. He instinctively thought of success – at least social success – as a matter of arbitrary luck and hereditary money. For the wealthy, it was easy to be both popular and good. The Trollopes were neither.

In his career in the Post Office, Trollope enjoyed a middling, slogger's success. But when he was 51, and within sight of the top of the Civil Service pyramid, a younger man was promoted over his head, and Trollope resigned. "I have long been aware of a certain weakness in my own character, which I may call a craving for love," wrote Trollope in his *Autobiography*. He coveted popularity "with a coveting which was almost mean". He wanted desperately to shine – to revenge himself on the cruel, dismissive judgments made on him all those years ago by his family and his schoolmasters. When he was 53, he stood as Liberal candidate for the parliamentary constituency of Beverley. For the middle-aged Trollope, as for the young Phineas Finn, the prospect of becoming an M.P. was "a beautiful dream". Trollope himself said, "I have always thought that to sit in the British Parliament should be the highest object of ambition to every educated Englishman."

But the electors of Beverley loved him hardly any more than his schoolfellows at Winchester and Harrow had done. The fortnight he spent canvassing in the borough was "I think, the most wretched fortnight of my manhood". He waded through the slush of a York-shire winter, speechifying feebly. His skin wasn't thick enough for him to be a politician: he was deeply hurt by the taunts of his opponents. "I felt myself to be a kind of pariah in the borough, to whom was opposed all that was pretty, and all that was nice, and all that was – ostensibly – good." Trollope came bottom of the poll.

In life Trollope cut an ungainly, donkeyish figure. When he was sent to the United States, his American hosts found his bluff clubland humour merely boorish. It was when he was alone with a pen and a ream of foolscap that Trollope was able to triumph. Writing in the early mornings, he anatomized the society which excluded him from its counsels and from the full warmth of its affection. His style has little surface brilliance: it is a style of long-term, detailed, in-depth investigation. It misses nothing. Its wit – and Trollope is a genuinely witty writer, with the great wit's awareness of the tragedy lurking round the corner of his every joke – is slow burning. When it goes off, you realize that the fuse was lit hundreds of pages before and that you had never noticed the smell of charred string beneath the bright tinkle of conversation. In his writing, Trollope worked over the material of his own social failure, and reconstructed it as a glittering fiction.

A year after his defeat at Beverley he published *Phineas Finn*, effectively the first Palliser novel. Since he could not himself take a seat in Parliament, he got the Speaker's permission to sit in the gallery; and for two months he sat there, watching debates and gathering together a cast of characters for his novels.

Although Trollope's characters are nearly all drawn from the "Upper Ten" – that thin, rich layer of cake icing on the top of English society – his sympathies are always with those who have failed, or been excluded, or have found their own fragile success suddenly crumbling under their feet. His best characters are invariably outsiders in an insider's world. It is for this reason that, a hundred years before the Women's Movement, Trollope wrote better about women than any male novelist in English. He understood their bitter sense of exclusion from the important centre of society. When Lady Laura Standish says, "I envy you men your clubs more than I do the House – though I feel that a woman's life is only half a life, as she cannot have a seat in Parliament," the remark is not a pleasantry. Lady Laura, like Glencora, is fuelled by a passionate anger at her own powerlessness. When Trollope's women devote themselves to parties, improvident love affairs and escapades that embarrass their husbands, they do it with the considered fury of people who have been prevented by society from being themselves.

Every one of his male characters carries the seed of his own failure within himself, like a field-marshal carrying a private's tin of dubbin in his knapsack. When Ferdinand Lopez, the luckless social climber in *The Prime Minister*, chucks himself in front of a train, he is only doing what Phineas Finn, Frank Tregear, even Plantagenet Palliser himself, have avoided doing by the merest hair's breadth. One emotion is more important than any other in Trollope's writing – and it is the feeling of *dread*. He makes society a terrible, unkind and difficult place to live in. He makes failure frighteningly easy. As no other novelist has ever quite done before or since, he makes us dread for the sanity and happiness of all his people. In his life, Trollope knew it was much easier to fail than to succeed; his greatest success was to convey that apprehension so deeply that his novels seem to shiver with it.

It is strange that, since *The Pallisers* was first shown on television, British political life has started to look as if it had been written by Trollope. How uncensorious he would have been about John Stonehouse! How subtly he would have written that story! I suspect that whenever Britain seems especially hard to live in, when we are brought face to face with our own failure, when society looks as if it might break up, then, again, we rediscover Trollope. For Trollope is the only English novelist who would really understand our own difficulties, our own particular dread.

1976

III

Trollope the novelist is wonderful at exposing the tender inner selves of people whom society has written off as being unattractive, contemptible or just plain dull. Josiah Crawley, the tormented clergyman hero of *The Last Chronicle of Barset*, is first described (in *Framley Parsonage*) as "unpleasant"; and it was from the ranks of the "unpleasant" that Trollope drew his finest and most sympathetic characters. When the novelist delicately unpeels the hard and unattractive social carapace from a Lizzie Eustace or a Ferdinand Lopez, he educates the reader into feeling keenly for people whose defences against the world have been so anxiously built up as to repel all ordinary attempts to love them.

Yet the tender inner self of Trollope the man remains one of the unexposed mysteries of literature. No biographer has penetrated much beyond the front door of the Trollope family household in Waltham Cross. The available snapshots of Trollope abroad in society show a gruff, choleric figure, riding to hounds, bent over his cards at an afternoon game of whist at the Garrick, or browbeating a dinner party. James Russell Lowell's famous description is typical ". . . a big, red-faced, rather underbred Englishman of the bald-with-spectacles type. A good roaring positive fellow who deafened me." W. D. Howells called him "the finest of artists" but "the most Philistine of men".

In his posthumously published autobiography, Trollope gave away everything and nothing about himself. He confessed that as a child he had bored his own mother, that he had been miserable at Winchester and generally regarded as a very dim boy. His assiduous career at the Post Office had been soured by the mutual dislike that existed between him and Rowland Hill. He wrote frankly that he had always had an inordinate need to be loved; then, with characteristic gruffness, he proved that this need had been satisfied by listing the London clubs to which he'd been elected. The pity is that, unlike Mr Crawley, Mr Trollope has had to go through the world without the benefit of Trollope the novelist to make the reader feel for him.

So in prospect at least, his letters have more than usual interest. In his novels, letters are always being used to reveal character; and one goes to N. John Hall's beautifully edited collection* with high hopes, expecting intimacies and revelations.

But it's no dice once again. Trollope's letters are duller, far duller, than those of any major writer, of any century, in any language. They are so superlatively dull that they qualify as one of the wonders of the literary world. For long stretches, they have all the intrinsic interest of old gas bills or the sort of circulars that begin "Dear Barclaycard-holder . . ."

It is true that they supply a good deal of evidence that will be useful to the specialized scholar of the commerce of literature in the 19th century. They dot the i's and cross the t's of the account sheets that Trollope rendered up in his autobiography (perfectly accurately, as it turns out). They document his laborious and uninspired editorship of *St Paul's Magazine* from 1867 to 1870 ("'Without the choking' does not recommend itself to me . . . Chill is a bad epithet for locks"). They show him acting, with extraordinary forbearance, as an unofficial literary agent for society ladies with unpublishable novels on their hands. He agrees to go to dinner, he declines to go to dinner; he hunts, he travels, and he works – and works and works. The letters confirm everything one already knew of Trollope, from his beefy good manners to his relentless busyness.

He began a letter to one correspondent, "I wrote you a horrid scrawl yesterday". Trollope was not indulging in false modesty: his letters usually are horrid scrawls – slovenly, full of decorous cliché, far too hastily written to bother with the games, conceits and rehearsals for fiction that make the letters of most professional writers worth reading.

* N. John Hall (ed.), *The Letters of Anthony Trollope* (California: Stanford University Press).

Even his letters to his wife and a handful of close friends do little to open the horny clamshell in which Trollope kept himself safe from the world. He was enchanted by the glamorous young American, Kate Field, and his fond notes to her are more intimate than anything else in this collection; yet they are hardly more than bearishly playful. "My dear Kate," he wrote, upping the stakes from "my dear Miss Field", "The great distance [from Waltham Cross to Boston] added to my bald head may perhaps justify me in so writing to you . . ." It is a giveaway remark. Trollope was embarrassed at close quarters: he needed distance to express himself. The further away his correspondents were from him, in years and geography, the nearer he dared to come to them in writing. No wonder, then, that his frankest work, the *Autobiography*, was written with the grave intervening between himself and his readers.

On one subject, though, he was always frank, sometimes woundingly so. When he wrote about writing, he came clean, without an ounce of gush or flannel. "It wants a plot and is too egoistic," he told Kate Field when she sent him a story. Her next effort was "worse" and "more pretentious". The moment he had a story or a poem in his hands, he unbuttoned himself and laid in with the cruel directness of a lover, as if candid criticism was a substitute for candour of the heart.

That, perhaps, supplies a clue to the intensity and warmth of Trollope's fiction. Writing novels, he was able to experience an intimacy singularly lacking in his life outside fiction. His converse with his characters was pillow talk. He loved them, and said so. His letters, like his "roaring" talk at dinner, belong to the injured and thwarted side of Trollope's life – the side that worked like the weights on a pressure cooker, to build up steam for the fiction within.

N. John Hall has done everything one could ask of an editor. He has collected every last scrap. His introduction is first-rate. He has wisely included a number of letters to and about Trollope. His footnotes are both diligent and economical; and the tales the footnotes tell, of long-dead rumpuses in publishing, the theatre and the Civil Service, are usually far more engaging than the letters they annotate. The small print at the bottom of the pages makes these volumes unexpectedly readable: their raw material is lacklustre but they are an editorial triumph.

1984

CHARLES KINGSLEY

What an extraordinary man Kingsley was. Even by the high standards of clerical oddity set by people like Sterne, Gilbert White, Sydney Smith, Lewis Carroll and the Rector of Stiffkey, Kingsley stands out as *the* clergyman-amateur of all time; an enthusiast, a bungler, a visionary, something of a buffoon, riding wildly high on that most peculiar of privileges, "parson's freehold".

In the 19th century, there was no occupation so suited to a man with a minor talent, no safer refuge for an eccentric, no better platform for an ideologue, than the job of being a Church of England clergyman. The draughty country rectory was like an offshore island, half adrift from the rest of society. With his stipend and his pulpit, the parson had a unique freedom. Lacking property and the duties attached to property, he was able to devote himself to causes, hobbies and the unlimited cultivation of his own personality. From the gentlemanly fastness of his study, with its heavy cumulus clouds of pipe smoke, its minutely labelled collections of fossils, butterflies, wild flowers, its racks of rods and guns and shelves of old sermons, came a steady stream of books about everything, madcap theories, scientific inventions (parsonage attics are full of pipettes and bunsen burners), homilies, new kinds of trout fly, letters to *The Times*.

In his last year as a Cambridge undergraduate, Kingsley wrote to his mother:

> If you rejoice that you have born a man into the world, remember that he is not like common men, neither cleverer nor wiser, nor better than the multitude, but utterly *different*.

That sentence alone should have qualified him for ordination; its combination of innocence, egotism and unctuousness, together with Kingsley's ferocious natural energy and wayward intelligence, promised great things in the curious sphere of the Anglican Church, where conceited idiosyncrasy and a sense of being not as other men were only proper in someone who was going to fill out the large, lonely spaces of a parsonage.

He lived up to that promise splendidly. There were the books and poems – *Alton Locke, The Water Babies, Hypatia, Hereward the Wake,*

Yeast. Yet even as a literary man, he was an amateur; his one certain contribution to literature was that he annoyed Newman sufficiently to provoke the writing of *Apologia Pro Vita Sua*. He published a delightful children's guide to the flora and fauna of rockpools. Victorian gentlewomen found themselves awash in a deluge of his lectures, sermons and essays on sanitary reform – though the initial result of mains drainage was a network of fast freeways for the germs it was supposed to eliminate. He campaigned against tight stays and cold lavatory seats. He was made Regius Professor of Modern History at Cambridge, and one professional historian complained, not without some justice, that he could see "no more reason why [Kingsley] should be made a Professor of History than why he should be set to command the Channel Fleet". He dabbled in science, Chartism and theology. As Rector of Eversley, he was a thoroughly effective parish priest. He was a passionate husband and an unusually kind father.

His life was a turmoil of fads and crazes. He never quite achieved excellence in anything – there was always a streak of the cranky amateur about his activities, an air of having been cooked up too excitedly and too fast in the heady atmosphere of the rectory study. Until now, too, his character has remained an infuriating puzzle. The poems and novels open weird, slantwise glimpses: a rather embarrassing relish for nakedness and babyhood, an obsession with washing and purification, a repeated prurient interest in the details of the torture of crucifixion, a flirtatious canoodling with the idea of disease and death. But it has all gone unexplained. Una Pope-Hennessy, in her fine and sensible 1948 biography of Kingsley, ended the book by frankly confessing her puzzlement at his "uniquely experimental life". He was, she wrote, "propelled by irresistible spasms of sympathy to lavish his energies on one objective after another"; his "career was unpredictable for his star traced no recognisable orbit". And that has been as much as anyone could say of this wandering star, zooming about the sky propelled by irresistible spasms – a conclusion no biographer could find satisfying.

But now Susan Chitty has been allowed access to more than 300 letters written by Kingsley to his wife Fanny. Some had been printed in a heavily expurgated form by Fanny herself in her *Charles Kingsley: His Letters and Memories*. Their interest lies almost exclusively in the passages she suppressed, and *The Beast and the Monk*,* despite its

---

* Susan Chitty, *The Beast and the Monk: A Life of Charles Kingsley* (London: Hodder & Stoughton).

scarifying and quite irrelevantly allusive title, is the first book about Kingsley to reveal that his life did, indeed, follow a tight and regular orbit; an annual cycle of mania and depression, lived out inside a vivid and terrible private iconography.

As soon as he became engaged to Fanny, Kingsley invited her to join him on this dangerous rollercoaster. On his instructions, every Thursday night they lay in their separate beds imagining themselves in each other's arms and thinking, in Fanny's words, of "delicious nightery". On Friday nights, Kingsley took off his clothes and flogged himself with a switch. Fanny wrote in her diary: "Oh, how I long to kiss away those stripes!" On All Saints Day, the new curate of Eversley went into the local woods at midnight, stripped naked, and threw himself among thorns. He wrote to Fanny:

> When I came home my body was torn from head to foot. I never suffered so much. I began to understand Popish raptures and visions that night, and their connection with self-torture. I saw such glorious things.

He designed matching hair shirts for himself and his fiancée. For a wedding present to her, he wrote and illustrated *The Life of St Elizabeth*. Over the naked body of an instantly recognizable Fanny nailed to a cross, Kingsley drew, in ornamental gothic lettering, the word "Darling!" Another picture shows Kingsley and Fanny bound to a cross floating on an ocean wave; another shows them as naked angels, ascending into heaven as they seem to copulate. But when one looks closely at both drawings, one sees that the normal sexual position has been reversed; the woman is locked chastely between the man's legs.

Their honeymoon was an ecstasy of self-denial. Fanny anticipated the wedding night in a letter:

> We will undress and bathe and then you will come to my room, and we will kiss and love very much and read psalms aloud together, and then we will kneel down and pray in our nightdresses. Oh! What solemn bliss! How hallowing! And then you will take me up in your arms, will you not? And lay me down in bed. And then you will extinguish our light and *come to me*! How I will open my arms to you and then sink into yours! And you will kiss me and clasp me and we will both praise God alone in the dark night with His

eye shining down upon us and His love enclosing us. After
a time we shall sleep!

And yet I fear you will yearn so for *fuller* communion that
you will not be so happy as me. And I too perhaps shall
yearn, frightened as I am!

Copulation was holy – indeed, Kingsley believed that eternal life consisted of the unceasing bliss of sexual union. To make the body fit for
divine pleasure, it must first be scourged. Fanny was his martyr. He
saw Christ's wounds in her flesh, and he worshipped her, just as she
lived willingly in his crazed fantasies of bliss and punishment – fantasies
that most Victorian women would have found alien and obscene.

For every ecstatic vision, there was a corresponding spell of inert
and empty depression. Projects died on him by the dozen. He craved
drink, and punished himself for it. Then he would be away again,
scribbling uncorrected through the night, high as an addict on his
own body chemistry. He had one lifelong obsession, and it came at
him again and again with the force of a manic hallucination. He saw
Britain rinsed through with clean water, criss-crossed by drains – a
whole country of naked water babies playing in the crystal shallows
like a giant shoal of rainbow trout, purified, ready at last for an
eternity of innocent copulation.

Surely his attack on Newman, his abhorrence of Papists and ritual,
was a depressive revulsion from the glittering icons inside his own head.
At the top of his fever, writing of the crucifixion of Santa Maura –

I cannot stir. Ah God! these shoots of fire
Through all my limbs! Hush selfish girl! He hears you!
Whoever found the cross a pleasant bed?

– he was a whole Catholic Church unto himself. He had had his own
visions, and was elated and terrified by them. Other people's visions
repelled him. He would write furious, disgusted marginalia in his
hymnal against the words of, for instance, Wesley's "Jesu, Lover of
my Soul", which he found nauseatingly carnal. When he detected
idolatrous or fleshly fantasies in the minds of others, he wanted to
dowse them in his universal specific, cold water. Newman must have
enraged him, simply because Newman could accommodate, with
cool reasonableness, the very things that drove Kingsley out on to
the hysterical edge of manic obsession.

1975

MARK TWAIN

The Innocents Abroad is that freakish thing, a travel book which is also an important turning point in the history of a national literature. Twain's jaunty satire on an early American package tour made his reputation. Writing it, he hammered out a style of plainspoken moral scepticism; intimate in tone, funny, deflating and superbly flexible. This is the book in which Twain found his voice – a voice which America at large immediately recognised as her own.

The reasons why *The Innocents Abroad* was such an instant contemporary success need some exhuming. When the cruise liner *The Quaker City* left New York Harbor in June 1867, bound for Europe and the Holy Land, it was barely two years since Lee had surrendered to Grant at Appomattox. The wounds inflicted on the country by the Civil War were still largely undressed. "Reconstruction" was turning into a synonym for inaction, revenge and widespread graft. If no hint of the ugliness and difficulty of that period creeps into the opening pages of Twain's book, with its rather over-cheery portrait of New York life, it is because no contemporary reader needed to be reminded of it. After a devastating war, what better than Twain's beguiling promise of "a giant picnic"?

Twain was 32. He had just published his first book, *The Celebrated Jumping Frog of Calaveras County*, a collection of short stories in the vein of Josh Billings and other "Southwestern" humourists – campfire tall tales, relying on comic rural dialect and crackerbarrel witticisms. The cruise of *The Quaker City* supplied him with a magnificent, profoundly topical subject.

For aboard *The Quaker City*, a group of representative American citizens, who had so recently been at war with each other on their home ground, were going to be literally all in the same boat. "Pilgrims from New England, the South and the Mississippi Valley . . ." The phrase sounds innocuous now; in 1867 it would have had an odd and dangerous novelty.

I had always suspected Twain of inventing the name of the ship, it is so eerily apposite to his purpose. The Quaker city is Philadelphia, where the Declaration of Independence was signed in 1776. For Americans, trying to reunite into one nation nearly a century later, the name of the ship must have been a talisman, standing as it did for peace, concord, national identity. Pleasure cruises have always been prescribed for invalids recuperating from long illnesses: on the voyage of *The Quaker City*, America's health was on the mend – and would be seen to be on the mend by the rest of the world. The jubilant nationalism that pervades the book is sometimes solemnly, sometimes facetiously expressed, with every available reference to the ship's flag, to the singing of "The Star Spangled Banner" and to the Declaration of Independence (see Chapter V) press-ganged into service.

No wonder that the cruise itself caught the American imagination. Twain himself embarked on it as a correspondent for a bunch of newspapers, including the *Daily Alta California*, the New York *Tribune* and the New York *Herald*. It was a sharp editorial move, to post off a young humourist to cover the cruise; in the hands of anyone more sententious than Twain, the subject, with its penumbra of inevitable symbols, could have made deadly reading.

For Twain himself the excursion was at least as much a literary as it was a territorial one, and, whatever the official itinerary, he meant to take it into uncharted waters. "I offer no apologies for any departures from the usual style of travel writing that may be charged against me," he writes in his preface; and it is in those departures that the continued life of the book survives.

American literature was already replete with books of European travel. Franklin, Washington Irving, Emerson, Hawthorne, along with dozens of lesser writers, had been here before. The proper tone had been firmly set. A becoming humility was expected from the "innocent" traveller from the New World as he made his reckoning with the complex cultural antiquity of the Old. The encounter with Europe set him standards of urbanity that the American visitor must be on his best behaviour to match. The European landscape, with its ancient architecture and hallowed places, commanded a style of suitable romantic sublimity. The great model here was Washington Irving's *The Sketch-Book*; and when Irving visited Westminster Abbey he was, in effect, teaching Americans how to walk, on reverent tiptoe, through Europe at large:

> We step cautiously and softly about, as if fearful of disturbing the hallowed silence of the tomb; while every footfall whispers along the walls, and chatters among the sepulchres,

making us more sensible of the quiet we have interrupted.

It seems as if the awful nature of the place presses down upon the soul, and hushes the beholder into noiseless reverence. We feel that we are surrounded by the congregated bones of the great men of past times, who have filled history with their deeds, and the earth with their renown.

Like Becky Sharp chucking Johnson's *Dictionary* out of the window of the carriage at the beginning of *Vanity Fair*, Twain, in effect, hurls *The Sketch-Book*, along with Emerson's *English Traits & Representative Sentiments* and the rest over the taffrail of *The Quaker City* as she leaves the dock. *His* intention is to tramp over the hallowed ground of Europe in hobnailed boots, leaving a shameless trail of cigar ash behind him as he goes.

He was, in part, settling an old score. Several European visitors to America, most famously Frances Trollope in her *Domestic Manners of the Americans* (18), had portrayed the United States as an extended farmyard of cussing, spitting, tobacco-chawing hogs. In *The Innocents Abroad*, it was the turn of the hogs to exact their sweet revenge.

Arrived in the Azores (after a superbly described ocean crossing), Twain begins as he means to carry on. "The community is eminently Portuguese – that is to say, it is slow, poor, shiftless, sleepy and lazy . . ." Venice is "a paradise for cripples":

This the famed gondola and this the gorgeous gondolier! – the one an inky, rusty old canoe, with a sable hearse-body clapped on to the middle of it, and the other a mangy, barefooted guttersnipe, with a portion of his raiment on exhibition which should have been sacred from public scrutiny . . .

The Civita Vecchia in Florence is "the finest nest of dirt, vermin, and ignorance we have found yet, except that African perdition called Tangier, which is just like it . . ." This is Twain writing in a nicely-judged version of the second person plural; half guying the prudishness of the tourists, half speaking in his own voice as a genuinely disconcerted observer. Putting on the accent of a Missouri hick, he finds a way of telling the truth – and the performance is, at its best, exquisitely balanced midway between parody and earnestness.

This doubleness is at the heart of the book. Twain was fascinated by the language of romantic description, and by the picturesque lies which that language could enshrine. He could turn it out to order, by the yard, in wickedly accurate pastiche:

Towards nightfall the next evening, we steamed into the great artificial harbour of this noble city of Marseilles, and saw the dying sunlight gild its clustering spires and ramparts, and flood its leagues of environing verdure with a mellow radiance that touched with an added charm the white villas that flecked the landscape far and near. (Copyright secured according to law.)

The sentence in parentheses at the end is needed because the passage is not so very different from other passages in the book which go unflagged with ironic warnings. *This* is a bit of fine writing to be jeered at. But what of this?

The island in sight was Flores. It seemed only a mountain of mud standing up out of the dull mists of the sea. But as we bore down upon it, the sun came out and made it a beautiful picture – a mass of green farms and meadows that swelled up to a height of fifteen hundred feet, and mingled its upper outlines with the clouds. It was ribbed with sharp, steep ridges, and cloven with narrow canons, and here and there on the heights, rocky upheavals shaped themselves into mimic battlements and castles; and out of rifted clouds came broad shafts of sunlight, that painted summit and slope and glen with bands of fire, and left belts of sombre shade between.

Even the latest of electronic irony-detectors would be hard put to register a tremor here. It is in earnest – and it's good; one of the best descriptions of making a landfall that I know. Yet it is a close cousin to the romantic fribbling whose copyright was secured according to law.

The two passages, at once so close and so different in intent, demonstrate Twain's genius as a writer for mocking what he revered and for maintaining a sneaking reverence for what he mocked. They help to explain the uniquely experimental nature of *The Innocents Abroad* – a book in which Twain was trying out a whole succession of different voices, testing them against experience, rejecting some, developing others. So, in the space of a few pages, he will have a go in the manner of Irving at his solemnest, undermine it with a few choice remarks made as if by a hay-sucking rube, try a touch more serious colour, mix a noble sentiment with a dry sarcasm . . . This is not so much an uncertain search for a voice of one's own as a deliberate exercise in literary anarchy.

He must have read Sterne's *A Sentimental Journey*. There is certainly a great deal of Mr Yorick in Twain's make-up; his continuous verbal playfulness, his somersaults of tone, his implicit trust in the contradiction as the most truthful sort of utterance. You need to be wary to read Twain well. His most innocent-seeming sentences frequently turn out to be bombs, timed to explode in the next paragraph.

The wonderful thing about these protean pyrotechnics is the way they enable one man to embody a whole shipload of tourists. Some of them are piously moved, so *he* is piously moved; some snigger, and *he* sniggers; some are enchanted, *he* is enchanted; some are bored, *he* is bored; some are knowledgeable, *he* is knowledgeable; some are ignorant, *he* is ignorant. He *is* the package tour on the move – a voice for America, speaking at once in all of America's many tongues.

The progress of the tour is beautifully done and strikingly up to date, with its obsessive harping on restaurant meals, prices, hotel rooms, exchange rates, tummy upsets, greedy and mendacious local guides, train times, tickets and the universal fact that all foreigners are amusing ragamuffins. Europe and the Near East turn out to be a vast, fusty museum, around whose most famous exhibits the tourists are made to trail until they are practically dead of exhaustion. When Twain gives voice to the general conclusion of the *Quaker City* pilgrims, he might be Mr Midwest 1988, interviewed at Minneapolis airport at the end of his European vacation:

> The people of those foreign countries are very, very ignorant. They looked curiously at the costumes we had bought from the wilds of America. They observed that we talked loudly at table sometimes. They noticed that we looked out for expenses, and got what we conveniently could out of a franc, and wondered where in the mischief we came from. In Paris they just simply opened their eyes and stared when we spoke to them in French! We never did succeed in making those idiots understand their own language. One of our passengers said to a shopkeeper in reference to a proposed return to buy a pair of gloves, "*Allong restay trankeel – may be ve coom Moonday;*" and, would you believe it, that shopkeeper, a born Frenchman, had to ask what it was that had been said . . .
>
> The people stared at us everywhere, and we stared at them. We generally made them feel rather small, too, before we

got done with them, because we bore down on them with America's greatness until we crushed them . . .

It was inevitable that, in some inconsolably pompous quarters, Twain was charged with having brought America into disrepute with *The Innocents Abroad*; he had portrayed himself and his countrymen as a gang of oafish rubbernecks. More generally, the book was loved and chuckled over. It was the most joyful, funny and vivid act of Reconstruction so far. Its confident tone (made up of such a melange of individual voices) was what the nation needed. For Twain himself, the book was a voyage of literary discovery. To speak in an authentic American accent, to be wise and gullible in the same breath, to be full of wonder and scepticism . . . he found all this in the writing of *The Innocents Abroad* and he would return to it again in his masterpiece, *Huckleberry Finn*.

There is another irony worth noting here. It has been said often, and said snobbishly, that package tourism has killed "real travel". In his book *Abroad*, Professor Paul Fussell laboured this point into the ground, and explained that what it meant was that the travel book is dead. The argument may sound all right until one remembers *The Innocents Abroad*, and the fact that one of the great classics of nineteenth century travel (the golden age of "real travel") happened to be about a package tour of the kind that "real travellers" have always so heartily affected to despise. (Evelyn Waugh's *Labels*, as it happens, was also about a package tour aboard a cruise ship in the Mediterranean, and owes a good deal to *The Innocents Abroad*). One of the pities of modern package tourism is not so much that it has killed the travel book but that so far no Twain - or Waugh - has come forward to chronicle it.

1988

II

"Huckleberry Finn" is *the* American Classic. Uneven and bitty, it is no masterpiece in the ordinary sense: at least half the book is skimped and facetious, the storytelling labored, the jokes flat. Yet it is the only novel in American literature that has the permanent, enchanting and mysterious power of an ancient myth. The vision at its center – of the skin-and-bones son of the town drunk floating down the Mississippi on a raft in the company of a runaway slave – goes side by side with images like that of Prometheus chained to the rock; it embodies, as much by luck and magic as by conscious art, something fundamental in the experience of being human. The voice at its center – Huck himself talking in the lazy, cracked, down-home accent of Pike County, Mo. – has an extraordinary surviving vitality. It speaks to the reader with the intimacy of a lover sharing the same pillow (*"Everything was dead quiet, and it looked late and smelt late. You know what I mean - I don't know the words to put it in"*), yet it is as famously public, as definitively "American," as the voice of Lincoln at Gettysburg, speaking for the Nation. "Huckleberry Finn" is a miraculous collision of circumstances: a unique and serendipitous case of exactly the right author for the job finding himself at exactly the right historical moment in exactly the right geographical spot.

For much of the time when he was working on the novel, Twain hardly seemed to know what he was doing. He kept on putting the manuscript away and fishing it out again, returning to Huck's story out of compulsion but lacking an adequate design with which to execute it. He cobbled it together, in spurts and scraps, between 1876 and 1884, reassembling the fragments of an obsessive dream. Reading the book, you can feel Twain groping in the dark, trying new components on for size, rejecting whole chunks of the plot, improvising his way through as if the book were writing him rather than vice versa. Unlike "Tom Sawyer," where the author is firmly – rather too firmly – in control from beginning to end, "Huckleberry Finn" got the better of Mark Twain; it insisted on being told, and on being told in a way that Twain himself didn't completely understand.

What he clearly knew was that somewhere in his own life on the Mississippi there was the germ, at least, of pure legend. He'd grown up as Samuel Clemens in Hannibal, Mo., had been employed as a steamboat pilot in his 20s, working the river between St Louis and New Orleans, and had taken as his pen name the leadsman's cry of "mark twain!" for two fathoms of Mississippi water. In his 40s the literary tycoon of Hartford, Conn., with his magnificently vulgar steamboat-gothic mansion, was imaginatively preoccupied with his own childhood and with the lost vigor and innocence of the river itself.

For Twain's youth coincided with the heyday of the Mississippi as the first great interstate highway of American life. The river had been the western boundary of the United States, the muddy end of things, before the Louisiana Purchase; it was split in two by the Civil War, a fracture from which it never fully recovered; but in the 1840s and '50s the river was a wonderfully lively and cosmopolitan mainstream. The refueling stops for the stern-wheelers turned into boom towns, with wharfside bars and brothels and pseudo-Greek hotels. The traffic was thick and various: coal and grain going south from Wisconsin, Minnesota, Illinois; fancy imported goods going north from New Orleans; rafts full of settlers drifting down from Chicago on the Illinois River, which joins up with the Mississippi above St Louis, and from Pittsburgh and Cincinnati on the Ohio River, which links in to the Mississippi system at Cairo; speculators, show people, gamblers, European immigrants – the Mississippi was mid-century America afloat.

Yet the river was also a huge and untamed wilderness. It wrecked ships on its shoals and sand bars; it carried away whole towns when it was in flood; it left other towns high and dry and miles inland when a sudden "cutoff" closed the loop of a bend. It was society and solitude, culture and nature, all at once, and it brought the values of the big city and the values of the open frontier face to face.

When Twain set Huck and Jim adrift on the Mississippi, he placed them in a landscape of terrifying and topical complexity. For the river in the book is nothing less than the current of life itself: it carries the raft along on an epic voyage in which idyll turns into nightmare and nightmare into idyll by turns.

For long stretches, the boy and the slave are quite alone, living by instinct, as at home in nature as a pair of raccoons; then the river spits them out abruptly into the middle of society, where they have to deal with a multitude of con men, bigots, thieves and kindly aunts. As the current quickens under them, so Huck has to deal at firsthand with the dilemmas of America in the 19th century: the issue of slavery, the divide between the North and the South, the limits of individual liberty and the steady encroachment on the wilderness of "civiliz-ation" in the form of the narrow, philistine, god-fearing, law-abiding small town.

No wonder that Huck gets into such a tragic muddle. The boy from Pike County is confronted by the Mississippi with questions that continue to defeat Presidents and their cabinets. Trying to work things out on his finger-ends, painfully naming his experience to himself in his own plain words, Huck fails as an ethical philosopher, but he succeeds – dazzlingly – in defining what it means, in Henry James' phrase, to share the complex fate of being an American.

He also brings the river itself alive – more alive than any single place that I know in any literature. I first read Twain's book when I was 7, in an English village 4000 miles away from Hannibal. The Mississippi then was more real to me than the landscape outside the window: I could see the "chutes" where the lighted steamboats tumbled on rainy nights; the submerged trees turned to "sawyers," waving and drowning; the broad, cocoa-colored pools and archipelagoes of green islands.

Some of that magic landscape is still left. The steamboat towns have been in retirement for more than 60 years now. Some have been washed away, some have been deserted by the river, many have just shut their doors and windows and turned in on themselves. Hannibal, with its Tom 'n Huck Motel, Huck Finn Shopping Center, Mark Twain Pet Center and Injun Joe Campground, has very nearly succeeded in burying a great book in plastic and sentimentality. But the river is still intact. Below St Louis, after the U.S. Army Corps of Engineers lock-and-dam system stops, the Mississippi is the same beautiful and scary place that I first visited in Twain's novel. Camped out on a sand bar, with owls and catfish for company, I have myself watched dawn come up over the river, and it was just as Huck says:

"The first thing to see, looking away over the water, was a kind of dull line – that was the woods on t'other side; you couldn't make nothing else out; then a pale place in the sky; then more paleness spreading around; then the river softened up away off, and warn't black any more, but gray . . . and by and by you could see a streak on the water which you know by the look of the streak that there's a snag there in a swift current which breaks on it and makes that streak look that way; and you see the mist curl up off of the water, and the east reddens up, and the river. . . ."

I can't even copy out the words on the typewriter without wanting to be there. That is what "Huckleberry Finn" does: it makes you live intensely inside it. It is incomparable.

1987

RUDYARD KIPLING

Kipling has always cut a more powerful figure in English culture with a small *c* than in English Literature with a big *L*. He has been in repeated need of rescue, not from obscurity but from the distractions of his wider fame. In each literary generation after Kipling's own, at least one leading member has come forward to reclaim him as a lost colleague – a "real" writer of far more subtlety and richness than his embarrassing legend allows. T. S. Eliot, Angus Wilson, Kingsley Amis and now Craig Raine* have each unveiled a new Kipling whose temperamental preoccupations have turned out to strangely mirror those of Eliot, Wilson, Amis and now Raine.

Raine has borrowed Eliot's tactic, of spearheading a personal anthology of Kipling's work (28 stories dating from the 1880s to the 1930s) with a detailed introduction which talks in fighting terms. The strategy works well. You find yourself continually leafing back from the end of a Kipling story to check out what Raine has to say about what you've just read – and he is unfailingly nimble and provocative.

By the end, most readers will emerge happily flushed, after a long, enjoyable and constructive quarrel. Right or wrong – and he seems to me to be as often wrong as right – Raine is worth reading. His selection of stories, with one invidious exception, does Kipling proud. For anyone without the complete shelf of claret-cloth elephant-and-swastika editions of Kipling's work, this is an anthology to treasure.

Raine's Kipling is a democrat: he "extends the literary franchise to the inarticulate". Admittedly, some of the gloss of this liberal impulse does tend to fade when one learns that Kipling extends the same franchise to machines – the aitch-dropping classes share their ballot box with wireless sets, motor cars and steam turbines. Just so. One might as easily reverse the order of that claim and say that Kipling's obsessive genius for making you see, hear and smell the ship's engine or the mechanism of a lighthouse was merely extended to cover people. When Private Ortheris appears, in a snow shower of apostrophes and a devilish code of phonetic spellings, he is a weird and wonderful machine. His technical intricacies are expounded by Kipling with exactly the kind of expert's relish for his subject that is likely to exhaust the reader's patience. *This is how he works – and look, there's a button here . . .*

Democracy it isn't, but Raine is on sure ground when he shows how Kipling paid more attention than any other writer in the language to the problem of making people talk on the page. His ear was superb, his transcriptions were as precise in their timing as musical scores – and he taught his successors how to listen to English vernacular speech, just as he taught them how to cast an intent and

* Craig Raine (ed.), *A Choice of Kipling's Prose* (London: Faber & Faber).

alienated eye on the surfaces of things. Kipling wrote brilliant Martian postcards, like the one about Mackie's blood drying on the barrack-square in "Love-o'-Women":

> The hot sun had dried it to a dusky goldbeater-skin film, cracked lozenge-wise by the heat; and as the wind rose, each lozenge, rising a little, curled up at the edges as if it were a dumb tongue.

In Kipling, the world's surface is shimmeringly alive. The problem lies in what's below the faultless talk and thrilling similes. Raine, focusing on the puzzle-stories like "Mrs Bathurst" and "Dayspring Mishandled", finds a web of ingenious complications which he claims are deep and psychologically complex.

On one level he is wholly convincing. Scampering assiduously round the text, fielding every hint and clue, Raine proves that Kipling's artistic method was much the same as that of Torquemada. Every seemingly casual detail is a vital part of the large cryptogram. As fast as Kipling buries an allusion, Raine digs it up again and demonstrates its function in the covert plot of the story. Yet the stories themselves are curiously diminished by the act of exegesis: at the end of the game, they have the spent quality of solved crosswords. All that's left is a handful of unclued lights for the reader to fill in according to taste (who is the other charred figure in the teak forest? did Vidal's mother have syphilis?).

Kipling himself toyed a great deal with Hidden Depths. Scratch the material world in his stories, and you expose ghosts, fairies, telepathy. It is a very mechanistic version of the supernatural: Kipling's *faerie* is feebly conventional compared with Sylvia Townsend Warner's; the sweet-natured child sprites in "They" are flavourless and pastel-coloured, a nursery of ghostly jelly babies. When Mr Shaynor tunes in to the spirit of John Keats, or Charlie Mears remembers a previous incarnation as a galley slave, Kipling touches no great mystery: he simply presents us with a pair of otherwise stock characters who happen to work like radio sets with faulty condensers.

There is one story which goes deeper than any other into private passion and grief: "Without Benefit of Clergy". It isn't here – its place having been usurped by the much flashier, colder, more superficial story on a parallel theme, "Beyond the Pale". I find that judgment baffling. Does it really mean that Raine prefers conjuring tricks with bloody stumps and blind alleys to serious artistry? Conceivably.

He writes: "[Kipling's] work remains ignored by the literary intelligentsia, largely for political reasons." *No* – and *no*! Kipling's sometimes facile politics, his contempt for Jews, his glib Social Darwinism, have always been seen as products of a more fundamental defect of sensibility. "The talent enormous, but the brutality even deeper seated," wrote James; "it is all bright and shallow and limpid," wrote Stevenson. *That* is the core of what Raine calls "the case against Kipling", but Raine doesn't counter it, choosing instead to go off at a tangent, tilting at anti-imperialist windmills.

Nor is Kipling ignored, even by the clerisy. He is read, taught on university courses and figures as a reference point in every survey of 20th-century literature I can lay my hands on. If he is not vastly revered in academe, he is cherished by practising writers as a supreme technician. Much more than Joyce, James, Chekhov, or any other of the great names to which Raine has coupled Kipling's, he is a writer whom people learn from.

His legacy is here and now – in the exact grammatical distortions of the talk in Kingsley Amis's novels; in Paul Theroux's treatment of know-how and "shop"; in Raine's own crisp metaphorical one-liners; in almost everybody's treatment of the landscape of Abroad. There are strong grounds for the complaint that, far from being ignored, Kipling has proved to be the most durable and influential writer of his age.

1987

MAX BEERBOHM AND WILLIAM ROTHENSTEIN

"Your affectionate Max," wrote Beerbohm. "Your devoted Will," wrote Rothenstein. The inequality in their signatures was a measure of the inequality in their friendship. In 1893 Rothenstein was the "bolt from the blue" who "flashed down" on Beerbohm's Oxford; by 1931 an anonymous reviewer in, of all things, the *Inverness Courier* was voicing the world's ignorant, unkind but more enduring appraisal. "Mr William Rothenstein, whose book *Men and Memories* came from Faber and Faber last Thursday, is a character in Max Beerbohm's story, 'Enoch Soames'." It was Max himself who sent

Rothenstein the clipping. It had a single sentence attached: "Couldn't you contrive to be a little more real?" Poor Rothenstein. Despite his vitality as a draughtsman and painter, despite the enormous, generous energy which he threw into his job as Principal of the Royal College of Art, he had become almost as insubstantial as the hapless Enoch Soames himself. This superlatively edited collection of letters goes a long way towards righting the balance. For it is Rothenstein who comes across as vastly the more interesting character of the two. Awkward, craven, self-effacing, often crashingly wrong in his artistic judgments, he succeeds in eclipsing the man whose shadow he believed himself to be. Late in the day, shadows fall longer than the people who cast them.

Through the Nineties, they carolled at each other like a pair of schoolgirls out on the town. Both were up to their ears in society, drawing, painting and cartooning the fashionables of the time. But it was Beerbohm who was himself caricatured by Sickert for *Vanity Fair*. "*You* have not appeared in *Vanity Fair*, my lad!" he wrote to Rothenstein from Bognor in 1897. But this sort of innocent puffery was beginning to sound in poor taste by the turn of the century, when it became clear that while Beerbohm was destined for extravagant honours, Rothenstein could expect no more than respectable, middling success. Where before they had swapped joshing, comradely compliments, Rothenstein started to bathe Beerbohm in an adoring shower of praise. "I am getting nearer each day," he wrote in 1907, "to a more perfect understanding of your work and of your soul." Of an exhibition of new caricatures by Max, he said: "You are one of the few people living who can give abstract qualities and forms and you must not prefer a man's gifts to a God's."

The strain of receiving homage so unremittingly ardent from a contemporary and friend must have been considerable. In 1909, the God took it into his head that He had been grievously slighted by His worshipper. Beerbohm's side of the correspondence is missing, but Rothenstein's is an avalanche of self-abasing apology. "I am so upset and grieved and humbled that I feel incapable of saying more . . ." Two days later, he was writing in the accents of a small boy at the feet of a heavy Victorian father. "I suppose I got into bad habits before other people and went too far." Max forgave him, and administered a brisk ticking-off.

> Evidently you hanker after the dignity and picturesqueness and pathos which go with failure and which are so lamentably

lacking to success. But you can't, dear Will, have it both ways.

This row should, perhaps, have cleared the air between the two men of the haze of reverential incense which Rothenstein had sprinkled so liberally on it. It didn't. Rothenstein was even more admiring than before. When Beerbohm sent a copy of *Zuleika Dobson*, Rothenstein wrote to him:

> Your book came as a fierce joy to me . . . You, Max, are Puck and Ariel combined; you have escaped from Prospero, for whom most of us still slave, and we can only turn yearning and admiring eyes towards Rapallo . . .

Beerbohm was temperamentally incapable of responding in kind. He could, of course, turn an exquisite compliment, but there was always a niggardly honesty lurking at the bottom of it. His estimation of his own work was admirably cool. When two of his *Seven Men* had been stupidly subbed at the offices of the *Century*, he wrote to the editor demanding that his own punctuation be restored: "I am very well aware that I am not a great or heaven-inspired writer. But I am equally well aware that I am a very careful, conscientious, skilled craftsman in literature."

To Rothenstein, he would start out on a flight of hyperbole, only to end it in a puncturing exactitude. "Your creative, suggestive, fertilizing mind has enormously helped me," he wrote, and then added frankly, "from time to time." His praise of Rothenstein's *Men and Memories* peters out in lame remarks about how Rothenstein's judgments are "never pompous". And to the man who had called him Puck, Ariel, God and many more names besides, he said: "You have always appeared to me such an exquisitely adjusted dynamo, warranted to work for ever without a trace of friction."

It may even have been Max's imperviousness to praise which brought out Rothenstein in such a froth. There is a curious passage in a letter he wrote to Beerbohm about Rabindranath Tagore:

> It is a misfortune for a poet to be too handsome; and even the Gods sometimes take praise too seriously, not to mention the Goddesses. After all the boasting about Jupiter and Diana, the poor earthly lions really did more harm to the Christians than the thunderbolts from heaven. Perhaps, dreadful thought, Lady Colefax has destroyed more souls than Lucifer himself. Perhaps adulation is a habit – I mean

the receiving of it – like smoking, and Tagore can't do
without it.

That parenthetic "I mean the receiving of it" was a giveaway. It was
the giving of it which was Rothenstein's own habit, and in Beerbohm
he had found a perfect, safe recipient. He needed the assurance of
the courtly lover that the lady's head would not be turned. Nor was
it. "Will," said Beerbohm at Rothenstein's memorial service in 1945,
"was assuredly a giver, a giver with both hands, in the grand manner."
During their friendship, Beerbohm had learned how to be the most
gracious of receivers.

Minor art requires a warm, humid climate. Beerbohm and Rothenstein cherished each other's self-esteem and nursed each other's
talents. But if one takes their friendship as a window through which
to look out on the world at large, what an odd scene it presents.
Nothing of major importance is in sight at all. Rothenstein was away
sketching in India when Roger Fry mounted the London exhibition
of Post-Impressionists in 1910. Back in London, Rothenstein wrote
to Fry, confidently dismissing Post-Impressionism as a passing fad.
But to Beerbohm, who had just put on a new show of political
caricatures, he was idolatrous: "You have reached great heights
and can now regard the world beneath you with serene eye . . ."
Beerbohm, writing from the safe distance of Rapallo, replied that he
supposed Rothenstein's own exhibition of Indian drawings must
have been an artistic triumph. They had a genius for backing weak,
well-groomed horses. When Shaw, Wells and Galsworthy were in
the running for the O.M. in 1929, Galsworthy was, of course, their
man. He got it, too.

Somewhere at the back of the house, a massive revolution of
taste was taking place, but they loftily ignored the noise and put
it down to childish horseplay. By the teens of the century, they
were both pickled in a kind of artistic aspic. Already crusty in
their thirties, they kept the company of old men. When they
sought a jury of public opinion, they looked to the Athenaeum
rather than to more down-at-heel joints where criticism was
sharper. As early as 1907, Rothenstein, then aged 35, was able to
bluster about "these days of so-called realism and ugliness worship",
sounding for all the world like an *Any Answers* Wiltshire colonel.
Yet at 21, hot from Paris, he had himself been the harbinger of
everything new, modern and up-to-date. The wave of fashion, on
which he'd ridden like a surfer, had tumbled him; and he was

understandably bitter. Beerbohm was far luckier. A much loved "character", he was able to float his books and drawings on the powerful current of his social reputation.

Both would surely have been pleased with *Max and Will.** Like their own work, it is a splendid piece of craftsmanship, done with great elegance and tact. Mary Lago and Karl Beckson have written two lucid and sprightly biographical introductions. Their notes are everything that notes should be. Brief, informative, and excellently placed in relation to the text, they are the visible eighth of what must have been an enormous iceberg of research.

1975

V. S. PRITCHETT

In "As Old as the Century", his soliloquy on being eighty, V. S. Pritchett writes:

> It seems to me that my life as a man and as a writer has been spent on crossing and recrossing frontiers and that is at the heart of any talent that I have.

Lest this conjure an image of the writer as a man who has to dodge armed guards, searchlights, and wolfhounds, before an average day's breakfast, Pritchett adds:

> It cheers me that I live on the frontier of Camden Town and Regent's Park.

His frontiers are the truly dangerous ones, of the kind that thousands of people habitually cross without ever acknowledging their existence. They are very British frontiers, where a barely perceptible shift of accent, dress, or architecture can signal a human gulf just as cold, bland, and intimidating as Checkpoint Charlie. For nearly sixty years now, V. S. Pritchett has been mapping these rifts and seams of English society, and his *Collected Stories*† have an extraordinary completeness to them. Here is a book that really does work like a world.

---

* Mary M. Lago and Karl Beckson (eds), *Max and Will: Max Beerbohm and William Rothenstein, their Friendship and Letters 1893–1945* (Cambridge: Harvard University Press).

† V. S. Pritchett, *Collected Stories* and *The Turn of the Years: "As Old as the Century"* (New York: Randon House).

It contains virtually all classes and conditions of men, from rich old boys in the port-and-leather nurseries of their clubs to the hapless refugees who grub an impromptu life on the city's dingier streets.

Everyone who lives in the book has his own spiky particularity; he is a unique creature, to whom his author has given the inalienable right of self-determination – however frequently that right is exercised at the expense of authorial design. Taken together, this tumbling crowd of individual characters and their entwined stories compose a larger narrative about the world we have made for ourselves, from our cocky days in the 1920s to the hurts and recriminations of Britain under Mrs Thatcher. They are our history, and we could not have asked for a more wise or vivid one.

Pritchett's "realism" is so successful, his artistry so self-effacing, that he tempts the critic into merely gossiping about what happens in his stories, as if his characters were people who lived on one's own street. The moral philosophy and the literary artifice by which these characters are brought into being are cunningly hidden from the reader. The seemingly inconsequential talkiness of tone, together with Pritchett's habitual air of just being a plain man with an anecdote to tell, are devices that conceal an art as rigorous and deeply thought out as that of Henry James. Beware of Pritchett's homespun manner: it is an elaborate camouflage.

It is rare for Pritchett to speak directly to the reader, and one should attend carefully when he announces that "When My Girl Comes Home" is his own favourite among his stories. "When My Girl Comes Home" is a moral fable disguised as a casual memoir: it occupies the same key place in Pritchett's work as "The Lesson of the Master" does in James's. The lesson taught by "When My Girl Comes Home" is the arbitrary nature of social reality and its transformation in literature.

The story is set in Hincham Street. The name itself, like so many names in Pritchett, has particular resonance. Like England in 1947, for which it stands, "Hincham" is pinched and short of dignity. It sounds like an illiterate abbreviation of some other, grander name (Hinchingham? Hindlesham?). Yet Hincham Street, underlettered, underfed, grown sceptical on a surfeit of wartime propaganda, has a firm grasp of reality. It knows what's what, and knows exactly what is too exotic to be real. Hincham Street is the mean, penny-wise capital of English common sense.

When Hilda Draper returns to Hincham Street after thirteen years away, she is extravagantly, preposterously unreal. The street has prepared itself to receive the ravaged victim of a Japanese P.O.W. camp. The headline that appears in a newspaper the day after Hilda's return reads: A MOTHER'S FAITH. FOUR YEARS IN JAPANESE TORTURE CAMP. LONDON GIRL'S ORDEAL. Yet the Hilda who comes back to Hincham is not at all the Hilda of LONDON GIRL'S ORDEAL. "She shone with money," says the local librarian who tells the story. Her very suitcases are an affront to Hincham notions of reality. She has been everywhere – India, Tokyo, Hawaii, San Francisco. She has been married, certainly; but was it to an Indian called Singh, or a Japanese called Shinji? Were they one man or two?

More puzzling still, there are two further men on the fringe of Hilda's picture, a Mr Faulkner and a Mr Gloster. Mr Gloster is an "American" and a "writer" (both equally improbable species in the world of Hincham Street); and "a book" is to be written about Hilda's "life". "We were all flabbergasted," says the librarian.

> Her life! Here was a woman who had, on top of everything else, a life.

Hincham Street finds Hilda a thoroughly unconvincing character. Her stories all have the clear ring of untruth about them; her behaviour displays a weakness for gothic melodrama of a sort that doesn't fit in at all with the ingrained realism of inner London suburbia. Hilda disappears in a cloud of unlikeliness. The last paragraph of Pritchett's story reads:

> But Mr Gloster's book came out. Oh yes. It wasn't about Japan or India or anything like that. It was about us.

All Pritchett's characters would, like the residents of Hincham Street, be "flabbergasted" to find themselves in a book. They would protest that their lives were so ordinary, so "real", as to be beyond the range of stories. They are frontierspeople, as far outside the folklore of traditional working-class culture as they are outside the genteel manners of the established middle class; shabby, urban, very full of themselves, pure Pritchett.

He allows us to see that Hilda, "unreal" as she may seem to her relations and neighbours, is pure Hincham Street. For Pritchett's people all teeter on the edge of extravagant selfhood; Mr Fulmino and Constance and Bill Williams and all the other residents of the street have more in common with Hilda than any of them would care, or dare, to admit. Given half a chance, any one of them would go in for kid suitcases, studded jewel boxes, improbable journeys abroad, and madcap marriages. The gaiety of Pritchett's world springs from his ability to show that everybody in it, however bound or reduced his social circumstances may make him seem, is rattling the chains of class – another shake, and the whole tottering system will fall apart.

This conviction has literary consequences. In English fiction, the technique of realism has usually been just one more means of keeping the working classes in their place: it has imprisoned them in class accents, class clothes, class districts, class brand names. Give the British realist a voice, a make of shirt, or a neighbourhood for his character to live in, and he will construct a complete cosmology, working from the outside inward. Pritchett does exactly the reverse. He uses the class system, with all its intricately coded symbols, as a challenge, to test his characters' innate powers of individualism.

In story after story he unmasks the sublime ego of someone who, elsewhere in our literature, would be no more than a diagrammatic face in a crowd. Evans, the evangelizing odd-job man in "The Wheelbarrow", Muriel, Colin, and Mr Humphrey in "Sense of Humour", Thompson in "The Sailor", crusty George in "The Skeleton", Mrs Pliny in "The Camberwell Beauty" – they are all figures whom Pritchett has liberated from stereotype.

The tenor of Pritchett's style slyly asserts that this is the world as we already know it, as it really is; that the author, like the narrating librarian in "When My Girl Comes Home", is only a humble archivist. Everything that can happen in direct speech does: dialogue is neutral evidence, and dialogue is Pritchett's primary medium. On every possible occasion he makes his characters speak for themselves, as if their creator were a passive witness to their activities. Much of his writing looks, on the surface, merely like stage directions, to place and inflect the central flow of talk. *She said, with excitement . . . He said seriously . . . He smiled scornfully at me . . .* He is puritanically sparing with metaphor, preferring rather the kind of observant detail from which another writer would construct a metaphor, but which Pritchett likes to present as tangible fact:

> He hated the glazed, whorish, hypocritically impersonal look
> of telephone booths. They were always unpleasantly warmed
> by the random emotions left behind in them.

(Who, after reading those two sentences, will use a pay phone again without thinking of them?)

Pritchett's prose style hinges on the pretence that it never tinkers with the world, never sacrifices the world's oddities and protuberances for the sake of literary rhetoric. He deliberately lets his sentences become clogged and saturated as they try to carry the burden of the world's details. Often they have the tone of inventories, with objects and people piling up, higgledy-piggledy, one on top of another.

> London was cabbaged with greenery. It sprouted in bunches along the widening and narrowing of the streets, bulging at corners, at the awkward turnings that made the streets look rheumatic. There were wide pavements at empty corners, narrow ones where the streets were packed. Brilliant traffic was squeezing and bunching, shaking, spurting, in short disorderly processions like an assortment of funerals. On some windows the blinds of a night worker were drawn and the milk bottle stood untouched at the door; at the Tube, papers and cigarette litter blowing, in the churchyards women pushing prams . . .

It is at once exhaustive and exact. To test its precision of phrase and observation, set it beside any descriptive passage in Dreiser, and Pritchett's artistic cunning will be at once apparent.

His stylistic method is that of a classic realist. Pritchett is temperamentally empirical, Aristotelian, a man who has the air of living humbly in the world as it is. Yet that is a deceptive pose. For every story makes an imaginative appeal for the lives of the characters – of which it pretends to be a straightforward archive – that is absolutely foreign to the conventional assumptions of realism. All the stolid details are there to prove a very unrealist case: that each individual life marvellously transcends its given circumstances, that we are creatures of the spirit, only superficially and temporarily encased in suburban accents and shiny suits.

Sometimes the marvellous happens quite literally, as in "Citizen", when a bronze 19th-century statue takes to the streets of Rome to answer to the needs of a neurotic spinster. More often, it is there as a constant force working on the inner lives of Pritchett's characters, suddenly showing itself in their humour, their capacity to surprise themselves, their unbidden, childlike springs of playfulness and wonder. The delirious ending of Pritchett's most famous story, "Sense of Humour", is a perfect example, with the salesman and his girl jaunting along in the hearse that carries the body of the girl's previous lover:

Through all the towns that run into one another as you might say, we caught it. We went through, as she said, like royalty. So many years since I drove a hearse, I'd forgotten what it was like.

I was proud of her, I was proud of Colin, and I was proud of myself. And after what had happened, I mean on the last two nights, it was like a wedding. And although we knew it was for Colin, it was for us too, because Colin was with both of us. It was like this all the way.

"Look at that man there. Why doesn't he raise his hat? People ought to show respect for the dead," she said.

Humphrey and Muriel, dazzlingly alive, dazzlingly themselves, as morally indifferent as cats, are a glorious creation. Tough, unlikely emblems of the human spirit, they occupy a saintly place in Pritchett's world; just as the famous sanctity of that hero of Christian Science, Mr Timberlake, in "The Saint", earns him a comically low position in the moral order of things.

All this makes V. S. Pritchett the strangest and least easily categorized of modern British writers. He may strike the reader as "English" to a fault with his quizzical mildness of manner, his insistent emphasis on the trifles of speech and social life, his effacement of his own power as an author over the lives of the people he has brought into being. Yet his nicely modulated Englishness is employed in the service of a way of thinking and feeling that is much closer to the 19th-century French and Russian writers of whom Pritchett has been the most readable of critics than it is to, say, Wells or Galsworthy, his most obvious British ancestors. In this too he is a frontiersman: Camden Town turns out to adjoin Paris and Moscow as well as Regent's Park.

As he points out in the title of his memoir, he is "as old as the century"; and the habit of living on one frontier or another has equipped him with his unplaceable, chameleonlike agility in adapting himself as a writer to more decades than it seems decent to list. Each of his stories is rooted in a specific place and period, but Pritchett himself has gone comfortably striding on, as exact about the 1970s as he is about the '20s and the '30s. Over the long continuing arc of his career, the larger story that he tells is not a consoling or a cosy one.

The early stories in the collection hark directly back to the childhood world he has described in *A Cab at the Door*, and it is easy to see how Pritchett's visionary humanism, his stance as a protesting unrealist, chime with his own upbringing. Pritchett's father, though he lacked the subtlety, the intelligence, and the reading of his son, recognized no limits to selfhood. In that most British of phrases, he was always getting above himself, with his dizzy business ventures, his new automobiles, his devout conversion to the transcendentalism of Mrs Eddy, and the young Pritchett grew up in a milieu that was happily innocent of the conventional constraints and taboos of class. The injuries of class that he suffered were inflicted outside the home; and as he became an expert on the delicate lunacies of English society so his expertise was that of someone who was essentially an outsider, with an outsider's ability to perceive the comedy at the heart of the pain.

Stories like "Sense of Humour" rejoice in the England they describe, finding in it a place at once absurd and possible. Pritchett's clerks and salesmen of the '20s and '30s, with their hair pasted flat on their skulls, their loud checks and faded new slang, are all kin to his own father, they are ebulliently busy getting above themselves, and their author is able to smile on them and find them good. They enter the book in a swirl of exhaust fumes, coming out of ribbon developments of ugly brick houses and art deco saloon bars: a succession of unlikely saints and rain kings for whom the world is their oyster.

Then something happens. It is not a change in Pritchett himself; he is as tolerant, as keen to love his characters, as ever. It is a change in the texture of the outside world. In "As Old as the Century" Pritchett writes:

> At eighty I look at the horrible state of our civilization. It seems to be breaking up and returning to the bloody world of Shakespeare's Histories which we thought we had outgrown . . .

This is not the predictable rumbling of an old codger; it is something more serious. One finds its evidence painfully documented in later stories like "Tea with Mrs Bittell" and "On the Edge of the Cliff", where the characters are struggling for survival like victims of a shipwreck, where cruelty and violence come casually out of the blue.

Pritchett never deals directly with public life, but one can sense it in the background of these private encounters as a spreading infection that extends from the body politic into the body personal. In "Tea with Mrs Bittell" what starts as a rumour about an I.R.A. bomb in a London restaurant ends as a grotesque and bloody battle between an old woman and a young thief in a South Kensington flat. As in the early stories, what happens has the air of being unwilled by the author, of surprising him with its cruelty as earlier events surprised him with their grace. As a version of our own history it is all the more ominous because one is certain that this is not the history Pritchett ever wanted to write, and that only honesty now compels him to set it down. The frontier on which his latest stories are set is an England trembling between civilization and savagery; an unhappy setting and a frighteningly truthful one.

1982

EVELYN WAUGH

I

The publication of Waugh's diaries* ought to be an important literary event, not the tiresome social function which it threatens to become. The cards, however, are already out on the mantelpieces of the almost-dead, and the same voices which were heard in 1973 when the *Observer* colour supplement printed its selection of extracts from the diaries, and were heard again last year when Christopher Sykes brought out his biography, are being raised once more. Who, it will be debated, was the more exquisitely nasty: Waugh or Bowra? Ancient triumphs and humiliations at White's will be fondly revived, and the nursery nicknames of the English upper class will be flicked like bread pellets across the review pages of the Sunday papers. Nothing that Evelyn Waugh is reported to have ever said or done is actually nastier than the prospect of his admirers rolling joyfully on their backs in the mess of 30-, 40-, and 50-year-old gossip which he and his set have left behind.

Against these voices will be raised ones equally repulsive – those of the detractors who speak of Waugh as if he were some undesirable social institution, like pay beds in N.H.S. hospitals, of which any liberal society should feel ashamed. Enraged by what they perceive as Waugh's snobbery, they descend to terms which outface their object in affected superiority and snobbishness. In a recent review of a television programme made by Auberon Waugh, Clive James remarked that Au-

---

* Michael Davie (ed.), *The Diaries of Evelyn Waugh* (London: Weidenfeld & Nicolson).

beron "is a fake squire like his father". The brush-off administered to Waugh Sr is of exactly the same order as a Mayfair "cut". It's also (except by the any-mud-that-sticks standards of these irredeemably social affairs) wildly inaccurate. "Fake" suggests a degree of servile imitation of which Evelyn Waugh was simply not capable. With his ear-trumpet, his three-inch-square red check suit, his inexhaustible capacity for rudeness, his fulminations about the "grey lice" of the Attlee administration, he may have been a travesty but he was certainly not a fake.

None of this would matter much if Waugh had been just another Chips Channon, Cecil King or Harold Nicolson. People who make a full-time career of living in Society deservedly end up as gross cartoons – preserved (or not, as the case may be) in the careless distortions of social gossip, like freaks in bottles. With Waugh, the shame is that he had a very much more important career as a novelist, and we are now in some danger of altogether losing sight of the writer behind this overpowering smog of gossip. Fine English novelists have been thin enough on the ground lately, and we can ill afford to abandon Waugh to the Paul Slickeys.

It is tempting to be saddened by the Waugh family's decision to publish the diaries. Too many people will be hunting up their friends and enemies in the index and cackling over the old monster's gibes; even more will bask vicariously in the better-forgotten inanities of that world where Babe and Terence and Pansy and Olivia and Zena frisked over cocktails at the Ritz and said the most utterly crymaking things about one another. Yet for all their dubious incidental appeal as scandal, the diaries are vital literary documents, and in a less snobbish and nostalgic climate than our own they would enhance and deepen Waugh's reputation as a novelist. Perhaps, though, we shall have to wait for a later generation to read them with the care and disinterestedness that they deserve.

They begin in 1911, when Waugh was seven, and continue with intermittent breaks and changes of format to 1965, a year, almost to the day, before he died. Reading them, I was reminded of that curiosity of the cinema, *London to Brighton in Three Minutes*. In the course of a few hours one watches the weird metamorphosis of a chirpy prep school boy fattening out, hardening, and exaggerating his own mannerisms until he is eventually transformed into a senile La Rochefoucauld. From beginning to end there is a resistant core of personality which survives the endless succession of experimental masks and costumes with which Waugh adorned it. The eleven-year-old who wrote

> In the evening we went to church. We struck a horrible low
> one. I was the only person who crossed myself and bowed
> to the altar . . .

is recognizably the same person as the prematurely aged man who
finds himself increasingly alone in a horrible low world. In fact,
Waugh retained a disproportionate amount of schoolboy in his
make-up, right through to the end: a schoolboy cruelty, a schoolboy
obsession with the digestive system, a romantic schoolboy honour
and a schoolboy talent for friendship. Plenty of small boys have
indulged in the insolent verbal savagery of

> We had 3 classics today which was something awful Mr
> Hynchcliffe is getting more obnoxious every day and his
> nose is getting pereceptably longer every day. He spent
> the greatest part of the first Latin in slobbering over the
> unfortunate Spenser who has the bad luck to be the favorite
> of a man like Hynchcliffe.

No one except Waugh has elaborated the same style into a supple
medium for extended fiction. When, in *Black Mischief*, Basil Seal
consumes his mistress in a cannibal stew ("You're a grand girl,
Prudence, and I'd like to eat you." "So you shall, my sweet . . .
anything you want."), the sheer awfulness of the irony bounces us
back into the schoolroom. For Waugh the novelist, this odd closeness
to the cruelties and extremities of boyhood was an essential strength;
it was a constant source of metaphor and invention which Waugh
was able to tap at will throughout his career. For Waugh the man,
it was perhaps his most painful encumbrance; it was certainly the
quality in him which caused most pain to others. Like the unhappy
Bultitudes, in *Vice Versa*, it was sometimes difficult to tell whether
he was a grown-up squashed into a striped cap and short trousers or
a child masquerading in the sombre uniform of an adult. In his
biography of Waugh, Christopher Sykes recounts how, near the end
of his life, Waugh confided to Lord Antrim that he spent his mornings
"breathing on his library window and then playing noughts and
crosses against himself, drinking gin in the intervals between play".

This disconcerting, sometimes vengeful, sometimes pathetic, childishness gives all Waugh's writing an odd innocence, a kind of brazen
incorruptibility. His cult of the noble (which was much more a dream
of living in a Burne-Jonesish world of sunlit castles and pure chivalry
than it was a toadying after titles), his fiercely traditionalist Catholi-

cism, his horror of the urban proletariat, were too wide-eyed to be either dangerous or mean. His sensibility had the extravagance of a brilliant child's: adult moderation never got in the way of clarity. When he admired, he worshipped; when he disapproved, he was appalled. The bourgeois virtues of common sense and good manners (the besetting vices of so many modern English novelists) were totally foreign to him – not because he was a snob but because he never forgot what it was like to be a child.

Perhaps this is why there is no serious break in tone over the whole stretch of the Waugh diaries, no point at which the adult decisively emerges from the child. Rather, there is a deliberate cultivation of a manner of speaking, a sense of self, which is evident even in the most babyish of the early entries. There is an important gap between the end of Waugh's Lancing diary in 1921 and the diary begun on coming down from Oxford in 1924, but it is clear that by the time Waugh left university the broad outlines of his style were already firmly fixed. From 1924 onwards, the diaries bristle with sentences whose structure rings instantly familiar to a reader of the novels.

> Pink men chased a fox about the park and excited the mad boys.

> The school in Notting Hill is quite awful. All the masters drop their aitches and spit in the fire and scratch their genitals. The boys have close-cropped heads and steel-rimmed spectacles wound about with worsted.

> A Scotsman covered in blood came to dig a pond in the garden.

These are clear practice runs for the writing of fiction. Their bizarre simplicity, their relish for incongruous detail, hark straight back to the nursery. If they have any formal literary antecedent, it is *Alice in Wonderland* (from which Waugh drew the epigraph of *Vile Bodies*). They are also quite intimately related to two other forms in which Waugh was interested: the cinema and drawing. It's revealing to learn that he loathed Chaplin and loved Harold Lloyd. Lloyd's simplicity, his air of being an inexpressive waif at large in a monstrous world, comes very close to Waugh's characteristic posture in his novels. In his drawings too, he shows the same delight in a purity of statement won from between the teeth of experience: everything is economized into a decorative outline. The illustrations which Waugh drew for his novels were of a piece with their literary style – candid, childlike, obsessively precise.

When teaching at Aston Clinton in 1927, Waugh noted: "Next Thursday I am to visit a Father Underhill about being a parson. Last night I was very drunk. How odd those two sentences seem together." That kind of juxtaposition rapidly became a conscious manner, tried out in the diaries and soon absorbed into the novels.

> . . . Mrs Y's brother, a typical ineffectual younger son. He had lost his money in South Africa and been rescued by the family. Now he spends his time drawing pear trees.

> Kit Wood has committed suicide. The Duchess of York has had a daughter. Birkenhead is still alive.

In Waugh's writing, depth comes from the matching of unlikely simplicities of this sort – a setting of one bold, flat colour against another. In his early work – especially in *Decline and Fall* and *Vile Bodies* – the calculated exactitude of patchwork quilting sometimes sounds priggish or arch. But at best his style affords a way of being faithful to an off-key world of wild moral and social disparities without losing authority or poise. The diarist and the novelist merge perfectly in an entry describing a house party at the Sitwells in 1930:

> The household was very full of plots. Almost everything was a secret and most of the conversations deliberately engineered in prosecution of some private joke. Ginger, for instance, was told that Ankaret's two subjects were Arctic exploration and ecclesiastical instruments; also that Alastair played the violin. Sachie liked talking about sex. Osbert very shy. Edith wholly ignorant. We talked of slums. She said the poor streets of Scarborough are terrible but that she did not think the fishermen took drugs very much. She also said that port was made with methylated spirit; she knew this for a fact because her charwoman told her.

If Waugh makes the Sitwells sound absurd, he does so by reporting on them with the deadly accuracy of an unsmiling child. He uses the same technique, the same jumpy but controlled prose rhythm, when he writes of Archie Schwert's party in *Vile Bodies*:

> There was a famous actor making jokes (but it was not so much what he said as the way he said it that made the people laugh who did laugh). "I've come to the party as a wild

widower," he said. They were that kind of joke – but, of course, he made a droll face when he said it.

Miss Runcible had changed into Hawaiian costume and was the life and soul of the evening.

She had heard someone say something about an Independent Labour Party, and was furious that she had not been asked.

There were two men with a lot of explosive powder taking photographs in another room. Their flashes and bangs had rather a disquieting effect on the party, causing a feeling of tension, because everyone looked negligent and said what a bore the papers were, and how *too* like Archie to let the photographers come, but most of them, as a matter of fact, wanted dreadfully to be photographed and the others were frozen with unaffected terror that they might be taken unawares and then their mamas would know where they had been when they said they were at the Bicesters' dance, and then there would be a row again, which was so *exhausting*, if nothing else.

With Waugh in this vein, one is never very far from Daisy Ashford and Mr Salteena. But he has another style, of which we see only hints and glimpses in the diaries. Self-consciously "grown-up", with its magisterial periods and elaborate parallelisms, it's a style which Waugh reserved (in his fiction) for speaking about country houses, history and the Church. In his most accomplished work (*A Handful of Dust, Put Out More Flags, Work Suspended*, and parts of the *Sword of Honour* trilogy) he could switch from being an innocent abroad to being Tiresias at the turn of a sentence. Yet the grown-up and the childlike are always kept distinct, in a private and purposeful dissociation of sensibility. It was as if Waugh the child yearned for the dignified serenity of his own mock-eighteenth-century prose, while Waugh the grown-up found himself in a world where only children were at home. Once, in *Brideshead*, this yearning for amplitude swamped a whole book and turned the entire novel into an extended purple passage. *Decline and Fall, Vile Bodies* and *Black Mischief*, by contrast, are written almost completely in the naif idiom, and are the weaker for it. It was not until *A Handful of Dust* (1934) that Waugh really gave vent to the tension in his own character which made him a novelist rather than a lightweight social comedian.

The nature of this tension has never been properly explored, but the diaries offer some useful clues. There is an entry made in 1926:

> I suppose that the desire to merge one's individual destiny in forces outside oneself, which seems to me deeply rooted in most people and shows itself in social service and mysticism and in some manner in debauchery, is really only a consciousness that this is already the real mechanism of life which requires so much concentration to perceive that one wishes to objectify it in more immediate (and themselves subordinate) forces. How badly I write when there is no audience to arrange my thoughts for.

The sentence goes hopelessly to pieces after "and in some manner in debauchery", as Waugh loses himself in a smokescreen of abstractions. But the initial insight holds, and it is significant that Waugh found it impossible to pursue it further. His attempt to immerse himself in the social life of the 1920s and '30s was touched with heroic dedication. He gave himself up to the round of parties and drinking bouts with a priestly fervour, as if by doing so he could engage with a world from which he felt deeply alienated. Waugh had been unpopular at school (as he records in *A Little Learning*); and in the army he was heartily disliked by his men and by many of his brother officers. He might well have made a successful pious anchorite. But he chose instead to be a social lion and a chronicler of social manners, and he went into society rather as an inexperienced missionary might go into the jungle, with gritted teeth and terrible enthusiasm. Waugh the socialite, drowning in a succession of bats and one-night-stands, was just as extreme a pose as the one he adopted in the 1950s and '60s, when he acted out the part of an aged aristo withdrawing in horror from the modern world. He threw himself into London society, then into travel, then into the army, with the kind of moral determination that only comes from doing something against the grain of one's own nature.

The novels – unlike the gossip and most of the anecdotes – reveal that he never fooled himself with these forays into social service. Even at their most gleeful, there is something in them which shrinks from the world they record, a constant undercurrent of distress and loss. Yet when Waugh tried to indicate what *had* been lost, in that "mature" prose of syrup and aloes, his own language betrayed the unreality of the vision. As he later admitted, his belief in the Marchmains had been a sentimental aberration. In *Brideshead*, he had tried to describe the Great Good Place before and after the Fall, but had succeeded only in piously burning candles to a dream. (In his preface to the second edition of the book, Waugh noted, somewhat ruefully, that the most evident features of Brideshead life had been its sumptuous menus and extensive wine cellars. On the one occasion when he had attempted to create a moral ideal, it had come out in terms of knowing about vintages and being a good judge of properly cooked grouse.) In *Brideshead* he had tried to show a society where he felt he might have been at home; but the truth was that Waugh was, in the deepest sense, homeless – a displaced person. His best work doesn't flinch from that fact.

His quest for a home, for a point of rest and reconciliation, was Ulyssean. He threw himself into the hyperactive swirl of society, into globetrotting, into active service, with manic restlessness, as if tranquillity could only come from sheer physical exhaustion. His stamina was immense. Just to read the bare record of the travelling and partying which he did in the 1930s is tiring. But one never loses the sense that this *was* a quest, even though its purpose is never made explicit. One short entry stands out. Waugh was in British Guiana in 1932: "General impression of Georgetown that I don't mind how soon I leave it. Too diffuse."

That was what was wrong with the world. "Too diffuse." Waugh yearned for precision and clarity. Occasionally he found it, in experiences that matched the simplicity and extremity of his own style. In the Brazilian jungle he hit on what was to become both the metaphorical theme and the literal ending of *A Handful of Dust* – the situation of a civilized man who finds himself among savages. When he himself was anticipating Tony Last's trip up river, his diary entries suddenly sharpened. For the moment, life was sufficiently brilliant and exact to write about and be at home in.

> Large abandoned store: counters, cupboards, a weighing machine, floor of sawn planks full of jiggers and fleas, thatch roof full of spiders, bats, etc. Continuous falls in Chinapeng from where we met it to here. Water deep and fast and cold. Indians turned up at 4.10, those who left today before those who left yesterday. Bathed, drank rum. Rations supplemented by yesterday's kill = 1½ macaws.

In both his diaries and his fiction he loves lists like that; a world of bold substantives and clear actions. At such times, Waugh himself is wholly absorbed in externals; nothing of the self – bristling, bored, troubled with conscience, melancholic – obtrudes. The self-extinction of the mystic, lost in contemplation of the object, is not so very far away. The real trouble with the diffuse is that it leads one inescapably back to self.

Perhaps Waugh's Catholicism answered the same need. Army service certainly did. And when, after the war, he came to "settle down" in England, first at Piers Court, then at Combe Florey, he did so in a characteristically extreme fashion. No one in history can have made buying a country house in Somerset look so much like a trip to Abyssinia as Waugh did. He equipped himself for his new role much as William Boot kitted himself out for Ishmaelia with cleft sticks and collapsible canoe. The eccentric squires in Thackeray and Fielding look tame beside the twice-life-size figure of Waugh in full cry. It's impossible not to suspect that his life and his fiction had become dangerously mixed up by the 1950s, and that the Gilbert Pinfold episode was the price he had to pay for that confusion. Certainly there was a remarkable consistency between the way he observed life and the way he actually lived it. In 1955, he entertained Lord Longford at Piers Court:

> Frank made a splendid entrance to Sunday breakfast his face, neck and shirt covered with blood, brandishing the Vulgate, crying, "Who will explain to me 2nd Corinthians 5.16?" (or some text). Of every name mentioned Frank asked: "What chance of their coming in?" (to the Church). He was much concerned for the welfare of Trevor-Roper's soul.

In his biography, Christopher Sykes suggests that many of the more extreme anecdotes in the diaries may have been "hallucinations". Was Longford's entrance to Sunday breakfast a hallucination? Or was it a slight bending of reality to fit a vision of life which had already been long established in Waugh's literary style? Waugh's own life was lived increasingly on this heightened scale; its hard edges and over-bright colours may have been an affront to social conventions in a decade of frightened orthodoxy, but they kept faith with the deeper truth of his best fiction.

By the end, though, his life had become unbearable to himself. He was only just over sixty when he died, but his manner was that of a senile octogenarian. Depression, boredom and remorse at the insulting extravagances of his own behaviour haunted him. He had never clearly grasped the effect of his personality on other people, and was still capable of being surprised and hurt by the discovery of his unpopularity. There is an entry written in 1962: "Clarissa writes to Ann Fleming: 'The Haileses found Evelyn W. rather a bore'. I thought I had charmed and delighted them."

Later in the same year he reflected:

> *Abjuring the realm.* To make an *interior* act of renunciation and to become a stranger in the world; to watch one's fellow-countrymen, as one used to watch foreigners, curious of their habits, patient of their absurdities, indifferent to their animosities – that is the secret of happiness in this century of the common man.

He had always, in some sense, been a stranger in the world. In his writing, he had succeeded in making that interior act of renunciation: his style is a triumphant submission of the self to the object. Waugh the novelist enjoys a godlike poise and calm behind the frantic activity of his created world. But as a man, he would never escape being a creature of the realm he longed to abjure.

In one of the last entries in the diaries (Easter 1964), Waugh wrote:

> When I first came into the Church I was drawn, not by splendid ceremonies but by the spectacle of the priest as a craftsman. He had an important job to do which none but he was qualified for. He and his apprentice stumped up to the altar with their tools and set to work without a glance to those behind them, still less with any intention to make a personal impression on them.

This is just how he would have liked to have been as a novelist, one feels. If only the gossip had not got so incriminatingly in the way of the books, that, perhaps, is how he might be remembered. Stephen Dedalus's God wisely went off to pare his fingernails behind his handiwork; it was Waugh's personal tragedy that he made the mistake of coming down out of the clouds and getting drunk in his.

1976

II

Officially, Evelyn Waugh took the popular view that journalism was a very low trade indeed and that journalists were witless toadies. Unofficially, his writing tells an altogether different story. It is not just that Waugh was an unusually effective journalist himself, or that in *Scoop* he produced the funniest novel ever written about the Street of Shame. It is that his fiction is deeply rooted in the style and method of journalism. When he went to work for Beaverbrook for a seemingly unproductive few months in 1927, he learned more of his craft as a novelist than, understandably, he would ever care to admit. It is Mr Chatterbox's gossip column (Tom Driberg's William Hickey) which supplies the basic style in which *Vile Bodies* is written. The most telling connection, though, is the way that Waugh's novels are built – like feature articles – around topics. Several of them, including *Black Mischief* and *The Loved One*, had already been worked over in journalism before Waugh sat down to fantasticate them in fiction. All of them tend to subordinate their characters to an essentially journalistic argument and have plots which resemble nothing so much as the point by point structure of the didactic article.

Journalism, with its bald simplicities and violent logic, suited Waugh's temperament. Impatient of the shades and ambiguities which absorb most novelists, he craved for certitude and clarity. Catholic theology partially satisfied this craving; so did Waugh's mad, parodic brand of high Toryism. In the arts, he loved whatever was simple, elegant and clear-cut – virtues that he first tried to practise in his own drawings, and later discovered in the work of an oddly assorted crew of modern heroes, like Harold Lloyd, P. G. Wodehouse, Max Beerbohm and Mgr Ronald Knox ("No major writer in our history has ever shown such an extent of accomplishment"). He had a neurotic antipathy to the mess and clutter of modern life and, like a demented housewife, he wanted to tidy, straighten and stuff as much of this bungled civilization as he could into garbage bags. His saving genius lay in his anarchic sense of humour and his manic glee in pure invention; otherwise, one can imagine that he might have been most happily employed in the writing of pamphlets for the Catholic Truth Society.

It was the absolute logic of Catholicism – its reductive, icy clarity – that held Waugh's imagination. He used theology like an axe and tried to chop his way out of the confusions of the modern world. When he recalled his conversion, he wrote of how he was admitted to the church "on firm intellectual conviction but with little emotion". Father Martin D'Arcy, who instructed him in 1930, later said of his pupil:

> He was a man of very strong convictions and a clear mind.
> He had convinced himself very unsentimentally – with only

> an intellectual passion – of the truth of the Catholic faith,
> and that in it he must save his soul . . . He was perhaps
> inclined to be too literal about The Last Things, and the
> message of the Gospel.

If Catholicism supplied Waugh with a line of cold, and often pre-
posterous, logic, journalism offered him its most natural form of
expression. The short paragraph, the authoritarian insistence of
points (a) and (b) and (c), the flying leap between the second and
third stages of the syllogism, the shocking simplicity of the conclusion, would have been anathema to almost any other imaginative
writer one can think of. For Waugh, these rigid procedures were like
the elegant discipline of the sonnet; they bore a fearsome correspondence to the way in which he instinctively thought about things.

Even before his conversion, the habit of mind is clearly there. For
a *Spectator* article on "War and the Younger Generation", published
in 1929, he was writing:

> In the social subsidence that resulted from the War a double
> cleft appeared in the life of Europe, dividing it into three
> perfectly distinct classes between whom none but the most
> superficial sympathy can ever exist. There is (a) the wistful
> generation who grew up and formed their opinions before
> the War and who were too old for military service; (b) the
> stunted and mutilated generation who fought; and (c) the
> younger generation.

The giveaway words are "perfectly" and "can ever", betraying both
the pleasure and the prescriptive vehemence of a man who first chops
up the world in order to make a pretty pattern, then dares it to
reassemble itself on pain of logical excommunication. Indeed, here
as elsewhere in Waugh's work, logic and aesthetics are cunningly
scrambled: the one being used as an instrument of law enforcement
to protect the other.

Thirty years later, in a *Daily Mail* piece called "I See Nothing But
Boredom . . . Everywhere", Waugh was tickling his readers with this
announcement: "I must confess that I face the immediate future with
gloomy apprehensions . . ." Tame enough, that. Was the old white
rhino off form?

> I am not the least nervous about the much-advertised threats
> of the nuclear scientists: First, because I can see nothing

objectionable in the total destruction of the earth, provided
it is done, as seems most likely, inadvertently . . .

Waugh takes three more sentences to dispose of the holocaust on
theological grounds, then goes on to prove at length that the world
faces a far greater threat: Waugh, it turns out, should be earning
£20,750 a year in order to continue to live in the manner to which
he was accustomed in the 1930s; actually, he finds it "hard work to
earn half that amount". This was the kind of stuff for which editors
– and readers too – were baying: Waugh was an institutionalized
monster, half shibboleth, half figure of fun. He was, in a word
more usually applied to stand-up club comedians than to novelists,
"outrageous", and it was enjoyably hard to tell whether he was just
joking or whether he really meant the awful things he said.

Theological jokes are hard to decode in a secular world, as Waugh
well knew. They are not even exactly jokes. Their humour, as they
shove the little, mutable universe of man in humiliating proximity to
God's eternity, is cold and literal. They have the deadly seriousness
of slapstick; they have no truck with civilized irony. In his introduction to this collection,* Donat Gallagher summarizes an unreprinted
piece by Waugh, calling it "an article on Wilberforce, pointing out
some of the advantages of slavery". The formulation sounds like
Swift, just as Waugh's Augustan clarity of style often superficially
resembles Swift's. (He was once commissioned to write Swift's
biography.) But Waugh is not like Swift at all. His immodest pro-
posals, though they masquerade in cap and bells, are totally in earnest.
He is an ironic writer only in the lightest social and conversational
sense: the heart of his comedy is knockabout farce, while its soul is
pure theological ice. He "means" his indifference to the holocaust,
just as he "means" his hatred of Tito, his horror at the imminent
collapse of the class system, or his observation that almost the only
benefit to be derived from the invention of photography is its
revelation of the stains on the Holy Shroud of Turin. In all these
subjects he also found something grotesquely funny. No doubt God
does too.

When we think of "Christian" writers, Waugh does not immediately leap to mind. He is a millennium away from the gentle, forgiv-
ing, modernist, ecumenical version of Christianity; much closer in
spirit to the cruel piety of the gothic monk carving gargoyles and
misericords. His Manichean sensibility, with its broad choleric

---

* Evelyn Waugh, *A Little Order*, ed. Donat Gallagher (Boston: Little, Brown & Co.).

humour, comes out most clearly in his book reviews. He gloats over the sumptuous binding and fine paper of a Dropmore Press edition of *The Holkham Bible*; he treats a little book of homilies by Mgr Knox in a manner that verges on idolatry; on Cyril Connolly and Stephen Spender he turns into a jeering Inquisitor, showing rather too lingering a pleasure as he tears their wings off with his fingers one by one. At the same time, his carefully constructed tortures are so craftsmanly that one relishes them even in spite of their unfairness.

> At one stage in his life Mr Spender took to painting and, he naïvely tells us, then learned the great lesson that "it is possible entirely to lack talent in an art where one believes oneself to have creative feelings". It is odd that this never occurred to him while he was writing, for to see him fumbling with our rich and delicate language is to experience all the horror of seeing a Sèvres vase in the hands of a chimpanzee.

In this review of *World Within World*, Waugh handles Spender with exactly the same slow, delighted malignity that he accords to Atwater in *Work Suspended* – one of the most brilliant and relatively neglected of his fictions. The narrator of that novella (Waugh rarely used the first person) is himself oddly monkish; pious in the exercise of his narrow craft, at one remove from the modern world. Waugh's journalism is, in one sense, a further fleshing-out of the character of John Plant.

This selection of what Waugh called his "beastly little articles" is regrettably meagre. An essay on Venice and the superb piece on Forest Lawn Cemetery which became the springboard for *The Loved One* do not fairly represent Waugh's travel writing. Nor has Mr Gallagher dredged up anything from the period in 1927 when Waugh was a full-time Beaverbrook hack (did his name ever appear in the *Express* at that time?). Within the cramped space at his disposal, Mr Gallagher has got together a fair spread of different kinds of writing, but his preference is for the formal essay over the newspaper "feature". Given the way in which Waugh's novels derive from and treat daily journalism, it might have been more interesting if the balance had been tipped in the opposite direction. Mr Gallagher's own editorial matter is usefully informative, but written as if in mud with a cleft stick. His suggestion that the *Spectator* "is the favourite reading matter of Church of England clergymen" is entertaining, but suspect. In my experience, they prefer the *Investor's Chronicle, Yachting Monthly* and *The Vole.*

1977

III

In September 1953, Evelyn Waugh wrote to Nancy Mitford:

> I am reading an enormous life of Dickens, by an American professor of course, which gives details of every chop he ever ate and every speech at every public banquet. Did you know that he was a perfectly awful man?

The point is not that in any prize stakes for sheer bloody awfulness Dickens would run at far longer odds than Waugh, but that no revelation about Dickens the man – no chop, no speech, no diary entry, no letter – could conceivably damage the unassailable glory of the novels which he wrote. Is the same true of Waugh?

In his books, Waugh's style was more pure, his wit saner, his invented societies more animated, than those of any other British writer of his time. His novels were brilliant distillations of a life which was peculiarly messy and riddled with paradox. Every *roman* had its *clef.* At the most obvious and trivial level his books are all "about" particular circumstances in his life. Beginning *A Handful of Dust*, he wrote to the Lygon sisters that the opening was "about Sponger", who is now footnoted as Major Murrough O'Brien (1910–   ), better known to us as that marvellously feeble and ingratiating character called John Beaver.

Yet the art was a fantastic refinement of the life. Knowing readers have always been able to spot people like Cyril Connolly, Harold Acton and Brian Howard behind the comic masks which Waugh fashioned for them, but these are trifling distractions in a body of fiction whose main driving forces are its intense good humour, its nostalgic sense of chivalry, and, at its heart, a childlike capacity for taking delight in a wonderful, if fallen, world. Gossip about the man has contradicted the fiction at every point. The good humour, so one is told, was irritable melancholia; the chivalry mere snobbism; and as for the childlike capacity etcetera, that was really spiteful misanthropy.

It has become harder and harder to read Waugh's novels without finding them being elbowed off the table by the importunate character of Waugh himself. His autobiography, *A Little Learning*, mildly enhanced the fiction by its very blandness. Christopher Sykes's intimate biography added a legitimate amount of pepper and spice to one's sense of the writer behind the books. It has been the publication first of the diaries, edited by Michael Davie, and now of the letters, edited by Mark Amory,* which together have made the novelist loom so destructively over his own novels, like Prospero ending the revels with a lecture on dreams and death and baseless fabrics.

Yet, like Prospero's speech, the diaries and letters contain some of the best bits in the whole bewildering play; and the letters are much the more consistently riveting of the two. It was not simply Waugh's famous aversion to the telephone which drove him to write such a towering heap of correspondence (for this Bible-sized book, Mark Amory has chosen less than one in five of the letters made available to him). He used letters as an athlete uses the gym, to limber up in, to try out risky leaps and handstands before exhibiting them in public. Even in the most ordinary business note, language is there to be played with.

He loved to construct sentences whose bald simplicity of grammar was in calculated discord with the outrageous disparity of the (very dubious) facts they reported: "He had a sister called Hermione who lived in sin with a genealogist who kept pet squirrels."

He could turn the dullest acquaintance into an amazing freak for the entertainment of his friends. His own daily rounds became atrocious adventures, with himself cast as a kind of languid Harold Lloyd at their centre, at once weary and wide-eyed. There are more rounded characters, too. In February 1940, he described to Laura Waugh how he had been dragged off to Sunday lunch by his brigadier. The letter is a superb example of Waugh's knack of turning fact into hilarious fiction; and in 1952, in *Men At Arms*, both the lunch and the brigadier (Ben Ritchie-Hook) turn up again hardly changed at all since their first, epistolary appearance.

These glimpses of the novelist doing his morning exercises are fascinating. They are overshadowed, though, by a darker story which starts to emerge in the book in the early 1930s immediately after the break-up of Waugh's first marriage and goes on, getting blacker and blacker, until his death in 1966. In his writing he was always a consummate actor, a genius at putting on funny faces and funny

* Mark Amory (ed.), *The Letters of Evelyn Waugh* (New York: Viking Penguin).

voices. By the time that he proposed to Laura Herbert in 1936, he was perfecting the voice which was to carry him to a tragically premature senility. "You would be taking on an elderly buffer," he wrote to Laura, ". . . I have always tried to be nice to you and you may have got it into your head that I am nice really, but that is all rot."

The elderly buffer was then aged 32. To many friends who were closer to his own age, especially to Lady Mary Lygon, he was still acting the part of the dazzling boy; for several years more, his skittish letters might have been written by a ferociously talented undergraduate. To Laura, though (who was nearly 13 years younger than Waugh), to his juniors during the war, and later to the world in general, Evelyn Waugh became the elderly buffer; out of date before his time, rigid in politics and theology, constitutionally low in spirits, grave in manner, tired to death with life itself. To begin with, he played alternately at being buffer and boy. Letters of the same date to different people show the undergraduate face to one correspondent, the crusty old soak to another. Bufferism had started as a joke, a try-on; it turned into a horridly distorting mask which Waugh was unable to remove.

The later letters are full of sentences which seem to take the same energetic pleasure in what is anomalous as the early ones. So close in construction are they that an ignorant reader might altogether mistake their intent. When Clarissa Churchill, brought up as a Catholic, married Anthony Eden, a divorcé, Waugh wrote to her on her honeymoon:

> I don't suppose you deliberately chose the vigil of the Assumption for your betrayal or deliberately arrived in a Catholic capital on the Feast. But I am sure Our Lady noticed . . . You must now and then in an *antiquère* have seen a crucifix. Did you never think how you were contributing to the loneliness of Calvary by your desertion?

The line between what had once been outrageously funny and was now outrageously cruel and intolerant was dreadfully thin.

One suspects that Waugh himself was incapable of recognizing when he crossed the boundary from the one to the other. Eight months before he died he reported to Lady Diana Cooper that he'd been reading Nigel Dennis's life of Swift. "I found many affinities with the temperament (not of course the talent) of the master." That seems right on both counts. Like Swift, Waugh impaled himself on the hook of his own irony; unlike Swift's, Waugh's work is not quite great enough to disentangle itself and float free of the character of the man who wrote it.

In the same letter, he wrote: "No, there's no 'reward' in this world. Perhaps retribution hereafter." At the end, there were no games or masks. Waugh found himself facing death and life with the same dull fear and repugnance. His last letters – bereft of art – make sorrowful reading. I found myself wishing that I had not been allowed to intrude on the ending of this particular story. Picking up *A Handful of Dust*, I tried to re-read it for, I suppose, the seventh or eighth time. It has not been spoiled, quite. But it seems somehow thinner, the pathology of its artifice wanly exposed. The publication of these letters will add to Waugh's stature as one of the stranger English characters of the century; it may unnecessarily dent his reputation as a novelist – a disservice which his books have done nothing to deserve.

1980

ANTHONY POWELL AND PETER QUENNELL

All over England, from converted croquet huts on well-trimmed lawns, from attic studies, and from studios overlooking Chelsea Reach, comes the soporific rattle of a dozen electric typewriters. The Men of Letters are knocking out their memoirs. Each leather-topped desk bears – or so one might justifiably suspect – a printed memorandum, prepared, perhaps, by the Regent School of Successful Writing. Headed "Your Autobiography: Hints and Wrinkles for the Tyro", it runs, in part: "Genealogy (see accompanying leaflet), Your Household (Mother, Father, nanny, housemaids, etc.), Schools (unhappiness at school has been overdone, so treat it lightly), Oxford in the 1920s (mention John Sutro and the Railway Club, Cyril Connolly, Brian Howard, Hugh Lygon, Maurice Bowra, 'Sligger' Urquhart, the Hypocrites Club, boast of drinking exploits), Your first sexual experience (a tart in Paris in the long vac), country house weekends (preferably Garsington, but the Sitwells in Yorkshire will do at a pinch), London parties (remember Inez Holden), foreign travel (rehash your old travel books for this section; they're safely out of print), portraits of celebrities (dig out all the essays you've written lately for Festschrifts and memorials) . . ."

The section headed "Style" is interesting. I quote only a fragment:

> Recall the immoderations of your youth in a manner of unflappable irony. Remember that it all happened a long time ago and doesn't matter now. Adopt as many old-fashioned locutions as you can. Refer to the recent past by such phrases as "of late years". Cultivate a tone of gentlemanly boredom with life. At your age, a certain weary snobbery is most becoming.

Finally, a useful tip on indexes. They should run, roughly, from Acton, Harold to Yorke, Henry, and if throughout the text you have been referring to, say, Chubby or Gumbo, his title and country seat should be included in full in the index. Thus: Gumbo, see Chatterbourne, Basil Mountcalm De Clairvaux, 14th Earl of Gloom, of Hartletop Hall, Lincs.

It is perfectly possible to produce a book of sorts by following this prescription, but it is no recipe at all for autobiography. This is the stuff of which *memoirs* are made – and the plural noun gives all away. Events are included merely because they happened to happen. There is no narrative drive, no passion, and only the most genteel and cursory of attempts at self-examination. Beside real autobiography (*The Education of Henry Adams, Father and Son, Memoirs of a Foxhunting Man, My Father and Myself, A Cab at the Door*) such books have the desultory, synthetic flavour of crushed soya beans. The chemical formula to which they are manufactured ought to be printed clearly on their dustjackets.

Anthony Powell is widely regarded as our most accomplished living novelist. *Infants of the Spring** is the first volume of an autobiographical epic of as yet unspecified length entitled, ominously, *To Keep the Ball Rolling* (presumably an allusion to an I.B.M. Golfball). It is a book so boring, reticent and formulaic that it would hardly be a creditable effort had it come from the hand of an idle brigadier jotting down his Notes of an Old Soldier or Tales of an Officer's Mess. Mr Powell begins by tracing his family tree back to Old King Cole and Rhys the Hoarse, constructs a complete stud book of Powells and Wells-Dymokes, then embarks, in a style of stultified

---

* Anthony Powell, *Infants of the Spring* (London: Heinemann).

discretion, on a rambling, much interrupted account of his own life. Ten pages short of the end (apropos an undergraduate gaffe he once committed in the presence of Bowra, Maurice, Oxford don) he remarks:

> One learns in due course (without ever achieving the aim in practice) that, more or often than not [*sic*], it is better to keep deeply felt views about oneself to oneself.

This is, no doubt, an excellent precept for anyone who wishes to pass unscathed through the world of Wadham or White's; as a rule of thumb for an autobiographer, it is about as desirable as Maule's Curse. In *Infants of the Spring*, Mr Powell achieves his stated aim with leaden regularity; he eradicates himself from his story with such clinical thoroughness that by the end the reader is left with a faint whiff of antiseptic in his nose as the only evidence that a human being has been there at all. He is simply neither frank nor caddish enough to bring off even a passable autobiography.

Edmund Gosse (who was sufficiently frank to be superbly caddish) has a striking passage in *Father and Son*:

> Through thick and thin I clung to a hard nut of individuality, deep down in my childish nature. To the pressure from without, I resigned everything else, my thoughts, my words, my anticipations, my assurances, but there was something which I never resigned, my innate and persistent self.

It is precisely this quality which is missing from Anthony Powell; he offers us the life and times of an immaculate zero. That this zero is a deliberate and evasive mask is quite clear from his peppery character studies of his contemporaries. In a series of set-piece portraits of Henry Yorke, Cyril Connolly, George Orwell and Maurice Bowra (some of which have seen the light of print in other contexts, and which severely disrupt the frail narrative on which *Infants of the Spring* is strung), Powell reveals himself as sceptical, sardonic, alert to pretensions and absurdities in his friends which he resolutely refuses to detect in himself. The character of Anthony Powell remains undramatized – a pair of eyes and ears mutely abroad in society.

This elusiveness (which has won him so much acclaim in his fiction) is perhaps a more positive quality than it seems at first sight. The social world into which Powell was absorbed, first at Eton, then at Oxford, was one which had a high esteem for eccentricity but not much regard for character. Powell approvingly quotes Bowra's system of social classification in which people were "Able", "Upright", "Nice Men", or "Shits of Hell". In a world (like that of Powell's own fiction) of manners and conventions rather than of morals and psychology, this infantile code sufficed; but, not surprisingly, it seems to have rendered its users incapable of self-examination. Nice men – like oneself – are all but invisible. They are more acted upon than acting. Their decencies are negative qualities, exposed by the general awfulness of the world around them. Waugh's Tony Last in *A Handful of Dust* is a nice man cast among the shits of hell; Powell's narrator in *The Music of Time* is a nice man cast among the able, the upright, the "unpresentable" (another Bowra word) and the mildly shitty.

The main question raised by this numbingly silly version of morality is why writers as gifted and intelligent as Waugh and Powell should have been so unerringly drawn to it. Their ideal of gentlemanliness looks simple-minded when set beside the much more complex values of their immediate literary predecessors like Thackeray and Trollope. Yet unlike Thackeray and Trollope, Waugh and Powell have been able to believe that there are very few gentlemen left; that the world is increasingly vulgar and louche, and that nice men are as rare as golden eagles. It was surely a mistake for Powell to write *Infants of the Spring*; by attempting an autobiography of a nice man he has exposed the vapidity of his ideal in a way that could seriously damage the status of his fiction. For all its charm as an epic of beautifully orchestrated gossip, there is a shallowness at the heart of *The Music of Time*, an absence of anything that could be called a moral intelligence. *Infants of the Spring* charts the growth of that absence with disturbing pride.

Peter Quennell is an exact contemporary of Powell's. They made friends at Oxford, and their indexes tally. But *The Marble Foot** is a much better book than *Infants of the Spring*, partly perhaps because Quennell's father weaned him at an early age from the cult of gentlemanliness. Quennell Senior was an architect turned freelance author:

> Snobbery was not among his failings. He had become, however, an inverted snob, a particularly English type, and was fond of telling stories, and delivering pronouncements that illustrated our modest position in the world. "Don't

---

* Peter Quennell, *The Marble Foot: An Autobiography 1905–1938* (London: Collins).

forget," he enjoined me at a family meal, "that *you* are a member of the *lower* middle class!"

The Quennell household was one in which children were encouraged to think of themselves as "highly strung" and *sui generis*. Their father, a humorous, irascible, largely self-educated man who lived by the gospel of hard work and was much given to impulsive crazes, moved on the fringes of the Berkhamsted intelligentsia – an oddly assorted group which included R. H. Tawney, W. W. Jacobs, G. M. Trevelyan and Mrs Humphry Ward. People who grow up on social margins have to make an early reckoning with their own characters, without benefit of the protective custody of family trees and class manners.

By the time Peter Quennell arrived at Oxford he was evidently more fully formed and self-aware than any of his contemporaries except, perhaps, Connolly. He was already known as a promising poet; he was beginning work on a biography of Blake; in the prevailing climate of mild public school hellenism, Quennell stood out as a determined heterosexual. Sir Alec Douglas-Home (then Lord Dunglass) wondered if he was "quite decent" and Brian Howard dropped him. A certain caddish intransigence of character kept Quennell a little apart from the braying herd of gentlemen. Yet as he chronicles his gradual assimilation into smart literary society, first at Oxford, then in London, so this character begins to leak out of his book. He too becomes an invisible man. When he describes his first two marriages, the women are vividly done but Quennell himself is no more than a ghostly cipher, too innocent, too all-ears-and-eyes to be believable.

Powell appears to have surrendered himself to a conservative nostalgia for Society; Quennell's surrender has been made to Style – to the cold pleasures of making phrases. "My love of the English language," he writes, "has become a superstitious cult." He is a Stylist as another man might be a french polisher. Every distancing irony is placed just so. The even rhythm of his prose is fastidious and impeccable. His metaphors gleam as if they lay under several coats of clear varnish. The total effect is one of lifelessness and impersonality. Quennell has successfully practised the embalmer's art on his own person.

These strange unacknowledged attempts at self-surrender seem characteristic of a whole generation of English writers. Evelyn Waugh spent his life acting out such impulses on a scale so grand that it was at once heroic and absurd. Why have so many middle-class intellectuals, now in their seventies, craved this absorption into an archaic vision of society or an equally archaic vision of literary style? Perhaps only history and biography will explain. For lives like theirs, autobiography is a singularly unilluminating form: it would appear to be too much of a contradiction in terms.

1976

EUDORA WELTY

The American South likes to lap itself in a sentimental and protective mythology. Southerners (as they will hasten to tell you themselves) live in splendid wooden mock-ups of the Parthenon: where the rest of the United States is ingenious, dollar-wise, go-getting and philistine, the South is steeped in its own history. It has manners, charm, hospitality. It has Culture, with a big and flourishing C. The myth is a fine and even truthful one, so long as one remembers that all myths are attempts to reconcile intolerable contradictions.

The contradiction of the South is that, ever since the ritual humiliations of the "Reconstruction" period after the Civil War, it has been miserably bereft of the two things which have done most to shape modern American history: industry and finance. The South is rich only in the goods that money can't buy. Its natural landscape is tropically abundant with singularly uneconomic commodities like magnolia, bog-myrtle, mosquitoes, alligators and giant coypu. Most important, the South has made itself immodestly rich in language.

The greatest of the 20th-century Southern writers, William Faulkner, came from Mississippi, a state which hasn't had much more than two nickels to rub together since 1865. Faulkner looted the coffers of the verbal millionaires of literature from Shakespeare to James Joyce, and dressed his grubby sharecroppers in such a finery of language that they live in his books as peasant kings, trailing robes of expensive rhetoric through their native dust.

British readers tend to find Faulkner hard going. His thunderously metrical prose, his florid symbolism, his love of metaphor for metaphor's own sake, all seem excessive, even embarrassing. Yet their excess is their point. Faulkner is no realist. His "Southernness" consists of the way in which he transforms the real South beyond all recognition, into a gaudy wonderland of words.

Faulkner was a writer of overbearing genius; a creator of master-pieces that one is glad one doesn't have to re-read. Eudora Welty (also from Mississippi) is the one Southern writer whose gifts are comparable to those of Faulkner. Her imaginative concerns run in close parallel to his. If she lacks Faulkner's unapproachable stature, she far outreaches him in humour, tenderness and exactitude. This is very much her year. Here is the glittering treasury of her *Collected Stories*.* In the spring, Virago will reissue three of her novels, *The Robber Bridegroom, Delta Wedding* and *Losing Battles*, with more to follow in 1983. We now have no excuse for failing to accord Eudora Welty her proper place in modern literature. She should be known as widely in this country as she has been, for forty years already, in the United States.

The human territory in which Miss Welty's stories take place is even more bare and impoverished than Faulkner's Yoknapatawpha County; a long, inhospitable swathe of Mississippi and Louisiana, dotted with hamlets of "shotgun houses" – two rooms planted on either side of a front door and a narrow passage, with a tin awning overhead, and a verandah just big enough for a rocker with leaky stuffing. Some of her characters are black, some white; but their colour hardly matters by comparison with what they have in common – their few, precious sticks of furniture, their cheap ornaments, patched clothes and sleepy pride.

For these gimcrack cabins are not where Miss Welty's characters really live at all. Inside their heads they are aristocrats of the spirit with endless space, time and luxury at their command. Their author has given them a language of such elaboration and refinement that their inner lives are as opulent as their external circumstances are pinched. It is a language which is constantly reaching upward and outward, using random associations as stepping stones to the high altitude at which these people are most at home. Metaphor (in prose, at least) is usually a means of returning us back to the everyday, the near at hand. In Eudora Welty, metaphor is habitually speculative and oblique; it wanders dreamily away from the object it seems to describe. Here, for instance, is a husband watching his wife:

> . . . she sat self-hypnotised in her own domain, with her "Get-out-of-my-kitchen" and "Come-here-do-you-realise-what-you've-done," all her stiffening and wifely glaze run-ning sweet and finespun as sugar threads over her.

* Eudora Welty, *Collected Stories* (San Diego: Harcourt Brace Jovanovich).

EUDORA WELTY · 131

That "wifely glaze" is common enough. But to the husband it suggests other glazes – the glaze of icing on a cake and the precise intricacy of its making. The wife herself is almost completely lost to view as the husband drifts, at liberty, among the sweet words in his head.

No wonder that such characters find it difficult to talk to each other. They are always drifting and forgetting. When (in "The Wide Net") half a town turns out to drag a river for the body of a missing woman, the event turns into a delirious picnic as everyone, including the supposedly bereaved husband, splashes about in the water, each pursuing his own private imaginative trail. The dialogue in these stories has the simplicity of lines from a ballad: when people connect directly with each other, they talk of elemental, necessary things:

> "Sonny," said the woman, "you'll have to borry some fire."
> "I'll go git it from Redmond's," said Sonny.
> "What?" Bowman strained to hear their words to each other.
> "Our fire, it's out, and Sonny's got to borry some, because it's dark and cold," she said.
> "But matches – I have matches."
> "We don't have no need for 'em," she said proudly. "Sonny's goin' after his own fire."

Spoken words come hard. Yet behind everyone's voice there is the powerful presence of an incommunicable life, subtle, tacit, full of implications and odd imaginings.

This governing vision, that in Eudora Welty's world there is always much, much more than meets the ear or eye, gives her writing its obsessive, searching exactitude. A page is often too short a space in which to explore a second or two of time. Every detail is handled as a vital clue, and her stories demand to be read almost as painstakingly carefully as they have been written. They offer no handy resolutions. They deal with people who look uncomplicated enough on the surface: a travelling shoe salesman, a racial bigot, a sulky teenage lifesaver, a vain old dandy, a lonely widow . . . Each life is delicately opened out to reveal its marvellous store of secrecies and contradictions. The stories are at once intricately eventful and plotless. They are more like dreams than tales.

Sometimes, as if to redefine her own world as a writer, Miss Welty puts herself behind the eyes of visitors and tourists to the South. In

"No Place for You, My Love", a couple drive southwest from New Orleans, shocked and thrilled to find themselves in a landscape of such outrageous fecundity, full of insects, dead turtles, a live alligator, "violent-green grass", poinsettias and oleanders. It is a place that most of the characters in Miss Welty's stories take comfortably for granted. The couple from the North see it as a lurid map of their own dangerous and confused feelings. And so it is. What Miss Welty has done is to give the people of her South an inner richness, a mental abundance to match that of the nature they live in. It is a great and generous achievement.

1982

SAUL BELLOW

I

The Vesuvian eloquence of Saul Bellow is one of the glories of modern literature. Very few living novelists can match the way he brings crowds of characters to instant life on the page; fewer still have his hugely observant genius for place. He can furnish an apartment in a sentence and make it smell dustily lived-in; his city streets are oppressively real, full of raw particularity, dangerous for his readers to walk on after dusk.

These, though, are predictable novelists' gifts, even if Bellow has them in superabundance. Where no one can touch him is in his relish for ideas. He wallows in them – an intellectual hippo of a type quite foreign to the English-speaking world. From Rousseau and Hegel down to Schumacher and the latest notion in *Scientific American*, ideas in Bellow's work topple over each other, some earth shattering, some downright bad, all grist to the mill of the novel in hand. He is a champion argufier, creating in print the impression of a stream of brilliant talk.

It would be wrong to call his writing ambitious. Ambition suggests a sense of limitations transcended, but Bellow writes as if he'd never noticed limits in his imaginative precinct. For him the novel has been the supreme form of discourse – a genre in which to conjure, wrangle, confess and speak his mind. He has told tales when it suited him (in early books like *The Victim* he proved himself a marvellous story-teller); since *Herzog*, though, he has moved as much in the tradition of the sermon, the lecture, the essay, the prayer, as in the tradition of narrative fiction.

So *The Dean's December*,* despite the faint Trollopian echo of its title, is not so much a story as a work of passionate, brooding ratiocination. It is an exhortatory study in which the illustrative figures merely happen to be imaginary people. Its structure is dialecti-cal: its events occur as stages in a logical argument. One turns its pages, not to find out what happens next but to see how this point is going to be answered, that position bolstered by evidence. It manages – as only Bellow can manage – to be simultaneously mag-nificent and dull.

The Dean is Albert Corde: one-time journalist, now Chicago professor, full-time amateur of the human race. December is the present – the wintry twilight of civilization. The Dean's particular December is a month in Bucharest, where his Rumanian mother-in-law is dying and he has the time and distance to reflect on the turmoil of modern life around the Loop.

Fresh from the stir created by his articles for *Harper's* on the blight and corruption of inner-city Chicago, still entangled in the trial for murder of a black accused of killing one of his students, Corde is yet another of Bellow's ravaged, dangling men, suspended between the "hard nihilism" of his temporary perch in Eastern Europe and the "soft nihilism" of the United States. Where Joseph, in *Dangling Man*, waited for his army draft, Corde waits for revelation, for apocalypse now. His wife, Minna, is a famous astronomer. "She did boundless space, his beat was terra firma."

Now, though, the earth is anything but firm, and Corde is a helpless onlooker in a world of murder, rape, terrorism, philistine self-indulgence and cold bureaucracy. The one slim prospect of revelation lies in the work of a boyish geophysicist called Beech who enlists Corde as a professional "communicator" to spread the word that mankind is poisoning itself with lead: "Man's great technical works, looming over him, have coated him with deadly metal. We can't carry the weight. The blood is sobbing in us. Our brains grow feebler . . ."

---

* Saul Bellow, *The Dean's December* (New York: Harper & Row).

Beech supplies the statistics. Corde comes up with the rhetoric, spinning a miserable poetry out of the fatal afflictions of the late 20th century. Chicago, in all its rush of grievous details, turns into a symbol: the city comes to represent the "slum of innermost being", the ultimate poisoned place to which leaden, modern man naturally gravitates. Bucharest too. The city of the East and the city of the West share the same poison. The globe shrinks, Corde broods and Bellow writes a new novel.

The book itself is a brilliant sermon pinned to this impoverished text. From anyone but Bellow, it would have been a cover-to-cover disaster. That it is not is because of Bellow's mastery of incidentals. Zig-zagging fast and continuously between the two cities, he fills out the novel with people and places; cold-water flats in Bucharest, over-stuffed ones in Chicago, riveting grotesques, like the elderly secretary who is trying to "put the sex back into sexagenarian" or the famous Washington columnist who unbuttons his shirt in a café to reveal the plastic bag where his stomach should have been.

As an energetic impresario, Bellow is faultless. He rushes around behind the scenes in the book, arranging rapid revolves, new lighting effects, egging on the bit-part players to come up with showstopping one-liners. There isn't a page which doesn't bear the impressive, always intelligent, always observant mark of the Nobel prizewinner.

Yet everything and everybody in the novel is there as a kind of visual aid to the text: they exist only to illustrate what is, in essence, a windy editorial on the decay of the body politic. It is for *the sake of the text* that Valeria dies a humiliating, vegetable death in a Bucharest hospital, that Minna is an astronomer, that Chicago rots, that Corde's sister has to marry a flashy judge, that Corde himself must be attacked by his students and vilified in the newspaper columns of his childhood friend. The didactic pattern of the book allows the characters no other reason to exist or behave; but the text, in whose service they are brought into existence, is not one worth living or dying for.

The end of the book is a wonderfully described set-piece in which Corde accompanies his wife to the icy kernel of the Mount Palomar observatory. He is – the text dictates – through with his rum notions about the salvation of humankind. Now, only the glittering, gigantic vacancies of the solar system will answer to his needs. World-weary, he shivers and looks at the stars from the steel catwalks of Mount Palomar. Standing there, soothed by outer space, he suspiciously resembles a novelist who has grown tired of the human welter of his own books, bored by the restlessness of which he is so brilliant an analyst. It is, one hopes, a passing mood.

1982

II

Few writers are less at home with the usual conventions of the short story – its delicate architecture and well-timed obliquities – than Saul Bellow; and "stories" is not quite the right word for these five magnificent virtuoso pieces. Structurally they are built on the same principle as waterfalls: they simply pour from a great height until they hit bottom. They interlock, one on top of another, to form a book of more consistent vigour and concentrated intelligence than anything that Bellow has done since *Herzog*, twenty years ago. *Humboldt's Gift* and *The Dean's December* both gave one cause to worry that Bellow was getting musclebound; there isn't a hint of that in *Him with His Foot in His Mouth*.* Its torrential drive leaves one shaken by and grateful for the man's extraordinary and lordly way with the language.

The pieces are connected by dozens of fine strands held in common. Their capital city is Chicago, whose rancid brick- and lake-smells permeate the collection. Their central characters are intransigently themselves, and each is given an occupation (music professor, art critic, writer, tile contractor, legal consultant) and a name (Shawmut, Wulpy, Zetland, Selbst, Ijah) that reflect his sturdy quiddity; Bellow is far too passionate a romantic individualist to allow his people to become shadows of each other. They are all, though, pushing, or just past, the age of 70 (Bellow himself was 69 last week). They go back a long way – to the world of the ghetto (and its nearness to "the sphere of Revelation"), to billiard parlours under the tracks of the El, to crimson streetcars and billboards advertising Lydia Pinkham's Vegetable Compound. They all share their creator's prominent fleshy underlip, likewise his fondness for Kant and Hegel. Snappy traces of Yiddish still cling to the rhythm of their English sentences, and when they suffer from fits of American grouchiness, they give it the dandified French name of *ressentiment*.

* Saul Bellow, *Him with His Foot in His Mouth* (New York: Harper & Row).

Their minds have never been in better, or more furious, shape (as Shawmut says, "People seldom give up the mental capital accumulated in their 'best' years"), but their bodies are cracked vessels. They are afflicted by hypertension, cardiovascular disturbances, arthritis and cold feet. They are approaching "the end of the line, the outskirts of the City of Life"; and each is seen to be squatting on his long experience like a treasure hoard. Age and history have turned the characters into rememberers, witnesses, tallymen for whom writing and talking have become urgent necessities. The world only survives in so far as these old men can make it real in the telling; and the pieces in the book show them as compulsive and absorbed as spiders in their webs of words, spinning to live and living to spin. Age makes every man his own novelist, as it makes the shaping and rearranging processes of fiction into his sole defence against the Void.

Never has Bellow's genius for writing in a style that looks and feels like the act of thought itself been put to more forceful use. It is a style of lyrical parenthesis, in which memory is continuously crowding in to interrupt the sentence; a style in which the footnote and the *esprit d'escalier* impose themselves on the foreground of the text. It zig-zags back and forth in time, endlessly resourceful in its attempts to remember, compare, argue, justify. Events as such dissolve in it as they dissolve in memory; it is an impossible instrument for telling any kind of simple story. It sustains itself plotlessly, on the power of metaphor, on the surprising twist of thought at a sentence-end, on the peculiarly musical quality of Bellow's way with grammar. In each of these pieces, the style *is* the character: it is a man in the act of bidding for his life.

"As usual," says Cousin Ijah, "I gave more information than my questioner had any use for, using every occasion to transmit my sense of life." That is the common, redeeming fault of all of Bellow's older men. In an epic, Herzogian letter of belated apology to a retired lady librarian, Shawmut cannot resist such pieces of information as, "As a boy, Philip was fat. We had to sleep together when we were children and it was like sharing a bed with a dugong." And, "My behind is like a rucksack that has slipped its straps." The sense of life (and the stuff of fiction) lies in the department of excess information, over which Bellow presides like a rain king. Among the "unnecessarily circumstantial particulars" that assail Cousin Ijah is a by-the-way memory of Lake Zurich, Illinois: "Like the dish in which you clean watercolour brushes, Lake Zurich is yellow-green, the ooze is deep, the reeds are thick, the air is close, and the grove smells not of nature but of sandwiches and summer bananas . . ."

Places, people, things are all recollected with the same entranced verbal ecstasy. A Swedish interior in 1920s Chicago: "There were Bibles and pictures of Jesus and the Holy Land and that faint, Gentile odour, as if things had been rinsed in a weak vinegar solution."

The most minor characters are brought alive in major similes: "He was a huge man dressed in velvet dinner clothes, a copious costume, kelly green in colour, upon which his large, pale, clever head seemed to have been deposited with a boom." In recollection, the faces and features of the absent and the dead are caressed with the attention of a 19th-century phrenologist feeling a skull: "Only the unshavable pucker in his father's chin was a sign of pathos." This intense tenderness for the corporeal – for the way the flesh falls on a face, for "avid" veins and old smells – is not just something that Bellow is (and always has been) astonishingly fine; in *Him with His Foot in His Mouth* it has become an explicit theme. The tenderly attentive metaphor is as near as man can come to working the godly miracle of resurrection.

Vesting so much in the improvising power of style alone has led to some oddities. One piece here ("Zetland: By a Character Witness") just stops dead, as if Bellow had gone out to dinner and forgotten it. Another ("Cousins") fans out to encircle a family like a tide rising over mudflats; at high water, it ceases. Perhaps a book which dwells on old age as this one does simply could not bear to have too strong a sense of an ending.

Yet the most completely magical piece in the collection, "What Kind of a Day Did You Have?", is also the most nearly conventional. It is told through the eyes (and the nose and the fingers) of a plump suburban Chicago divorcee who is jumping to the beck and call of her old "celebrity" lover, Victor Wulpy, the art critic. Her story is by turns bewildered, enchanted, frightened and smug as she gentles the monstrous Wulpy and is dragged round three cities in the course of 18 hours, is subjected to Wulpy's old fights and old glories, treated to his learned witticisms, almost killed in an air crash, taken on a grand conversational tour of world cultural history, and has her own bid for "creative" life (she is writing a children's story about an elephant) taken less than wholly seriously. That is the kind of day *she* has; and it is a pretty average diurnal round for an old man in a Saul Bellow story, but rather a strain for a chicken like Katrina Goliger. It reads as if Bellow had taken an ironic longsight on himself and his

characters through the eyes of one of his devoted Book of the Month
Club subscribers. It is immensely funny, and it throws the other four
pieces into brilliant relief. This is a marvellous book.

1984

ROBERT LOWELL

I

Pity the biographical critic who takes on Robert Lowell. He has a
crushingly experienced rival in the field. For Lowell spent his entire
literary career in writing what amounts to his own exhaustive critical
biography. His collected poems are his Authorized Life; and Lowell
himself found his life a peculiarly volatile and intractable substance.
His poems strain at every line's end in the struggle to contain it.

The turmoil is insistently there on the page. The barest reading of
the poems draws one into a world of continuous bone-shaking
turbulence. Lowell wrote simply about what he knew, but what he
knew was complication and difficulty. He never cultivated obscurity
as some of his contemporaries did; obscurity, however, tended to
cultivate Robert Lowell, and in his poems he makes the business of
ordinary living look like tightrope walking – an art which calls for
the utmost guile, grace and concentration. There is not a moment in
his work when we are out of sight of large, terribly legible warnings
of what happens to those who stumble: the gates of the mental
asylum; the smashed marriage; the chemical void of depression. Nor
are these merely warnings. In Lowell's poems, falling is the daily
occupational risk of being human, and the flight of thankful joy on
one page presages the arrival of the men from the locked ward on
the next.

Perhaps Lowell led no more than an averagely rumpled life. Its
distinction lay not in the extremes which it touched and his poetry
registered but in the extraordinary status he accorded to it. It was to
be the material for a modern Ulyssean epic – an epic of lost battles
and wrong turnings. By all normal odds, the project should have
turned out to be an egotistic folly, but Lowell had extraordinary
qualifications for the job. He had a tremendous gift for comedy (his

critics, a deadly solemn crew, rarely notice that his poems about himself are actually very funny; Ulysses is only half a step away from Sancho Panza). His intelligence was exact and playful. He was superbly well read, and carried his learning with easy assurance. He had a pure genius for language unrivalled by any poet since Yeats.

We can look back now over the completed epic, which started in 1944 with *Land of Unlikeness* and ended last year with the posthumous publication of *Day by Day*. Inevitably, there is a price to be paid for Lowell's determination to settle for nothing less than greatness. There are passages of windy bluster, odd lurches into bathos, lines so clogged with the attempt to load them with meaning that they lie on the page swollen, inert, beyond comprehension. Yet on balance the enterprise reveals itself as a triumph of nerve and calculation. Here is an exemplary 20th-century life with an exemplary measure of muddle and defeat, an exemplary measure of passing glory. It's a life lived in full conscience by a man of preternatural quickness and sensitivity and candour. We can all count ourselves lucky that Lowell happened to be around in our messy stretch of history; more than any other writer he has got down on paper what it feels like to be morally alive in our particular snakepit.

In his last ten years, in *Notebook* and after, he burrowed into the sources and techniques of his own writing with the same searching precision as he used to excavate the rest of his life. In a succession of poems-about-poems he tried to tease out what was going on in his work. He revised, then revised his revisions, as if somehow the literary critic in him might discover what the autobiographer had missed. He had been schooled in the heyday of the New Criticism, and the general temper of his mind was instinctively critical, in the reflexive, speculative style of Tate, Winters, Jarrell, Empson and Richards. Many of his later poems resemble a new *Seven Types of Ambiguity* in verse, in which Lowell's own poetry provides the raw material for a polemical, and often dazzling, critical inquiry.

It was all part of the same epic enterprise. There is a rage for explanation in Lowell's work, an obsessive conviction that somewhere there must be clues to be decoded, that experience, however impossibly tangled, can be made intelligible.

> For
> the hundredth time, we slice the fog, and round
> the village with our headlights on the ground,

> like the first philosopher Thales who thought
>   all things water,
>   and fell in a well . . . trying to find a car
>   key . . . It can't be here, and so it must
>   be there . . .

A life so fully written, and a work so fully annotated, leave very little space for the latecoming critic. Yet a really good critical biography of Lowell would be an immensely valuable book. For Lowell is a bewildering figure. His poems show him bewildered by himself. It's easy to know the "Robert Lowell" who is the hero of the epic, but the man who created him remains stubbornly outside the grasp of the poems. Lowell ransacked his own memory in the attempt to come to terms with this troubling character; he tried to hunt him down in history; finally he tried to pin him out with criticism. The results were inconclusive. There is a magnificent body of poetry which Lowell left behind in the process of his search; yet at the end of it all there's a tantalizing blank where Lowell himself ought to be.

At this point, Steven Gould Axelrod steps in on cue. *Robert Lowell: Life and Art*** is the first book on Lowell to be completed since his death. As its pre-emptive title suggests, it promises great things in the way of general perspectives and long-term critical assessments. With Lowell dead, the time has come for tape measures and post-mortems. Biography, though, unlike the undertaking business, involves a direct encounter between two lives; and it's not wholly irrelevant to inspect what Axelrod lets fall about his own.

He is an associate professor at the University of California, Riverside campus. His book on Lowell has occupied him for, we gather, six years. This has not, happily, been a solitary labour: he acknowledges the help of "my wonderful research assistants, Joyce McLean and Denis Jones". Eleven scholarly colleagues have been through his manuscript for him, and "saved me from more errors and infelicities than I like to . . ." etcetera. Librarians from 20 libraries have been bustling in the stacks on his behalf, while the Riverside Research Committee has chipped in with a helpful wad of greenbacks. Axelrod's acknowledgments page offers a telling, if sketchy, self-portrait of the author as academic corporation man. That by no means disqualifies him for the job on hand, but it does point up the gulf which lies between the world of Steven Gould Axelrod and that of Robert Lowell.

---

* Steven Gould Axelrod, *Robert Lowell: Life and Art* (New Jersey: Princeton University Press).

This gulf comes to seem ever more important as one reads on. For Axelrod has made sense, of an academic, corporation kind, of Lowell's grandly dishevelled life. He has turned it into a Horatio Alger story, about a poor boy from an unhappy family who wanted to make good in the world of poetry and eventually succeeded in achieving tenure at the state university of Parnassus. It's quite a touching story in its way, and it at least has the virtue of dogged simplicity.

The early chapters are about Learning to Write. The young Lowell was in search of Teachers who would also serve as Substitute Father Figures. He was lucky to find two of these undoubtedly useful characters in Allen Tate and William Carlos Williams. Tate taught him "the disciplined ecstasy" of "the poetic act"; Williams "persuaded Lowell to trust in the authority of the self". The big problem on young Cal's agenda was to get all this together; it was hard going for the youthful poet as he tried to trust in the disciplined ecstasy of the authority of the self while it was engaged in the poetic act. Nevertheless, these were exciting times, and like Alger's Tattered Tom he stuck to his task. Occasionally we are afforded privileged glimpses into the Poet's Mind: "In Maine, his mind churned with the new ideas he had encountered and with the new possibilities they seemed to open up." Sometimes, though, all this churning proves too much for our hero. "The intensity of this creative surge sent him back for a brief rest at McLean's."

"A brief rest at McLean's" is Axelrod's coy euphemism for a period of forced incarceration in a mental hospital during an attack of mania. Perhaps Axelrod means to be tactful – if so his tact is surely misplaced. These recurrent bouts of temporary insanity brought Lowell down once a year for more than 20 years. They humbled and weakened him in life; in his poetry, they were made to serve his purpose. His illness defines the margin of the habitable world, while the "myopia" of insanity is a way of seeing which Lowell uses again and again in his work – a bemused and solitary form of vision to which the sane are just as much prone as the mad. In one phrase, Axelrod both devalues Lowell's illness and makes it one of those romantic diseases which only poets catch: it is brought on by "the intensity" of a "creative surge". It wasn't.

In the story, Lowell recovers from his brief rest and publishes *Life Studies*. The book, says Axelrod in the pop-eyed tones of a drum majorette, "became the poetry event of the year". It's a little hard to see why, since in Axelrod's lengthy examination of its contents *Life Studies* "affirms the value of human experience". One would have thought that it would have been more of an event had it denied it.

Axelrod's method, such as it is, is most clearly on display in the long chapter he devotes to *The Dolphin*. In his discussions of the earlier works, he is able to rely heavily on other critics of Lowell, especially on Hugh B. Staples, Marjorie Perloff and Jerome Mazzaro. With *The Dolphin*, Axelrod is out on his own, a solitary critical voyager in the wilderness of literature which has not yet been established on the syllabus. He wades through the book, poem by poem, reducing Lowell's life and lines to a prose garble which is pure, 22-carat Axelrod.

> Lowell arrives in England in early 1970 and takes up residence on Redcliffe Square in the Earl's Court section of London. The mid-Victorian buildings take getting used to, for they are foreign and ugly. But they are also curiously familiar. They are the image of Lowell himself.

Well, Lowell did look a bit odd, I suppose, but not *that* odd . . .

> On a stormy night soon after arriving in London, Lowell becomes reacquainted with Caroline, whom he first met years before in New York. The two begin an affair which is at first sensually pleasing but emotionally "estranged", so estranged that he contemplates Aztec rites of human sacrifice . . .

This fascinating allegation is, alas, not justified by the text. Axelrod has mixed up (and misread) two different sonnets.

> The elegiac tone deepens; his wings contract. His new life has come to seem rather uncomfortable.

One would imagine so: contracting wings is a notoriously painful condition.

> Lowell's doctors love him and wish he would stay always . . . Caroline, however, does not love him any longer.

Nevertheless, this really is an Alger story, and we can all feel a warm glow at the end:

> After a lifetime of kicking against the pricks, Lowell in a moment of spiritual insight, unconditionally accepts his world and himself.

After which Axelrod goes on to a cursory disfiguration of *Day by Day*.

Robert Lowell: Life and Art is laughably inadequate. It is hard to imagine how anyone could write a worse book about Lowell, and it will soon, no doubt, be supplanted by better ones. Yet Axelrod's grotesque failure, with his two wonderful research assistants, his six years' hard labour, his army of advisers and his travels through the university libraries of America, stands as a minatory warning to the critics and biographers who are going to follow in his path. His book serves much the same purpose as a particularly bloody road accident seen at the beginning of a long car journey.

For many of the causes of Axelrod's failure lie in the nature of the subject. Lowell's poetry resists criticism precisely because it incorporates an extremely delicate and sophisticated critical system into the texture of the verse itself. His life has already been phrased in the poems, with more resonance and authority than any biographer is ever likely to attain. There remains a great deal which is undescribed, unexplained and perplexing. I doubt if anyone who knew Lowell well would claim to have understood him. He was, in the deepest sense, an unknowable man. It would indeed be a fine thing if criticism and biography were able to make him more accessible; it is more likely, I suspect, that he will prove to be a kind of Bermuda Triangle of modern literature, in which more and more earnest Axelrods will disappear without trace.

1979

II

No one has ever managed to catch the flavour of Robert Lowell's glorious tabletalk. It was too slow-burning, too dependent on timing and delivery, to lend itself to quotation. One would need a supreme mimic to bring off Lowell's teasing playfulness, his spontaneous ignition of bright metaphors and unlikely likenesses, his long strangulated pauses and sudden hectic rushes of enthusiasm, and his voice – back-of-the-throat, cigarette dry, a Tennessee drawl that actually came from Boston. He made every sentence sound like an uncertain chemical experiment that might end in a bigger bang than he'd planned.

Here is Lowell talking again. On Robert Frost: "He wasn't quite a farmer even in his early, isolated years. He didn't quite make a living; he got up at noon. He said the cows got used to his hours more easily than his neighbours . . ." On Ford Madox Ford – "large, unwieldy, wheezy, unwell, and looked somehow like a British version of the Republican elephant"; on John Berryman, who had "the almost intimate mumble of a don"; on George Santayana, who "wore a shabby chocolate dressing gown and resembled an emeritus Franciscan general"; on Longfellow – "Tennyson without the gin"; on "mountainous" Henry James with his "reckless urbanity"; on Emily Dickinson's verse – "frayed and mussed and wilful". Lowell's laughter, his utterly unpredictable quickness of mind, his sureness of heart and eye, shine through his prose exactly as they shone in conversation.

The big surprise of his *Collected Prose** is the suddenness with which Lowell became himself, in 1955 when he was 38. In February 1954 his mother died in Rapallo; in July, Lowell suffered an attack of mania and was admitted to the Payne-Whitney Clinic of New York Hospital; in April 1955, as Robert Giroux records in his introduction, Lowell asked for – and signed – a formal contract for a prose autobiography. This businesslike gesture was wildly out of character, and Giroux, his friend and publisher, was understandably puzzled by it. The contract was merely a convenient symbol for another, more important pact between Lowell and his family – that tumultuously strained relationship which (or so his Freudian therapists said) had led to his mania. It was the beginning of the project that was to last him for the rest of his life, from *Life Studies* through to *The Dolphin* and the final poems – a long, frank, brave and intimate quest for his own selfhood that would explore what it meant to be one troubled man living through the middle of an afflicted century.

Before 1955, his prose was formal, high toned and on its guard – hardly his own at all. The early pieces in the book, from a 1935 school magazine effort on Homer through a scatter of poetry reviews in the 1940s, show Lowell in dutiful thrall to his tutors. He sounds some-times like John Crowe Ransom, sometimes like Randall Jarrell, sometimes like R. P. Blackmur; an assertive, slightly embarrassed New Critic in a rather too recognizable mould.

Then the dam bursts. The first sign of the new style comes, not in an explicitly autobiographical piece but in an exuberantly argued essay on English verse translations of Ovid. One phrase conveys the tone: Dryden's Augustan couplets "roar like an unmuffled Vespa",

---

* Robert Lowell, *Collected Prose*, edited and introduced by Robert Giroux (New York: Farrar, Straus & Giroux).

which is pure Lowell, with the first, the 17th and the 20th centuries casually mingling, with new Italian scooters kicking up a din in the Roman Republic and Dryden ribbed as if he were a Kenyon classmate.

For in coming to terms with his family Lowell found a style in which he could write, not just about Cousin Harriet and Uncle Devereux but about that spacious mental world where the living share their quarters with the vivid dead. Elizabeth Bishop once enviously observed that Lowell had made his own family belong to History; equally, he saw the historical past forming a kind of extended family, whose members could be loved, joshed, borrowed from and wrangled with on kissing cousin terms. To write about Lyndon Johnson in "Waking Early Sunday Morning", he'd enroll Marvell as a companion in arms; just as Sylvia Plath would remind him of Sir Walter Raleigh, or Racine of Robert Bridges.

There was an element of inspired purpose in the most seemingly cavalier of these associations. "We live in a hard and cracked world", he wrote. Lowell was on the side of softness, always trying to mend and reconnect – first his own disjointed life, then the severed arteries of 20th-century literature, with its suicidal rejection of the past. Lowell's work, like his life, was a constant struggle to keep in touch. He had to fight to see what he saw. Plagued by myopia, as by mania, he scrutinized the world through thick glasses (a clever poster for a Lowell reading once showed only a pair of spectacles alone in a white void). His handwriting (of runic, unjoined letters, scratched on to the page) made writing itself look like mild torture; a holiday postcard from Lowell had the appearance of being wrung from the heart. Philip Larkin inscribed a copy of *High Windows*, "To Robert Lowell from Philip Larkin – a drought to a flood"; but the flood belonged to the realm of public illusion, the words came hard, every happy connection was won from the teeth of chaos. Each flight of inspired articulacy was a triumph over his innate "boiled" shyness and reticence.

The prize pieces in the book are the three fragments from Lowell's unfinished autobiography – "Antebellum Boston", "91 Revere Street" (already known from its publication in *Life Studies*) and "Near the Unbalanced Aquarium". This last, with its cinematic crosscuts between Lowell's boyhood and his incarceration in the Payne-Whitney Clinic, is the quarry from which several of the *Life Studies* poems were excavated, almost word for word. The genius for treating his own life with the same toughness, sympathy and large humour that he brought to writing about Dryden, or Ford, or Frost is in magnificent shape:

> When the head nurse came gliding into the lounge, I pretended that I was a white-gloved policeman who was directing traffic. I held up my open hands and said, "No roughage, Madam; just innocent merriment!" Roger was getting to his feet; I made a stop signal in his direction. In a purring, pompous James Michael Curley voice, I said, "Later, he will thank me." The head nurse, looking bored and tolerant, led me away to watch the Liberace program in the men's television parlor. I was left unpunished. But next morning, while I was weighing in and "purifying" myself in the cold shower, I sang
>
> > *Rex tremendae majestatis*
> > *qui salvandos salvas gratis*
>
> at the top of my lungs and to a melody of my own devising . . .

The book is a wrench to read, because in it Lowell is so insistently alive – and well, and just turned seventy.

1987

TOM WOLFE

There's an enduring American compulsion to be on the side of the angels. Expediency alone has never been an adequate American reason for doing anything. When actions are judged, they go before the bar of God, where Mom and the Flag closely flank His presence. It's an attitude which has bred a dubious craving for moral heroes, along with a confusing readiness to dump those heroes as soon as circumstances change, and new angelic warriors are called for.

In the motel room where this piece is being written, there's a card instructing me to turn out the lights when I leave. I'm asked to perform this simple act "as an American", concerned – "as is every American" – about the Energy Crisis. "We know you'll join us in doing your part," wheedles the motel management. Virtue, patriotism, personal honour, at present reside in switching things off, saving gas, building solar ponds, and lagging the family roof.

Strings of T.V. ads present a new hero for the times: cautious, bespectacled, undersized, wise, his very lack of muscle and chutzpah a rebuke to those burly, promiscuously wasteful figures who have generally dominated the moral Hall of Fame. In this climate, it's no accident that Tom Wolfe's *The Right Stuff** has been sitting squarely on the best-seller lists for weeks. Officially, it's a book about the astronauts on the Mercury Programme; actually, it's a riveting sermon on the sins which led America to her present state of born-again enlightenment.

The Cold War and the fear of Soviet domination of the "high ground" of space produced that squad of improbable angels – John Glenn, Wally Schirra, Gus Grissom, Deke Slayton, Scott Carpenter, Gordon Cooper, Al Shepard. Tom Wolfe now unmasks them as the last of the big gas guzzlers. He has chosen his moment well, hitting the exact point at which America needs to look back on its heroes of a decade ago with ironic condescension. The tone of *The Right Stuff* is artfully balanced between satiric jeering and the excited squeals of the fanzine. It answers perfectly to the order of the day – putting the astronauts down while maintaining a decent American regard for heroes and hero-worship.

The men who queued up to be picked for the Mercury Programme were "fighter Jocks", dedicated to an ethic that Wolfe labels "Flying & Drinking and Drinking & Driving". They owned, or at least dreamed of owning, hot cars like Shelby Cobras and Maseratis, in which they buzzed each other on the freeways outside their Air Force bases. Posted away from home, they subscribed energetically to any double standards that were going: chasing tail was an all-American activity. Having the right stuff meant manliness in the Midwestern, heartland mould – an appetite for the pig-roast, the beerfest, the coon hunt, big cars, big broads and drawled laconic phrases.

Wolfe's central story is about how this prime beef was transformed into the-astronaut-as-hero. It was not obviously promising material. The Mercury craft didn't actually need pilots at all. The spacemen were there to add a dash of human interest to what was essentially a demonstration of purely technological power – a series of explosive experiments with huge quantities of fuel, steel, and electronic hardware which would, according to Kennedy and his advisers, frighten the Reds and keep the Free World free. Glenn, Schirra, and the rest had already been preceded by two chimpanzees; and like Ape 61

---

* Tom Wolfe, *The Right Stuff* (New York: Farrar, Straus & Giroux).

("Ham"), and Ape 85 ("Enos"), they were sent into the blue sprouting catheters from every orifice. On the ground, they spent most of their time producing urine samples and studying inkblots under the supervision of N.A.S.A. psychiatrists. They were little more than a representative assortment of kidneys, brains, bowels and ventricles.

They became heroes as the result of an adoring collaboration between the American public, N.A.S.A., and the press and television. *Life* Magazine bought their stories and packaged them for mass consumption. Walter Cronkite wept live tears for them on C.B.S. They turned into creatures of a necessary American fiction: their simple physical presence had converted the space programme from a war dance into an evangelical crusade. When Gus Grissom grunted out a few monosyllables, America listened spellbound: words from an astronaut, however stiff and banal, were *de jure* gospel.

The United States had needed moral heroes to license an expensive, conspicuously consumptive style of foreign policy: it got them. The rewards to the astronauts themselves were paid in the right stuff: Shelby Cobras, big suburban houses, coast-to-coast parades, N.A.S.A. groupies. When the policy changed, the heroes were shelved. When the astronauts crop up on television nowadays (plugging autoparts and other manly accoutrements) they are barely visible behind the subtitles required to explain to America who they were.

There is one significant exception: John Glenn, "The Presbyterian Pilot". Glenn wasn't interested in hot cars, preferring to drive an economical French biscuit tin. Glenn's sententious moralism had made him an outsider on the Mercury group, it equipped him perfectly for the traumatic passage from the 1960s to the 1970s. He now sits in the U.S. Senate, an essential, solitary figure of continuity spanning two mythological eras. His survival is a reassuring, if erroneous, symbol of the idea that America, for all her somersaults of ideology, is not as fickle as she seems. Glenn is the man who at once burned all that gas *and* switches off the last light in his hall.

The Right Stuff is Wolfe's best book. All his sharpness as a chronicler of social style is here. So, in abundance, is his genius for making yesterday look like something out of an infinitely remote tribal past. Wolfe, too, is a bridging figure between two opposed decades. His style has the sprawl and repetitiousness of the incontinent Sixties. When he turns a resonant phrase, he repeats it remorselessly until it turns into a slogan. By the time one finishes the book, Wolfe's sentences are famous in the way that Alpo Dog Food is famous, for being advertised. Some of his coinages do survive this shameless plugging; "Flying & Drinking and Drinking & Driving" is one. Many (like his characterization of the press as "that ever-seemly Victorian Gent") die a hundred deaths before their final interment in the end papers. Like Glenn, Wolfe is really a hometown moralist. The idiosyncratic flash is a stylistic trick. His true strength lies in his pussycat adroitness at keeping abreast – and only just abreast – of the times. A penetrating expert on yesterday, he is careful to leave all of today's illusions intact.

1979

II

Tom Wolfe has cultivated his own public image with a skill more often found in politics than literature. His grin, in his writing as in his photographs, is so disarming that it seems churlish to take him seriously. His style – peppered with exclamation marks, underlinings, catch phrases and funny noises of the kind one used to see in children's comics – aims for the breathless intimacy of a schoolgirl's letter. He is supremely worldly, yet somehow contrives to sound as if he'd just stepped off the train and can't quite believe the evidence of his own eyes. He has the vote-catching charm of the down-home kid who's conquered the big city but still retains his open-handed country manners.

It's a finely calculated act, and it is rooted in assiduous market research. No writer has devoted himself so whole-heartedly as Wolfe to the study of what's up, what's down, what's coming in and what's on the way out. There's a price tag and a brand name to be attached to everything, from socks and ties to ideas, social groups and individuals. Wolfe has a brilliant investor's eye for the human market, and always picks exactly the right moment to unload his stock. In 1970 (*Radical Chic*) the smart money moved out of Bernsteins and trendy liberalism; in 1979 (*The Right Stuff*) it got out of high government spending on the space programme. The targets on Wolfe's agenda, from pretentious art pseuds to Black Power, have always been good grass-roots populist ones: scratch the funky style of a Wolfe essay, and you expose a bedrock of simple fogeyism. His talent is for imparting the gloss of the new, the hip, the glisteningly particular, to a view of the world that is at best conventional, at worst downright banal.

His new book takes the form of an old-fashioned snakes-and-ladders saga of New York life of the kind made popular by John O'Hara and Louis Auchinloss, but Wolfe is far too full of himself as an ebullient monologuist to write a real novel. He is interested in characters only to the extent that people come in handy to illustrate general points. As a storyteller, he is a tyrant, shaping the destinies of his creatures by brute force to make them fit the predetermined logic of his theme.

His chief victim is a Wall Street bond broker (last year's worst-buy brand of human being), whom he consigns from an opulent apartment on Park Avenue to the lower depths of a jail in the Bronx. The downfall of Sherman McCoy is presented as a Hogarthian progress, allowing Wolfe to mount a series of luridly vivacious tableaux representing high- and low-life in New York in the 1980s. These colourful and noisy crowd scenes are by far the best things in the book, and give full rein to Wolfe's skill as an extravagant verbal cartoonist. Reporting from an unruly political meeting, a courtroom in uproar, a celebrity party in full bay, a newspaper office, a fashionable restaurant, a police pen stuffed to bursting-point with the jaibait of the ghetto, Wolfe is inexhaustibly vivid, funny and scarifying. Working with broad strokes from a distance of ten yards or so, he captures the uniforms, the voices, the ugly mood of the crowd, with scabrous accuracy. There are scenes in *The Bonfire of the Vanities* that pop up as you open the page and will frighten a nervous reader half to death. There are even individual human beings here, seen in medium-to-long-shot, who have every semblance of life, like the foul-mouthed little Judge Kovitsky who's paid $65,100 a year to preside over the mayhem of the Bronx County Court.

It's when Wolfe moves in close, when he shifts from being a jauntily detached reporter to pretending to be a novelist, that the book reveals itself as a shallow and meretricious performance. The way he treats his hapless fall-guy is typical of Wolfe's technique. He starts at the top and the bottom ("thick brown hair"; "$650 shoes from New & Lingwood of Jermyn Street"), then moves towards the middle by way of a "rubberized British riding mac" and "blue-gray nailhead worsted suit". Under these outer garments is a musculature of "deltoids", "trapezii" and "pectorals". Beyond that, there is – nothing. Like everyone else in the book, and to an exactly equal degree, Sherman McCoy is driven by the clockwork promptings of lust, greed and fear, but he is no more a person than the $48,000 two-seat black Mercedes sports car which serves as his roach-like outer carapace. There *are* differences between the characters in *Bonfire of the Vanities*: some wear Nike as against Reebok running shoes; some are "bald", some "balding", and one is "com*pletely* bald". McCoy's wife is a head of rich brown hair and shoes "with tiny black grosgrain caps"; his mistress is a head of bobbed black hair, plus "high-heeled pumps with a black-and-white checkerboard pattern worked into the leather". In the interests of critical discrimination, it has to be said that Wolfe is a lot better on footwear than he is on heads: on hearts, he is a dead loss. His people, squirming in heaps in their jail cells and round their expensive dinner tables, are no more than laboratory rats, kitted out by Wolfe in carefully-labelled human vestments. That some rise in the pecking-order while others fall is a matter of merely zoological interest.

English readers are used to taking Wolfe's astounding social expertise for granted; he is, at least, the crowned king of fabrics, prices, status symbols and class manners. This book may give one pause, since a good deal of its foreground is occupied by the scurrilous activities of a gang of Brits who run a New York tabloid called the *City Light*, whose drunken star reporter is a "widow's peak of longish wavy blond hair", a Blades blazer, a poplin raincoat with slash pockets and, perhaps significantly, no shoes worth mentioning. Every time Wolfe tries to take off a British accent or turn of phrase, it comes out slightly but definitely wrong. The *City Light* sections are characteristically spiced with arcane bits of social knowhow, but none ring true. Holland Park Comprehensive is not the British byword for academic excellence; prefects in English boarding schools are not known as "proctors"; fenders (of the kind that go round fires) are not most typically to be found in country houses in "the west of England"; there is a crucial difference, not grasped by Wolfe, between being "pissed" and being "pissed off"; Sir Gerald Steiner (known in England, apparently, as "that Jew Steiner") would be hard-pressed to father a daughter called Lady Evelyn. Etcetera. In another book, by another writer, these would be just fluffs, attributable to lazy editing; but Wolfe has staked his whole reputation on his command of small social and cultural distinctions, and every slip he makes about the English tends to weaken one's faith in his encyclopedic mastery of the comparable details of American life.

The Bonfire of the Vanities is as long as *Middlemarch*. By the end, the reader has never been faced with an issue with two sides to it, never been made to feel one pang of moral doubt. Instead, all his gut-prejudices have been expertly massaged and returned to him as witty, glittering and original *aperçus*. The ghetto *is* a terrifying place. The blacks *are* out for blood. Lawyers are shits. Brits are shits. Rich socialites are shits with nothing between their ears. Highly-paid yuppies really stink (and have no consideration for their dogs, either). The legal system is in a mess. Local politicians are corrupt. Only vulgar people buy Louis Vuitton luggage. New York City is one hell of a place to live, and any guy who survives in that jungle deserves a Purple Heart.

This is the technique not of the novelist but of the popular columnist - to use "style" like paint, to tart up the numbingly commonplace perception and make it look daringly new. Wolfe is endowed with a wickedly sharp eye, great good humour, an enviable fluency of phrase; it is a crying shame that his mind appears to have been transplanted from the corpse of Archie Bunker.

1988

JOHN UPDIKE

"This reviewer" is how John Updike usually styles himself when on assignment in the book pages of the *New Yorker*. The bulky pronoun with its echo, to an English ear, of Ed Murrow broadcasting from wartime London, is not a casual reflex; worn by Updike it is a liberating mask for a writer who rarely seems quite at his ease with the naked "I".

It's noticeable that all the less successful pieces in this vast – and on the whole vastly successful – collection* are written in the undisguised first person. The lectures on Hawthorne, Melville and Whitman are as genial and intelligent as one could wish, but they are somehow tainted, partly by the whiff one gets of Updike's personal celebrity as a platform guest and partly, perhaps, by the baleful loftiness of the halls in which they were aired. (Who could suppress a yawn in the Xerox Square auditorium of the Rochester, N.Y., Public Library?) The prefaces to Updike's own books suffer from their rather too finely calculated charm: writing about himself he can come perilously close to being winsome.

As "this reviewer", writing about other people's books, he is a joy and a relief. For the book review, in Britain especially, has become a

---

* John Updike, *Hugging the Shore: Essays and Criticism* (New York: Alfred A. Knopf).

relentlessly first-person form. The best-known reviewers are as chattily full of themselves and their hobbyhorses as television columnists. Against all this, Updike brings a novelist's stealth and negative capability. He dissolves himself in the books he reviews as artfully as he does in the glisteningly real suburban households of his fiction.

If Updike were to review himself he would probably say that the landscape of Brewer, Pa. (Rabbit Angstrom's briar patch) was "made palpable". It is the most frequently used term of praise in his critical vocabulary, a modest but reliable touchstone of excellence in writing. As a critic, Updike makes books palpable. He treats them exactly as if they were imaginary characters: tweaking them alive, adding happy dabs of colour and detail, exposing their weaknesses not so much in dispraise as in the interests of roundness and depth. A book reviewed by Updike has been vividly recreated on the page. You respond to it – or rather to its crafty likeness – much as you would to a person in fiction. There is very little superior authorial commentary: palpability is the thing, and the book stands acquitted or condemned by what looks deceptively like its own behaviour, as if Updike hadn't been there at all.

As befits true characters, books have very particular physical identities. They are to be recognized by the clothes they wear. One seems almost to remember, with affection, the borrowed library copy of *Memoirs of Hecate County* which the 14-year-old Updike ransacked for its enlightening dirty bits: "That slightly sinister volume, a milky green in the original Doubleday edition, with the epigraph in Russian and a three-faced Hecate opposite the title page." Likewise, on the shelves of a professorial friend: "The slim, sans-serif spines of Grove Press's paperback editions of Samuel Beckett, complete. The books looked bought at one blow and, if not pristine, used delicately. So enshrined, they composed a canon . . ."

He brings the same evocative precision to the insides of books: he can recollect a whole style in a phrase, as when he points to Iris Murdoch's "sly and glossy spookiness" or talks of Saul Bellow's "lavish, rippling notations of persons, furniture, habiliments and vistas". In his criticism as in his fiction Updike is a three-dimensional realist.

It is tempting (as it always is with realists) to dwell on the phrase-making, the web of details and exactitudes, and *Hugging the Shore* is packed solid with these small, telling successes. They are, though, always being put to work in the service of a vision of life and literature which is generous, comprehensive and intellectually well-found. It is a Christian vision in the broadest sense, with an acute theological grasp of the metaphysical implications of doubleness and paradox. The unshakeable civility of Updike's manner as a writer is Christian, too. He is both a superb unraveller and a superb accepter of the contradictions of the world. He is – to borrow two more of his favourite terms – attentive to creation.

All the best pieces in the book come to grips with the contrary fabric of things with a kind of intelligent wonder. In his brilliant essay on Céline, for instance, Updike makes polished sense of how the gentle Parisian doctor, a fastidious reviser of his own sentences, could at the same time be an extreme and odious anti-semite and, in his fiction, make an "infernal mess" of the world. The Céline review, like Updike's retelling of the barbed and sad friendship between Nabokov and Edmund Wilson, has the form and density of a short story as it shapes itself around the conflicts of the life it uncovers. It is this charitable eye for reality that makes Updike so thoroughly convincing on the badnesses of good books and the goodnesses of bad ones.

He is full of surprises. It is predictable that he should admire other elegant realists and pattern-makers – Nabokov, Calvino, Murdoch, Henry Green, John Cheever, Anne Tyler. Who, though, would guess that Updike writes better than anyone has ever done before on William Burroughs and Kurt Vonnegut? That he warms, warily, to Roland Barthes and Robert Pinget? That his piece on *The Origin of Table Manners* is a miraculously sane and clear exposition of Lévi-Strauss's structuralism?

To call Updike a model reviewer is to suggest that he is imitable. He's not. We should simply be grateful that he is there, with his fine, discriminatory prose working its way through the columns of the *New Yorker* between ads for whisky, mosquito hats and Caribbean vacation communities. The blandness of that context may, perhaps, remind one of just why he is so good: he makes reading books as real, as ordinary, as intermittently dramatic a part of civilized life, as worthy of the novelist's attention, as suburban adultery or the getting of money. He puts books in the foreground of creation.

1984

III

Of course Shelleyblake wants to write plays. How could he not? Most of his working life is spent alone in a room, not so much writing as trying to write – going fishing in his head for sentences and getting no bites. When he stops to make coffee, there are no colleagues to share it with, no one to gossip to, no one to rib. On workdays, he has to live by extension, over the telephone. He might as well be a patient in an isolation ward. He wouldn't dream of relinquishing his singular freedom, but still pines for company. When he visits the offices of editors, agents, publishers, he envies them their easy sociability, their ability to palm off a pleasant conversation as a serious job of work. He's only paid for finished pages; they're paid to talk, have lunch, talk some more, read a little, and put their signatures on letters.

But playwrights, Shelleyblake observes, have the best of both worlds – solitude and society. The first reward of writing a play is the companionable busyness of long lunches, script and casting conferences, rehearsals. The writer is enrolled into a hectic and, on the whole, happy industry. Talking with the producer, the director, the set designer, the actors, he feels he's part of real life again; he even has his own chair to prove it.

The business that actors call "The Business" has a seductive fascination for many writers who have no special talent for it at all. The lonelier the writer, the more prone he is to succumb. Writing can come to seem a very solitary vice; but to write for people and to work with them, to enjoy the warmth of a shared community, to be reintegrated into society . . . so goes the dream, and so the play's begun.

In the 1960s and early '70s, it was often said (mostly, admittedly, by T.V. producers), that television drama was the "real" national theatre. There was a lot more point to the claim then than there would be now. In the main auditorium the work of writers like David Mercer, Simon Gray and Dennis Potter, all of whom then wrote more or less exclusively for television, was in repertory. There was also a large and hospitable fringe – several weekly slots for single plays (which could be of almost any length from half an hour to an hour and three-quarters), a large number of young producers (some of whom were employed by the T.V. companies, while others worked for independent outfits that were under contract to supply the big companies with seasons of new plays), and a great deal of money. The producers could afford to experiment with untried writers, commissioning many more scripts than they needed to fulfil their production schedules. Being an unproduced television playwright could turn into a well-paid permanent job.

I found a berth with Kestrel Films, a company set up by Tony Garnett, Ken Loach and Kenith Trodd, who had worked together at the B.B.C. making the "Wednesday Play" series and who were now largely funded by London Weekend Television. They had offices in a tall stucco house off Kensington Church Street, where they established an atmosphere that combined the severity of a revolutionary cell with the opulence of a rising property developer's headquarters.

Temperamentally, they were serious men for their medium. Trodd, with whom I dealt, was a Cambridge Leavisite with haggard eyes and haggard mouth. Politically, they were of the New Left. Aesthetically, they were committed to a style of realistic documentary, making films to shock, to rouse consciences and change consciousnesses. Their best work at the B.B.C. had been the production of pieces like *Cathy Come Home* and *The Lump*, together with the feature film *Kes*, from which the company took its name. They had evolved a style in which television drama could make news (as *Cathy* certainly did) because it looked so like News that viewers couldn't draw the line between the fact and the fiction in the picture.

Television then was still, just, in black and white, which made reality easier to fake. By using newsmen's handheld cameras and characteristic camera angles, along with sparse and intermittent dialogue, it was possible to achieve a seamless transition between the News, which preceded the "Wednesday Play", and the play itself. Loach and Garnett dominated English television drama in the late '60s, creating a much-imitated dialect of grainy, underlit footage, apparently snatched from reality on the wing, like pictures from a running war. The style was effectively killed by the introduction of colour, which overexposed the artifice involved and made such plays look self-consciously faked.

Trodd was the company's literary man. He'd worked with Simon Gray and Dennis Potter at the B.B.C., and at Kestrel Films he was interested in wordier, more formal scripts that could be videotaped in a studio, with a ration of only seven or eight minutes of film to 50 minutes of tape. So it was for tape, not film, that I was trying to write; for the more traditionally theatrical conventions of the studio set, whose unrealism permitted a corresponding artificiality of language, or so I thought.

A play for Kestrel was commissioned, written, budgeted and not done. I'd included, in my allotted eight minutes of film, a fire spreading through the clapboard houses of an East Anglian village – far too expensive an effect for a beginner's effort. Another script was commissioned, paid for, but found too verbose and pretentious to be put into production.

Trodd left Kestrel Films, and I caught up with him again when he was producing plays for Granada Television. I had another go, this time with a play about the gentrification of a square in Islington. It seemed to work on paper, and Trodd put it into production.

The *on paper* was the problem. The would-be playwright ought to hear alarm bells in his head when he finds that he is getting more pleasure from writing his stage directions than he is from writing his dialogue. The talk of the characters was lavishly supported by huge paragraphs of Shavian description – of their clothes, furniture, facial expressions and secret motives. So long as it remained a script only, it read convincingly enough: a story was told, the characters were adequately filled out. Shafts of particular sunlight filtered through on to piles of particular builders' rubble on a particular staircase. The smell of an abandoned tomcat was named, so was the baconfatty complexion of its elderly Irish owner. And so on. The reader of the script was lulled by the surrounding description into believing that the dialogue was doing far more work than it actually was.

The first readthrough was in a huge and gloomy rehearsal room in Vauxhall. I drove over Vauxhall Bridge in a state of seraphic elation, a just-about-to-be-performed playwright at last. I fetched coffee from the machine for Hermione Baddeley, and did my best to make friends with her miniature dog. The social joys of the playwright's life were beginning, with Baddeley on one side of me and Edward Fox on the other. The dog was the only fly in the ointment.

When the director said "Let's go from the top", I settled down to enjoy hearing the lines of the play enriched and transformed by a cast of talented actors. That, so I had read, was what all playwrights felt at readthroughs, as their words suddenly began to belong to other people.

Every line sounded forced and dead. It was like listening to the sound of someone trying to play a waterlogged piano; a succession of tuneless bonks and ploinks. I looked across at Trodd: his eyes were shut and his lips were deeply indrawn. There wasn't much to deduce from his expression, but it certainly wasn't amused and it certainly wasn't moved.

What we were listening to was just – dialogue. It wasn't talk, it was lumps of spoken writing, of a kind meant only to exist on a page. All the ironies of inflection and shades of double meaning lay in the accompanying prose of the stage directions. Made to stand on its own, in the mouths of the actors, it wobbled and fell flat.

It was, Trodd said later that morning, just a readthrough. You could never tell from readthroughs, and he'd heard many that were even worse. Give it a week, and the magic of production would restore the play to life. But it didn't. It couldn't. From readthrough to final take, the lines remained stolidly unamenable to resurrection. On the night the play was transmitted, I hid in a pub in Crouch End that didn't have a television.

It was a total failure that still had in it the faint, tantalizing smell of what success might be like. Within a week, I'd started another play, for radio. Television had been a punishing medium. It studied lines in close-up and searched them for overstatement and false notes on camera. It set standards of literal realism that I couldn't match up to. It was all showing and no telling.

Radio was much kinder. It could handle speech at a greater distance from the ear, could afford more in the way of exaggeration and stylization. You could narrate on radio, using similes and metaphors, because the radio close-up, the intimate *sotto voce*, entailed an exchange of confidences with the listener, and not, as on television, an act of indecent exposure. On radio you could freely zig-zag about in time and space. No need to fly to Africa to film it, when a stock recording of cicadas would get you there in one small adjustment of the ear to a change of scene; no need to overfurnish a studio with 1940s tat, when a scratchy 78 record of Vera Lynn, with the sound of a steam train shunting in the background, would, on radio, overfurnish an entire decade. All of radio's cues and signals were both far more stylized and far more simple (and cheap) than those of television. It was more obviously hospitable to ornate language. It was as elastic in its rules and conventions as the printed page itself.

At the next readthrough, people actually laughed at each other's lines, and in the stereo studio at the top of Broadcasting House the play began to take off. The same lines were read again and again, each time with a slightly different cadence and emphasis. Recordings were compared. A web of aural detail was spun around the words. A 60-minute radio play gets four days of rehearsal and recording; they are packed days of close listening and sifting and experiment. The B.B.C.'s radio drama department is staffed by obsessives. Hardly any publicity attends their work. Their plays literally fade into thin air after their second or third broadcast. It's chastening to discover the infinite trouble that they're prepared to take in order to make a play sound right. So much craft, so much fine tuning, so little public response. By the time the producer has spent two further days editing his tapes, the play as broadcast will have had an hour of intense work devoted to every minute of its transmission. It may get a couple of brief reviews. And that will be it.

I wrote seven plays for radio, and six of them were produced by Richard Wortley. Tinkering all day in the studio with intonations and noises off, he would build the play up layer by layer, until the texture of its sound was thick with colour. Watching – or rather, listening – to him work was much like seeing an Empsonian critic teasing meanings from a text. Coaxing an actor to dip his voice in the middle of a line, adding a shade of echo, fading out an intrusive effect, he would succeed eventually in making even the flat line, the writer's failure, surprise one as it came back on the control room speakers. He was bent on enriching the words in front of him, and, again like the Empsonian critic, he was – is – prone to go over the heads of his audience in his search for subtleties and elaborations. No one outside the small group inside the studio can have heard everything that Wortley meant them to hear. He was creating something to be listened to intently in a darkened room, when most of his audience had half an ear for the play as it leaked out of a tiny car radio on a motorway or from a transistor in the kitchen.

The people we were really making plays for were the blind. Most theatre audiences, and many people who watch television, are prepared to attend to what happens on the stage or screen with a degree of concentration not far short of that which went into the preparation of the play. The blind listen to radio like that, and so do a small coterie of radio listeners who are prepared, in effect, to blind themselves for the duration of a programme. But they are very few and far between.

Sitting in the studio, listening to a line delivered with an expertly paced twist for the sixth time round, I did suspect that we were getting far more interest and excitement from the play than any listener at home would. It was like being in a workshop, learning from experiments conducted in secret. For the writer, at least, they were engrossing sessions, these master-classes in dialogue, with first-rate actors trying one's lines out on the air.

Radio seemed such a generous and elastic medium to work in that I probably exaggerated the rigidity of television. It seemed too narrowly realistic, too glaring, too bound by the unities imposed by limited numbers of studio sets and reels of film. Invited to contribute to a series of 30-minute plays on B.B.C.2 – to write a televisual short story – I tried to work out the ground rules beforehand, and see if the rules themselves would yield an idea.

> 1. *It has to be done in the studio, so use one set – a single room.*
>
> 2. *Try to find an action that would only take about half an hour in real life.*
>
> 3. *Characters must be the sort of people who go in for fancy talk, so that I can get away with "unrealistic" dialogue.*

At the time I was playing a lot of late-night snooker at a London club. The brilliance of the table at the centre, the shadowy figures of the men who came to watch, sitting in line on leaking horsehair settees, the figures of the two opponents, one crouched over the table, the other retiring back in the shadows, all looked as if they could be transferred intact to television (which had, fairly recently, discovered snooker as the most photogenic of all sports). In real life, the talk was both witty, in a laboured, otiose, public-school way, and pungently misogynistic. It was 1974, but from the slang, the mannered style of circumlocution, the constant undertow (which grew stronger as the brandies piled up into the small hours) of contempt for and fear of women, one might have guessed it to be 1920. Datedness and artificiality could become part of the subject of the play.

The best thing about the idea seemed to be the way that the table itself, the shots, the lie and movement of the balls, would command the viewer's attention, so that much of the talk could happen off camera. Or the conversation could come as a rumble out of the darkness, where the spectators sat on their bench. Following my earlier, disastrous effort for television, I was determined to distract the cameras, to make them film something else while the characters were actually speaking. It looked like the best of both worlds – radio with pictures.

That wasn't how the director, Claude Whatham, saw the piece, but it did enable it to get written. Whatham injected a degree of surprise and spontaneity into the performance of the play by deciding to film (or, more precisely, tape) the game on the hop. Neither actors nor cameramen would know where they'd be for the next shot; it would depend on how the game went and whose balls went where. There were no chalk marks, and few rehearsed gestures. The two opponents, Michael Cadman and Julian Holloway, stalked each other round the table, playing some serious snooker, while the cameras followed, just as they would have done on *Pot Black*. It was noticeable that neither Cadman nor Holloway ever delivered the same line in the same way twice. Their positioning and the distance between them were always different, and their delivery was constantly having to be altered to fit new circumstances. It was fluently done, and Whatham's direction earned the tape a place in the National Film Archive.

I wrote five more plays for television. Three of them were put on, but they all creaked, one much more badly than the others. The failing playwright finds himself riding an increasingly familiar see-saw: first the hope and the belief that goes with the writing of the play, then the surge of disappointment at its performance. Here *again*? But, cries the playwright, that's not what I wrote at all! Which is the penalty he pays for having dreamed of working in a collaborative medium. You wanted other people, says a second voice inside him, so you got other people – you got yourself a director, a cast, a set designer, a whole bunch of guys, and now all you do is bitch about how they've taken your toy away and bust it. What kind of a toy busts so easy? It was junk in the first place.

I kept on having not quite enough failure to make me retire. The next play was always going to be better written than the last; actorproof, directorproof, reviewerproof. Then the theatrical producer Michael Codron intervened, with a contract for a full-length stage play. It was a splendid contract. It promised 5 per cent of the gross weekly box office receipts on the "UK tour prior to the West End", 10 per cent of the gross weekly box office receipts in the West End after "the recoupment of the cost of the production", and "Two pairs of house seats at the first night in the West End at the Manager's expense". The play ("untitled") was almost as good as on already, and I walked along Shaftesbury Avenue, sizing up theatres to house it.

It seemed to write itself, which is – in long retrospect – never a good sign. I read it aloud to a friend, doing all the voices. She loved it. Codron hated it. Plays, unlike books, don't elicit temperate emotional responses; they are loved or hated, loved *and* hated, and between the love and the hatred lies a hairline crack of pure indifference. Codron hated it, but the artistic director of the Bristol Old Vic loved it. Another contract was drawn up ("It is further agreed that the name of the Director shall never be larger in size type and degree of boldness and prominence than the name of the author . . .').

I drove the length of the motorway between London and Bristol in much the same state of manic serenity as that in which I'd driven over Vauxhall Bridge seven years before. (Shelleyblake, *be warned.*) The steep-galleried theatre was old and beautiful, the model of the set a masterpiece of changing backcloths and revolves. Ten minutes into the readthrough, the play suddenly died, as if overtaken by a coronary. *Bang* – and it was all over bar the notices, which were obituaries of the kind that have no respect for the feelings of the family, but remorselessly rake over the dead man's sins. As Kenith Trodd had said to me at Vauxhall, "When a play works, the actors get the praise, and when it doesn't, the writer gets the blame."

It was a death from which there seemed to be nothing to learn. Several people experienced in the theatre, including Richard Cottrell of Bristol and Alec McCowen, who'd wanted to direct it for another London management, had read the script and been confident that it would "play". But it didn't. On such occasions, the writer inevitably thinks that the director's name should go into a larger size type and degree of boldness and prominence than his own; he feels his words have been misread, misconstrued and misappropriated. The truth is that they were not "his" words. They belonged just as much to the director and the cast as they ever did to him. That is what the shared community of the theatre is about.

In Bristol, the actors bravely played through their allotted month. Eric Thompson, the director, nursed them through the shower of bad notices. "You don't want to take any notice of those," he said to me; "the critics always get it wrong." Only the writer broke ranks from the company and left the play to rot quietly away on the boards.

Only the writer was free to be so disloyal – everyone else had to grin and bear it. They huddled a little more closely together in their encampment. They cossetted each other with "Darlings" and "You were wonderfuls" and surprise bouquets of flowers; a stranger would have mistaken them for one of those sprawling happy families that you read about only in children's books, and the writer marvelled at them from a distance that seemed at the time to be the exact dividing mileage that separated fact from fiction. I knew the play was bad; they had the much harder job of keeping themselves persuaded that it wasn't.

I took off – to travel in Arabia for a book and kick the habit of writing plays. It has been like giving up alcohol or tobacco: you boast about how long you've managed to stay off it. Ten years, so far, with one bad lapse. At least, that's how the record stood until yesterday when, writing about playwriting, I found myself scribbling five lines of dialogue, divided by a long pause, into a notebook. Only five lines. But it lies there like an unlit cigarette.

IV

Shelleyblake writes for what are annoyingly called the little magazines. They pay little (and irregularly), and their circulation figures are small – between 1000 and 3000 copies, probably. The only people whom Shelleyblake knows who subscribe to them are other writers. They tend to fizzle out abruptly, leaving unpaid printers' bills and writs pinned to their office doors. The magazines are chronically impoverished in mundane ways, but extravagantly generous in more unworldly ones.

They have space – space to print far longer and more detailed pieces of work than Shelleyblake could possibly hope to have accepted by the commercial press. Their editorial standards are both relaxed and sophisticated; they are dedicated, in theory at least, to "good writing", not to topicality, relevance, reader-identification or the other sacred cows of workaday journalism. They offer counsel and criticism – not just "Can you lose 80 words to make it fit?" They are meeting-places. Contributors drop in, especially during licensing hours. Working for newspapers, Shelleyblake makes money; working for a little magazine, he makes friends. If he's a regular dropper-in, he's likely to see himself described somewhere as a member of a notorious London literary conspiracy. This means that the little magazine is reasonably successful, that it exerts some influence on the larger literary world.

In 1969, Ian Hamilton was editing the *Review* from a first-floor room in Greek Street. He'd started the magazine seven years before in Oxford, and it had built up a coterie reputation for tough critical articles and poems pared down to the bone. In a decade which was soft on crap, the *Review* was about cutting the crap out of contemporary writing and talking about literature in plain English. It scorned most forms of modernism, pop poetry, Beat poetry, poetry by all the windy descendants of Ezra Pound. It printed poems as short as haiku (by Michael Fried, Peter Dale, Colin Falck, David Harsent, Hugo Williams, John Fuller and Hamilton himself) and its reviews were snappish.

Hamilton had another job; he was Poetry Editor of *The Times Literary Supplement*, where he was famous for his skill as a crap cutter. He had so improved the leisurely 3500-word essay of one distinguished professor of literature that it eventually appeared as a 100-word "short notice", or so people on the *TLS* claimed. The *Review*, in sharp contrast to the prevailing trend of the moment, was sardonic, serious, straight and closely edited.

It also had a pub next door. The Pillars of Hercules was the magazine's main office; Hamilton's room was only resorted to when the pub closed. For the freelance writer, new to London and new to the precarious solitude of writing as a job, the *Review* offered – much more valuably than space, or books to carry away for review – a habitable version of life.

The magazine's finances were as uncertain as my own. Bailiffs haunted the premises like blowflies. It had the "shabby independence" that Johnson claimed as the duty and privilege of being freelance. It took its own stand on things. Its hours were irregular. Its editor and contributors were the first people whom I'd met who didn't seem to think me eccentric for having cut and run from a salary and a pension scheme. They lived much as I did, scribbling alone in rooms, selling review copies to pay for dinner at L'Escargot and sleeping-in till ten in the morning; they'd stuffed their pensions, and appeared perfectly happy to have done so. They had read more widely, and talked more intelligently, than any group of people that I'd run into before. Their tone was exactly consonant with that of the magazine – tough, funny, deflating.

It was like finding a continuous party that you could join more or less whenever you pleased; but a party with a point to it, with irony and hard edges. The sole qualification was that you should take writing seriously, and it was constantly being enlarged to admit newcomers. There was no whiff of fashionability, or exclusiveness about it; it was a spontaneous assembly of people who had regard for Hamilton and the magazine – and the *Review* was inevitably a minority taste. It wasn't cosy (like the huddling actors at the Bristol Old Vic) because the magazine itself was pitted against cosiness. Its tone was brisk and cool.

The *Review*, in its original form, as a magazine devoted to poetry, was wound up in 1972, after ten years of policing the scruffy frontiers of modern verse. Financed – in part – by the Arts Council, Hamilton set about turning a little magazine into a big one. The single room swelled to a shambling cluster of offices in the same building. The format of the magazine grew correspondingly, from, as it were, pamphlet-octavo to *Vogue*-sized A4. The *New Review* was designed to accommodate plays, fiction, profiles, reportage and argument, as well as poems and reviews. Where the old *Review*, theoretically a quarterly, had made sporadic guerrilla appearances, the *New Review* was to come out once a month, and claim space on news stands with the other glossy magazines. Why should literature be seen to cringe in littleness when women's fashions, food, yachting, photography and car ownership hogged the foreground in W. H. Smith's? Hamilton founded the *New Review* on the idea that serious writing could compete with commercial monthly journalism on its own terms, and without losing the critical standards on which the *Review* had stood so firm. Its first issue included things by Edna O'Brien, Robert Lowell, George Steiner, Al Alvarez, Martin Amis, Julian Mitchell, Douglas Dunn, Caroline Blackwood, Russell Davies, Clive James and Dan Jacobson, with photographs by Fay Godwin. *Vogue*'s "feature pages" – any magazine's feature pages – should be so lucky.

Yet where the *Review* had been treasured by the few, the *New Review* instantly incurred the malice of many. Its glossiness was held against it as a clear sign of fallen morals. Its grant from the Arts Council (which covered barely half the expenses of each issue) earned it the reputation of a welfare-scrounger living at the state's expense. Its size offended. Literature was all very well, but in the *New Review* literature was getting uppish. *Private Eye* and the gossip columns of the Sunday papers decided that the magazine was sneerworthy before it had been launched.

It might have been criticized on subtler grounds. The size of the page, and the number of words that could be printed on one page (from 1400 to 2000, depending on the type-size used), made it difficult to display the kind of poem promoted by the old *Review*. A tightly whittled six-liner now looked like a starveling orphan, and the *Review* poets had to set themselves to writing epics. The page soaked up words. Full-length plays by Harold Pinter, Simon Gray and Dennis Potter shrank to a few pages in the *New Review*. A long novella by Paul Theroux looked, at first glance, like a brief short story. Robert Lowell had a joke about Tolstoy publishing *War and Peace* in the *New Review* and nobody noticing.

Once you started reading the magazine, of course, it was different. Its uninterrupted swathes of print made it the perfect showcase for plays and extended pieces of prose – and for long poems, too. But the *New Review*, having set so much store on its own appearance, was being judged by appearances. Though it was big, it was conspicuously thin (72 pages, against *Vogue*'s 240). *Vogue* and *Harper's* were artificially fattened on advertising matter, but the twelfth issue of the *New Review* (a fair test case) carried just ten ads, one of them for its patron the Arts Council. It was *all writing*. Every month it published about 75,000 words; the equivalent of a 200-plus-page book. But passers-by looked at it and saw that it was thin.

It was the most handsome literary magazine to be published in England, and its rocky finances (the bailiffs were more in evidence than ever) gave it the sympathetically fugitive air of a little magazine still. During its lifespan, from 1974 to 1979, the Pillars of Hercules turned into a living room for dozens of the *New Review*'s friends, who were many, though never quite many enough to allow the magazine to enjoy a life of bourgeois comfort and security. That was probably a good thing. Hamilton himself seemed born to live on knife-edges. He dodged the bailiffs by posing as a rival creditor and lay low in the Pillars until the crisis overhead had passed (for that day, anyway). He ignored all letters in brown envelopes with windows, and got on with the job of editing the magazine.

The definite article was important. The *New Review* was never "his"; it was always "the" magazine – a cause held in common by the editor, the office staff and the contributors. The values it stood for were clear as bells: catholicity of taste, excellence in writing, and no indulgent crap. If you were on the side of its programme, then you had a personal stake in the magazine. If it foundered, that was going to be everybody's fault, and if it worked, everyone was going to share in its success. Hamilton had the gift of convincing the contributors that writing for the *New Review* was like joining a crack regiment on the eve of battle; it was a cause that you might have to shed blood for. That the magazine lived with the imminent threat of closure gave it an air of urgency and adrenalin: if you were late with a piece, you might arrive in Greek Street to find the office padlocked and no magazine to publish in.

He made people feel that *their* contribution was crucial to the *New Review*'s survival, that they must write at the top of their bent in order not to let the magazine down. He was, by all normal standards, hopeless with money: it was simply stuff you spent, and that was that. This left him unusually free to wrangle about writing over lunches that lasted into the twilight. A cannier editor in his position would have found himself never out of the company of lawyers and accountants; Hamilton had made the simple decision that good writing was more interesting and important than mere solvency, that the magazine would be saved more effectively by its writing than by its financial advisers, and so he spent his time with writers, saying *have you thought of . . .?* and *why don't you . . .?* and *that doesn't work.*

A staunch community grew up around the *New Review*. We knew how good the magazine was (whatever its detractors said), and that it was worth fighting for. When the *New Review Anthology* was published in 1986, seven years after the magazine's death, several of its reviewers seemed bemused by how much richer the collection was than they had expected. They should have bought the magazine when it came out, instead of noting sourly that it wasn't as fat as *Vogue*. Its eventual closure left a hole in the literary landscape that hasn't been filled since.

The *New Review* managed to solicit disappointingly few regular advertisements. One of them, on its back cover, had the inscrutable slogan, *Writing of Quality For a Magazine of Choice*, and was headed "Some of these writers write for the *New Review*. All of them write for the *Radio Times*". There followed a list of names, laid out as on a war memorial. It included Kingsley Amis, Margaret Drabble, Ian McEwan, Paul Theroux, Angela Carter, V. S. Naipaul, Julian Mitchell, Frederic Raphael, Andy Warhol, P. J. Kavanagh and Ian Hamilton. *Dulce et decorum est pro tempora radii scribere.*

It was a curious list, since *Radio Times* has always been a publication that people look at rather than read, and consists mostly of routine programme puffs and star interviews. However, under the editorship of Geoffrey Cannon it went through an interesting paroxysm in an unexciting history.

Cannon was an Oxford contemporary of Hamilton. They had worked together on several undergraduate magazines. Appointed to oversee the weekly production of programme pages sandwiched between two slabs of anodyne editorial matter, Cannon took a more exalted view of his role than his employers did. He would use B.B.C. money to become a literary patron, and he'd fill his paper with Prose. Nobody much would actually read it (those who did tended, for a variety of reasons, to take a dim view of it), but Cannon would print it, defend it, and lay his job on the line for it.

By comparison with other English editors, Cannon was as rich as Mr Toad. He could pay up to £400 for a piece of 1800 words in the middling-1970s, which was rather more than was on offer from, say, the colour supplements of the *Observer* and the *Sunday Times*. This was roughly what I was being paid for half-hour plays for television and 75-minute plays for radio; it was at least six times as much as I could earn from a book review. It was no wonder that Cannon was able to engage his crew of poets, novelists and short story writers: a piece for the *Radio Times* would settle the gas bill, the phone bill, the electricity bill and the month's mortgage all in one. It was writing for jam.

It got Cannon into trouble with his masters, for *Radio Times*, instead of obediently hyping the programmes of the B.B.C., began either to ignore them altogether or to ironically debunk them. Often the only thing in common between the programmes and the pieces in *Radio Times* was a vague general location. If *Dallas* was beginning, a novelist might be despatched to Texas in order to turn in an essay on his encounters with Dallas lowlifers in a succession of dives. Interviews with popular talk show hosts would hinge on their dumb bad taste in furniture, books and politics. The programme makers (who, under earlier regimes, had written their own articles to boost their products) began to see *Radio Times* as the B.B.C.'s Fifth Column, and Cannon spent an increasing amount of time at frosty meetings with senior management.

But Cannon and his editorial staff endeared themselves to a lot of writers. They commissioned them to go off to improbable places, meet improbable people, and left them blessedly free to write what they pleased. Balked in the middle of a book or play, you could call Cannon's office and beg for a temporary release from your study. There was nearly always something on hand that would take you away from home for a few days and give you a taste of a life that you'd never have dreamed of living on your own account. The cant word was that journalism should be "fresh", and Cannon interpreted this to mean that the best possible qualification for writing about any subject was total prior ignorance of it.

So, because I knew nothing at all about horse racing, I spent a week hobnobbing with jockeys, trainers and owners to write an Aliceish piece about the opening of the Flat season. In a Tudor mansion in Sussex, taking sherry before lunch with a lady owner, I thought I'd found a patch of dearly-needed common ground when I noticed a copy of Iris Murdoch's latest novel on the table between us. "What do you think of it?" I asked. "Oh," she said, dragging the poor little word out so that it had at least four separate vowel sounds, and staring at *The Sacred and Profane Love Machine* as if it was a displaced garden slug, "I haven't *read* it." She looked out sadly beyond the roses to the stables. "They just *come*, you know – the books. From Heywood Hill."

Posted for ten days to Monte Carlo, I trailed in the entourage of the nightclub owner, Regine, and watched the very bored and the very rich dancing and drinking, drinking and dancing. I met an unfortunate in Barnsley who was dedicated to refighting the American Civil War, by himself, on the slag heaps behind his council house, and spent his free time dressed in the uniform of a Confederate general. His wife said that she thought it was nice for a man to have an interesting hobby. In Los Angeles, I sat in the studio at the top of the tower of Aimee Semple MacPherson's Radio Church of America, where prayers (though they sounded more like medical prescriptions and peremptory injunctions to me) were beamed to God, 24 hours a day, on His personal M.F. wavelength. I floated down the Euphrates on a raft with Freya Stark, sailed from Gloucester to the Isle of Wight on a converted Baltic Trader, found class warfare in the village of Cerne Abbas and sunken treasure in the Scilly Islands. These assignments were occasional and irregular – about a dozen altogether, scattered over a period of four years. They came not as work but as escapes from work; liberating breaks from the long spells of solitary confinement that more serious writing demands.

Connolly called journalism the Blue Bugloss, the "deadliest of the weeds on Crabbe's heath", and it's easy to be seduced by journalism's promise of instant distraction, instant publication, instant payment. The most damaging aspect of feature journalism is the way it turns life into a series of larks. A few days spent in someone else's world (however dismal, violent, pretty or even boring that world may be) is simply not enough to experience it as real. It is too tightly framed by one's own domestic normality. Wherever you are today, you know that next Monday you'll be home, and from the perspective of home today will seem too exaggerated, too highly coloured, too remote to take quite seriously. So the writer slips into a style of mechanical facetious irony as he deals with this wrong-end-of-the-telescope view of the world. The perfervid similes that are the trademark of the hardened magazine writer betray him as he tries to make language itself mask and make up for the fundamental shallowness of his experience with its synthetic energy. The more extravagant the similes become, the more you smell the writer's basic disengagement from the world he is describing. He is fatally engaged by the mere business of description, by that verbal manufacturing industry in which skies are always being turned into bolts of shot silk, or gunmetal, or eiderdown, or anything else that will demonstrate that a professional writer has been to work on them.

It isn't only journalists who are prone either to mechanical irony or to routinely ingenious simile: novelists and poets – often very good novelists and poets – tend to be susceptible to these tricks of journalese. But the nature of journalism is such that it forces the writer into a purely professional relationship with his subject. Emotional disengagement, self-conscious observation, the capacity to quickly turn a muddle of not very deeply felt sensations into a neat and vivid piece, are part of the necessary equipment of the writer as journalist. His book, if it is worth writing at all, will insist on being written for its own sake, will make a creature of its author. Rarely if ever does a commissioned article take on that kind of mysterious, autonomous life. It is rooted in technique, not compulsion, in being able to tell a story to order.

Too many such commissions, lightly assigned and lightly taken on, are likely to teach the writer secrets that are better not learned. He will suddenly find he has access to a set of useful codes, for expressing pity, anger, admiration, scorn, wonder, when in fact he feels nothing much at all but his deadline looms. He'll know how to tart up a dull landscape with well-gauged dabs of acrylic colour, and how to convey the illusion of easy intimacy with someone he's spoken to for all of 15 minutes. He'll wake up one morning and discover that he's not a writer but a forger.

The stylistic pitfalls of incidental journalism are dug very deep and it's easy to fall into them, but the rewards of the business make the pitfalls worth risking. It gets you out of the house, introduces you to people whom you'd never otherwise meet, in places you'd never otherwise see. Writers, especially when they live in London, are likely to find themselves living in an amiable, self-contained society that consists, almost exclusively, of publishers, editors, agents, producers and other writers. By the time they reach the third-novel stage in their career, they drift into writing a book about a character, living in London, who is writing a novel, because that is the only kind of character they now really know. It is surprising how quickly your horizon can shrink in radius until it's too small to contain anything bigger than a medium-sized literary party. Journalism – a friendly working relationship with the features editor of a reasonably liberal and easygoing magazine – is a wonderful specific against that condition.

"If you want to get on with your book, that's okay; we'll find someone else. But if you'd like to fly to Damascus on Thursday, we'll send the tickets round by messenger . . ." Very few editors would be so indulgent, but that was the style of *Radio Times* under Geoffrey Cannon, who was in my experience unique among professional journalists in that he actually thought that books were more important than magazine pieces, even when the pieces were for his own magazine.

Parachuting into someone else's life for a few days does not, on the whole, yield anything very deep in the way of experience. But it offers glimpses, hints, possibilities. The turned door handle admits a crack of light, and you can always return later to open it wide, step inside, and take up serious residence in the room you spotted on that flying visit.

Radio Times let me go to the Middle East for a fortnight. It was the first time that I'd been abroad, really abroad, in a culture whose language, religion, dress, economy and politics were so different from my own that I couldn't begin to guess at what people might be thinking and feeling. It was a fortnight of fascinated, infatuated estrangement, and it afforded a taste, faint but definitely addictive, of what it might be like genuinely to lose oneself in someone's else's world. Six months later, I was back in Arabia, to wander, get deeply lost, ask toddler's questions in my new nursery Arabic, and write.

Another *Radio Times* piece sparked off two books and an obsession that I still can't rid myself of. I rather reluctantly agreed to join a sailing ship for three days (it was being used as a prop in the B.B.C. T.V. series, *The Onedin Line*), when I heard that I'd have to bring my own Dunlopillo and sleep with the rest of the crew in the unconverted cargo hold. But a novel had died on me after two chapters, and anything seemed better than staring at Chapter 3's blank first page and knowing I was living with a corpse. The boat fulfilled most of my worst expectations of the hearty, gumbooted life. Life aboard was like that of a floating boarding school on the Gordonstoun model, with school food, school jokes and a prevailing spirit of schoolboy machismo. I spent most of my time trying to get out of the way of people shouting things in incomprehensible nauticalese and searching for a quiet place to read somebody's critical book on Trollope. Late at night, somewhere off Lundy Island in the Bristol Channel, the wind began to caterwaul in the shrouds, and the boat took to dipping her scuppers in the increasingly violent swell. The crew were being sick into buckets. To my great surprise I found myself wondering about the propriety of making myself a bacon sandwich. Having dreaded seasickness, and prayed for a calm passage, I was inordinately proud of my apparent immunity to the boat's motion as she corkscrewed her way through an averagely rough sea. In the morning, we were edging along the Cornish coast. From three miles or so offshore, England looked as foreign as Arabia – a long, low, moody, gorse-clad island, its towns skulking in fissures in the rock, its edges rimed with breaking surf. Seen from this angle, Home was Abroad, and the sea a wilderness as truly wild as a great desert or rain forest. The idea lodged in my head and wouldn't budge. Four years later, I was sailing alone past the same stretch of coast in a solid seaboat of my own.

With luck, with imaginative commissions, journalism nourishes rather than vitiates the writer's other work. Its technical demands are absorbing. How, for instance, do you make a real person, with a verifiable address and phone number (not to mention a smart solicitor, well versed in the law of libel), talk on the page with the veracity of a character in fiction? Literal transcriptions of tape-recorded speech may be accurate in the legal sense, but they are curiously lifeless. Shorn of gesture, emphasis, timbre and cadence, they are the empty husks of what was once a real conversation. Often, they make their speakers sound completely half-witted. What was said with an ironic twist of the voice now reads as a solemn pontification; what was said with intense seriousness comes out as a passing aside. Read almost any newspaper interview, and you'll conclude that the dialogue of real people is more stilted and implausible than the dialogue of invented characters. Trying to make real people sound real on the page is necessarily an exercise in impressionism. Nothing teaches one the subtleties of punctuation so well as an attempt to take a skein of actual speech and restore to it the pauses, ellipses, switches of tone and speed, that it had in life. Lumbered with a rough and ready supply of dots, dashes and stops, you ache for a system of musical notation: if only this word could be written as a semi-quaver ascending, on a series of rising notes to that word, a breve . . . You isolate the speaker's tics and tricks of speech, his keywords, and make him say them slightly more often than he did in fact; you give him small bits of stage business to mark his silences; you invent lines of dialogue for yourself to break up a paragraph of solid talk that looks too long to be believable. You are trespassing, perhaps, into writing fiction, but the fiction will still be truer to the man and to the occasion than the literal transcription.

Here the tightrope act begins. For the generic line between fact and fiction is fuzzier than most people find it convenient to admit. There is the commonsensical assertion that while the novelist is engaged on a work of the creative imagination, the duty of the journalist is to tell what really happened, as it happened – to tell the truth and nothing but the truth. That distinction is easy to voice but hard to sustain in logic. For imagination and memory are Siamese twins, and you cannot cut them so cleanly apart. Writing from memory, trying to re-create events on the page as you remember them, and building them into the form of a story, is an act of imagination, however closely you try to stick to what seem to have been the facts. Only in the writing, as the story unfolds and the events fall into place, do you discover what actually happened. *But did it?*

I see the writer arraigned before an inquisitorial Select Committee on Untruthful Activities:

Q: This – ah – *object* is a piece of journalism?
A: It is.
Q: All the events described in it took place?
A: They did. At least, I believe they did.
Q: Did they take place in the same order as described?
A: Not necessarily.
Q: Did other events take place at the same time, which you have failed to mention here?
A: Yes, many. Many, many more than I described.
Q: Why then did you omit them? Is this a matter of what I believe journalists call "space"? Was there no "space" for them?
A: They simply seemed irrelevant to the story.
Q: "Story". Another piece of journalistic slang, I take it?
A: Not entirely. It is a story in the sense that it's a narrative. It's got a beginning, a middle and an end. I hope, too, that it has a forward drive, a shape, a point, some kind of conflict, some sort of resolution. That is what stories – unlike most of life – usually have.

Q: This committee has already heard that some of the people mentioned in this "story" of yours disagree, one of them quite violently, with your version of these events.

A: Of course. Point of view is everything. His point of view and mine were very different.

Q: Yet you claim to be telling the truth. Are you therefore accusing the previous witness of lying?

A: Not at all. Truth in description is a very tricky business. I once caused deep offence to someone by describing him as bald. He looked bald to me, but it's true that he still had a few wisps of hair around the tops of his ears. I perceived him as a bald man; he perceived himself as a hairy man. Neither of us were technically deceiving ourselves, or telling lies. He had sufficient evidence for his perception, just as I had sufficient evidence for mine. In description, one can only be true to one's own perceptions. Another person would see things in quite another light.

Q: You mean another writer might have produced an entirely different version of the events you have described here?

A: Inevitably.

Q: So this hypothetical other writer might well have omitted every single so-called "fact" recorded in this piece as written by you?

A: It's possible. In any case, the events themselves would have panned out differently. The fact of *my* being there instead of him or her being there altered the nature of the occasion.

Q: Hasn't it taken rather a long time for you to come around, at last, to the use of the word "fact"? So at least you accept your own presence as a fact in this matter?

A: I do. But I'd hesitate to claim that the quality of the light on the trees, or the expressions on people's faces, or even the precise meaning of their words as I interpreted them, were facts in any legal sense. Almost everything I have written here belongs to the realm of personal perception rather than to the realm of ascertainable fact.

Q: You nevertheless persist in your claim that this piece is a work of non-fiction?

A: Well, that's how it will, I suppose, be generally perceived by its readers. The world is hooked on categories, and it's comforting for most people to think they know whether what they're reading is "true" or whether it's "made up". This particular piece is clearly not "made up", so, yes, I think . . .

Q: Stop bamboozling and answer the question. Is this fiction or is it non-fiction?

A: I take the Fifth.

Q: Your memory, in your life as in your writings, seems to be both selective and self-serving to an unusual degree. We are in England now. We have no Fifth Amendment.

A: I'm sorry. I forgot.

Q: As you forget many things. Now, please, return to the point. Fiction or non-fiction?

A: I'm afraid I shall bore the committee.

Q: We shall have to bear with being bored. Answer the question.

A: I don't suppose you happen to have read Wittgenstein, have you?

Q: Is he another of your slippery media types?

A: No, a philosopher. Now dead. But interesting. Okay, I'll skip Wittgenstein – he'd only get me into deeper trouble. But there's a good case for arguing that any narrative account (have you read Carlyle's *The French Revolution*, for instance, or Gibbon's *Decline and Fall of the Roman Empire?*) is a form of fiction. The moment that you start to arrange the world in words, you alter its nature. The words themselves begin to suggest patterns and connections that seemed at the time to be absent from the events the words describe. Then the story (I'm sorry, I know you hate that expression) takes hold. *It* begins to determine what goes in and what's left out. It has its own logic and it carries the writer along with it. He may well set out to write one story, and find that he's writing quite another—

Q: Telling lies, you mean?

A: No, not telling lies at all. Trying to tell the truth. The piece you are investigating has no wanton inventions in it. I haven't made anything up in order to spice a dull tale. But I have told a story. Like all stories, it is selective, patterned, interpretative, finite. It is not "the facts"; if it were, it would be an exhaustive inventory, unimaginably long. The facts of just five minutes of this committee's hearing would probably fill all the volumes of the *Encyclopedia Britannica*. The fact that you are now picking your nose surreptitiously, for instance, the fact that—

Q: You impertinent hack!

A: —you were picking it with the index finger of your left hand. That is a perfectly fair example of a fact which happens to be irrelevant to our particular story. But in someone else's story, about, say, the tedium of select committees, it might figure as central to the action. The point I am trying to make is simple, and much misunderstood. I take it that you went to the sort of school where you were made to learn a bit of Latin. Do you know the etymology of *fiction*? No? It's from *fictio*, which means a fashioning. Any verbal account is a fashioning of events. The more self-consciously language is used, the more responsive the writer is to the medium in which he works, the more elaborate that fashioning is. The naive storyteller will burden you with a mass of irrelevancies, which get into the story just because he remembers that they happened to be there; the sophisticated storyteller will fashion his contingencies so that they support and move his story forward. That is fiction making.

Q: You will be trying to tell us next that *Hansard* is a form of fiction?

[*Laughter*]

A: No. Though it is ruthlessly selective. It records only what is said in Parliament; it leaves out most of the ums and ers, and the cattle-trough noises. But it is not a fashioning in the sense that I mean. It is not one person's moulded perception of events, or an attempted recreation of them; it is a record of some of the many words that get spoken in this building every day. That is what many newspaper reporters honourably try to do – to supply a reliable record of who said what to whom. But this piece of mine which you have singled out is not a report, not a record. It is rather an attempt to dramatize, to fashion, an actual experience, and give it the ring of reality on the page.

Q: This smacks to me of passing counterfeit coinage. One moment you say that your readers think that what they're getting is the truth, the next you say that you can only supply it to them in the form of fiction.

A: I agree. That is rather a sticky problem.

Q: If, for a moment, we accept your argument about the lies, or rather fashionings that go on in the piece itself, are you not still lying to your readers about the basic nature of the product you are offering them?

A: I think not. People instinctively understand the conventions of storytelling. They know that the first-person narrator is a potentially unreliable witness, and that he is there to be judged along with the other characters in the piece. They know that the convention of total recall – that ability to seemingly remember every smell, every slant of light, every word of dialogue – *is* a convention; that it's part of the storyteller's necessary licence. *They know perfectly well that they're reading a story.* Because the text is full of signals saying that "this is a story, this is my tale of these events". But they are also, I hope, convinced that this is a story that really happened – to me, to its narrator; that it is securely rooted in the stuff of the actual, that I haven't simply dreamed it up.

Q: Aren't you asking your readers to solve your moral problems for you?

A: No. Reading is a craft, like writing. I'm trying to write for skilled readers.

Q: So this is what my granddaughter calls the New Journalism, is it? Tom Wolfe, Norman Mailer, Gay Talese, Hunter Thompson – all those Americans who go around saying that they've written "factions" or "non-fiction novels" or some other damned contradiction in terms?

A: Not at all. The kind of thing I'm talking about is as old as Mrs Aphra Behn, Defoe, Smollett, Richardson. It's at least as old as the beginnings of the Novel, which, you may possibly remember, used to be thought of as a species of journalism.

Q: It's no good trying to cower behind the names of the famous dead. We are concerned here with one thing, and one thing only. Are you, or are you not, telling the truth?

A: I am. Or I'm trying to.

Q: Yet technically, according to this Mr Witwatersrand, or whatever his name was, you tell the truth by inflicting on the public a form of potentially misleading and inaccurate fiction?

A: Yes. I do.

Q: Thank you. You have irritated this long-suffering committee quite long enough for one morning. You may step down.

LIVING ON CAPITAL

I suppose that everyone is really the father of their own family. We make them up, these private sanctuaries, prisons and sunny utopias. Visiting other people's families, I've always found it hard to square what I've seen with the legend as it was told to me in the car on the way. The characters are always much bigger or smaller, nicer or nastier, than they ought to be. It's like seeing a play performed by a weekly rep working from the wrong text. One's own legend is doubly distrustable. One has all the ruthless impartiality of a critic writing up a show in which he has been both casting director and one of the stars. Legend it must be, not accountancy or gritty realism; and like all genesis myths, its garden, its rib and its fruit of the tree are symbols. When it comes to his own family, no one can afford to be a fundamentalist.

Once upon a time, before the idea of "family" ever took hold, there was just my mother and I. We lived in a sweet cocoon, and it was much like having an idyllic extramarital affair. My father was away "in the war": he was a photograph on the mantelpiece; he was the morning post; he was part of the one o'clock news on the wireless. He was not so much my father as the complaisant husband of the woman I lived with – and I dreaded his return. Meanwhile, we made hay while the sun shone. I had contracted a wasting disease called coeliac, and I was fed, like a privileged lover, on specially imported bananas and boiled brains. We learned to read together, so that I could spell out paragraphs from *The Times* before my third birthday. We stoved in the bottoms of eggshells, so that witches wouldn't be able to use them as boats. We saved up our petrol rations, and drove to my grandmother's house in Sheringham. My mother's Ford Eight, AUP 595, had been bought in 1939 with money she'd earned writing love stories for women's magazines, and it was the perfect vehicle for conducting a romance. Bowling along Norfolk lanes at a hair-raising thirty, with the windows down and the smell of pollen, leather and motor oil in my nose, I felt that this was the life. I meant to keep on as I had started; riding in the front seat with kisses and confessions, and the Ribena bottle conveniently near the top of the hamper.

I was a bag of bones. But I had already acquired the manner of a practised gigolo. My illness gave me the right to constant attention. With my forehead in my mother's hands, I was sick until my throat bled. When I wasn't being sick, I was being loquacious. Since my mother had only me to talk to, I'd picked up an impressive vocabulary which I was perpetually airing and adding to. Too weak to play with other children – whom I regarded from a distance as rough, untutored creatures – I looked to grown-ups for the concern and admiration that were clearly my due. I feared the mockery of the few children who were allowed ("No rough games, mind!") to enter my bone-china world. My one friend was the doctor's son, who'd been crippled with polio and went about in a steel frame that was almost as big as himself. When I was three, my mother told me that children like him and me would go on scholarships to nice schools, but that the village children would all go to knocky-down schools like the one up the road. I saw myself and my mother sailing out in my scholar ship, its sail filling with the offshore wind on the beach at Sheringham, its prow headed into a romantic sunset, away from the line of jeering, unkempt children on the shore.

I hadn't reckoned with my father. I had once made my mother cry, when I had enquired whether he was likely to be killed by Germans; and I was often puzzled by the depth of her engrossment when a new batch of letters arrived from North Africa, then Italy, then Palestine. Curiously, I have no memory at all of my father coming back on leave. He must have blended into the other occasional visitors – many of them in uniform – to our house. Was he the man who took us both out to lunch one Sunday at a Fakenham hotel, where I remember the stringy rhubarb and a fit of sickness in the lavatory? I'm not sure.

At any rate, he was a complete stranger when he turned up late one morning, carrying a khaki kitbag across Hempton Green – the moment at which family life began for me. My first impression of him was of an unprepossessing roughness. The photo on the mantelpiece showed a junior officer so boyish he looked too young to shave. My father's jowl was the colour and texture of emery paper. His demob suit, too, seemed to have been woven out of corn-stubble. When my mother and he embraced, right there in the open on the green, I was mortified. I studied the faded white lettering on his bag: Major J. P. C. P. Raban R.A. By what right did this tall soldier in his ill-fitting civilian suit horn in on our household? The question took me several years to even begin to answer.

My father must have been a bit shaken too. His spindly, solemn son can hardly have been the beamish three-year-old he might have looked forward to. He was obviously unused to children anyway, and had had no practice at dealing with precocious little invalids who cried when he spoke to them. He brought with him the affectedly hearty manners of the mess, and tried to make friends with me rather as he might have jollied along a particularly green subaltern. On the afternoon of his arrival, he carried me by my feet and suspended me over the water-butt in the back garden. As I hung, screaming, over this black soup of mosquito larvae, my mother rushed out of the house to my defence.

"Only a game," said my father. "We were just having a game." But

I knew otherwise. This terrifying Visigoth, fresh from the slaughter, had tried to murder me before we'd even reached teatime. I ran bleating to my mother, begging her to send this awful man back to the war where he so clearly belonged. My father's fears were also confirmed: unless something pretty firm in the way of paternal influence was applied here and now, I was going to turn out a first-rate milksop, an insufferable little wet.

My father's feelings about "wets" may have been streaked with anxieties of his own. Before the war, he had been a shy young man who had scraped through School Certificate at a minor public school. From there he had gone to a teachers' training college, and had done a probationary year of teaching (at which he had not been a success) before enlisting in the Territorial Army. In the army, he blossomed. He was rapidly promoted. He got married. He found himself suddenly a figure of some considerable poise and authority. When the war ended, he had hoped to transfer to the Regular Army but had been discouraged from doing so. By the time we met, he was 27, already at the end of a career he had been able to shine at. He had, along with his forced officer-style jocularity, a kind of preternatural gravity; he had learned to carry his own manliness with the air of an acolyte bearing an incense-boat. My father in his twenties was a profoundly responsible young man who had grown up late and then too quickly. He was stiff, avuncular and harsh by turns. I think that he felt my namby-pamby nature obscurely threatened his own manhood, and he set about toughening me up.

I was frightened of him. I was afraid of his irritable, headachey silences; afraid of his sudden gusts of good humour; afraid of his inscrutable, untouchable air; and afraid, most of all, of his summary beatings, which were administered court-martial fashion in his study. A toy left overnight in the path of the car got me a spanking; so did being unable to remember whether I had said "thank you" to my hostess after a four-year-old's birthday party. He introduced me to a new cold world of duties and punishments – a vastly complicated, unforgiving place in which the best one could hope for was to pass without comment. Perhaps my father had cause to believe that the world really was like this, and was simply doing his best to rescue me from the fool's paradise unwittingly created for me by my mother. I felt then that he was just jealous of my intimacy with her, and was taking his revenge.

For weeks after the war he hung about the house and garden. He clacked out letters to potential employers on my mother's old portable Olivetti. He practised golf swings. He rambled round and round the birdbath in his demob suit. He made gunnery calculations on his slide rule. I played gooseberry – a sullen child lurking in passageways, resentfully spying on my parents. I felt cuckolded, and showed it. When my father eventually found a job, as the local area secretary of TocH, his work took him out of the house most evenings: when he drove off to Wisbech and Peterborough and King's Lynn, I would try to seduce my mother back to the old days of our affair. We listened to *Dick Barton* on the wireless over cocoa, and then I would launch into an avalanche of bright talk, hoping to buy back her attention and distract her from the clock. I felt her joy at having my father home, and I think I did sense her distress at my conspicuous failure to share it. I also felt a twinge or two of shame at our snugness. From my father, I was beginning to learn that my behaviour was distinctly unmanly, and these cocoon-evenings were clouded with guilt. When my father said, as he did several times a week, "You are going to have to learn to stand up for yourself, old boy," I shrank from the idea but knew it to be unarguably right.

But my father and I grew grim with the responsibilities that had been placed on our shoulders. I think we both felt helpless. He had inherited a role in life which he could only conceive in the most old-fashioned terms: he had to become a Victorian husband and father, a pillar of the family, the heir to the fading Raban fortunes. I had inherited *him*. And we both chafed under the weight of these legacies, both of us too weak to carry them off with any style. He bullied me, and he in turn was bullied by the family dead. If I feared him, he had Furies of his own – the ancestors and elderly relations who had set him standards by which he could do nothing except fail.

My father was not an eldest son, nor was his father. It must have been just his seriousness, his air of being the sort of young man who could take responsibility, his obvious dutifulness towards his own father, that marked him out. Whatever it was, it seemed that every dotty uncle and crusty great aunt had named him as an executor of their wills. Whenever anyone in the family died, my father got busy with auctioneers and lawyers; and our house began to fill with heirlooms. Vans arrived with furniture and pictures and papers in tin boxes. Things went "into store", then had to be brought out because it cost too much to keep them in the repository. We were swamped by my father's ancestors.

They looked down on us disapprovingly from every wall. In vast, bad, oxidized oil portraits, in pencil-and-wash sketches, in delicate miniatures, in silhouettes, they glared dyspeptically from their frames. There was the Recorder of Bombay. There was General Sir Edward. There was Cousin Emma at her writing desk. There were countless Indian Army colonels and mean-mouthed clerics. There were General Sir Edward's military honours mounted on velvet in a glass case. On top of the wireless stood the family coat of arms (a raven, a boar's head, some battlements and a motto that I don't remember). They were joyless, oppressive trophies. They represented a hundred-and-something years of dim middle-class slogging through the ranks of the army and the church. The faces of these ancestors were like their furniture – stolid, graceless but well-made in that provincial English fashion which equates worth with bulk. There was no fun in them, and only the barest modicum of intelligence. They looked like people who had found the going hard, but had come through by sticking to the principles that had been drummed into them at boarding school.

We revered them, these implacable household gods. We tiptoed around their hideous furniture ("*Don't* play on the games table; it's an *antique*—"); we ate our fish fingers with their crested forks; we obediently tidied our own lives into the few humble corners that were left behind by the importunate family dead. My father bought books on genealogy (*How to Trace Your Family Tree* by L. G. Pine), and buried himself in index cards and the 1928 edition of *Burke's Landed Gentry*. Summer holidays turned into sustained bouts of ancestor-worship of a kind that might have been more appropriate to a pious Chinese than to an English middle-class family on its uppers. In a Bradford Jowett van (my mother's Ford had been sold, and I now rode second class, in the back) we trailed through Somerset, hunting for churchyards where remote cousins were supposed to have been buried. My father scraped the lichens off tombstones with a kitchen knife, while I looked for slow worms under fallen slates. On wet days, he took himself off to the record offices in Taunton and Exeter, where he ploughed through parish registers, checking births, marriages and deaths in 18th-century villages. "We come," he said, "from yeoman stock. Good yeoman stock."

Then there were the living to visit. Most seemed to be elderly women living with a "companion", and they stretched, like a row of hill forts, across southern England from Sussex to Devon. Each holiday, my father appeared to discover a new great aunt. Their houses were thatched, and smelled of must and dog. The ladies themselves were mannish, always up to something in the garden with a hoe and trug. The few men were immobilized, wrapped up in rugs, and talked in fluting falsetto voices. My grandfather, Harry Priaulx Raban (grown-ups called him "H.P."), had retired from his parish in Worcestershire to a Hampshire cottage where, on his good days, he used to celebrate an Anglo-Catholic mass of his own devising in a little room that he'd turned into an alfresco shrine. I sometimes acted as his server on these occasions, piping the responses to his piped versicles. A plain crucifix hung above the improvised altar, surrounded by framed photographs of Edwardian boys at Clifton College. At Prime and Compline and Communion, my grandfather paid homage to his own past in a way that had come to seem to me perfectly natural – for anyone in our family.

My father was barely thirty, yet we lived almost exclusively in the company of the old and the dead. Sometimes his old regimental friends would call, and there was a steady stream of youngish clergy-men and colleagues from TocH; these contemporaries brought a boisterous, irresponsible air into the house, a hint of fun which seemed alien to it. Its proper visitors were aunts and elderly cousins – people who nodded at the portraits on the walls and left their sticks in the rack by the front door. In private with my mother, my father had a lightness I have not done justice to. He liked *Punch*, and told stories, and spent a lot of time in the garage tinkering with the car: there was a boyishness about him which was always being forcibly squashed. The lugubrious solemnity was practised as a duty. He behaved as if it was incumbent on him to appear older, stuffier, more deferential than he really was. The silly world of gaiety and feeling was my mother's province, and I think my father felt a stab of guilt every time he entered it. It was *not manly*, not quite worthy of a serious Raban. So he overcompensated, with a surfeit of aunts and ancestors, and made his amends by constructing a vast family tree which he kept rolled up in a cardboard tube. Each year, new lines appeared; forgotten cousins many times removed were resurrected; our yeoman stock inched steadily back through the Georges and into the reigns of Queen Anne and Charles II.

I was five, then six, when my younger brothers were born. These additions to the tree struck me as needless. With ancestors like ours, who needed children? But I had been cuckolded before, and had learned to live with infidelity. Our household was already bulging with family, and my brothers simply added to the clutter. Though my own status was eroded. My mother constantly mixed up our names, and the two leaking babies and I got rechristened, for convenience's sake, as "the boys", a title that made me cringe with humiliation. I hated their swaddled plumpness, their milky smell, and felt that their babyhood somehow defeated what little progress I had made in the direction of manliness. Lined up with them on the back seat of the Bradford van, surrounded by their cardigans, their leggings, their bootees, their plastic chamber pots and teated bottles, I used to daydream myself into a state of haughty solitude. I acquired a habitual manner of grossly injured dignity.

If I have a single image of family life, it is of a meal table. There is a high chair in the picture, dirty bibs, spilt apple puree, food chaotically laid out in saucepans, a squeal, a smack, my father's suffering brow creased with migraine, my mother's harassed face ("Oh, *Blow!*"), and the line "William's made a smell" spoken by my younger brother through his adenoids. And over all this, the ancestors glower from their frames and the crested silver mocks from the tabletop. It isn't just the noise, the mess, the intrusive intimacies; it is that hopeless collision between the idea of Family as expounded by my father and the facts of family as we lived them out. We had ideas that were far beyond our means.

At this time my father must have been earning about £600 a year. Like most other lower-middle-class households, we were overcrowded, we had to make do on a shoestring budget and we had neither the money, the time nor the space for the dignities and civilities that my father craved. "We are," he reminded us, "a family of *gentlemen*." Was my teacher at school, I asked, a gentleman? No. A nice man, certainly, but not quite a gentleman. Was Mr Banham up the road a gentleman? No: Mr Banham was in trade. People in trade were not gentlemen: gentlemanliness, it was explained, had nothing to do with money; it was a matter of caste, taste and breeding – and we were gentlemen. This distinction caused me a great deal of anxiety. The few friends I made never turned out to be gentlemen. Some were "almost"; most were "not quite". Their fathers were often much better paid than mine, their accents (to my ears) just as clear. My mother was always keen to stretch the point and allow all sorts and conditions of men into our privileged class; but my father was a stickler for accuracy and knew a parvenu when he saw one. Consequently I was ashamed of my friends, though my mother always welcomed them, at least into the garden if not into the house. They didn't have ancestors and family trees like ours, and I half-despised and half-envied them their undistinguished ordinariness. Once or twice I was unwise enough to let on that I was marked by a secret distinction invisible to the eye – and the consequences tended to support my parents' conviction that the state system of education was barbarous and fit only for young hooligans. I was, predictably (especially since I started to get asthma the moment I stopped having coeliac), a thoroughly unpopular child. At primary school, I started to keep a score of the number of days I had lasted without crying in the playground. It stayed at zero, and I gave it up. But I always believed that I was bullied because I was "special". That too happened to you because you were a gentleman.

There was another family on our horizon. Uncle Peter – my mother's brother – lived on the suburban outskirts of Birmingham, and we saw him twice or three times a year. I was his godson, and after I was seven or eight I was occasionally allowed to stay at his house. For me, he was pure legend. Balding, affable, blasé, he would drop in out of the blue in a Jaguar car, smelling of soap and aftershave. Like my mother, Uncle Peter had been brought up by my grandmother in Switzerland, in the last days of servants; but somehow he had managed to escape being a gentleman. He'd taken a degree in engineering at Birmingham University, and during the war had served in the R.N.V.R. If Macmillan had wanted a symbol of postwar meritocratic affluence in the age of You've-Never-Had-It-So-Good, he might well have chosen Uncle Peter, with his car, his sailing boat, his first-in-the-road T.V. set and his centrally heated suburban villa. Uncle Peter had real class – with a flat *a* – but he was entirely innocent of the suffocating class snobbery which ruled our roost.

Staying at Uncle Peter's was like being admitted to Eden. There was no smell of guilt in the air, no piety to a lost past. Where we had ancestors, he had Peter Scott bird-paintings and framed photos of ocean racing yachts on his walls. Where we had shelves of family books (sermons, Baker's *Sport in Bengal, The Royal Kalendar,* first editions of Jane Austen, a Victorian *Encyclopedia Britannica*), Uncle Peter had copies of the *National Geographic* magazine, *Reader's Digest* condensed books and greenback Penguins. I had often been enchanted by the bright theatre of an illuminated department store window at dusk – the impossibly soft rugs, the virgin upholstery of the three-piece suite, the bottles and glasses set ready on gleaming coffee tables, the glow of steel standing lamps . . . a room designed for immaculate people without memories or consciences. The inside of Uncle Peter's house was like one of those windows come to life. It was my Brideshead. I was dazzled by its easy, expensive philistinism;

dazzled, too, by my girl cousins with their bicycles and tennis rackets and the casual, bantering way in which they talked to their parents.

On Sunday morning, no one went to church. I half expected a thunderbolt to strike us down for our audacity, but in Uncle Peter's family church was for weddings, funerals, baptisms and Christmas. Instead, we sat out on the breakfast patio, sunbathing. Uncle Peter stretched himself out on a scarlet barcalounger, put on dark glasses, and settled into his *Sunday Express*. I was nearly delirious. I hadn't realized that it was possible to break so many taboos at once, and Uncle Peter was breaking them all without so much as a flicker of acknowledgement that he was doing anything out of the ordinary. I also felt ashamed. I was so much grubbier, more awkward, more screwed-up than these strange people with their Californian ease and negligent freedom; like any trespasser in Eden, I was always expecting to be given the boot.

Given his belief in stock and blood-lines, it would have been hard for my father to be too openly critical of Uncle Peter. My mother's family (doctors and Shetland crofters) was, of course, not quite up to Raban standards, but Uncle Peter was still definitely a gentleman. So my father limited himself to a few warning shots delivered from a safe distance. "Don't suppose he gets more than 15 to the gallon out of *that car*." "Can't think what he must be paying for moorings for *that boat*."

"He's always going abroad to conferences," said my mother.

"One conference, dear. One conference that we actually *know* of."

To me, he was spoken of as "*your* Uncle Peter", which gave me a certain pride of possession, as I happily took responsibility for the 3.8 Jag, the decanter of Scotch and *that boat*. At Christmas and on my birthday he sent postal orders, and I was briefly *nouveau riche*, happily about to squander the money on status symbols on my own account, like fixed-spool fishing reels and lacquered cork floats. "You'd better put *that* in your post office savings. Hadn't you, old boy?" So Uncle Peter was laid up where neither moth nor rust corrupted. I loathed my savings-book. When, years later, I first heard the phrase "The Protestant Ethic", I knew exactly what it meant: it was my father's lectures on the subject of my post-office savings account.

"It's all very well, old boy, your wanting to throw your money down the drain in inessentials now. But when it comes to the time, what are you going to do about the Big Things, eh? Now, that money you've got in the post office; that *grows*. Sixpence in the pound mounts up, you know. Suppose . . . suppose, in, say, three or four years you want a bicycle. Where do you imagine that bicycle is going to come from? I'm afraid, old boy, that bicycles do not grow on trees."

But in Selly Oak I had ridden in the Jag, and skipped church on Sunday, and a splinter of doubt had lodged in my mind. There were, I now knew, places in the world where bicycles did grow on trees.

When it was announced ("Daddy has had a calling") that my father was going to seek ordination, I lay on the floor and howled with laughter. I can't remember why – it certainly wasn't in any spirit of satire. I think it may have been straightforward nervous hysteria in the face of the fact that my father was on such intimate terms with God. The question had been put to Him, and He had made His position clear. It all sounded a bit like having an interview with one's bank manager. But I was awed and proud. We were high Anglicans – so high that we could almost rub noses with the Romans. The priest, in his purple and gold vestments, was a figure of glorious authority. He was attended by boys swinging incense. He chanted services in plainsong. High in the pulpit, his surplice billowing round him, he exercised a mystique of a kind that, say, a politician could not hope to match. Had my father said that he was going to stand for parliament, I would have been impressed; when he said he was going to be a priest, I was awestruck. I grew intensely vain on the strength of his vocation. I was not only a gentleman; I was about to be the son of a priest. When bullied in the playground, I now thought of myself as a holy martyr, and my brows touched heaven. "Daddy's vocation" had singled him out from the ruck of common men, just as I expected soon to be singled out myself. I waited for my calling, and pitied my persecutors. At night, I had vivid fantasies in which God and I were entwined in a passionate embrace. By day, I spent my time staring out of the classroom window in a fog of distraction. I was not a clever child. My distinction was a secret between myself, my ancestors and God.

My father was thirty-three – a year younger than I am now – when he became a theological student. For the first time in my life, I realized that he was not actually as old as he had always seemed. We took a rented house on the outskirts of Bognor, and my father bicycled the six miles between there and his college in Chichester, staying in the house only at weekends. He wore a college scarf and went about in cycle clips; he played for the college cricket team and swotted up his notes. Now that he was more often away from the family than inside it, he lost his irritable hauteur, and I began to lose my fear of him. On Saturday afternoons, my mother brought my brothers and me to support his team from the boundary, where we were the centre of a group of pious, hearty young men with the arms of their white sweaters tied round their necks. At college, I think my father must have recaptured some of the ease that he'd felt in his wartime regiment. Most of the other students were younger than him, and he was like an easygoing adjutant among subalterns. I sensed – again for the first time – that he was proud of his family, and we were proud of him.

For those two years we were "living on capital" – an ominous phrase which meant, in effect, that my parents were blueing their post-office savings; and this hectic, once-in-a-lifetime gesture seemed to liberate and frighten them in equal parts. They went on a spree of economies, putting one gallon of petrol at a time in the car and buying everything in quantities so small that my mother appeared to be going shopping round the clock. They also hatched what was as far as I was concerned their greatest folly. They decided to scrape their last pennies together and send me to public school.

For once, I was happy at school. At Rose Green Primary I had made some friends (no gentlemen, but with my father now a student we were turning into daring bohemians). With private coaching, I muddled, a little improbably, through the eleven-plus, and had a place waiting for me at the grammar school in Chichester. But my parents were expecting to move house at least twice within the next three years, and at ten I had already attended four different schools (a dame, a prep and two primaries). That was the rational side. The irrational side was all to do with ancestors, gentility and manliness.

"Take this business of your asthma, old boy. It's all psychosomatic, you know. Psychosomatic. Know what psychosomatic means? In the head. It's all in the head. It means you bring it on yourself. Public school will clear that one up in no time."

The brochure arrived. My father had been at King's in the 1930s, and we pored over the blotchy photos of rugger pitches and the cathedral green. My father showed a new, alarming levity; we were boys together as he pitched into a slightly mad peroration about the joys of doing "The Classics" and taught me the basic rules of rugger on the drawing room carpet.

"Pass the ball behind you – like this. Always pass the ball behind, never in front."

His own fondest memory of King's had to do with being put into a laundry basket and having his arm broken. Somehow as my father told it it came out as pure pleasure. Every Sunday we checked over the public school rugby results where they were listed in small print at the back of the *Sunday Times*. When King's won, there was a celebratory air around the breakfast table; when they lost we were downcast too. My mother had some Cash's name-tapes made up: J. M. H. P. RABAN SCHOOL HOUSE. In the evenings, she sewed them into piles of socks, pants, shirts and towels, checking each item against the matron's printed list.

When we made our annual trek from aunt to aunt, I basked in the phrase, repeated like a litany, "Ah – Jonathan's off to public school, you know." God, I was special. Suddenly elevated out of "the boys", I towered with distinction. I could barely speak to my old friends at Rose Green – common little boys who played soccer and went on Sundays, if they went at all, to nonconformist churches.

At my confirmation service, the Bishop of Chichester preached on a text from Paul's Epistle to the Ephesians:

> I therefore, the prisoner of the Lord, beseech you
> that ye walk worthy of the vocation wherewith ye are called.

No one that year was walking more worthily than me. Already I was nursing my own calling and talking regularly to God. I walked in imaginary vestments, a halo of distinction faintly glowing round my person.

As my father pointed out, sending me to public school was going to mean sacrifices – enormous sacrifices. My mother was not going to be able to buy clothes; my brothers would have to live in hand-me-downs; with the price of tobacco as it was, my father was going to have to think seriously about giving up his pipe. This did frighten me. Despite the fact that I was living in an ever-inflating bubble of persecuted egotism, it did break in on me that the probable result of all this sacrifice was going to be that I was going to let everybody down. At nights, I strained to see myself sprinting away from the scrum towards the touch-line to score the winning try for School House; but the picture would never quite come right. When my father talked about the famous "house spirit", I was troubled by a stubborn image of myself skulking grubbily, shame-faced, on the fringe of things. I had always been the last to be picked for any side.

Would public school really change that? I tried fervently to believe so but some germ of realism made me doubt it. Certainly I felt singled out for peculiar honours, but my vocation was for something priestly and solitary; it wasn't for team games. I was scared by the other children whom I now affected to despise – and the prospect of living in a whole houseful of my contemporaries was frightening. I was beginning to suspect that I had my limits, and my faith in miracles was shaky. But with General Sir Edward and his cronies on one side, and the hand-me-downs and shiny skirts on the other, I went off to King's, teased by the notion that it was I who was the sacrifice.

One memory of being miserable at boarding school is much like another – and none are quite believable. I went when I was eleven; I left when I was sixteen; and I spent an unhealthy proportion of that five years wishing that I was dead. The usual story. For the holidays, I came home to beat my puzzled younger brothers black and blue. I was their monitor; they were my fags. So I was able to share with my family some of the benefits of going to public school.

Our family life seemed full of anomalies and bad fits. There was the problem of my father's age – one moment he was boyish, the next testily patriarchal. There was the mismatch between our actual circumstances and our secret splendour. There was the constant conflict between the superior Victorian family to which we were supposed to belong and the squally muddle of our everyday life. We were short on education, short on money, short on manners; and the shorter we got, the taller grew our inward esteem. In the Anglican Church, and in the succession of clergy-houses that we moved to, we found a kind of objective correlative for our private family paradoxes.

In the 1950s, the Church of England had not changed all that much since George Herbert was a parish priest. It hadn't yet been hit by "existential theology" or the decadent tomfoolery of the Charismatic Movement. It still stood firm on Parson's Freehold and the idea that the priest was third in line to the squire and the doctor. Even on urban housing estates, where churches were plonked down in the middle to be vandalized before they'd had a chance to be consecrated, the vicar was expected to behave as he would in an agricultural village. The Church was smiled on by the housing authorities presumably because it was felt that it might introduce a cheery, villagey note of "community" into these godforsaken places. Put a beaming cleric in dog-collar and cassock in Churchill Crescent or Keynes Road, and you are halfway to creating another Tiddlepuddle Magna. In one sense, the clergyman was expressly hired to be an anomaly. Like our family, the Church had a grand past but was down on its luck. Like our family, it was succoured by a sense of its own inner virtue and stature in the face of utter indifference from 90 per cent of the rest of the world. Like my own, its public face was one of superior injured dignity.

My father was given the curacy of a council estate just outside Winchester, and we turned into a parsonage family. To begin with, the ancestors were moved into a council house, disdainfully slumming it in the cramped lounge-diner. They had probably known worse. Long-suffering, ox-like men, their schools, like mine, had prepared them for temporary quarters and outposts of Empire. The Weeke Estate was much like an Indian hill station, with hard rations, lousy architecture and nothing to speak of in the way of society. It was no accident that the one author whose works we possessed in their entirety, in the uniform Swastika edition, was Kipling.

The parsonage was an island. People came to it when they wanted *rites de passage* – to be baptized, married and buried. Or they were in distress: tramps with tall stories on the look-out for a soft touch; pregnant girls, dragged there by grave, ashamed parents; middle-aged women who cried easily; and lots of shadowy people, talking in low confessional voices beyond the closed door of my father's study. When they came to the house, their manners were formal; often they had put on best suits for the occasion. What is it that people want from a priest? Understanding, surely, but not ease or intimacy. Most of all, I suspect, they feel that only a priest can clothe a bitter private hurt or mess with the gravity and dignity that they would like it to deserve.

My father seemed cold and inhibited towards me as if he found our biological connection an embarrassment. But to his parishioners he was able to show a sympathy, even a warmth, that perhaps depended on the formal distance which lay between him and them. In mufti, he was often stiff and blundering. In the uniform of his cassock and his office, he was gentle and considerate. The very things that might have marked him as a misfit outside the priesthood enabled him to be a good priest. I've known a number of people who have told me how much they have admired him, been grateful to him, and thought of him as a consummately good man.

At that time, though, for me he was pure Jekyll and Hyde. I thought of him as a hypocritical actor. Offstage, he seemed to be perpetually irritable, perpetually swallowing aspirins, never to be disturbed. His study – a chaos of papers under a blue pall of St Bruno Rough Cut tobacco smoke – was a place I was summoned to, for a long series of awkward, sometimes tearful, occasionally violent interviews. Once I tried to knock him down, and in my memory he collapses in an amazed heap among the parish magazines, narrowly avoiding cracking his skull on the duplicating machine. But that is probably an Oedipal fantasy. What really happened, I'm afraid, is that the amazement was on my face, and that the collapse too was mine – into weeping apologies. Usually, though, these confrontations followed a pattern as cold and stereotyped as a chess gambit. I stood; my father sat, shuffling papers, filling his pipe. While he stared beyond me out of the window, he would talk with tired logic about my misdemeanours (terrible school reports, insolence, laziness in the house, rumours of girls). The final line was always the same.

"I'm afraid that the trouble with you . . . old boy . . . is that you appear to have no thought for anyone except yourself."

Long, long pause. Sound of pipe dottle bubbling in a stem. A faint groan from my father. A muttered monosyllable from me.

"What did you say?"

"Sorry."

"Sorry – *what*?"

"Sorry . . . *Daddy*."

Another pause, while my father gazes sadly out over a landscape of sandpiles, stray dogs and upturned tricycles.

"I do wish you'd make *some* sort of an effort."

I did see his point. The sacrifices that were being made on my behalf were all too visible. My father's clothes had been worn to a bluebottle sheen. His shoes gaped. And I was at public school. Worse, I knew that I was wrong, perhaps even evil, when I accused him of hypocrisy. Here he was, wearing himself through on my behalf, and driving himself to nervous exhaustion in the parish; what right had I to ask even more of a man who was clearly twothirds of the way to being a living saint? It was further evidence – as if I needed any more – of my own selfishness. With the help of a Penguin book on psychology I diagnosed myself as a psychopath.

The parsonage became a refuge for a number of people who, as social casualties go, were the walking wounded. Most had been left stranded – as we had – in the wrong age or the wrong class.

Schoolmistresses, social workers, district nurses, they attached themselves to the fringe of the family, dropping in unannounced with small presents and staying on into the night talking with my father. The closest, most persistent ones were made honorary aunts, and they liked to busy themselves in the house, clucking over my brothers, "helping" my mother, and making strained conversation with me, until my father, his cassock flapping round his heels, came home from his rounds.

"Hello, dear!" Having spotted the parked Morris Minors round the corner, he had the cheeriness of someone walking through the French windows in a drawing room comedy. He always discovered the lurking aunts with delighted surprise. "Ah, Elspeth!" And Miss Stockbridge, or Miss Winnall, or Miss Crawley, glandularly mountainous in tweeds, would produce a tiny, astonished little Bo-Beep voice – "Oh, he*ll*o, Peter!" – as if their meeting was a stroke of wild coincidence. From my room upstairs, I would hear my father's "Hmmn . . . hmmn . . . yes . . . yes . . . yes . . . *Oh*, dear. Ah. ha-ha," while the high, put-upon frequency of the adoptive aunt was lost to all except my father and the neighbourhood dogs.

Much later, when they'd gone, I'd hear my mother's voice. "Oh, poor old Elspeth – the *poor* soul!" And my father would answer, "I'm afraid the trouble with *that* one . . ."

The social worker's dealings with his client do have some formal limits. But with a clergyman, nothing is out of bounds. People came to my father for reassurances of a kind no doctor or psychiatrist could offer. This meant that everyone who arrived at the parsonage – even those who came in the guise of my parents' friends – presented themselves as crocks and casualties. The ones who came and came again had things wrong with them that were far too vague to ever cure. They were spiritual things – weaknesses and discontents for which the doctrine of the Resurrection was the only answer. My father had put himself in the position of Miss Lonelyhearts, but he had more pride and less saving cynicism than the columnist in Nathanael West's novel; and his view of this world to which he'd opened our door was one of compassionate condescension.

"We in the parsonage . . ." "In the parsonage family . . ." "As a son of the parsonage . . ." My father's lectures nearly always started out with one or other of these riders. We were expected to be exemplary. Our standards of moral and social decorum – unlike those of the natives among whom we'd been posted – were supposed to be beyond either criticism or pity. Another favourite was "More people know Tom Fool than Tom Fool knows"; and I went about the council estate aware that it was full of spies behind curtains. One slip from me, and my father's standing in his parish could come a cropper. On the estate as on the rugger field, I was always letting our side down. At twelve and thirteen, up to no particular good with boys of my own age from the youth club, I sometimes came face to face with my father on his rounds, and pretended not to see him. He misinterpreted these gestures, and thought I was trying to "cut" him. I wasn't. I was simply ashamed to be caught fraternizing with the children of his problem families – boys who, as he pointed out, had not had my advantages, and whose obvious shortcomings deserved compassion, not uncritical collusion.

On the far fringes of the parish, where the houses stood back from the road behind trees and rhododendrons, the gentry lived. Like the ancestors, they were retired colonels and commanders, admirals and generals. Their children went to boarding schools. Their houses smelled of flowers, dry sherry and wax polish. They weren't problem families; and we visited them shyly when bidden, like poor cousins, trying as best we could to tiptoe through their loud gravel. It usually took fifteen minutes for me to find myself out on the back lawn with their daughter, where we would both stand awkwardly scuffing our heels and smiling fiendishly.

"Do you play tennis?"

"No."

"Oh what a pity. When Henry's here, we play a lot of tennis. But Henry's at Dartmouth, you know."

"Oh, dear."

"Mummy said she thought you might play tennis."

"I'm sorry."

"Oh – not to worry!"

Desperation. With an hour to kill, we would inspect abandoned tree-houses like a pair of undertakers visiting a cemetery on their day off.

"I say, you didn't hear a bell, did you?"

"I don't think so."

"I could have sworn . . . I suppose Mrs Hawkins must be late with tea. Awfully boring for you, I'm afraid."

"Oh, no! No, no, no!"

'Are you in YF?"

"Er . . . I don't think so."

"Ah, there's the bell. Good-oh."

Then, quite suddenly in the middle of the 1950s, a lot of bells began to ring. The first one I remember hearing was Frankie Lymon singing "I'm not a juvenile delinquent", which went to the top of the hit parade sometime in 1955, I think. Bill Haley and his Comets made their first British tour, and in Worcester, where I was at school, there was hardly a seat left intact after *Rock Around The Clock* was shown at the Gaumont. I read *Look Back In Anger*, Joyce's *Portrait of the Artist*, and Anouilh's *Antigone*, and somehow managed to muddle them together into a single work of which I was the hero. There was the Chris Barber band and the Beaulieu Jazz Festival. There was C.N.D., which for me meant the triumphant end of the C.C.F. All at once it was possible to think of oneself as a member of a generation and not as a member of a family; and the generation provided me with new standards that were even more liberated than Uncle Peter's. It seemed that overnight my minuses had all changed to pluses. The generation loathed my ancestors even more than I did; it despised team games; its heroes were sulky, sickly solitaries like Juliette Greco in her death-mask phase. At sixteen, I discovered that the inchoate mess of my relations with my father had been all the time, unknown to me, a key battle in the coming revolution. And I was on the winning side. It was like having my dream of scoring the winning try in the house match come true. We continued to have rows – about my wearing a C.N.D. badge at family meals, about bringing *that* rag into *this* house (the *New Statesman* into the vicarage), about girls ("Not really the kind of girl you'd wish to introduce to Mummy, is she?"), about the width of my trouser-bottoms (18 was permissible, but 16 was "teddy boy"). But I too now wore an expression of distant superiority through these wrangles. An outsider looking in might have seen us as a pair of quarrelling mirror-images – two glazed faces speaking in the accents of the same old school.

I was much too absorbed in the enthralling process of my own adolescence to notice that bells had begun to ring for my father too. Something happened. Perhaps it came about on his parish rounds, as he found himself drawn in to the tangle of other people's lives, unable, finally, to maintain his distance. Perhaps it had to do with the difficulties he found himself in when he skirmished with the local worthies who regarded the church as an extension of their own drawing rooms. Perhaps he just strayed one day from under the oppressive shadow of the family past and found the air clearer and the going easier. At any rate, he changed. The first thing to go was his Anglo-Catholicism, which he dropped in favour of a kind of basic, ecumenical Christianity. Sometime in the 1960s, he slipped out of his ancestral family toryism and became a Labour voter. He exchanged his living in a Hampshire village for a vast parish of tower blocks in Southampton. His passion for ancestor-hunting turned into a scholarly interest in social history. On holiday one year, he grew a beard. It was as if a row of buttons on a tight waistcoat had suddenly given way.

I have written about him as if he was dead – the oedipal fantasy again. But when we see each other now, I find it hard to detect more than shadows of the man I remember as my father. The ancestors are still hanging on the walls of his vicarage, but they have the air of inherited lumber now, and have lost their power to hex. We talk easily. We both think of ourselves as victims of our upbringing – and beneficiaries of it too. The solitariness of his priesthood and my writing is a shared legacy: we have each had to learn how to be alone in society in the practice of our odd, anomalous crafts. A little more than ten years ago, we both suddenly realized that we were chips off the same family block – and I think that the discovery surprised him as much as it did me. When I showed my father this piece in galley proof, he said: "What you've written here is really a confession on my behalf."

It is certainly a confession on mine. Looking at the other man, it occurs to me that he may have been a wilful invention of my own. Did I conceive him on the green when I was three as a jealous, defensive fiction? And did I let this fiction die only when I was old enough to leave the family and do without a father to be afraid of?

Perhaps. I don't know. "There's some *slight* exaggeration – I hope," my father said, handing me back my galley sheets. I'm afraid so.

1977

LIVING WITH LOOSE ENDS

One of the oddest features of western Christianized culture is its ready acceptance of the myth of the stable family and the happy marriage. We have been taught to accept the myth not as an heroic ideal, something good, brave, and nearly impossible to fulfil, but as the very fibre of normal life. Given most families and most marriages, the belief seems admirable but foolhardy. People rattle together inside one house, continually at cross-purposes. Some take to sopping gin in the afternoons. Some get taken away in vans. Outsiders feel cruelly excluded from the companionable glow within, while insiders feel the constriction tighten like an asthmatic lung. Really happy marriages rapidly become legendary as freaks of nature. After supper at the Goodhearts, the guests disperse, simultaneously elated at having been in the presence of the myth made flesh and bleakly depressed at how shoddy their own more compromised arrangements seem by comparison. Even the worst marriages, as Meredith showed with tactless brilliance in *Modern Love*, can forge a flawless counterfeit of the ideal when occasion demands it.

> We,
> Enamoured of an acting nought can tire,
> Each other, like true hypocrites, admire;
> Warm-lighted looks, Love's ephemeriae,
> Shoot gaily o'er the dishes and the wine.
> We waken envy of our happy lot.
> Fast, sweet, and golden, shows the marriage-knot.
> Dear guests, you now have seen Love's corpse-light shine.

Saint Paul, like most bachelors, was over-sanguine. Many people marry and burn. So it was not really surprising that when the B.B.C. documentary, *The Family*, was screened on television, there were two opposed waves of reaction to it. One was a burst of predictable fury at seeing a sacred myth defiled. The other, much more powerful and long-lasting, was a huge sigh of relief at seeing an ancient taboo broached at last. The Wilkinses, with their painful inarticulacy, their slablike silences, their spasmodic outbreaks of affection and concern interspersed with long wounding passages of hostility, their air of suffocating for lack of space to be themselves, their capacity to suddenly turn and maul whoever happened at that moment to be the weakest member of the pack, were, after all, much like us. A number of reviewers (I remember particularly Joan Bakewell in the *Listener*) took the series as an opportunity to make a personal confession, an acknowledgement of what had been until then an almost entirely unacknowledged life. *The Family* was an important clearing of the air; it brought out into the open something that had always been known in private but rarely talked about in public. (It still isn't. I just rang a friend at her office to check the name of the Wilkinses, and overheard her asking a colleague, "Do you remember the name of that *awful* family who were in *The Family*?" I have stayed with her family. They are certainly not "awful", but if they admitted a hand-held camera into their life for a couple of months, they would not look so different from the Wilkinses. Their voices are classier, their tactics perhaps a little more oblique; their one real point of difference is that they have the middle-class knack of sounding determinedly gay about themselves – a tiresome habit which would quickly get them labelled as "awful" by those numerous members of the population who are accustomed to less indirect methods of social intercourse.)

Giving credence to the unacknowledged life of society should not mean that we have to demolish contemptuously the myth of marriage and the family. Recognizing one's kinship with the Wilkinses does not automatically make one a disciple of David Cooper's hysterical demythologizing. The myth is both an heroic and a necessary one. Most ways of living in society outside the family are more strenuous, more unhappy, more likely to cripple the individual with an over-weening sense of his inadequacy before the rigours of the world. But we have made the myth the object of such exclusive and fanatical belief that too many people are quite unnecessarily shamed and made guilty by their inability to live up to it.

It bestrides us, exerting a slow, continuous, enervating pressure on our lives. Those who live outside the conventional family have to learn to develop the mentality of conscious deviants; at best trying to relish a freedom they do not wholly welcome, at worst feeling that they have been gratuitously debarred from participating in the only reality which society at large recognizes as being properly real. Out of the family, it is often hard not to feel like the astigmatic child who had been left behind after the teams have been picked. Inside the family, one is made insistently aware of the widening gulf between the squally here-and-now and the bright arc of the myth as it sails, oppressively yet unattainably, over one's head. The *possibility* is forever being attested to – in television advertisements, in fictions of every kind, in the small change of everyday language, and, occasionally, in the real lives of acquaintances and friends. (Though, somehow, it always seems to be one's acquaintances and not one's friends who manage to live on this mythological scale; families tend to look at their best when seen from a distance.)

In life, these issues are the proper province of those who have to deal with mental illness and breakdown. I am more concerned here with some of their implications for literature – or, more particularly, for novels and autobiographies. Poetry, with its ritual independence of social convention and its easy emphasis on the supremacy of the first person, has not been notably enslaved to a vision of family life. But the novel has. Pulp romantic fiction conventionally ends with a wedding, as if all the turmoil and uncertainty of life ceased with marriage – as if characters stopped being interesting individuals at that point and became creatures of predictable history. To be a parent, to grow old, to amass wealth, is to take one's place in the cycle of shared public rituals, and so to drift out of the novelist's hands and into those of the mythologist. The interest of the romantic writer is focused on the prehistoric life of people before they become full members of society.

Even the picaresque, the form of fiction which appears to deal most squarely with life outside the family, grants that life a status which is merely temporary and provisional. If the catalogue of adventures is to assume a meaning, then it demands to be seen from a retrospective point of moral equilibrium – from within the family. Marriage and death serve equally well as devices by which unruly heroes can be brought to book before the stern jury of father, mother, wife and child. Remember how the last sentence in *Pendennis* ends:

> Knowing how mean the best of us is, let us give a hand of charity to Arthur Pendennis, with all his faults and short-comings, who does not claim to be a hero, but only a man and a brother.

When Thackeray extends that hand of charity on behalf of "us", he speaks as the father of the family which is English society. Pendennis is restored from fiction to life by being made to bear the responsibilities of being a husband and father himself.

> His children or their mother have never heard a harsh word from him; and when his fits of moodiness and solitude are over, welcome him back with a never-failing regard and confidence.

And such is the elasticity of the family, that there is virtually no act of rebellion or revenge that cannot be tolerated as a little fit of moodiness or solitude.

The special case of the picaresque novel reveals a larger truth about novels in general. For to have a narrative to tell at all one needs the continuity of relations, the stake in the future and the fixed point of moral certitude which the family provides. The novel does not thrive on one-night stands. If, as Iris Murdoch argued in her study of Sartre, prose fiction uniquely accommodates the inherent contingency of life, it's also true that it cannot bear too much contingency. Some lives are simply too random, too accidental, too lacking in moral or historical direction, for novels to make much sense of them. And literature, even the most serious literature, is as prejudiced against these lives as the censorious matrons of both sexes who set themselves up as custodians of society's morals.

Loose-ended lives conventionally belong to the sub-plot; case histories, there to illustrate what happens to people who drift out of the mainstream and land up in the stagnant creeks where the feckless, the unfamilied, the criminal and the psychopathic foregather. In Trollope's *The Prime Minister*, for instance, the unsuccessful adventurer and social climber Ferdinand Lopez is given the exemplary career of the man who lives above his means, takes chances and trusts his luck. He comes to a particularly bloody end, throwing himself under an express train at Tenway Junction. But before smashing him to atoms, Trollope allows him to marry – to submit to the final test of whether he can conceivably make a proper member of society. He fails as a family man just as surely as he failed as a bachelor: the railway terminus therefore awaits him as his inevitable fate. Trollope's description of Tenway Junction is important here – it is one of his light, clear passages of symbolism, handled with such ease and deftness that one barely notices the symbolic weight it carries so effortlessly.

> From this spot, some six or seven miles distant from London, lines diverge east, west, and north, north-east, and north-west, round the metropolis in every direction, and with direct communication with every other line in and out of London. It is a marvellous place, quite unintelligible to the uninitiated, and yet daily used by thousands who only know that when they get there, they are to do what someone tells them. The space occupied by the convergent rails seems to be insufficient for a large farm. And these rails always run one into another with sloping joints, and cross passages, and mysterious meandering sidings, till it seems to the thoughtful stranger to be impossible that the best trained engine should know its own line.

This seems to me one of the most concise, exact and illuminating descriptions of English society that I have read anywhere in 19th-century fiction. From it, one grasps instantly the real nature of Lopez's downfall. He failed to do what he was told. A poorly trained engine (his foreign ancestry, of course, gets him into a great deal of trouble with Father), he did not know his own line. Trying to leap from one milieu to another, travelling arrogantly and alone, he is finally crushed into the rails of the social labyrinth. When Trollope shifts to a description of the other passengers waiting on the plat-forms, we see the people who belong to the mainstream of the novel from whose ranks all central characters are drawn.

> Men and women, – especially the men, for the women knowing their ignorance are generally willing to trust to the pundits of the place, – look doubtful, uneasy, and bewil-dered. But they all do get properly placed and unplaced, so that the spectator at last acknowledges that over all this apparent chaos there is presiding a great genius of order.

But the only way of placing the Lopezes of the world is to arrange for their extinction. Trollope's description of the station platforms is a thumbnail sketch of every novel of society. In such novels, the presiding genius of order expresses himself by putting on a festival of nuptials in the last or last-but-one chapter, and woe betide those characters who, like Lopez, prove themselves to be unmarryable.

The logic of prose narrative in English fiction is rooted in the institution of the family. The unfamilied life is inherently minor, or tragic, or aberrant. Sometimes, in Jean Rhys's novels for instance, it is allowed to occupy the foreground of the book, but it never succeeds in losing the bohemian taint of oddity and extremity. *After Leaving Mr Mackenzie*, *Voyage in the Dark*, and *Good Morning, Midnight* are like sub-plots which have escaped from much longer and more conventional novels. Outside the family, life takes on a jumpy arbitrariness. Miss Rhys's style is one in which connections of any kind are hard to come by. It seizes on physical objects like a drowning man clutching at a lifebelt – as the only constants in a pathologically fluctuating world. Between one sentence and another, one chapter and the next, lies a void of chance in which anything might happen. The narrative moves in a series of nervous hops and jumps. Most importantly, it has no confidence in conclusions, no sense of an ending. What we are given instead is a kind of pivotal caesura, the hypothetical dead spot in the turning circle which signals only that the whole ghastly business is about to begin all over again. The closing sentences of *After Leaving Mr Mackenzie* and *Voyage in the Dark* indicate this perfectly:

> When their voices stopped the ray of light came in under the door like the last thrust of remembering before everything is blotted out. I lay and watched it and thought about starting all over again. And about being new and fresh. And about mornings, and misty days, when anything might happen. And about starting all over again . . .

> The street was cool and full of grey shadows. Lights were beginning to come out in the cafés. It was the hour between dog and wolf, as they say.

The string of *ands*, the line of dots, the tone of apprehensive provisionality – these are the stylistic marks of the unfamilied life. So too is the cyclonic plot – a whirlwind of events which will at some unspecified time on the far side of the future bear its victim to extinction. Tenway Junction waits as surely for Miss Rhys's heroines as it did for Lopez.

Yet these techniques announce, almost in every sentence, just how far this kind of life diverges from what it consoles us to think of as the normal. In the shadows behind Jean Rhys's fiction lies a vision of the family, that safe, conclusive institution from which her characters have had the bad luck to have been expelled or have rendered themselves ineligible to join. Both literally and metaphorically, they are exiles, with the exile's cruel memory of that alternative life which he has lost. In *Voyage in the Dark*, Anna Morgan imaginatively conflates the ideas of the family, England, and a corny advertisement on a street-hoarding.

> I got into bed and lay there . . . thinking of that picture advertising the Biscuits Like Mother Makes, as Fresh in the Tropics as in the Motherland, Packed in Airtight Tins, which they stuck up on a hoarding at the end of Market Street.
>
> There was a little girl in a pink dress eating a large yellow biscuit studded with currants – what they called a squashed-fly biscuit – and a little boy in a sailor-suit, trundling a hoop, looking back over his shoulder at the little girl. There was a tidy green tree and a shiny pale-blue sky, so close that if the little girl had stretched her arm up she could

have touched it. (God is always near us. So cosy.) And a
high dark wall behind the little girl.
    Underneath the picture was written:
        The past is dear,
        The future clear,
        And, best of all, the present.
    But it was the wall that mattered.
    And that used to be my idea of what England was like.

Vulgar, sentimental, insidiously powerful, that notion of family
life, with its attendant view of a well-ordered personal history, haunts
all those who are on the margins of society. It is their lost Eden, the
Great Good Place from which they have been cast out. Condemned
to live on the wrong side of the wall, they learn to regard the texture
of their own lives as being temporary and freakish; the result of an
accidental warp in the social order. Even in the hands of a writer like
Jean Rhys, such lives are not granted the power of mere ordinariness.
    It seems distinctly odd that novelists should be so ready to collude
with that view of the family promulgated by domestic moralists like
Mrs Whitehouse and the anonymous authors of Oxo and Bisto
advertisements. Yet the sweet dream of the Family as an ideal appears
to be resolutely impervious to modification by experience. Writers
whose own families have been hell to live in – Dickens, for instance
– have been among the most strenuous propagandists for the family
in their fiction. So too have writers who haven't really had a family
at all – Jane Austen, E. M. Forster, Ivy Compton-Burnett. It's worth
mentioning that Thackeray, who loved to pass himself off as the
supreme family-man in his novels, spent rather more time than he
should have done in escaping from his ailing wife in the Boltons to
the alcoholic company of his cronies in the Garrick Club. If the idea
of the family has been essential to the development of the novel, a
great deal of bad faith has gone into sustaining a continued belief in
it.
    Perhaps no writer in recent times has exposed his own unfamilied
life as clearly and forcefully as J. R. Ackerley did in *My Father and
Myself.* Yet the book is so badly scarred that it sometimes seems
miraculous that Ackerley should have been able to write it at all. Its
style is stiff with Ackerley's sense of his own oddity. There is a
peculiar flatness and coldness of tone in his writing; he has the
wounded solitary's habit of repelling sympathy because sympathy is
something he has learned not to expect or rely on. "I care for nobody,

no, not I, and nobody cares for me," sang the Miller of Dee with deceptive jollity; and a remark made by Ackerley about his social manner reveals a good deal about his tightly-buttoned literary style:

> I . . . wear a defensive mask, a deadpan look; when I think I have betrayed, under strain, the sickening anxieties and nervous fears from which I often suffer, I am praised for my coolness and self-possession, the rabbit within is not suspected.

The language of feeling is given short shrift in *My Father and Myself.* What we are given instead is facts – thousands of them, scrupulously marshalled and observed. One is reminded of those English Compositions that teachers like to set in primary schools: describe a day in your life to a Martian. Ackerley writes for Martians. His book is burdened by the evident conviction that his experience is so remote from that of the people he assumes will be his readers, that it cannot be properly shared, only exhibited and catalogued. His epic, unrewarding, homosexual odyssey, his eventual domestic peace in the company of Tulip, are light-years away from the "normal" life of marriage and the family. They are so distant, indeed, that Ackerley seems uncertain whether they can be meaningfully conveyed in language at all. The book is peppered with self-derisory scatological jokes, as if the author was trying to milk a sneer from his reader, in place of the more conventional libation of a tear. ". . . Others, to whom this superficial sketch of myself may be of value when I lie under another sort of sod." Again and again, Ackerley tempts one into a gratuitous alienation from his life. Triumphantly, he fails – in spite of all the opposition he has himself erected against the reader's sympathy.

My Father and Myself, like the novels of the unfamilied life which I have mentioned, is controlled, even persecuted, by the knowledge that what it describes is freakish and aberrant. It takes the form of a self-excoriating parody of a romantic novel, as Ackerley chases the receding vision of his Ideal Friend through the book, and ends up wedded, in the appendix, to an Alsatian bitch. This curious nuptial scene, with its happily-ever-after finality, stands as a rich symbol of the gulf which separates those with families from those without. It also indicates how even the most solitary men find themselves living in the shadow of the marriage they were unable to make, the family they couldn't belong to. At the heart of *My Father and Myself,* there is a profound conviction of shame and failure. But there is also something unreasonable about it. Ackerley, as he says himself, was so intensely self-absorbed that there was no room in his life for anyone else. He had his sexual adventures, his literary friendships, his dogs. Why should he have been so tormented by this notion of the Lost Family? Is the loose-ended life of the kind that Ackerley lived really so cold and arid? Or was Ackerley simply the victim of social propaganda? He was himself the child of a bourgeois marriage, and was brought up in a family which was founded on a liberal quota of lies and secrecies. I suspect that he absorbed its mythology all too well; and the mythology caused him to suffer a quite unnecessary amount of guilt and misery.

Ackerley's father maintained another household in Barnes. He had three illegitimate daughters by a woman called Muriel whose real surname is still obscure, though she took the name Perry. From this second household – which couldn't by any stretch of the imagination be called a bourgeois family – has come another book, written by A. R. Ackerley's youngest daughter, Diana Petre. *The Secret Orchard of A. R. Ackerley** is utterly different from *My Father and Myself*. Miss Petre writes as if the usual conventions for describing the unfamilied life did not exist. She also writes so finely, with such dramatic resonance and completeness, that *The Secret Orchard of A. R. Ackerley* reads more like a novel than an autobiography. Had it been a novel, I think reviewers might well have seized on it as the most original piece of English fiction to have been published this year: as it is, it had been politely complimented on being almost as good as *My Father and Myself*. It is very, very much more interesting than that.

In her preface, Miss Petre writes of her mother:

> She was brought up in an age of intrigue and sexual secrecy and she never questioned the mores of her time. Her life was not a happy one; indeed, it was often almost too much for her, and the story I have tried to tell is a rather upsetting one. I have done my best to expose her secrets in the belief that her ineradicable shame was mistaken; on the contrary, I see her courage and loyalty as matters for pride, and her long struggle with her own difficult nature as a story that deserves better than the modest oblivion with which she did all in her power to stifle it.

* Diana Petre, *The Secret Orchard of A. R. Ackerley* (London: Hamish Hamilton).

That statement is true, I think, not just of Muriel Perry but of J. R. Ackerley, Jean Rhys's "Anna Morgan", and of a vast number of people in both life and fiction who have lived outside the conventional family. Their lives have been hidden in shame, secrecy and oblivion. When they have been exposed at all, they have usually been given the pathos of failure or the unnatural dignity of tragedy. Diana Petre, in her exploration of the lives of her mother, herself and her two sisters, has restored them to the much more important dignity of ordinariness. She has lived in a world of loose ends and found it normal.

Muriel Perry was silly, flirty and abstracted; at her best in hotel rooms, which she sprayed with Guerlain's "Jicky" to make them smell like home. In 1912, as soon as she had given birth to Diana Petre, she abandoned the house in Barnes, leaving her children in the care of a Dickensian crone called Miss Coutts who dressed in black, pored over her bible, stank of pee, and turned her filthy room into a treasure trove of goods purloined from her charges. Their father, A. R. Ackerley, would turn up in a chauffeur-driven car bulging with presents which they were never allowed to enjoy. He was "Uncle Bodger" and "William Whiteley, the Universal Provider", and danced the children on his knee; a practice that Miss Coutts regarded with grim Presbyterian disapproval, though she enjoyed having her nipples stroked by Diana. Muriel, meanwhile, was gadding about London and Europe. She ran a troop-kitchen during the war with notable bravery and efficiency. In Italy, she was decorated by the Duke of Aosta, and later became his mistress. After ten years of this erratic butterfly life, she suddenly arrived back in Barnes in a rust-coloured veil and a whiff of "Jicky". Her children – whom she had not seen since they were babies – were unrecognizable: "two giraffe-like creatures and a spindly small one, all freak-thin and poor looking". They had been so starved by Miss Coutts that they were suffering from rickets. Muriel moved back in, playing Mother, as if her ten-year absence had been a trip up the road to the corner shop. The household, with its two women and three girls, was hopelessly out of kilter; a feckless and unbalanced place whose inhabitants all drifted in their separate cocoons of privacy and indifference. "Sometimes," writes Miss Petre, "in a despairing effort to make contact with some living thing, I'd dig up the worms from the borders and lay them in a line on the lawn and kiss them one by one".

Muriel's ideas of middle-class motherhood were distinctly offbeat. For a treat, she would take her children off to Barnes Common, open a bottle of champagne, and regale them with her wartime escapades.

On her good days she lay in bed, holding an open salon in her boudoir. On her bad days she locked herself in her room and drank, only to emerge at night, weeping in a dressing gown, stoned out of her mind. She and her children lived in that other alternative society of the unfamilied; visiting the flats of her lone women friends, never trespassing into the world of the comfortably married and socialized. Miss Petre's description of her mother's acquaintances deserves quotation; it also illustrates how her book has the symbolic control and management of good fiction.

> They were all of the same type, rather beautiful, unmarried and childless, idle and lonely, disillusioned with life, solitary drinkers when we knew them, and they all seemed to live on money left them by mysterious men.
>
> Of these women Irene was the most striking, with her classic profile and porcelain skin. She lived in a flat off Baker Street and Muriel sometimes took us with her to lunch there. In the dining-room there was a small round looking glass hung in the most curious place, right up in the cornice; and it was hung at an abrupt angle, trained down like a camera on to the chair at the head of the table. Here sat Irene. When she was talking to Muriel she faced this little mirror in the ceiling, watching herself, and when Muriel was talking to her Irene was still gazing upwards, her lips drawn forward a little, as though for a kiss. She couldn't take her eyes off herself. Sometimes she would turn her head to one side as far as was possible while still maintaining her gaze in the mirror, but of course here in the dining-room the beloved profile was denied to her.

That image of solipsistic vanity attaches itself to nearly every character in the book. Everyone alternately stifles for lack of contact with anothing living thing and consoles herself with her own reflected face. On occasions, somebody vanishes out of the story altogether, into marriage. When this happens, it is as if they had gone behind a forbidden bead curtain; they are not mentioned again unless their marriage breaks and they return to the life of looking glasses and empty bottles. Somewhere behind the scenes, Miss Petre herself marries and separates during the course of the narrative, but the whole event takes place in two throwaway subordinate clauses. Real life, in *The Secret Orchard of A. R. Ackerley*, is essentially solitary. And Miss Petre has the solitary's gift for rooting out the solitariness in others. The genial major who lives next door in Barnes turns out to be a furtive pederast; and even the most minor characters, the governesses, maids and schoolteachers, are detected alone, each surviving in her different way on the fringe of the great married and familied world.

Actions are random and haphazard. People have a disturbing knack of suddenly upping sticks and taking on a new life. Motives and reasons are hard to come by. At the age of forty-one, Muriel abruptly married. She had already failed to marry a Major Deed, who presented her with a motor car, although she couldn't drive. (When given the car, it was typically obscure of her that she instantly enrolled for dancing lessons.) But she succeeded in getting wed to Colonel Alfred Scott-Hewitt, a man whom she had known for just a few hours in Italy during the war. In 1930, she read in *The Times* that Mrs Scott-Hewitt had died, and promptly moved into the widower's life. Time was of remarkably little account to her; a decade could pass as unimportantly as an hour.

> She was always amazed by coincidences and often gave occurrences little shoves into the realm of premonition. Thus, it was not enough that on that July morning she should discover that an old acquaintance of a few hours, encountered some twelve years before, was now in trouble at the precise moment that she herself didn't know where to turn: it was both omen and premonition.
>
> "When I woke up that morning I knew something was going to happen," she would say later, "I had a premonition."
>
> Muriel packed a bag and took the train to Cornwall.

A conventional novelist would have found Muriel an impossible character to handle. Just when the lines of the narrative are clear, and the scene set for a long, lonely middle age, she has a premonition, packs a bag, and takes the train to Cornwall. Not that there was anything very conclusive about her marriage to the colonel. When war broke out in 1939, there was more packing, and Muriel was in France, and later in detention in Germany. She was sublimely indifferent to the logic of plot, and to the necessary limitations imposed on one by being a single character. She was as unfit for narrative as she was for the family.

In her final chapter, Diana Petre tells of her last encounter with her mother. Muriel died of cancer. She had wanted her own remains to be as close to where Roger Ackerley had died as possible; and so her ashes were taken in a funeral urn to Southsea. Diana and her older sister got on the train at Victoria, armed with a bottle of cherry brandy, and lugging the urn containing their mother's ashes in a paper carrier bag. On Southsea beach, several cherry B's later, they tried to get rid of the thing in the sea. It wouldn't sink. They left it to float out to sea, and went to sunbathe on the shingle.

> We must have been there for half an hour, not speaking. I was sitting up, picking up stones and dropping them, bored and uncomfortable. I looked out to sea. And then I saw it.
> "Look!" I cried. "Just open your eyes and look!"
> Just a few yards out to sea, coming sideways and towards us, drifting merrily on the current, was Muriel's urn. In a few seconds it would be directly in front of us.
> "She's doing it on purpose!" I yelled.

She didn't even know how to be properly dead. The bizarre comedy of the urn is the perfect appropriate ending to the life of this woman who did not understand how to exist within her appointed conventions.

Miss Petre's mixture of sympathy and irritation as she describes that life, her cool tone, her emotional clarity, and her novelist's sense of possessing a whole world, make this book quite exceptional. It belongs to literature, partly because of its stylistic merits, but mainly because it does what most works of literature have long funked and evaded. It creates, with great brilliance, that neglected life outside the family, and sees it on its own terms – not from the synthetic perspective of "normal" family life. *The Secret Orchard of A. R. Ackerley* has broken an important literary taboo. Perhaps its strongest and most mysterious quality is the way it lights up life *inside* the family too. The house in Barnes, with its net of relationships so frail that they can be severed on an instant, its infuriating randomness, its dangerous dependence on luck, its deep solitudes, its pathological lack of motive and reason, is, after all, so like the family that most of us live in. It is not, *pace* Trollope, Thackeray, and practically every English novelist who's ever lived, only the tragic, the illegitimate, the unfamilied, who find themselves kissing worms.

1975

FREYA STARK ON THE EUPHRATES

I am a timid traveller. The Thames is my idea of a great river. Dorset amply satisfies my mild taste for the remote. I have often told myself that one can see all one wants of Arabia on the Earls Court Road. When I was asked to go to Syria to watch Dame Freya Stark sailing down the Euphrates on a raft, I looked up the place in an atlas and rang my doctor. "If I were you," he said, "I'd wear my gumboots . . . there's a lot of bilharzia about there." Bilharzia is a disease carried by water snails which starts at the feet and ends up by destroying your brain: it is just the sort of thing I expect of foreign parts, and a very good reason for never travelling further east than Norwich. Dame Freya and I do not come from the same mould, and I have always thought that globe-trotting adventurers like her must be touched with a degree of insanity – a kind of mad bravery induced, perhaps, by contact with a water snail at some early age.

So when I arrived – exhilarated by my own bravado – on the bank of the Euphrates, I was unequipped for what I saw. The Euphrates is not at all like the Thames, and it is decidedly not the place for gumboots. It is the colour of cappuccino and it has the texture of Scotch broth. It begins somewhere up in the mountains of Turkey and ends in the vast brown bog at the neck of the Persian Gulf. It is the town drain of Asia Minor – 1400 miles of water pouring through a landscape of shale and sand, of spiky olive trees, tamarisk, poplars, willows and bamboo, where the mud-banks are as big as the Chilterns and the river often as wide and treacherous as our domestic seas. It is as changeable as Proteus. In winter it is the original of Noah's flood; in summer it can turn to a dribble between scorched hills that in mid-winter were too far down to touch with the Arab boatmen's long sounding-poles. When calm, it looks like a skating rink, grazed and patterned by the powerful cross-currents which are constantly stirring in its depths. When the wind comes up, it is like the Irish Sea on a choppy crossing, with scuds of brown foam and heavy breakers, and conical sandstorms ripping along its banks.

I've never before seen anything that has so much of Nature in it as the Euphrates – nothing so beautiful, harsh and unpredictable. But that is to misunderstand it, because this huge, muddy river has always been a centre, an instrument, of civilization. It is, along with the Tigris, one of the two oldest super-highways in the world, and its cosmopolitanism is richer, and goes deeper, than anything to be found in Earls Court. An Arab river with a Greek name (from *eu-phratir*, which roughly translates into "the good fellowship river"), it has the big-city feel that comes from strangers continually criss-crossing each other's paths. Its inhabitants range from people with pale European skins (descended, perhaps, from the Circassian girls who were the jewels of rich men's harems) to people who are almost pure black, whose ancestors must once have been Nubian slaves. It is a kind of liquid Orient Express, and its first-class passengers have included (at somewhat different dates) Alexander the Great and Freya Stark.

Dame Freya had always wanted to make this trip down the central section of the river, from the top of Syria to the border with Iraq. Twenty years ago, when she was a young sapling in her middle 60s, she had a raft built of timber and goatskins, but the river shrank early that year, and the raft was left stranded high on the dried-out mud. She is now 84, and when *The World About Us* asked her what she would most like to do in Syria, she was insistent that the high point of her expedition must be the frankincense run down the Euphrates. The B.B.C. clubbed together with Syrian television; a raft was made at Jerablus, on the Syrian/Turkish border, just below the bridge which carries the old Berlin–Baghdad railway over the river. A couple of rather worried Arabs called Ibrahim and Muhammad were hired to pole the raft downstream; district governors gave permission; the Syrian Army provided escorts armed with Russian submachine-guns; and Dame Freya's godson, Mark Lennox-Boyd, came with his wife Arabella.

Freya Stark's superb history of the river is called *Rome on the Euphrates*; on the day of her arrival at the raft, everything looked set fair for a new work called *Knightsbridge on the Euphrates*.

The atmosphere was pure royal garden party. The entire town of Jerablus seemed to have turned out to squat on the mud banks around the raft. The men and boys, in dowdy skirts and headdresses, had bagged the banks with the best views, and sat there smoking, joking and eating nuts. The women and children made a bright kaleidoscope of synthetic colours in the background; their brilliant floral prints and gold cummerbunds looking too pretty to be real. The television crew, like latterday scribes and Pharisees, buzzed with the importance of their trade. The raft itself – the focus of all this commotion – floated in soft mud like an unfinished thatched cottage, hung with lanterns and baskets, furnished with coloured carpets and rush-seated armchairs. There was an odd touch of Casa Pupo about it. Arabella Lennox-Boyd had supplied an Aleppo rose in a rusty tin; the B.B.C. had provided something called a Porta-Potti, which was tastefully hidden behind a striped, yellow curtain. And Dame Freya was late.

When her car eventually did come bumping over the dunes, it was a thoroughly queenly arrival. Clapperboards snapped. Everyone clapped. Our first glimpse was of an enormous cherry-coloured Ascot hat, winged with pink chiffon. Then, with more people arriving every minute to squat on the mudbanks – some coming on foot, some on gaily decorated motor-tricycles, some in ancient Dodges and Buicks done out like tarts' bedsitters and hung with brocade curtains – we settled down to a champagne party on the raft. We toasted the raft. We toasted Dame Freya. We toasted the constructor of the raft, and provided him with a splendid testimonial written in Arabic and announcing that he was the finest raftbuilder on all the Euphrates. One by one, the empty champagne bottles were thrown into the river, and Arab boys dived off the banks to swim to save them. Everyone basked in sun and success. But the raft stayed firmly tethered in its inlet on the mud.

Next day, it was raining. A raw wind was blowing out of – I suppose – Persia. The ford which lay between our inn in Jerablus and the party on the raft was flooded. The river was rising. The promised motor launches had not even been sighted. Tempers were fraying. Hissing conversations were conducted through interpreters. People started to gesture like ham actors. They pointed to the sky, to the rain, to the raft, to the river, to the cameras, to the microbus, to the Range Rover, to the hotel, to the governor's office, to the soldiers with their submachine-guns. It was nearly lunchtime before we even reached the raft, where Dame Freya was sitting placidly out on deck, doing her embroidery on a round frame.

There is a word in Arabic which is used more than any other in the language. It sounds like *maaleesh* and one has to shrug and smile as one says it. It means, roughly, "Never mind . . . so it goes . . .", and it constitutes a whole way of looking at the world with a kind of good-humoured acceptance of its contrarieties. It's not a word that comes easily to B.B.C. T.V. crews, who are used to breaking their way roughly through the undergrowth of difficulties that beset them. You need to have that peculiarly Arab sense of the absurdity of most human endeavour in the face of anything as mighty and unyielding as the landscape of the Euphrates. That is exactly what Dame Freya has: a serene humour that can be maddening to the sort of people who live off nerves and sandwiches. She was quite unclouded by the sandstorm of alarm which was brewing up around her. *Maaleesh*.

During the day, things steadily darkened. The raft, some said, was not a good raft at all. It did not have enough oildrums underneath it. It was quite unmanoeuvrable. The current of the rising river would sweep over its decks and drown Dame Freya and the Hon. and Mrs Mark Lennox-Boyd in that ugly flood of ice-cold cappuccino. (The builder of the craft had sensibly disappeared up-country, taking his testimonial with him.) Others said that this was totally the wrong time of year for such an attempt. Others said that it could only be done with a *shaktur* (a *shaktur* is a Brobdingnagian bath-tub made of wood and is used as a cross-channel ferry for intrepid men and their donkeys).

After all sorts of documents had been signed, exonerating everyone from responsibility for anything, it was agreed an experimental launch would take place at 4 p.m. The local football club paraded ceremonially, holding up banners reading (so I was told), "The Glorious Revolution of 8 March" and "The Arab Nation Will Never Be Conquered", and a large gilt-framed photo of President Assad.

At exactly 3.50 a violent storm blew up. Thunder crashed; forks of white lightning snaked around the cliffs on the far bank; the surface of the river looked as if it was being stirred by a giant electric blender; and a wall of rain drove the crowds off the mudbanks. The last I saw of the photograph of President Assad, it was being held high over the head of a running Arab boy, doing poor service as an umbrella.

That evening, which was shrill with plans and post-mortems, I heard Dame Freya's voice sounding clear over the top of the hubbub: "The man who invented the omelette must have been a genius, don't you think?" *Maaleesh*.

The following day, the boatmen refused to sail. The raft was towed out into mid-stream and half sank. There was a sad sight on the bank: the Aleppo rose on top of the Porta-Potti, left behind after everything else had been loaded into a van. *Shakturs* were hired. Permissions were granted and refused. Wireless messages were sent. The project was off. The project was on. The diplomatic activity was as intense as if war had broken out. Vanities were flattered, compromises sought. While the television people parleyed, a gathering crowd of

Arab soldiers and townsfolk assembled to watch the discussions round the table at the inn. The Arabs love delicate negotiation. They seemed much more interested in the sheer process of the talking – the formal compliments, the sly knight's-moves – than in its outcome. They appreciate disaster with exactly the same courteous good humour that they accord success.

"I do so loathe the way people go on about the 'fatalism' of people in these countries," Dame Freya said. "Poor things – they could barely live without fatalism, could they?"

Her own Arab virtues shone through this maddening afternoon. With narrowed eyes, imperial, acquisitive nose, and a mouth creased with a lifetime of humorous enjoyments, she sat through it all, waiting, watching, evidently relishing even the fine points of argument that threatened to bring her expedition to an abrupt end.

And then, quite suddenly, it was all sunshine. *Maaleesh* . . . So it goes . . . The raft was afloat, making stately progress through the mustard-tree and poplar groves. Women came running from the cotton fields; shepherds brought their sheep to stare; boys in *shakturs* and tin coracles poled out across the river to take a closer look. Huck Finning down the Euphrates, Dame Freya was at one with Noah and Alexander; even from my perch on the deck of a Russian river freighter a quarter-mile across the stream, I could see her glowing in the splendour of her trip.

That night we camped on a bluff overlooking the river. The local baker visited us with a formal present of a bag of newly-baked bread. From the shepherd on the hill above us, we heard the sound of the Koran chanted at sunset. For a nation of chain-smokers, the Syrians have voices as beautiful as sad bells. The frogs honked in the marsh and cicadas chirruped in the fields. The television crew were 20 kilometres up-river at the inn, and we slept in the open, making long shadows under the moon, with the frog-chorus and the occasional tinkling of sheep bells for company. Pure enchantment. It was not until morning, woken by the sun coming up like a giant grapefruit over the river, that I saw that the shepherd with the beautiful sad voice was carrying it canned in a Sanyo portable tape-recorder. *Maaleesh*.

For a morning, I joined Dame Freya and the Lennox-Boyds on the raft itself. With the sleepy hiss of water under the boards and the sun on one's face, the landscape is what moves, not the raft. It rattles by at six or seven miles an hour: caves, cliffs and groves unrolling like a lovely unreal travelogue. If you throw the peel from an orange or an empty cigarette packet overboard, it stays incriminatingly bobbing beside you for mile after mile. We drifted on, happily out of time. Dame Freya, licking yoghourt off a spoon, said, "It's terribly optimistic to ever think one's going to make a rendezvous in this country." "Who would you really like as a raft companion?" I asked her.

"Well, Chaucer would be nice. Yes, I think he'd rather like the Euphrates. But it might be rather difficult getting on with him, don't you think? One would have to spend so much time explaining all the recent history and so on." She made seven centuries sound like last week's news. "No, I think one would have to restrict oneself to moderns, don't you? I'd love to have John Donne as a close friend, but I'm not sure he'd be right for the raft, do you? Meredith, I think. George Meredith. He'd be an awfully good companion on the river . . ."

White cliffs, a gold sparkle in the sand . . . If there is a heaven for agnostics, I hope it is sharing a yoghourt dip on a May morning on a raft on the Euphrates.

There were, of course, more parliaments. The raft got stuck on a gravel-bank and had to be towed off. There was the usual maelstrom of television film-making. But Dame Freya and her raft were floating free, a millennium or two in distance away from the rest of us with our planes to catch and our hares in the gate. When I last saw her she was heading downstream in the thick yellow light of a late afternoon, with a Crusader castle coming up fast on her port bow.

I'm glad the raft-builder got his testimonial. I have no great experience of Euphrates rafts, but his was without doubt the most magical, if not the most riverworthy, that I could imagine; and on the Earls Court Road I'm haunted by its image as it drifts serenely down that enormous river, turning slowly in the current, its rush thatch lifting slightly in the breeze. I wonder, too, if that image – or one like it – haunts those melancholy Arabs who hang around the tube station, perhaps remembering an alternative kind of cosmopolitanism to the tawdry version on offer in West London.

1976

FISHING

I am careless about unpacking. The bottom of my suitcase is a crumby tidewrack of old letters, holey socks, postcards that never got sent, broken malaria tablets, squeezed-out toothpaste tubes and scraps of fishing tackle. It is the fishing tackle which instantly takes me back, more pungent and precise than any other kind of souvenir. Here are two gaudy, pop-eyed bass plugs, given me by Jim Curdue on a squally day in Wabasha, Minnesota. (We caught no bass with them, but saw a basking black rattlesnake and disturbed a colony of huge snapping turtles.) A scarlet-tipped float of goosequill . . . a long, not-quite-sober afternoon on the Basingstoke Canal. The rusty sea-hook was dangled right in front of the nose of a grouper in the Persian Gulf; wisely, the grouper wasn't in the least bit interested. A sorry-looking trout-fly on a nylon cast – that was a brook in Devon, a few hours of truancy in a catastrophic weekend.

If baggage handlers actually handled baggage, instead of carving up one's cases with knives and forks and chewing them, the tidewrack would take me far further back than that. Somewhere in the bottom of the suitcase there should be a length of garden twine, a stick of bamboo or a bent pin, and a lightning short-cut to the summer of – what? 1947? 1948? At the end of the lane in our Norfolk village, the river Wensum spilled through the ruins of a mill, opened out into a smooth pool, then ran tidily through watermeadows of oxeyes and kingcups into Fakenham. At the far side of the mill-pool, the stream slowed and deepened, and I used to lie among the tree-roots, over-hung by elm and willow, staring in.

The water was a window. At the pool, I turned into an enchanted tourist, watching a world as queer and foreign as Africa. Down there, tantalizingly close, big roach dawdled against the current, their red fins spread like sails and gently shimmying. Sometimes a silver dace would stray into this backwater out of the mainstream in a flash of spilled mercury. The minnows – natural joiners of queues, crowds and mass movements – stayed close to the surface, where they conducted a neurotically hectic social life of fights and affairs. Once I saw a pike. The pool suddenly emptied, with the minnows skittering across the top in a characteristically misguided attempt to become airborne and the black U-boat shadow of the pike was printed on the gravel bottom. I could feel the fright of it, this brute invasion of my underwater pastoral by a classic spine-chiller, fast, stealthy, built to kill, all jaws, eyes and prehistoric armour. The pike wasn't hurried. For the Wensum, it was a big-time hood and it had a lazy, show-off style as it cruised by, close to the roots, checking the bolt-holes of the local citizens.

For me, fishing was a way of trying to make contact with this exciting, Technicolor world of the mill-pool. Had I been content just to go on gazing, with more curiosity and a little learning, I might have become a naturalist. As it was, I liked the way the river bottom shelved away into invisible, unfathomable gloom. There might be real monsters down there, and I wanted the deep water to keep its legendary quality and not get quantified into the literal stuff of natural history. When I cast my hook, I was like someone chucking out a message in a bottle: I hoped to get a reply from some really unlikely quarter.

I got very few answers at first. My home-made tackle was rough and splashy. Sometimes my cork float would wobble shyly for a moment, then go on down with the current, and I knew that I'd been acknowledged. I felt the same jump of excitement that, 10 years later, would come when I caught the quick, secret glance of a girl across a crowded room. Once the float dithered, bobbed, and sailed smoothly out across the stream. For just a few seconds, I felt the thrumming pull of the unseen fish, quivery and muscular, as it went down into the deep, green legend of the middle of the pool. Pure magic. We'd been in touch – that other element and me. The fish was lost (though not to my imagination, where it grew stupendously, gleaming and golden, its fins working like fluttered fans at a ball). I was hooked.

A dim, moonfaced, lonely child, I was singularly clumsy at getting on with people, and it was a great comfort to discover that I could, at least, communicate with fish. The mill-pool was my sanctuary, and there was a suspicious whiff of natural religion about my attendance there. I was seven when I got my first, proper, five-shilling fishing rod. It was more like a sacramental means than a toy. I laid its three pieces out on my bed, fingered the shiny lacquered whippings round the rings, flexed its springy tip, took in the heady incense-smell of cork, glue and freshly sawn wood. It was much the most precious thing I had, a slender arc of bamboo connecting me with that other world.

That was 30 years ago. My other superstitions have long gone. I don't avoid the cracks between paving stones any more, I've stopped assuming that the world was created by a Galilean peasant, but I'm still a practising believer in fishing. A simple fundamentalist, I'm wedded to the ritual and the magic, still casting, without much dexterity, into the legendary pool. There are big carp down there, truffling in the mud at the bottom and sending up streams of little bubbles which burst between the lily pads of what used once to be a monastic fish-pond. Rainbow trout come crashing into the sun in a swirl of silver, gold and violet. Barbel lie doggedly low, their heads against the current, under the weir. The places and the species change, but the pool stays the same, enchanted and mysterious, as full of possibilities as imagination itself.

Gone Fishing. There's no better notice to hang on your door. It's like announcing that you've gone into exile for the day, headed for a private Tahiti of the spirit. Alone, out of time, out of society, out of language, even, I'm back at my pool, in touch again with all those strange and beautiful shadows in its depths. I try to conceal my mania from my friends. Rather too often I've noticed in their eyes a look which ought to be reserved for freaks who ring one's doorbell, pester one with leaflets and babble solemn nonsense about the Second Coming. My few attempts at evangelism have ended badly. The last person I tried to convert spent the day lying in the willow-herb with a bottle of Niersteiner, a matchboxful of hash and a copy of *Day of the Jackal.* On the drive back to London, there was a terrible note of sympathy in his voice. "Do you do that often?" he asked, and for days I feared that he would put me in touch with someone who could help.

There have only been one or two people with whom I could share the pool. I used to go fishing with Robert Lowell, on errant schoolboy days when we slipped out of the city and into that other element where the clocks have been permanently stopped and anything can happen. By the standards of men who think of fishing as a skilful sport, we were both laughably bad at it. By that crabbed measurement, Lowell probably qualified as the worst fisherman in the world. His idea of fly-casting was to wave his line about until it tangled into a mare's nest, then chuck this mess at the water, where it fell with a tremendous splash and made frightened moorhens take to the trees for cover.

Frequently this splash was followed by another, bigger splash, when Lowell's enthusiasm for mysterious underwater kingdoms

got the better of him and the fish were joined by a whopping bespectacled writer, calling – unnecessarily, but not without pleasure – "I
fell in."

He fell into an Orkney loch. He fell into a trout-stream in Kent
which looked like a trench in the First World War. He fell into a
very pretty artificial lake on the outskirts of Guildford. I only knew
Lowell for the last seven years of his life, but I imagine that there are
few fishable waters in Massachusetts and Ohio which Lowell didn't
at some point fall into. Falling in was an essential part of Lowell's
fishing style; it was the inevitable consequence of the joyful abandon
of his fishing trips, when the grizzled poet, whose chief subject was
sorrow, turned, for a day, into a whooping boy.

Yet fishing for Lowell wasn't simply a temporary escape into
childishness. He needed to keep visiting the pool because it was a
reservoir of poetic metaphor. He was comically cack-handed with a
rod and line, but in his poems he wrote about fishing as a rehearsal
for life itself. He hardly ever landed a real fish, but his work is crammed
with trophies from these expeditions. The essence of freedom, mortal,
illusory and joyful, is the "rainbow smashing a dry fly/in the white
run . . ." Courting a wife across a dinner table turns into a fly
fisherman's hopeful, heart-in-the-mouth cast. Raging twentieth-
century man, in all his grossness and calamity, is the drunken fisherman crying, "Is there no way to cast my hook/Out of this dynamited
brook?" It is not surprising that Lowell was such a goof at managing
his tackle; when he went fishing he was lost in a realm of vivid simile
– and when he wrote poetry he was a champion fisherman, as
watchful and quick as a heron.

Lowell and I went fishing in the same pool, I think. When we
talked of what it had meant to us in childhood, our separate memories
clicked exactly into place. The pond near Boston where he first fished
for bass and my stretch of the river Wensum overflowed into each
other. In the "fogbound solitudes" of his boyhood I saw the most
precise description of my own. The deepest pleasure in going fishing
is the discovery that what the pool really holds isn't fish at all but
visions, dreams, the stirred-up mud of a life.

To other men, other pools. Sir Humphrey Davy abandoned science
to devote himself to fishing. When he wrote his fishing book
Salmonia, he borrowed its shape and surface style from Walton's
Compleat Angler. Yet, into *Salmonia* went all of Davy's philosophy
of science; it looks as if it's about catching fish – actually it is a
marvellous dramatization of the workings of a nineteenth-century

scientific mind, just as Walton's own book is a classic self-portrait of a very unscientific seventeenth-century humanist.

I remember (though I bet he doesn't) meeting Brian Clarke, the *Sunday Times* angling correspondent, on the bank of a trout lake in Hampshire a few years ago. When at last I succeeded in netting a rainbow trout more or less under his nose Clarke said, not unkindly, "There are always a few kamikaze pilots about, especially at the beginning of the season." He went on to show me, in a few dazzling passes, how to cast an imitation nymph to a trout lying under a tree at the far side of the lake. It was a very pretty and exact display, involving a knowledge of trout-optics and entomology as well as a lot of wristy skill. I admired it, just as I admire Clarke's books, but I have no desire to emulate it. Clarke and I fish in different pools, and I'd sooner cast in the ruinous high gothic style of Robert Lowell.

Less edifyingly, I met another man who owned a machine-tool business in the Midlands. He'd hooked a trout and was playing it on a short line, the tip of his brand-new carbon-fibre rod jerking down into the water below him. He was grunting irritably when he saw me watching him.

"I'm a hard man on a fish," he said. "Always have been. A hard man on a fish."

I knew the pool where *he* went fishing. It resembled a very old-fashioned school of business management. His dealings with the trout resembled his life in cartoon outline. The large hairless baby. The school bully with tabs on the politics of the playground. The porcine young man starting on the ground floor. And now the Boss, gloating in his authority as he slid an exhausted two-pound trout over the rim of his landing net. As he scooped it out of the water, what was he seeing? A cringing shop-steward? A recalcitrant son? He allowed himself a short whistle of pleasure as he killed his particular symbol with a single blow and cast his fly to catch another.

For fishing is a looking-glass which throws your life back to you without softening the pimples. I take no pride in being a hard man on fish, but I do kill them. There's a pocket in my fishing bag which holds a miniature cosh, called a "priest". Its leaden end is darkened with bloodstains and there are a few dried scales still attached to it, like flakes of scurf. When you kill a trout, blood seeps from between its gills. Its lovely colours dull in a few moments. It curls, and stiffens; in an hour or two it takes on the texture of the broken leather of an old shoe. At the end of all the wonder, the sense of communion with that other world, the rootedness in nature, one is left with a full-grown man, with smelly, bloodstained hands, standing over a small dead fish. *Pleasure?* Yes, but alloyed pleasure and perhaps one wouldn't even recognize it as pleasure if it weren't alloyed. One doesn't have to be a member of the League Against Cruel Sports to see that there really is something ugly and absurd in what one had thought to be one's pursuit of a private Eden.

The taint is real, but it's not a final deterrent. Now the reason has started I'll be down on one knee again at the edge of my pool. The fly drops on the water . . . a bright splash of impressionism, made of peacock herl, gold tinsel, pheasant crest and oiled silk. A purple shadow swims to meet it, swirls, breaks water, and we're in touch. As the shadow drives down into the weeds, I still don't know what it's a shadow of. Something remembered. Something strange. Certainly a marvel. I shall catch it if I can.

1980

V

"True and sincere travelling," wrote Thoreau, "is no pastime but it is as serious as the grave, or any part of the human journey, and it requires a long probation to be broken into it." Brief excursions, on commission, are a world away from travel in Thoreau's sense. They're too whimsically undertaken, too well planned (with the return half of your ticket tucked into your wallet), too limited and explicit in their intentions (to bag a piece of 2500 words on . . .), to give more than a faint whiff of what real travel might be like.

When the true and sincere traveller pulls the front door shut and turns the key in the lock, he casts himself adrift in the world. For the foreseeable future, he'll be a creature of chance and accident. He doesn't know when – or if – he'll be back. From here on, he submits himself to the current of things, dog-paddling with the stream and watching where it takes him. If he's wise, he'll have made no appointments and will carry no letters of introduction. Trying to keep appointments wrecks the natural rhythm of a journey, and letters of introduction nearly always introduce you to people who don't much want to see you and whom you would sooner not have seen anyway.

The writer's working conditions tend to drive him to travel, just as they often drive him to drink. Sitting alone in a room from nine till six, for several months on end, will bring on fits of aggravated restlessness in the most determined homebody. In theory, too, the job's uniquely portable – needing only paper, pen and maybe one of those microchip typewriters that are no bigger than the averagely slim first novel. So why be here at all? When you've spent an hour stuck for a word, with a pile of unanswered tax demands on the floor, the London rain drumming on the window, the builders using a chainsaw in the flat overhead, and a stuck burglar alarm yammering on the wall of a house across the street, the thought will come unbidden that Trollope used to do it on trains, rolling punctually through the shires, Stevenson did it in the South Seas in the sun, Nabokov did it in grand hotels with room service, and there is really no good reason why you should be failing to do it here in this damp, fretful and noisy corner of London S.W. Why not Iona? or Marrakesh? or on passage to the Azores?

The question is not so much *why go?* as *what keeps you?*; and the answer is the three heavy shelves of reference books, a few dates in a diary, the force of gravity that keeps sedentary people in their chairs. So you stay put, feebly daydreaming, but more provisionally attached to where you are than anyone in a proper office with in and out trays, Fax machines and a half-hour-by-half-hour engagement book.

Simple wanderlust is relatively easy to fend off, but when it starts to get tangled up with a literary motive it becomes irresistible; and literature and travel are anciently, inevitably tangled. Journeys suggest stories, stories take the form of journeys – odysseys, exoduses, pilgrims' and rakes' progresses. Any travelling writer, leaving home, must find it difficult to rid himself of the idea that he's embarking on a kind of real-life picaresque. Before him lie the education and adventures of a rolling stone. Pilgrim, Gulliver, Tom Jones, Mr Yorick have been here before. When last seen, disappearing into the Underground, lugging his overstuffed bag and wearing an incongruous tropical suit, the writer is heading just as much for a literary tradition as he is for his train.

Yet actual journeys aren't like stories at all. At the time, they seem to be mere strings of haps and mishaps, without point or pattern. You get stuck. You meet someone you like. You get a rude going-over in a bar. You get lost. You get lonely. You get interested in architecture. You get diarrhoea. You get invited to a party. You get frightened. A stretch of country takes you by surprise. You get homesick. You are, by rapid turns, engrossed, bored, alert, dull, happy, miserable, well and ill. Every day tends to seem out of connection with every other day, until living from moment to moment turns into a habit and travelling itself into a form of ordinary life. You can't remember when it wasn't like this. There is a great deal of liberating pleasure to be had from being abroad in the world, continuously on the move, like one of Baudelaire's lost balloons, but a journey, at least as long as it is actually taking place, is the exact opposite of a story. It is a shapeless, unsifted, endlessly shifting accumulation of experience.

The first thing it needs is an ending, for only in retrospect (and often in long retrospect) will the dust of travelling settle and the journey begin to emerge as a story, of sorts. There is a convention of guileless immediacy about literary travel books, a long established pretence that the travelling and the writing are part and parcel of each other. When Sterne's Mr Yorick writes his preface to *A Sentimental Journey*, supposedly inside the curtained *desobligeant* in which he is being driven about Calais, he is setting an example that subsequent writers have fallen over themselves to follow. But the actual interval between the making of the journey and the publication of the book reveals the truth of the business. It took Kinglake more than seven years to finish *Eothen* after his trip to the Middle East. Eleven years elapsed between Hilaire Belloc's cruise from Wales to Sussex and his writing of *The Cruise of the Nona*. The record (I think) is held by Patrick Leigh Fermor, who spent most of 1933 and 1934 on a walking tour from Amsterdam to Constantinople; he has just published the second volume of the trilogy which recounts that journey. Fifty years! I offer the figure to my own publisher as a fair example of just how long events may need to be salted down in memory before they can be recreated in words on the page.

For travelling is inherently a plotless, disordered, chaotic affair, where writing insists on connection, order, plot, signification. It may take a year or more to see that there was any point to the thing at all, and more years still to make it yield an articulate story. Memory, not the notebook, holds the key. I try to keep a notebook when I'm on the move (largely because writing in it makes one feel that one's at work, despite all appearances to the contrary) but hardly ever find anything in the notebook that's worth using later. Trifles are described at inordinate length. Events that now seem important aren't mentioned at all. The keeper of the notebook sounds stupid and confused. He grouses too much about tides and timetables, and all the forgettable mechanics of the journey; he fails to notice what I remember observing in near-photographic detail. When I'm writing the book, I get precious little help from him . . . the odd proper name, a date, an ascertainable fact here and there, but little or nothing in the way of intelligent comprehension of what he was doing at the time. Why was he so blind? Because he was travelling and I am writing, and the two activities are chalk and cheese.

Memory, though, is always telling stories to itself, filing experience in narrative form. It feeds irrelevancies to the shredder, enlarges on crucial details, makes links and patterns, finds symbols, constructs plots. In memory, the journey takes shape and grows; in the notebook it merely languishes, with the notes themselves like a pile of cigarette butts confronted the morning after a party.

I envy Leigh Fermor his fifty years – the time it has given him to forget, as much as the time it has given him to enlarge on his memories. In my own experience, the richer the journey, the longer it takes to resolve itself into a story which you can then begin to write. Magazine pieces are easy. Assigned to spend three weeks wandering at will round some unfamiliar bit of the world, you can find yourself writing the first paragraph on the plane home. But the real journey, on which you lose yourself for months on end and which comes to seem as impenetrable, delicate and complicated as a long marriage, won't wear that kind of summary treatment.

In 1982, I took six months to sail slowly round the British Isles, stopping at every place I'd known as a child and adolescent. A year later, I was still trying to begin the book that was based on the journey. I had 30,000 words, but they seemed forced and wrong. There was writing, but as yet no story worth the telling. There was a title, *Foreign Land*, but it didn't fit the writing. I began to add up the dog days spent at the typewriter, and the sum looked frightening. From a well-heeled American magazine, I conned a commission to spend three weeks in the Cape Verde Islands (somewhere I knew nothing about, but which looked interesting on the atlas; a cluster of dots off Africa, too near the Equator for comfort or tourism), where I saw what was wrong. I wasn't foreign enough to write *Foreign Land*; I was trying to cook up an alienation that I didn't feel. Had I been much older, had I spent most of my life abroad (in, say, the Cape Verde Islands), then it might have been different: England really would have had the strangeness that I was trying and failing to manufacture for it. I wrote the piece about the Cape Verdes (the magazine editor hated it), then wrote a novel, retaining the alienated title that had been meant for the voyage round Britain. It was about a man who'd spent forty years abroad, in a country much like the Cape Verde Islands, who returned to England and found it a genu-inely foreign land. Late on in the writing of that book, I found myself remembering my own real trip quite differently, as a story with a pattern to it, and the intractable voyage suddenly became writeable under a new and less aggressive title. To the idea that the "travel book" simply writes itself, or is a more or less decorated version of the ship's log: *hooey*!

It's easy to talk blithely about casting oneself adrift in the world; not quite so easy to do it in practice, when most methods of transport turn the would-be traveller into a human bullet. You become a creature, not of chance and accident, but of flight schedules, Apex fare tariffs, hotel bookings and all the rest of the machinery of package tourism and business travel. You have no function in the landscape, no job to justify your movement through it. You may see a great deal of the world without ever becoming a working part of it, and the world itself has grown very tired of the idle spectators who haunt its exotic, sunny, or picturesque fringes. There aren't many places left where strangers are still interesting just because they're strangers.

When Evelyn Waugh, Robert Byron, Peter Fleming and Graham Greene travelled, the going was still rough (Waugh said "good"). Journeys had to be improvised, day by day, without benefit of travel agents. Pistols, machetes and tents were essential items of luggage. For writers of my generation it has been very different – although Redmond O'Hanlon, hacking his way up an unmapped tributary of the Amazon, fearful (and not without good reason) of ending his days in someone's cooking pot, has managed to keep that tradition alive. When I last saw him, he looked like the last of the classic travellers: ravaged and yellow from a bout of infectious peritonitis, he held a glass of orange juice at a London party and talked sadly of whisky as a long-lost friend. Where on earth had be been? I asked; was there still some distant corner of the world as yet unpenetrated by Gamma Globulin? The great traveller – survivor of tropical snakes, waterfalls, hostile tribes of South American Indians, and all the other accoutrements of a *Boy's Own Paper* adventure – said no, actually, he hadn't been anywhere much; he'd contracted that great travellers' disease at a Chinese restaurant in Mill Hill.

O'Hanlon apart, the travelling writers have had to find less hard-boiled ways of keeping on the move at the right pace, of retaining their independence and of giving themselves enough to do to properly inhabit the world through which they pass. Paul Theroux found one way, in the makeshift and fluid society of the railway carriage; Gavin Young another, in the small cargo ships that still porthop round the globe. Too much ingenuity, and the thing turns into a stunt, like shooting Niagara in a cardboard box, which isn't travelling at all; too little, and you become a helpless passenger in someone else's system and might as well stay home watching the world go by in glamorous colour on T.V.

I had always liked boats, in an ignorant way. In harbours, and on lakes and rivers, I warmed to the sight of solitary figures in skiffs and launches. They looked as if they knew what they were up to. They looked at home on the water, as much a part of the landscape as the gulls and herons. Unlike motorists, they had the air of people who enjoyed being where they were; the water was a good place in its own right, not just a distance to be endured at maximum speed. There was nothing self-conscious about the way they handled their craft, nothing riproaring and daredevil; they just got on with what they were doing, quietly, knowledgeably and without spoiling the view. It looked like an enviable way of being alone and of making one's way through the world.

In 1979 I wandered down the Mississippi in a 16-foot open boat with an outboard motor. There was no element of stunt in the trip; it was the only possible way of encountering a great river at close quarters. I didn't camp out on sandbars, or pretend to be Huckleberry Finn; I stayed in motels, ate in restaurants and drank too much and too long in riverside bars.

Simple possession of a boat turned out to be a ticket of entry to the society of the river. Lock keepers, ferrymen, towboat captains, fishermen, duck hunters treated me as an insider. Within a month of setting off, I could gossip comfortably about chutes, sloughs, sawyers, silting-up bends, wingdams and drownings, adding my own ha'porth to the lore. By the time I was halfway down, and into the beginning of the Mississippi's wilder reaches, I was an accredited river man. Though the oddity of my accent in those parts sometimes marked me out, I'd never felt less of a tourist, or more easily able to drift into the lives of strangers. We had the river in common, and it was a powerful bond.

Navigating a tricky stretch of water, trying to relate the formal symbols of the chart to the breaking surf of a shoal ahead and the indefinite line, half a mile to your left, where the river blurs into the green of a cypress swamp, you observe with a serious purpose. This is about keeping afloat and staying alive. You're a part of this, not a spectator of it. The landscape is not dull, or pretty – it is a code that needs continuous practical interpretation, like a text.

After eight years away, I can still open the U.S. Corps of Engineers' ringbound charts of the Mississippi at random and see the water as it was on the day that I went by: the overcast; the south wind blowing against the grain of the current and raising short, sharp houndstooth waves; the mile-long freight train slowly keeping pace with the boat on the rusty stilts of the Chicago, Milwaukee, St Paul and Pacific railroad; the jetty at the end of Union Street, Albany, where I stopped to take on a six-pack of Bud . . . I can't remember any landscape that I've driven through by car with such obsessive clarity, but I have 2000 miles of the Mississippi imprinted in my head. Because I was always anxious, sometimes frightened, necessarily watchful, the river made me concentrate in a way that I'd never concentrated before.

When I dumped the unlovely yellow aluminium boat in New Orleans at the end of the trip, I thought I was through with boats in general. I'd spent too much time being afraid, expecting imminent capsize (at the time, I didn't know how safe I really was; the dangers were mostly illusory ones, but none the less powerful for that). The journey had been a good deal more interesting than I'd meant it to be, and I thought I'd better find some way of travelling that didn't keep one's concentration screwed to breaking point.

Back in England, I felt quite unexpectedly bereft. After a long night of confused passage making, dodging tows, skidding on boils and racing through chutes, I'd wake up in the morning and remember with a pang that I'd lost the river and the boat. There was only one way to stop the dreams coming, and for £350 I bought a scuffed 15-foot launch which I kept moored on the Thames at Hammersmith. I took it to Lechlade at one end of the river and Tilbury at the other in a succession of soft, suburban outings.

Boat begat boat. The Mississippi book did well in the United States, and I was able to spend £10,500 on a seagoing ketch and have it refitted for a voyage round the British Isles. The money – nearly £19,000 in all – was meant to be a temporary investment: when I reached Cornwall again the next autumn, the boat would be sold, leaving me perhaps £3,000 out of pocket, since boats, unlike houses, only go down in value.

Its market price is still on the slide. As for its larger value – I've found a way of keeping on the move that works, or seems to. Accommodation sufficient to contain an ordinary daily working life. A suitable speed at which to meet the world. Just enough danger to keep one's wits sharp. A vehicle dependent on the random chances and decisions of the weather. A happy cross between Noah's ark and Mr Yorick's *desobligeant*, his one-man chaise.

There's a basic library on board. A manual typewriter lives in the middle locker under the starboard-side settee in the saloon. Up in the wheelhouse I can make telephone calls to anywhere in the world via the V.H.F. radio. It is possible, but satisfactorily difficult, for other people to make telephone calls to the boat. Quietly at anchor, out of the way of things, the boat is a functional floating office; a perfect place for reading, a tolerable one for writing in. It is warm and well lit; it used to have a television but now has a stereo tape system with what must be the best collection of Schubert on the North Sea.

It travels at a Victorian pace. Under way, with a friendly tide and the wind behind it, it will manage seven to eight knots over the ground – say nine m.p.h. at most. At this speed, you can get to know each wave on intimate terms, and if land is in sight you can study it – you have to study it – as closely as a book. Searching for marks, taking bearings, you get to know a coast in the purposeful way of someone whose living literally depends on his comprehension of his own exact place in the landscape.

But it is the wind – the endlessly shifting gradients of atmospheric pressure – that makes travelling in a small boat into an *adventure*, in the sense defined by the *O.E.D.* ("That which happens without design; chance, hap, luck"). The wind blows you into places that you'd never meant to visit, and keeps you pinioned there. The wind is a mad travel agent, with a malicious and surrealist turn of wit. You want to go to France – the wind will maroon you for ten days in Dover. You want to go to the Shetland Islands, and the wind will make you spend a week in Bridlington as penance for your hubris. You can't move without the wind's consent, and when you do move, you find yourself suddenly rescheduled, headed for a destination that you hadn't heard of ten minutes ago. Every day the chart and the pilot book produce surprises; and if you have any sense, you always take the wind's advice and go where it listeth, to the obscure village or small town that offers shelter. Sometimes you have to stay out at sea, missing your original destination altogether. More often, you're driven in haste into harbours you'd overlooked, far short of where you'd planned to be that night.

Going by sea is a reliably constant adventure. It's a slow and unpredictable business. It requires patience and a promiscuous curiosity about those unregarded places in the world where you're forever finding yourself stranded. Since its original circuit of the British Isles, *Gosfield Maid* has taken me to Ireland, France, Belgium, the Netherlands, West Germany, Denmark and Sweden. In every country, the wind has taken control of the itinerary, landing the boat up, for days on end, in ports that I had no idea I was destined to visit.

From Girvan in Scotland to Höganäs in Sweden, they were chosen by the weather, these windfall-landfalls. It is true about any port in a storm: as you round the inner breakwater after a few hours out in a rough sea, the dingiest town seems a wonderful place to be. I've come humiliatingly close to kissing the stones of Grimsby fish dock, I was so glad to be there. The worse the weather, the more you love the town – which is useful, since you'll probably have time to learn the name of every single street before the wind will allow you to leave it.

So you settle in, gratefully. You work. You make at least one friend. Strangers come to visit, and you entertain them in the hastily tidied saloon. Aboard a boat, so much of your life is already with you that almost anywhere can seem like home by the time you've spent seven days there, so quickly do you get used to the smell and the rhythm of it. In Pwllheli, I met a man who had been sailing from Scotland to Brittany seven years before. Off Bardsey Island, a gale had blown up, for him as for me (just as a gale had blown up there for Hilaire Belloc), and he'd put into Pwllheli to shelter for the night. After five years, he'd moved out of his boat and into a bungalow. He was married to a Pwllheli girl, and they'd just had their first child. He spoke now with a slight Welsh accent.

"If I were you," he said, "I'd give in now. Forget the shipping forecast. There's a bungalow for sale on the estate . . ."

You never know. It is part of the adventure that once in port you might never put out again. Or you might, depending on the wind. Whatever. Going about the world by boat like a snail in its shell feels, at least, as close to true and sincere travelling as you can reasonably come in the age of Intercity and Super Shuttle.

THE JOURNEY AND THE BOOK

It's no wonder that up till now criticism has shunned the travel book. As a literary form, travel writing is a notoriously raffish open house where very different genres are likely to end up in the same bed. It accommodates the private diary, the essay, the short story, the prose poem, the rough note and polished table talk with indiscriminate hospitality. It freely mixes narrative and discursive writing. Much of its "factual" material, in the way of bills, menus, ticket-stubs, names and addresses, dates and destinations, is there to authenticate what is really fiction; while its wildest fictions have the status of possible facts. Because of this genial confusion, the travel book has always been a favourite haunt of writers, just as critics, with some justification, have usually regarded it as a resort of easy virtue.

As a reward for merely knocking on the door of this establishment in literature's red-light district, Paul Fussell deserves a laurel or two to add to the garlands he won with his previous book *The Great War and Modern Memory*. *Abroad** is an exemplary piece of criticism. It is immensely readable. It bristles with ideas. It disinters a real lost masterpiece from the library stacks. It admits a whole area of writing – at last! – to its proper place in literary history. Its general thesis is, I think, wrongheaded, even mean; but Mr Fussell argues it with such force and clarity that he makes it a pleasure to quarrel with him.

The English travel books of the '20s and '30s were, Mr Fussell says, written in the Indian summer of what is now a dead form. Evelyn Waugh, Graham Greene, Norman Douglas, D. H. Lawrence, Robert Byron were the last masters of an art which was to be killed off by politics and the tourist industry. History had put them in a unique position. Never had England seemed so frowsty and constricting as in the period immediately after the Great War. The very word "abroad" had come to assume a dreamlike, talismanic quality. It had been conceived in the frozen trenches of Flanders and brought to birth in the tired and spiritless streets of Britain's postwar industrial cities. It was raised, umbrella-fashion, over a whole cluster of concepts – of sunlight, liberty, innocence, sexual passion, the fantastic and the healing. When the English writer bought his ticket to sail on the cruise ship or ride on the famous Blue Train, which went from Victoria Station all the way to the Riviera, his real destination was more a restorative idea than a place on the map.

Most important of all, his nationality equipped him with a point of view which made "abroad" singularly containable as a literary construct. Four hundred years of imperial experience had given the travelling Englishman a very clear idea of where he stood in the world – bang at its moral centre. Foreigners, by definition, were funny, untrustworthy and childlike. To be English and abroad was to be the one tight-minded, right-minded sensibility at large in a confused society where more or less everything was comically lax and

* Paul Fussell, *Abroad* (New York: Oxford University Press).

wrong. That may have been a deplorable attitude in the realm of international politics, but it was a useful misapprehension to be under when it came to writing books. Snobbishly alert to the small nuances of social behaviour, quick to spot the "anomalous" details which form the basic grist of travel writing, the Englishman was, in more senses than one, a privileged observer.

It was only when they were abroad, though, that Mr Fussell's literary travellers were ever likely to be mistaken for typical English-men. There was something anomalous about each of them in their insecure tenancy of the upper-middling reaches of the class system. They were climbers, like Waugh, or sliders, like Norman Douglas. At home, they stuck out as "queer", "not quite", or "on the make", or simply Papist. In foreign parts, their Englishness was restored to them intact, a comfortable, fictional identity woven in superior Harris tweed.

So it was with Robert Byron, author of *The Road to Oxiana*, the lost masterpiece which Mr Fussell now dusts off as "the *Ulysses* or 'Waste Land'" of travel writing. Byron came from a fossilized Victor-ian country house. He was a fat bachelor, "less homosexual than neuter", whose enthusiasm for the Byzantine was a calculated affront to the classical bias of conventional English taste. He went to Asia looking for "coloured architecture" and returned with a clutch of marvellously funny and observant books. When Mr Fussell picks *The Road to Oxiana* as the archetype of the entire genre, it's a characteristically sure-footed move; understand Byron and you understand the nature of travel writing.

The book fits on every count. Unknown to formal criticism, it still has its addicted readers, as the cross-hatching of date stamps of my borrowed London Library copy proves. Its appearance of artlessness is highly contrived. It takes the form of a day-to-day notebook of odd jottings, as if Byron had sent his journal, complete with pressed flowers and inkblots, direct to the printers. One can almost see his handwriting wobble on the page as he snatches at a phrase on an Afghan bus or rattles off a hasty, present-tense aside. For "security reasons", the Shah of Persia is referred to throughout as Marjori-banks, lest the notebook fall into the hands of the authorities. The unwary critic, happening on *The Road to Oxiana*, might be forgiven for thinking that he hadn't found a book at all, only its raw material.

In fact *The Road to Oxiana* was the product of three years of constant writing and revision. Its casualness is an elaborate fiction. (Just as Alexander Kinglake wrote and rewrote *Eothen* over seven years, then claimed that the book was just a hurried letter of hints and tips to a travelling friend.) Byron painstakingly re-created the episodic bittiness of the journey itself in the form of his book for serious imaginative reasons. Life, as the most ancient of all metaphors insists, is a journey; and the travel book, in its deceptive simulation of the journey's fits and starts, rehearses life's own fragmentation. More even than the novel, it embraces the contingency of things.

The discovery of the form of the fake-notebook liberated Byron as a writer. He was an improviser of genius, a natural player-by-ear. Into *The Road to Oxiana* went scholarly essays, aphorisms, farcical playlets, wonderfully exact notations of moments of time caught and frozen in the particularity of place, along with documents like visa forms and newspaper cuttings. Mr Fussell's claim that the book deserves an important place in the history of literary modernism seems ungainsayable. It is a brilliantly wrought expression of a thoroughly modernist sensibility, a portrait of an accidental man adrift between frontiers.

As long as he sticks to reading the individual books of his travellers, Mr Fussell is the best kind of critic; sensitive, adroit, infectious. He falls from grace when he allows *Abroad* to become enslaved to two related big ideas, both borrowed from other writers, one brilliant and one downright bad. The first comes from William Empson who, in *Some Versions of Pastoral*, argued that the "proletarian novel" of the 1930s was a reworking of the Renaissance pastoral mode in its idealization of the relationship between the rich (who wrote it) and the poor (who figured as its heroes). Swains and nymphs all over again, said Empson in his customary tone of no-nonsense simplicity. Mr Fussell reapplies that insight to the travel book and discovers that Christopher Isherwood's German boys, Norman Douglas's Italians, Byron's Persians are really just Corydon and Phyllis under *noms-de-plume*. Well, up to a point. The trouble is that Mr Fussell, mistaking a fashion for the form itself, comes to identify the fortunes of the travel book as a literary genre with the condition of pastoral: only when the writer can condescend to "abroad", when the foreign landscape can be seen to stand for innocence and innocent adventure, is the literature of travel possible. After Munich, Mr Fussell says, foreigners lost their charm. They had certainly ceased to be funny. The shepherds and the shepherdesses all took jobs in munitions factories or joined the *Hitlerjugend*, and the travel book was dead.

The second much cruder idea is taken from Evelyn Waugh's grumpy preface to *When the Going Was Good*. Travel itself, let alone travel writing, had been killed first by World War II and then by mass tourism. In the one thoroughly silly chapter of his book, Mr Fussell bewails the growth of the tourist industry, littering his pages with a mass of banal and contradictory complaints. In our "plebeian age" travel is too easy. Finding hotel rooms is too difficult. It's hard to go places by boat. Touts, souvenir sellers and Boeing 747's have turned the world into a collection of "pseudo-places". The rise of the tourist has meant the extinction of the traveller; and tourists, by definition, can't write travel books.

This is bad-tempered nonsense. Two of the best books ever written in the genre, Mark Twain's *Innocents Abroad* and Evelyn Waugh's own *Labels*, happen to be about tourists on package holidays. Nor is the travel book necessarily a version of pastoral. The curiously undated tone of R. L. Stevenson's *The Amateur Emigrant* and *Across the Plains*, in which he describes his nightmare journey from the Clyde to San Francisco, is largely due to the fact that he literally couldn't afford to condescend to the strangers in whose company he made the trip. His book is a masterpiece of humbled realism in which the illness and poverty of the writer have forcibly modernized his prose.

Mr Fussell, though, would have us believe that the travel book, like verse drama, is a form which has been disenfranchised by historical circumstances. Having restored the travel book to critical life, he goes on to perform a premature burial service over its remains. His reading should have led him to a different conclusion. He has brilliantly demonstrated the resilience of the form, its omnivorous appetite for writing of all kinds – fact, fiction, drama, note, testament. Its one essential condition isn't a private income, rough terrain, English imperial hauteur, tramp steamers, Baedekers, the cheap franc or any other of the incidentals on which Mr Fussell dwells with valedictory nostalgia; it is the experience of living among strangers, away from home. When *that* ceases to be a matter of any interest or importance, Mr Fussell will be welcome to have his funeral.

Meanwhile, despite exaggerated rumours of its demise, the travel book continues to be read and written. Paul Theroux, the Naipaul brothers, Bruce Chatwin, Edward Hoagland, Ted Simon . . . none of them have the manners of graverobbers or Frankensteins. Nor, as I nudge the 120,000 word mark of a manuscript which threatens to be longer than Mr Burgess's last novel, and therefore should at least prove to be a handy thing to stand on if you have to change a high lightbulb, do I feel much inclined to raise a cheer for Fussell's thesis. What the travel book needs is not an elegaic history but the ground rules of an intelligent criticism.

At present the form stands in a similarly dubious position to that once occupied by landscape painting. As recently as 1800, landscapes were commonly thought of as a species of painterly journalism. Real art meant pictures of allegorical or biblical subjects. A landscape was a mere record or report. As such, it couldn't be judged for its imaginative vision, its capacity to create and embody a world of complex meanings; instead it was measured on the rack of its "accuracy", its dumb fidelity to the geography on which it was based. Of course this was nonsense, as Turner gloriously proved, and as the mainstream of 19th-century French painting went on to vindicate. In literature, though, the distinction between realistic fiction and the imaginative recreation of a real journey through life has been maintained with pedantic assiduity. The novel, however autobiographical, is *writing;* the book of travel, however patterned, plotted, symbolized, is just *writing-up.* It is a damnable and silly piece of class discrimination.

Travel, in any case, is the wrong word. At best it contains a grain of half-truth. For it singles out this category of literature as the one which is exclusively concerned with place and motion. In fact the literary journey is more likely to be about time than place. The voyage has a beginning and an end. I suspect that the real secret of its appeal to the writer is that it provides him with a usable past, a store of memory, as contained as a childhood. Life ravels on, but the trip is over, and it's the writer's business to tease its significance out in the long tranquillity of the study. His notebook may supply him with cues and prompts, but these bits and pieces of the random world are little more than scraps of wool on a barbed wire fence; they're there to be collected, spun and woven into the fiction of the book. Somewhere in that sealed past there is a story to be found. Characters who seemed minor and shadowy when met in real life elbow themselves into the foreground on the page. Events which were quite unrecorded because they appeared trifling then now turn into structural pillars of the narrative. The relationship between *then* and *now*, between the journey and the book, is tricky and paradoxical; and as he negotiates it the writer discovers, often to his embarrassment, that he is a fabulist who only masquerades as a reporter.

For memory itself, the old fallible and ingenious composer of fiction, has reassembled his experience in a form very close to that of a novel. In recreating his journey he must either be an artist in spite of himself (in which case he is likely to prove a bad one) or, like Robert Byron, he can embrace the duplicity and unreliability of the genre and make a whole-hearted fiction of his book, telling the truth by means of the winding stair.

I am indebted to a recent review by Stephen Gardiner in the *Listener* for a quotation by the French painter, J. F. Millet, which I've now got pinned up over my desk:

> One man may paint a picture from a careful drawing made on the spot, and another may paint the same scene from memory, from a brief but strong impression; and the last may succeed better in giving the character, the physiognomy of the place, though all the details may be inexact.

That is not the wording of a licence to be careless with one's facts; it is, rather, a statement of the essential difference between the man who makes an exact record of what happened on his journey because the journey itself is of public interest, and the man who turns his memory of a journey into a book because finally it will be the book, and not the details of the journey, which will count. Chris Bonington's *Annapurna* is of the first kind; V. S. Naipaul's *An Area of Darkness* is of the second.

Fussell has argued that mass travel has killed the travel book as a literary form. Far from it. It has liberated it. Too much of the writing in Fussell's golden age was taken up with dutiful reporting on the customs of remote people and with the details of arduous hikes. Most of the remote people aren't remote any more, and their customs have all been filmed by *World About Us* crews. The arduous hikes can be comfortably left to the mountaineers, the lone yachtsmen and those fearless cranks who are bent on proving that the Welsh sailed to Patagonia in coracles made of leek-skins. The travelling writers, as opposed to these writing travellers, have, happily, been left with the ordinary, easily-visitable world; with a past they can make by making the trip, with strangers, with solitude, and with the responsibility to bring back not information but a good book. Let travel books be judged as pieces of imaginative writing. By that standard, most of them will look inept, scrappy and callow; even so, the standard is the right one. If we begin to apply it seriously, we would at once restore a shelf-full of books to their proper place as works of literature. More importantly, at a time when the appetite of readers for realist fictions is being left unsatisfied by a generation of formalist writers, we would reveal that the modern book-of-the-journey is the legal heir of the *roman fleuve*.

KINGLAKE IN THE MIDDLE EAST

Eothen is such an easygoing book, so funny, so crisp and vivid in its handling of people and places, that the reader may well not notice that it is also a very slippery book indeed. It seems so lightly and spontaneously done, this quizzical self-portrait of an Old Etonian swanning idly around the Middle East in the 1830s. Its determinedly inconsequential surface masks a degree of artistic guile for which Kinglake has never received full credit.

"My excuse for the book is its truth," he announces in his Preface. One may let one's eyebrow lift a fraction at that statement, since the preface itself is an elaborate, and highly purposeful, lie. Kinglake passes off *Eothen* as a hastily written letter (a "scrawl") to a travelling friend. It was no such thing. The book took Kinglake a decade to write. It was revised and re-revised; its style of bright talk was the product of a long process of literary refinement. In the Preface, Kinglake rejoices in the book's "studiously unpromising" title and makes the assurance that it is "quite superficial in its character". For an ironist, the worst of all fates is to be taken literally – and Kinglake, adored though he was by generations of Victorian and Edwardian readers, has usually been taken, or mistaken, at his word.

He liked to pose as a gentleman-amateur of life and letters. "I, a lay-man not forced to write at all . . ." As an artist of considerable cunning and professional seriousness, he was drawn to the travel-memoir precisely because it had the reputation of being an innocent and artless form – a rag-bag of haphazard trifles, random observations, domestic details, notes and sketches. For Kinglake it was the perfect vehicle for his peculiarly devious kind of literary talent. In the travel book he could dissemble, improvise, mock his readers. Disguised as a humble reporter, he could tell tall and improbable tales. Recreating himself in the character of the Victorian Englishman Abroad, he could bring off one of the finest pieces of satiric portraiture in 19th-century writing. *Eothen* needs to be read with more subtlety than most readers have brought to it in the past. If one remains alert to its tone and responsive to its architecture, it reveals itself as a brilliant acid comedy, a sly masterpiece, as full of tricks as an Egyptian magician.

The ribs and spine of the book are provided by a real journey, from the Danube through Greece, Turkey, Cyprus, the Lebanon, Palestine, Egypt, Jordan and Syria. Its flesh is a controlled riot of embroidery and invention. Actual events (or what one presumes to be actual events) are treated as excuses and springboards for a marvellous succession of flights of fancy and imagination. Kinglake shows his hand very early on. Half of Chapter One is taken up by a hilarious, and wholly mythical, conversation between an English Traveller, a Dragoman and a Pasha ("Whirr! whirr! all by wheels! – whiz! whiz! all by steam!"). What *might* happen interests Kinglake just as much as what actually *did* happen, and that inspired piece of fiction sets a tone from which the book never falters.

For travelling, in *Eothen*, is as much a mental state as a physical condition. Liberated by the East from "the stale civilization of Europe", Kinglake – or, rather, his first-person hero – is free to let his mind wander. With his foot in the stirrup he is in much the same reverie of free-association as a patient on an analyst's couch. For this rich young Englishman, the East itself exists primarily as an exotic stage on which his own character can be more vividly illuminated than it ever was at home. So he soliloquizes, he recollects, he speculates. Sometimes his surroundings bear in on him with more force than his imaginings, but for the most part he is the chief actor in a sublimely egotistic drama.

Here Kinglake and his readers have usually parted company. The readers, eager only for more snapshots of oriental life, have cheerfully ignored the fact that the young man at the centre of the book is a distinctly callow and nasty piece of work. His chief memories are of school life at Eton. His only measure of landscape is a sentimental fondness for the Thames at Windsor, to which he refers on every possible occasion. He has an automatic condescension to all "orientals", and is utterly unmoved when they suffer (as they do in almost every chapter) pain and death.

Yet the young man is a triumph. With wit and skill Kinglake paints in his character as a representative Englishman, complete with all the representative *vices Anglaises* – the lolling hauteur, the moral indifference, the cold charm, the lazy scepticism. *Eothen* is not a "straight" autobiographical account of Kinglake's travels; it is a dramatic monologue. It creates the "Orient" as seen through the sensibility of someone who is a close blood-relative of Flashman.

What Kinglake prizes in him is his detachment. As a narrator, he is ideally ruthless. The great comic set-piece of the book, the visit to Lady Hester Stanhope in her fastness in the Lebanon, is a cad's tale, in which the malicious arrogance of the young man matches, point for point, the outrageous posturing of *Milèdi*. *Eothen*'s climax (carefully built-up-to, arranged to happen exactly three-quarters of the way through the book) is the description of the Plague in Cairo. It is an extraordinary stretch of writing: frightening, exact and funny in equal parts. Yet the exactitude, the terror, spring from the absurd distance that the narrator is able to put between himself and his appalling subject. There's no natural piety in his account: it is snobbish, pitiless, monstrously comic.

> I became quite accustomed to the peculiar manner which [Dthmemetri, his servant] assumed when he prepared to announce a new death to me. The poor fellow naturally supposed that I should feel some uneasiness at hearing of the "accidents" which happened to persons employed by me, and he therefore communicated their deaths, as though they were the deaths of friends; he would cast down his eyes, and look like a man abashed, and then gently, and with a mournful gesture allow the words "Morto, Signor," to come through his lips. I don't know how many of such instances occurred, but they were several, and besides these (as I told you before,) my banker, my doctor, my landlord, and my magician, all died of the Plague.

If Kinglake's tone sounds oddly familiar and up to date, it is because he, more than anyone, established the voice of the modern English literary traveller. Robert Byron's *The Road to Oxiana* draws so directly from Kinglake that there are moments when Byron comes close to plagiarism (as in his borrowing of the playlet involving the *whirr! whirr! whizz! whizz!* Pasha). Evelyn Waugh's *Labels* smacks of Kinglake. So does Graham Greene's *Journey Without Maps*. So, more recently, does Paul Theroux's *The Great Railway Bazaar*. Since its publication 140 years ago, *Eothen* has been teaching writers how to travel, how to be clever, funny and true. It is one of the most deliciously nasty books in English literature.

1982

STEVENSON: SAILING TOWARDS MARRIAGE

Too much of Stevenson's work is marred for the modern reader by its desolate and ingratiating charm. As John Bayley has said, it tends to smack of "what I did on my hols". Scotland, the Rhine, the Cevennes, the South Seas all rise from Stevenson's writing at its worst like images from a travel agent's brochure; over-coloured, drained of reality. *The Amateur Emigrant* is a triumphant exception to this general rule. It is a black book – Stevenson's blackest by far. As a document it is, quite simply, the best account ever written of *the* great European adventure in the 19th century, the passage to America, the New World. It is, though, far more than a document. It has the resonance and simplicity of a myth. Its secret subject is the nature of personal identity – the same theme that Stevenson pursued, in a schematic and sensational way, in "Doctor Jekyll and Mr Hyde". For the first and, regrettably, the last time in his career, Stevenson found in the form of the workaday travel book a marvellously subtle and elastic vehicle for his imaginative concerns. *The Amateur Emigrant* is a living nightmare, and a masterpiece.

The extraordinary quality of the book can be partly – and only partly – explained by the extraordinariness, for Stevenson himself, of the journey it describes. When he sailed from the Clyde for New York in 1879, Stevenson was not on his hols; he was travelling in deadly earnest. The decision to go to America was the most important one in his life.

He was 28. He had already idled wistfully with his donkey in the hills, and in a canoe on the Rhine waterway system, in *Travels with a Donkey* and *An Inland Voyage*. He was making a bare living as an essayist and reviewer. His lungs were in bad shape and he was chronically feverish; it was no accident that his writing up till now had mostly reported the peregrinations of an invalid in search of sun and fresh air.

Three years before, he had met Fanny Osbourne at Fontainebleau. Mrs Osbourne was an American, separated from her husband, with two children in tow. She and Stevenson fell in love; then she returned to San Francisco. In 1879, she telegraphed Stevenson in Edinburgh, begging him to join her. His father, appalled at the prospect of this scandalous match, refused to contribute a penny to Stevenson's transatlantic fare. After a violent row with his parents, the sickly young writer took ship. He was breaking with Europe, with his family, with his entire past. Despite the title of his book, there was nothing amateurish about his emigration.

He was poor, but it was love, and not poverty, that drove him to cross the Atlantic. Fanny Osbourne's telegram caused him to take part in the most important mass-odyssey of modern history, as he joined the poor of Europe in their search for a new life in a promised land. Embarking at Clydebank in the company of the unemployed of Scotland and Northern England, he was at one with the Jewish peasants sailing from Bremerhaven, Swedes from Gothenberg, Italians from Naples, Irish from Cork. Most travelled "steerage class" (named because the accommodations were originally around the rudder of the ship), in unventilated holds below the waterline. Disease spread easily in these beastly conditions, and many people died on the way.

The ordeal of the voyage (which lasted anything from ten days to four weeks) separated the two worlds of Europe and America in much the same way as Purgatory separates Hell and Heaven – at least, that is how it has been seen in literature. The miseries of travelling in steerage became a powerful symbol of the rift between the two continents, their cultures and histories, and of the profound sea-change wrought on the individual in his passage to becoming an American. Again and again in American fiction – especially in novels written by American Jews, from Abraham Cahan's *The Rise of David Levinsky* to Henry Roth's *Call It Sleep* – the Atlantic crossing was given the heightened meaning of a legendary event, a new chapter in the Book of Exodus.

No one, though, brought the authority of first-hand experience to these descriptions. Established writers did not travel in steerage; and the novelists were nearly all American-born, reliant on parents and grandparents for stories of how it was. Stevenson's position was unique: he went as a poor man; unlike the Jews of Eastern Europe, he was an English-speaker; and he was a professional writer with a notebook. The pressure of his own circumstances saved him from being a mere reporter or a tourist. As a result, *The Amateur Emigrant*, with its classic American subject, has a richness of detail and feeling that is unmatched in American literature.

It's clear that Stevenson did not mean to write a very ambitious book. He would have been happy, I think, if he had been able to cast his experience in the whimsical, digressive form that had brought him a good deal of success in *Travels with a Donkey*. The "Amateur" of the title has a bright, belle-lettristic ring to it; so do chapter-titles like "Steerage Scenes" and "Steerage Types". Early on, he tries to ramble gaily in his old manner, and there are a few passages of routinely "lyrical" natural description.

Yet something is obviously wrong. The formula won't fit. Whatever happened to Stevenson on the exhausting journey by boat and train to San Francisco, it was too momentous, perhaps too terrible, to write out in his usual style of limp dandification. Instead, the experience itself seems to have taken hold of Stevenson and dictated its own form, powerfully overriding the author's original intentions.

The form eventually taken by *The Amateur Emigrant* is that of a *rite de passage*; it has the ritual structure of a marriage service or a funeral. The old self undergoes a symbolic death; the soul is put to trial and shriven; a new self is born in glory at the end of the rite. It is an immensely strong and evocative pattern; everywhere in the book, Stevenson seems to be governed by it more by instinct than by any conscious will to shape his writing to its demands.

From the beginning, it is made subtly evident that the emigrant steamer and its human cargo have a significance that goes well beyond the literal and the journalistic. The ship is a close cousin to Brant's 15th-century *Narrenschiff*, the ship of fools.

> We were a company of the rejected; the drunken, the incompetent, the weak, the prodigal, all who had been unable to prevail against circumstances in the one land, were now fleeing pitifully to another; and though one or two might still succeed, all had already failed. We were a shipful of failures, the broken men of England.

The tone here is important. It is one of many passages where Stevenson is explicitly writing in the ceremonial language of the prayer book. Something solemn, important and universal is going on here; something way over the top of the conventional accuracies and details of realism.

Almost immediately, the old self of the emigrant starts to dissolve. First, he loses his class. In Europe he was a "gentleman"; on board ship, the only reminder of that lost status is a brass plate on the door of a lavatory:

> I was like one with a patent of nobility in a drawer at home;
> and when I felt out of spirits I could go down and refresh
> myself with a look of that brass plate.

Next, he loses his occupation. To the amusement of his fellow
passengers, he spends most of each day writing. Eventually, nailed
as "a writer", he is given the passenger-list and told to reproduce it
in copybook. Finally, on the train, he loses his name. He refuses to
tell it to a curious stranger, and takes the nickname "Shakespeare".

These are not, of course, just ritual losses. They are part of the
humiliating experience of every emigrant. In bare outline, they define
what it means to be uprooted from one's country and one's past. In
The Amateur Emigrant, though, one watches Stevenson conducting
a curiously Jekyll-like experiment. He is fascinated by the process of
becoming a nobody. "I was travelling . . . out of myself." Nameless,
jobless, shorn of his personal history, his identity becomes perfectly
fluid. At one moment, he is taken to be a seaman; at another, a
musician. The rigours of the trip turn Stevenson into a lost soul,
charging across America in the company of millions of other souls,
all equally lost.

This appalled, phantasmagoric vision makes Stevenson's account
of the United States read much like a report on Inferno. He has no
time at all for the usual 19th-century pieties about the Melting
Pot, Westward Expansion, or the notion of America as Liberty,
welcoming the poor of Europe with compassionate open arms. What
he sees are restless souls in torment:

> It was still westward that they ran. Hunger, you would have
> thought, came out of the east like the sun, and the evening
> was made of edible gold. And, meantime, in the car in front
> of me, were there not half a hundred emigrants from the
> opposite quarter? Hungry Europe and hungry China, each
> pouring from their gates in search of provender, had here
> come face to face. The two waves had met; east and west
> had alike failed; the whole round world had been prospected
> and condemned; there was no El Dorado anywhere; and till
> one could emigrate to the moon, it seemed as well to stay
> patiently at home. Nor was there wanting another sign, at
> once more picturesque and more disheartening; for, as we
> continued to steam westward towards the land of gold, we
> were continually passing other emigrant trains upon the
> journey east; and these were as crowded as our own. Had

all these return voyagers made a fortune in the mines? Were they all bound for Paris, and to be in Rome by Easter? It would seem not, for, whenever we met them, the passengers ran on to the platform and cried to us through the windows, in a kind of wailing chorus, to "come back". On the plains of Nebraska, in the mountains of Wyoming, it was still the same cry, and dismal to my heart, "Come back!"

This is the nadir of the journey, Stevenson's darkest night of the soul. In the enormous emptiness of Nebraska and Wyoming (where the settler's eye "must embrace at every glance the whole seeming concave of the visible world; it quails before so vast an outlook, it is tortured by distance . . ."), the sick emigrant, crouched in a corner of the railroad car, is shriven.

In the final chapter the rite of passage is completed; the emigrant reborn in the green landscape of northern California. Greeting the river, the pine forest and the coloured sky, Stevenson writes "It was like meeting one's wife". Indeed, a real wedding was in the offing; Fanny Osbourne, now divorced, married Stevenson in 1880. The marriage in the book, though, is an exact and brilliant symbol. The old European is dead, the emigrant purged. He comes to California as a bridegroom.

The symbolic structure of *The Amateur Emigrant* is vital to the book. It is its hidden engine, giving it the pace and depth of a fine novel. Yet the real marvel of the thing is the way that Stevenson keeps the book continuously working at two separate levels. On one level there is the story, Dostoevskian in tone and execution, of the dissolution of an identity in a landscape close to that of Hell. On another, there is a heartbreakingly vivid documentary account of a real sea voyage, a real train journey.

For Stevenson's temperament was instinctively sceptical and empirical. He hoarded detail for its own sake. He was an immensely careful and sympathetic observer of other people's lives. When he came to deal with the physical conditions of the ship and the train, and with the characters of the emigrants, he was a scrupulous miniaturist. Every page of *The Amateur Emigrant* is dotted about with the trifles of life – with smells, fragments of dialect speech, clothes, facial expressions. It has the dense and varied texture of a true record.

Stevenson never wrote anything like this again. His next essay in travel, *The Silverado Squatters*, goes straight back to the cheerful whimsy of *Travels with a Donkey*. His fiction is obsessed with the dangerous identity games that he first explored in *The Amateur Emigrant*, but there they are distanced, seen through the reducing glass of gothic mannerism.

The book looks now like a lucky accident of history. In 1879, Stevenson happened to be going to the right place at the right time. Chance threw him the subject of his life; the story that he made of it is, I think, the best book he ever wrote – a marvellous piece of writing, lakelike in its lucidity and depth, part fact, part fiction, a genuine original.

1983

BELLOC AT SEA

No one who now reads *The Cruise of the Nona* for the first time will respond to it without some sense of shock. Most people will come to it (as I did) because of its fugitive reputation as a sea classic; an enchanting story of a voyage in a small boat down the Irish Sea and up the English Channel, a book full of idyllic solitude, of sunsets, storms, oily calms, wet sleeping-bags, tide races, tangled ropes and the rest of it. Such readers, if they skip judiciously, will manage to find what they want, but they won't be prepared for what *The Cruise of the Nona* actually is – an extraordinary and disturbing can of worms and glories.

For Belloc's work has mostly been expurgated by the passage of time. His career as a politician has been forgotten; his novels and history books are hardly read at all now. In literary history, he is mainly remembered, rather vaguely, as the over-energetic hindquarters of that quaint pantomime horse called Chesterbelloc. The Belloc whom everybody knows is the genial, baa-lamb author of *Cautionary Tales* and the *Bad Child's Book of Beasts*.

The Belloc of *The Cruise of the Nona* is a very different figure – a genuinely dangerous character. The book begins softly enough, in the language of romantic escapism, but by the time it has run its course it has laid down a seductive programme for the regeneration of England. The programme is explicitly Fascist, and the real hero of this story is Mussolini, who had come to power in Italy in 1922, three years before Belloc's *Cruise* was first published. The politics and the romance of the book are intimately, powerfully twined together.

It is the weirdest imaginable blend of *Mein Kampf* and *Yachting Monthly*.

In his dedication to Maurice Baring, Belloc suggests with great charm and lucidity that his voyage should be construed as a metaphor. A man "will find at sea the full model of human life":

> The cruising of a boat here and there is very much what happens to the soul of a man in a larger way . . . We are granted great visions, we suffer intolerable tediums, we come to no end of the business, we are lonely out of sight of England, we make astonishing landfalls – and the whole rigmarole leads us along no whither, and yet is alive with discovery, emotion, adventure, peril and repose.

The form of the voyage, with its passages, its long reflective spells at anchor, its visits to ports, its anxious navigation, becomes the perfect vehicle for a reckoning with life at large. En route, Belloc comes to terms both with his own personal past and with the history of England, his adopted country. The sea supplies him with distance and perspective; it enables him to stand *aloof* – a nautical term, originally, meaning to "luff-up" into the wind, away from the shore. The *Nona*, his engagingly untidy, leak-prone little sloop, gives him an alternative home. The boat – sailing under no ensign – is really another sovereign state in its own right.

Afloat at sea, Belloc sees Britain as a sinking ship. His concern with the public realm goes far beyond the usual bounds of the conscientious man of letters. In spite of the fact that he was French-born (and was naturalized British only in 1902), he was elected M.P. for South Salford in 1906. He stayed on in Parliament, first as a Liberal, then as an Independent member, until 1910. He was also a historian with a distinctively European cast of mind, writing in the grand synoptic tradition of Taine and Michelet. He loaded the *Nona* with a bulky cargo of ideas and political experience. The boat is, in effect, the last repository of Belloc's notion of all that is best and sanest in European history and culture.

His cruise takes him far out into the most hazardous of political deep waters. By the 1920s his disillusion with parliamentary democracy was absolute. Watching England from a mile or two offshore, he saw a history and geography that he loved with a convert's passion, while at the same moment he saw a contemporary social order that be believed to be utterly degenerate. He characterizes parliamentary government as a treacherous delegation of authority to "the slime of the Lobbies".

> There is no form of parliamentary activity which is not deplorable, save in aristocracies.
>
> For, in aristocracies, which are of their nature, governments by a clique, a Parliament – which is a clique – can be normal and natural. In communities based on the idea of equality, and of action by the public will, they are cancers, under which such nations always sicken and may die.

Europe's tragedy, Belloc thought, lay in its return to the "vomit" of parliamentary rule at the end of World War I, "instead of continuing the rule of soldiers as it should have done".

Today it's very hard to swallow such facile advocacy of martial law as a moral imperative. In 1925 it wasn't so. When *The Cruise of the Nona* first came out, the *London Mercury* called it "the most beautiful" of Belloc's books, while the *Observer* said that Belloc "has never written better". The reviews help to remind one that Belloc was writing in a climate far warmer than ours to the idea of final solutions.

Belloc's solution, inspected with the unearned wisdom of living in the 1980s, is one of terrible banality. Heartsick of contemporary Britain (in which corrupt and lazy politicians and charabancs of day-trippers at Clovelly are treated indifferently with the same blind rage), Belloc dreams of, and prays for, a miraculous return to a "homogeneous" society; a nation of one race and one religion. The sole spark of hope on his horizon is the mirage of Italy under Il Duce.

> What a strong critical sense Italy has shown! What intelligence in rejection of sophistry, and what virility in execution! May it last!

The word *virility* is a key one in Belloc's vocabulary. It crops up in *The Cruise of the Nona* over and over again, as if the real choice before the nations of Europe was between impotence and erection. It lurks significantly in the background of his exclamatory description of Mussolini:

> What a contrast with the sly and shifty talk of your parliamentarian! What a sense of decision, of sincerity, of serving the nation, and of serving it towards a known end with a definite will! Meeting this man after talking to the parliamentarians in other countries was like meeting with some athletic friend

of one's boyhood after an afternoon with racing touts; or it was like coming upon good wine in a Pyrenean village after compulsory draughts of marsh water in the mosses of the moors above, during some long day's travel over the range.

Belloc's hearty, open-air approach to things often led him to make judgements of infantile silliness, and infantile cruelty too. His anti-semitism (violently expressed in *The Jews*, a book designed to clear himself of the charge of being an anti-semite) sprang as much, one feels, from the conviction that Jews were pallid, cerebral people who spent too much time indoors as from any more serious perception.

None of this helps to make *The Cruise of the Nona* a likeable book, though it does give it real status as a rather odious historical document. The trouble is that the splendour and vitality of *The Cruise* is directly linked to its always cranky, often ugly vision of history and politics.

For the *Nona* is held up as a tiny scale model of how an idyllic society might be; it is a ship of state in miniature, and the simple virtues of life at sea are set in counterpoint against the corruption and depravity of modern England as it slides by on the beam. The boat is Belloc's great good place – a temple of virility, comradeship and self-reliance. The sea is the immutable element: while the land gets ravaged beyond recognition by the products of industrial democracy, the sea remains the same as it has always been – a mysterious and lovely wilderness.

When he deals with the sea, Belloc writes at the top of his bent. All the most memorable stretches of *The Cruise* are full-length portraits of a particular patch of water – the Sound between Bardsey Island and the Lleyn peninsula in a high gale; the entry to Port Madoc on a still evening; the great tide-races of Portland Bill and St Alban's Head; sailing through Spithead with its naval history still vividly printed on the surrounding landscape. These set-pieces are beautifully done. There's precious little nonsense about topping-lifts and jib-sheets and the rest of the salty talk that tends to disfigure the writing of most amateur sailors. Belloc's writing is entirely free of heroics: it is a good, plain prose, full of wonder, surprisingly humble. The page-long hymn of praise to the sea, with which the book ends, is an exact distillation of the rewards of the voyage:

Sailing the sea, we play every part of life: control, direction, effort, fate; and there we can test ourselves and know our

state. All that which concerns the sea is profound and final.
The sea provides visions, darknesses, revelations . . .

There's an interesting comparison to be drawn between *The Cruise
of the Nona* and the other odd conflation of politics and sailing,
Erskine Childers's *The Riddle of the Sands*. For in Childers's case the
politics of the book (the paranoid fear of German invasion) have
dissolved away in time and left a small, purely maritime masterpiece.
I doubt if anyone now is detained long by the spy-story stuff: it is,
in any case, a very dim and feeble ancestor of the bureaucratic
nightmares of Deighton and Le Carré. One cannot say the same of
the politics of *The Cruise of the Nona*.

Belloc is still frighteningly topical. His loathing of "politicians" is
probably more widely shared today than it was in 1925. His sense of
the degeneracy of society in Britain has turned into a platitude in our
own age. His particular strictures on British institutions have an
unpleasantly familiar ring sixty years on. Belloc on the Press, for
instance: "By the very nature of the organism, this new instrument
of power, the mob Press, must be ill-informed, unreal, and – what
is not without importance – morally vile." If his remarks about Italian
Fascism and Jewry make him sound like a political coelacanth, Belloc's
basic line on the condition-of-England-question is bang up to date.
He would be very much at home in 1984; certainly more at home
than he was in his own time.

His cruise, too, strikes a deep latterday chord. When Belloc took
to the sea alone, he was one of a small company of gentleman-
oddballs. The motives that drove him – to escape from England's
overpopulous industrial society, to be self-sufficient and dependent
only on the forces of nature, to meditate – were out of the ordinary.
They have since become commonplace. Britain's domestic seas are
crowded with Nonas; and most of their helmsmen would come up
with a less articulate version of Belloc's story. Much of what in *The
Cruise of the Nona* is fresh first-hand discovery has now become part
of the rolling stock of cliché in the yachting press. To go to sea to
come face to face with the eternal verities, and to return to land as a
prophet of the Far Right, is now almost as conventional a career as
computer programming or chartered accountancy. For some reason,
the visions, darknesses and revelations of the sea never seem to turn
men into socialists.

So the book survives, still bright; partly for excellent literary
reasons, and partly (or so it seems to me) for bad political ones. For

every moment of enchantment in it – and there are many – there is a corresponding spell of Mussolini-worship or worse ("Eh, Rosenheim? Eh, Guildenstern?"). The two aspects of *The Cruise* are inseparable: each is the inevitable product of the other. Belloc self-deprecatingly calls the book "a hotchpotch", but it is far more artistically elaborate than that. Land and sea, society and solitude, history and the present, are intricately balanced and woven into a pattern; and the pattern reveals a message as unambiguous as a homily on an embroidered sampler – forsake democracy, or be destroyed by an antlike mass-culture manipulated by tycoons and politicos.

Yet the dominant image of *The Cruise of the Nona* survives in spite of the crudity of the book's political intentions. Belloc, sitting alone at the tiller of the *Nona*, piloting his boat through the tricky waters of England and Wales, is cantankerously alive. One shares his adventures; quarrels furiously with him along the way; and remembers his own epitaph on himself:

> When I am dead, I hope it may be said:
> "His sins were scarlet, but his books were read."

1984

WILSON IN EUROPE

In January 1946 Evelyn Waugh wrote to thank his literary agent for a sheaf of press cuttings and gloated, "We have shaken off Edmund Wilson at last." Waugh could have been speaking for England: no foreign literary visitor has ever stung the country with quite such painful and telling effect as Wilson. His powerful argumentative capacity as a critic, his novelist's shrewd eye for psychological undercurrents, his instinctive grasp of social nuance, his snappish wit and his determination to chasten England by going all out for her tender parts make him the most formidable Anglophobe on record.

For *Europe without Baedeker* is really a book about the British at home and abroad. Though its settings are frequently rocky and sun-baked, with olive groves and statuary, its main characters are the British officers, men and civil servants who patrolled Europe in their jeeps and staff cars in the last days of war and the first days of peace in 1945. It has not lost its sting. Forty years on, its depiction of the snobbery, hypocrisy and insensitivity that Wilson saw as our chief national characteristics can still make the English reader squirm with embarrassed recognition: it is not nearly so easy to shake off Edmund Wilson as Evelyn Waugh imagined.

When he arrived in London in April 1945, on assignment from the *New Yorker* to report on the "wreckage" of Europe, Wilson was nearly 50. He was the most distinguished American literary intellectual of his age. Photographs of him at this time show a sombre suited corpulent figure, high browed and balding, his stonelike features habitually cast in the expression of a bank manager declining to allow an overdraft to an old friend. He exudes an air of ponderous responsibility – as well he might, since for 30 years already he had been teaching his contemporaries how to read and think. Bunny Wilson was an American institution, a one-man university. He had schooled his generation (Hemingway, Fitzgerald, Dos Passos, John Peale Bishop) in the French Symbolist poets, in Freud, in Marxism, in native American literature. He was relied on as a latterday Oracle, and he had the brilliant journalist's gift of making his thoughts seem like news. It was inevitable that Wilson's thoughts on Europe were awaited in America with an unusual degree of respectful attention.

So his trip had some of the self-conscious weightiness of an ambassadorial progress. Wearing the tabs of an American war corre-spondent, Wilson was sounding out the health of European culture and finding it to be dreadfully, perhaps mortally, enfeebled. *Baedeker* – that universal symbol of travelling for the fun of it – was banished on the title page; on his tour of Europe, Wilson was on serious business.

Yet, like his gloomy taste in managerial three-piece suits, all this was something of a pose on Wilson's part. The grave diagnostician was also a thoroughgoing bohemian – a famously hard drinker, an indefatigable chaser after girls, a temperamentally footloose man whose country house in Wellfleet, Massachusetts, was proving an insufficient anchor to keep him permanently moored. His European journey was, as so many classic journeys are, a quest in search of love, adventure and distraction. The relation between its severe, official public face and its libidinous private motives is a curious one – and it helps to explain the tone of aggrieved passion which gives *Europe without Baedeker* its peculiar force.

When Wilson came to London, his marriage to Mary McCarthy was in ashes and he had already set his heart on McCarthy's likely successor – an English society beauty called Mamaine Paget. In the book she appears in disguise and *en passant* as "G, a London girl whom I liked very much". Despite Wilson's assiduous courtship, Ms Paget preferred Arthur Koestler.

This rejection must have been hard enough for Wilson to bear at an age when sexual vanity becomes notoriously prickly and given to offence, and it no doubt made England seem an unkind place; but this wasn't all. His arrival in Europe coincided with the publication of Evelyn Waugh's *Brideshead Revisited*. Until 1945, Wilson and Waugh had admired each other's work from a safe distance, and in April Cyril Connolly introduced them at a dinner party. The meeting was a disaster. Waugh, as so often, was patronizingly rude (in his journal he recorded that he'd met "an insignificant yank called Edmund Wilson"). Wilson, much hurt, responded with a reading of *Brideshead* which was witheringly accurate about the novel's defects. His 1946 *New Yorker* review treated the book as an unedifying triumph of social snobbery and sickly nostalgia. It is impossible to read *Europe without Baedeker* and not be reminded of that review: when Wilson writes about "England" he always attributes to it the besetting sins of *Brideshead* and the appalling manners of Evelyn Waugh on a bad day.

Snubbed by Waugh and jilted by Mamaine Paget, Wilson not surprisingly fell out of love with their country. The reader has reason to be grateful to them both. They sharpened Wilson's wits for a hatchet job that has a lasting and impressive amount of justice in it. This is a vengeful book, full of concealed partiality; but here is vengeance turned to a good use, constantly tempered by intelligence and clearsighted observation. Wilson's personal rancour is a cruelly magnifying lens which tells the truth with uncompromising plainness.

The form of *Europe without Baedeker* is deceptively casual and notebooky. In fact (as one can see by comparing it with Wilson's actual notebooks in *The Forties*, edited by Leon Edel) it is a work of canny retrospective artifice, a series of elaborate variations on a single insistent theme. A notebook for August 1945 states the theme as a categoric assertion: "Perfide Albion, *la morgue anglaise*, international reputation as hypocrite". From London across Europe to Greece, under a variety of differently coloured skies, in sketches and snapshots, in sustained flights of argument and one fully worked piece of fiction ("Through the Abruzzi with Mattie and Harriet"), Wilson fleshes out that telegraphic sentence. In the process he creates something close to a mythological landscape, a Waste Land whose dismal capital is London at the time of V.E. Day.

La morgue anglaise. Wilson savoured the French phrase for its illuminating ambiguity, the idea of arrogance and death cohabiting in the same word. London he saw as both the most arrogant and the most deathly place in Europe. Within the first few pages of the book it is seen as "dim ... shut-in ... claustrophobic ... muted ... submissive ... dwindled ... starved ... breathless and strained, ridden by fatigue and fear". The adjectives, tactically deployed, convey a city which is at the same time a tragic state of mind. The pretty intricacy of London parks and squares, the "moist air which softens form and deepens colour" are quaint, sad relics of civility which only serve to underline the extent to which the social climate of Europe has been polluted. "Our whole world is poisoned now" is the sentence from which Wilson's first chapter takes its tone, and his London is a system riddled with, and leaking, poison.

Yet Wilson's literary manners as he pokes about this romantically dreadful city where the prostitutes are unclean, where the poulterers' shops sell only racks of dead crows, where the people are unfailingly rude, resentful and browbeaten, are impeccable. He keeps up the front of the polite and inquiring tourist to deadly effect. "I had forgotten what a pleasant city London was," he remarks – as a prelude to noticing that the style of British civic statuary proceeds from memorials to the poets, to Victory, horsedrawn through the sky, to "the bleak unassimilable block" of "a huge howitzer gun". In all of his face to face encounters with the British, in their theatre, their Parliament, their great churches, their ration book dinners and literary parties, it is as if the guest was out to teach his hosts a much-needed lesson in the ordinary graces of social decorum.

It is only when he steps back to frame a shaping generalization that Wilson unbuttons himself. Re-reading Dickens, Thackeray and Samuel Butler, he finds himself confronting:

> The ... basic English qualities, with which after nearly two hundred years, Americans have to reckon again: the passion for social privilege, the rapacious appetite for property, the egoism that damns one's neighbour, the dependence on inherited advantages, and the almost equally deep-fibered instinct, often not deliberate or conscious, to make all these appear forms of virtue.

Or, from the same section, this eloquent tirade on the "desperate materialism" of the British:

> *We* find making money exhilarating, but we also find it exhilarating to spend it. Money for us is a medium, a condition of life, like air. But with the English it means always property. A dollar is something that you multiply – something that causes an expansion of your house and your mechanical equipment, something that accelerates like speed; and that may be also slowed up and deflated. It is a value that may be totally imaginary, yet can for a time provide half-realized dreams. But pounds, shillings and pence are tangible, solid, heavy; they are objects one gains and possesses. And in England every good value is bound up with the things one can handle and hold.

The leaden values of the British hang heavily all over Europe. Escaping from London to Italy, Wilson finds "brilliance", "cleanness", "freedom" and "exhilaration". With George Santayana and Ignazio Silone, he is in good company – but not for long. Italy is polluted by the officious presence of people like Harriet in "Through the Abruzzi", the ruthlessly insensitive county debutante, a model English do-gooder who works for U.N.R.R.A., and the ineffably pompous Sir Osmond Gower. Gower is Sir Ronald Storrs in wafer-thin disguise; and in these full-length portraits of English monsters, Wilson the satirist, the author of *Memoirs of Hecate County*, comes enjoyably into his own:

> While Sir Osmond sat back, being brilliant and wagging his white mustaches, the audience were supposed to applaud and laugh: that was the only use he had for his companions . . .

The further Wilson travels away from London, the worse the English become. It is when he is in Greece that he plumbs the nadir of the national character. Here the English are seen as cheats (fiddling goods out of American P.X. stores with forged cards), boors, war-mongers, ingrained colonialists, dyed-in-the-wool anachronistic conservatives. They meddle unforgivably in the politics of the country, while Churchill, still their leader, himself half-American, has –

> the qualities of a romantic American journalist in love with the achievements of England and with no very realistic sense of what they amount to or what they involve. He has always lived more or less in a historical novel for boys just as Theodore Roosevelt did . . .

Flatly stated, Wilson's assault on the British sounds too shrill and bigoted to be true. What makes it stick is the fundamental good sense and good temper of Wilson's writing, his passion for the palpable detail. When he sees two puppet-like sentries at the entrance to the British Army Headquarters in Athens . . .

> Whenever an officer went in or out, these sentries, instead of presenting arms, would convulsively lift the rifle butt and bring it down on the ground, at the same time stamping one foot – as if they had been mechanical contrivances controlled, like the doors at the Pennsylvania Station, by photoelectric cells. If you watched them, as I did, for a moment, the effect was absolutely gruesome. It reminded me of the goose-step.

"Goose-step" is a lethal accusation, but here it is perfectly justified, rooted in a close fabric of supporting details. On this occasion, as elsewhere in the book, British and German militarism turn out to be ugly kissing-cousins.

In a key passage Wilson identifies a major symptom of *la morgue anglaise* as the habit of "suppressing the first person", of using the word "one" where an American would say "I". This "impersonal passive" (at Delphi an officer remarks languidly that "most of the time is spent swimming") is the grammatical heart of so much of the rudeness and indifference that Wilson observed on his travels. Take away the first person and you take away the first-hand. The English-man, instead of speaking from his own feelings and experience, is inclined to speak out of the prejudices of his class. ("One hasn't been to Sheffield"), in a miserably impoverished code of stock responses and ready-made phrases. It is this secondhand quality in British speech, and its implications for British social and intellectual life, that infects half the characters in *Europe without Baedeker* with their peculiar inherited and incurable disease.

There is not much comfort to be had from reading the book today. "The class line-up" which "runs through the whole people like a fissure" is as aggressively here under the government of Mrs Thatcher as it ever was under the government of Churchill, even if the particular terms by which class difference is measured have altered. The lethargic resentfulness, first nailed here by Wilson, continues to be observed by the literary travellers, most recently by Paul Theroux in *The Kingdom by the Sea*, where he writes of the "insulted" look of so many of the people he meets. What has gone is the romantic glamour of walking through a landscape literally wrecked and ruined by six years of warfare, of finding the Waste Land in the here-and-now. Yet who today would not recognize this scene?

> My companion . . . remarked: "It's a kind of Hell – eternally waiting in the street while one watches all the people one most loathes getting into taxis and driving off." He was not naturally an unamiable man, and it seemed to me that his comment was typical of the general state of mind to which England was now reduced: a combination of competitive spitefulness with exasperated patience.

The British reader who is tackling *Europe without Baedeker* for the first time would be well advised to first unpack his hair shirt.

1985

YOUNG'S SLOW BOATS

Gavin Young's *Slow Boats to China** tells two tales in parallel. The first is the official story, of Mr Young's adventures on and off the high seas as he tried to make his way by cargo boat, launch, and ferry from Piraeus to Canton. The second story (just as engrossing) is about his adventures (almost as hazardous) with the travel book as a literary form. The two intertwine to make a vivid, flawed, revealing book whose botches and lacunae are as interesting as its flights of brilliance.

Both journeys started with the same liberating idea. Mr Young had been a journalist, the chief foreign correspondent of the *Observer*. In that role, he had travelled altogether too fast and too purposefully; a creature of deadlines, flight numbers, and assignments. He had gone wherever there was trouble in the world, to report wars and revolutions. In 1979 he set out to retrieve his own lost innocence of vision. As a child, he had grown up by the sea in Cornwall; when he travelled then (as a passenger on a coaster carrying china clay to Antwerp) he'd been content with the simple magic of the going, untouched as yet by the adult's hysteria over schedules and

* Gavin Young, *Slow Boats to China* (London: Hutchinson).

destinations. So, this time too, he would go by sea, slowly. He wouldn't travel as a journalist, but as a writer, with the writer's freedom to play truant and to follow his own nose rather than the cabled instructions of an editor. It was to be a return in two senses – to childlikeness and to places that Mr Young had seen before through the unchildlike eyes of the salaried correspondent.

It was a lovely plan; and of course it could only have worked out pat in an unfallen world, where it might have produced a dully innocent book. In fact, Young was in trouble from the beginning, wrestling with gods just as tiresome and unpredictable as the ones who made such a mess of Odysseus' itinerary. Red tape and timetables are the late 20th century's equivalent to fair and foul winds, and the parts of Aeolus, Zeus, and Poseidon are played, in *Slow Boats to China*, by a gang of shipping agents and consular officials. Passages and visas are granted and withheld in bewildering succession. The chief business of these bureaucratic godlings is to remind Mr Young that he is, after all, a grown-up in a grown-up world. Whatever fancy notions he may have had in his head, his fate is to stand in line and sweat and curse like everyone else.

He is only halfway down the Red Sea, at Jedda, when the godlings score with a vengeance. A complacent Saudi with a rubber stamp robs Young of 2800 miles of his voyage by making him take a 747 to Dubai. Eleven hundred miles are lopped off at Karachi; another 900 go at Goa. Nor is Young, the unwilling old hand at scenes of violence and political oppression, allowed to forget such things for more than a day or two at a time. On the *Al Anoud*, out of Beirut, men with bloodied heads are trying to kill each other. Travelling in the domain of really important godlings like Sadat, Khomeini, General Zhia, and President Marcos is not an innocent pastime; try as he does to evade his Furies, Young finds them constantly at his elbow, muscling in on almost every encounter in the book. On the rim of the prettiest landscape there is always the shadow of the political prison, the rusty stain, the figure of a thug in uniform.

We owe the godlings something. Thanks to them, *Slow Boats to China* is not a sentimental idyll; it is a real journey in which every passage of high elation by moonlight under a full sail or a rusty smokestack is counterpointed by another, of frustration, anxiety, or funk. Mr Young's long voyage is very much like life, and it's in the very lifelikeness of the voyage that Mr Young's problems as a writer start.

In his opening pages Young revels in two closely related kinds of freedom. The first is the exhilarating liberty of being afloat in the world, of casting off and leaving London far astern. The second freedom has to do with words: released from journalism, Young can afford to ride language playfully, absorbing himself in details, images, phrases that would never have found a place in his copy while he was a correspondent. So, in Patmos, appropriately enough, where Orestes fled to escape the real Furies, we are told that the Monastery of St John was founded in 1088, but it sits beside the much more beguiling piece of information that "the girls' braless breasts wobbled about under their T-shirts like hotwater bottles under a sheet". The 1967 coup by the three Greek colonels is eclipsed by the observation that ice cubes dropped in ouzo turn it slowly into milk. On the waterfront at Smyrna, Young spots the N.A.T.O. building. For a journalist, one could hardly imagine a more important place; but here it is crisply dismissed as a "dull gray filing cabinet". What is truly important in that chapter turns out to be a perfectly anonymous car-ferry with its ramp open on the wharf. It "looked like a hippopotamus refusing a pill" – a simile strong enough to bring the chapter to an end.

In her book on Sartre, Iris Murdoch points out that the novel habitually deals in the realm of the contingent rather than the necessary. That is even more true of the travel book. It thrives on truant felicities like hot water bottles, ice cubes in ouzo, and gulping hippos. Characters met by chance, details seen from the corner of the eye . . . it is a form which embraces the contingent as securely as reportorial journalism claims, at least, to bring back the necessary. The chief strength of *Slow Boats to China* is its alertness to all the quiddities of a marvellously, heroically unnecessary journey. Young's liberation as a writer is infectious. It's as if the foreign correspondent had been wearing a hood like a tethered falcon; writing the book, he's in flight, seeing the world for the first time without tunnel vision.

It's this literary freedom that has drawn so many writers to the travel book. It is the supreme improvisatory form: one can play it by ear; it will happily accommodate all sorts and conditions of writing. At its occasional best it works like a constellation, with autobiography, essays, stories, reportage mingling together in a single controlled blaze. More often it has the casual freedom of the scrapbook, into which any old thing can be pasted at will; a lifelike form, certainly, with all of life's contingencies, dead ends, and artlessness. *Slow Boats to China* is closer to the scrapbook than the constellation; it is too true to life for its own good.

Young does have the ingredients of a driving narrative here. A man goes to sea in middle age, half to escape, half to come to terms with a past that has given him an oversceptical and hardboiled view of the world. The godlings dog his passage. His past comes back, in the form of flashbacks to old wars. Intermittently, in the wheelhouses and fo'c's'les of tacky little ships, he comes to a private peace with himself, mostly in the company of gentle, uncomplicated men who share these travelling fragments of their lives with him. It is the common *Odyssey* plot, of a kind that might easily have made an autobiographical novel; and it's this story which keeps one reading *Slow Boats to China* through its doldrums.

Because he is writing a travel book and not a novel, Young doesn't stick to his story. Stories happen in the past; much of this book takes place in a hamfisted present tense. Take these sentences, for instance (and they could have been lifted from any one of a dozen recent books about journeys): "Harry Miller has lived in India since the war. He is an excellent naturalist . . ." "As a vision from the sea, Singapore is still exciting . . ." "Alex is a Greek Cypriot by birth and has represented the Associated Press in innumerable hair-raising forays . . ." "Izmir, or Smyrna, is the third largest city . . ." "Alan Webb has lived in Sarawak for nearly thirty years . . ." Such factoid knobs and protuberances announce that *Slow Boats to China* is both something more and something less than a work of the imagination. Its real locations survive the progress of the author through them, while the characters in it have names and addresses of a kind one could verify from a telephone directory. Their stubborn actuality simply won't boil down into the story, and they stick out at abrupt right angles to the central narrative thread.

Yes, of course they *are* real – they do live on in a tense beyond the reach of the book as a story. Yet when we meet them in the book, these people and places, the Alan Webbs and Harry Millers, Smyrnas and Singapores, are fictions. They are real to us only insofar as the writer can create them on the page, and it's not enough merely to assert that they exist and therefore need no creation.

This is the awkward question that every serious travel book must face. How far dare one invent what is already ascertainably there? Gavin Young's answer is easygoing to a fault. He invents when the mood takes him, and asserts when it doesn't. When the story flags, he fills in with a few paragraphs on Egyptian politics, a potted biography of an old friend, architectural notes, a stray memory. Then the voyage, recreated in imagination, picks up again.

The strongest sequences are those on shipboard. Young is marvellous at building up the small, self-contained community of a boat at sea: it is his great good place, and his writing works over its construction lovingly. Sailing from Dubai on the *Al Raza*, for instance, "that inelegant polluter of the breezes of the Arabian Sea", Young writes at the top of his bent as he explores the deep, calming harmony between himself, the ship, and its Baluchi crew. The vessel is a derelict tub: her engine breaks down; under sail, she slops about on a windless ocean. Yet Young turns her into a precious, sane corner of a crazy and frustrating world.

Aboard the *Al Raza* dialogue takes place in lyric pidgin. Its happy mish-mash of phrase-book Arabic, phrase-book English, embraces, and handshakes is the language of sanity. Young asks one of the hands if dhows like this one are often lost at sea:

> "Ooooooooh, often," said Sumar, waving his arms happily to indicate fatal storms. "Big winds" – phweee! Big waves – oooooow! They go over. Many, many. Oooh, yah."

A little later, Sumar points to where the coast of Iran smudges into Pakistan:

> "Before sometimes I go to fish in there." Sumar frowned indignantly. "But Irani militia there shoot at me – *tuk! tuk!* " He mimed a man firing a rifle. "I go away quickly – Khomeini peoples no good." He added scornfully, "Old man with beard."

In this seaborne dislocation from the political world, the simplicities of pidgin are able to tell a kind of truth which is unavailable to the language of the landsman. It is what being afloat is really about: the sea, and the small impromptu family aboard ship, restore Young to wonder – and to common sense.

The book is rich in characters like Sumar and in ships like the *Al Raza*. Against them, though, one must set the old chums: the administrators, planters, foreign correspondents – the Alan Webbs and Harry Millers. Few have any real life on the page. Where Young is excellent at creating dialogue for his deckhands and captains, he makes his journalists talk in unconvincing blocks of copy. At sea, he is a writer in the steps of Conrad; ashore, he goes back to his old haunts and his old role as a newspaperman, hammering out routine, and often disjointed, dispatches from foreign parts.

He has much the same difficulty when it comes to the problem of managing his own character in the book. Sometimes he is there, a fully invented picaresque hero. When pirates overtake his crippled launch on the Sulu Sea, it is Young who saves the day by grinning furiously and taking all their pictures with his Polaroid. As "Yong" or "Mr Gavin", he is one of his own best creations: a self-deprecating quickthinker, easily charmed, easily irritated, a craggy, wounded, affectionate man who is addicted to swimming out of his depth to find himself. As long as this engaging character is firmly in the centre of things, his book has the imaginative solidity of good fiction. Yet there are long, long stretches when the hero seems to have taken leave of the narrative altogether. The details keep on coming, the voyage continues to be recorded, but where has "Mr Gavin" gone? The answer is that he's regressed, to being just the observer from the *Observer*.

As anyone who has experimented with the form of the travel book will know, these are common problems. The relationship between the journey and the book, the reality and the tale, is a very tricky one indeed. Mythologize the experience too much, and veracity leaks, then pours, out of the story. Travel books need their raw edges. They cannot, on the other hand, afford to be simple inventories of everything that happened on the trip. Too many of the events and people in *Slow Boats to China* have earned their place in the book merely because they happened to be there in life. If only Gavin Young had lightened ship by throwing overboard everything that wasn't essential to the quest which should have governed his narrative, he would have written a really fine book. As it is, he has brought back a fascinating collection of souvenirs. As with all collections, some exhibits are boring, others gems. They provide all the material for a patterned story, but this book is not that story. At best, it is fragments, episodes, notes, drafts of a kind that would lead one to say that this is *going to be* a wonderful book.

The blurb announces that *Slow Boats to China* is indeed only half of a long story. Mr Young is setting off again from Shanghai and continuing eastward back to Cornwall where the idea of going to sea started. If he sacks the foreign correspondent in himself, if he attends more to the tale in the Jamesian sense, if he dramatizes himself more fully, and shapes and invents with more consistency, he will (I enviously suspect) turn that journey into a classic book of travel.

1982

PRIESTLEY AND BAINBRIDGE IN ENGLAND

All through the past summer in England we were getting someone else's weather and someone else's news. On television the freakish sun, falling from a bold blue sky, lit the glittering lines of police riot shields. Beyond them picketing miners dressed in pastel nylon summer clothes, were hurling rocks, bottles, pieces of timber. A close-up picked out a handsome young policeman, apparently battering the brains out of a striking miner with his club. The whole scene looked surreal – an engagement between well-drilled Romans and angry Visigoths.

The news item ended and was replaced on the screen by a picture of a reservoir that had run dry in the long drought. A village, drowned thirty years ago to provide water for a Midland city, was exposed to the gaze of curious tourists, who stood in knots on the cracked and scaly mud, looking out on the ruined main street, the crumbled pub, the little river bridge whose arch had fallen in. The ruins were unrecognizable. The tourists might as well have been staring at those dull, fenced-off bumps in the ground that are posted as neolithic settlements and Saxon forts. The village belongs to the rainbow trout now. It is an obscure piece of subaquatic archaeology.

The television picture was overladen with meaning. How inaccessible the past has become – even the recent past of the 1950s. The drowned village really is a world and a half away from 1984; its version of society is as irretrievable as something out of folklore. Meanwhile the pound slides magnetically downward, drawn to parity with the dollar. Unemployment goes on rising. Mrs Thatcher makes more and more ebullient speeches about how the government has set Britain right on target, as if the country were a missile and our destination a big bang in some far sky. To my English eye, accustomed to more hazy, ambiguous, watercolour tones, it all seems thoroughly unEnglish. *Where are we at?*

When one feels as if one is living in a foreign country, the situation calls for a journey of reconnaissance and rediscovery. The famous books about England are – not surprisingly – the products of periods of catastrophic change in British society. The Domesday Book of

1086 was a necessary reckoning with the country during its traumatic passage from Saxon to Norman rule; Celia Fiennes's journeys of 1685–1703 and Daniel Defoe's *A Tour through the Whole Island of Great Britain* (1724–1727) registered the crucial shift of power from the court to the provincial, commercial bourgeoisie. In 1933, the effects of the Depression stung J. B. Priestley into making his *English Journey*,* republished just before Priestley's death this August at 89. It is a fair measure of our present disquiet that the last couple of years or so have seen English journeys cropping up in publishers' lists as if they were a genre, like gothics or romances. Paul West . . . Paul Theroux . . . now Beryl Bainbridge;† and more journeys wait in the wings. England in the 1980s is running short of all sorts of resources; not least of which is the stock of English men and women who remain as yet uninterviewed by travelling authors and television journalists on the subject of their position on the condition of England.

For England is hardly big enough to make a proper journey around it at all. Half the size of Italy, a quarter that of France, it has almost exactly the same number of square miles to its name as North Carolina. (Even in a Raleigh bookstore, I suspect, the title "North Carolina Journey" would have a comically pretentious ring to it.) Yet, like all small islands, England has got into the insular habit of thinking itself enormous, continental. Nor is this simply to do with its late political importance in the world. Even now the English take their cardinal points very solemnly indeed. North and South are worlds apart, buffered by the Midlands, grandly pluralized. The West Country (hardly more than an hour's train ride from London) is regarded as florid, rural, quaintly backward; as remote as Provence or the Dordogne. British television, far from homogenizing these images, exaggerates them. Advertisements depict beer drinkers from the North, honest farmers from the West, go-ahead housewives from the balmy South; in doing so, they exploit every trifling difference they can find of accent, architecture, fashion, class. When geography fails us, we can always fall back on that multitude of social barriers and distinctions with which the English have cunningly enlarged their little acreage. Or vice versa.

When Orwell wrote *The Road to Wigan Pier*, his journey to Wigan was hardly necessary, since he could have found almost exactly the

---

* J. B. Priestley, *English Journey* (Chicago: University of Chicago Press).
* Beryl Bainbridge, *English Journey* (New York: George Braziller).

same social conditions prevailing just around the corner in, say, Whitechapel or East Ham; but the 180 miles that separate Wigan from London conveniently ratified and explained the gulf between the English middle and working classes. To an English audience, a certain louche exoticism inevitably attaches itself to the idea of poverty in Wigan. Like Samarkand and Calcutta, Wigan is a place that most of us visit only in books, and we'd be pleasurably credulous to learn that in Wigan it was common practice to go in for black magic, snake-charming, or the eating of children. A fundamental ignorance about the fringes of our own neighbourhood is one of the prerequisites of being English. Without it, we might actually wake up to the intolerable fact that we have nine times North Carolina's population crammed into North Carolina's space.

So the English journey is by nature an epical affair. The terrain to be surveyed is conceived of as vast. The route is arduous. The traveller is always unworthy of the great task before him. Defoe, prefacing his description of "the most flourishing and opulent country in the world", sets the tone nicely:

> In travelling through England, a luxuriance of objects presents itself to our view. Wherever we come, and which way so ever we look, we see something new, something significant, something well worth the traveller's stay, and the writer's care; nor is any check to our design, or obstruction to its acceptance in the world, to say the like has been done already, or to panegyric upon the labours and value of those authors who have gone before, in this work. A complete account of Great Britain will be the work of many years, I might say ages, and may employ many hands. Whoever has travelled Great Britain before us, and whatever they have written, though they may have had a harvest, yet they have always, either by necessity, ignorance or negligence passed over so much, that others may come and glean after them by large handfuls.

If one adds to Defoe the closing remarks of J. B. Priestley, writing two hundred years later, the join is seamless, the style and manner perfectly at one:

> Ours is a country that has given the world something more than millions of yards of calico and thousands of steam engines. If we are a nation of shopkeepers, then what a shop!

There is Shakespeare in the window, to begin with; and the whole establishment is blazing with geniuses. Why, these little countries of ours have known so many great men and great ideas that one's mind is dazzled by their riches. We stagger beneath our inheritance.

No wonder that most English travel books deal with the wastes and deserts of the world. England – at least the English idea of England – is so bulgy, so intractable, so multitudinous that it transcends the capacity of one man ever to put it in perspective. It was on Malta, another, even smaller, island, that Evelyn Waugh was defeated by a hotelier who kept on saying, "'Ullo, 'ullo. And 'ow's that book getting along? You don't seem to be seeing much of the island. You couldn't see a 'alf of it, not if you was to spend a lifetime 'ere, you couldn't." It is the proudest complaint of the English journeyer that he is unable to see the half of it even though he has spent a lifetime there.

In 1933, when Priestley made his English journey, the number of people registered as being out of work was 2,498,100. That is the dominant fact of Priestley's book. It sets him travelling and it colours almost every perception that he has of England. One sentence echoes through the book like a ground bass: "Never were more men doing nothing and there never was before so much to be done." This forthright apprehension of what was wrong with the country gives the journey point and clarity, turns it into a serious quest for a solution, and leads Priestley to the passionate flights of description of the decaying industrial landscape that make the book at least as vivid as anything else that Priestley ever wrote.

To begin with, it is true, he dallies for a while in the South; hobnobbing with on-the-make travelling salesmen on the new arterial roads, sipping ale in rosy Cotswold villages, making the acquaintance of an eccentric aristocrat in a great country house. But the book and the journey catch fire as he moves north to Birmingham, the Black Country, and beyond. Riding on the top deck of a Birmingham tram, he achieves the characteristic tone of warm indignation that will last him through the book:

> If I was tired and perhaps a little low-spirited when I began, I was still more tired and far lower-spirited before I had done. For there was nothing, I repeat, to light up a man's mind for one single instant. I loathed the whole long array of shops, with their nasty bits of meat, their cough mixtures,

their *Racing Specials*, their sticky cheap furniture, their shoddy clothes, their fly-blown pastry, their coupons and sales and lies and dreariness and ugliness. I asked myself if this really represented the level reached by all those people down there on the pavements. I am too near them myself, not being one of the sensitive plants of contemporary authorship, to believe that it does represent their level. They have passed it. They have gone on and it is not catching up.

If this sounds like Orwell (though *The Road to Wigan Pier* was not published until 1937), it is Orwell with a common sense and a common humanity that Orwell himself conspicuously lacked. With Orwell, one can always see through to the old Etonian for whom class disdain has been subtly metamorphosed into political anger. It is as much a matter of rebellious principle as one of personal feeling. With Priestley, though, one is with a man directly implicated in what he sees. The schoolmaster's son from Bradford, Yorkshire, is (by courtesy of the luck of a Cambridge education) only a whisker away from the people on the pavements. Priestley – and this can't be said of Orwell – is never a tourist in his own country.

In West Bromwich, Priestley is taken to see a warehouse in which a businessman stores sheets of steel. Children are throwing rocks on the roof, and Priestley goes off to meet them, but the small boys have fled.

> Where they could run to, I cannot imagine. They need not have run away from me, because I could not blame them if they threw stones and stones and smashed every pane of glass for miles. Nobody can blame them if they grow up to smash everything that can be smashed. There ought to be no more of those lunches and dinners at which political and financial and industrial gentlemen congratulate one another, until something is done about Rusty Lane and West Bromwich. While they still exist in their present foul shape, it is idle to congratulate ourselves about anything. They make the whole pomp of government here a miserable farce. The Crown, Lords and Commons are the Crown, Lords and Commons of Rusty Lane, West Bromwich. In the heart of the great empire on which the sun never sets, in the land of hope and glory, Mother of the Free, is Rusty Lane, West Bromwich. What do they know of England who only England know? The answer must be Rusty Lane, West

Bromwich. And if there is another economic conference, let it meet there, in one of the warehouses, and be fed with bread and margarine and slabs of brawn. The delegates have seen one England, Mayfair in the season. Let them see another England next time, West Bromwich out of the season. Out of all seasons except the winter of discontent.

Out of context, perhaps the prose sounds rather too ripe to be true. In context it doesn't because it is justified, first by the vigour of Priestley's description, secondly by the fact that it is couched in the language of urgent and immediate action. This is not empty rhetoric. For Priestley, the problem of West Bromwich is a soluble one: "this is not good enough", as he says of Leicester a little later; something can and must be done.

Half the trouble, as Priestley saw it, was a simple failure of comprehension. The southern middle classes didn't care about the plight of the northern working classes because they'd never made the short but epic journey up the length of England and never been shamed by what they saw as Priestley himself was shamed. ("They made me feel like a fat rich man. And I object to feeling like a fat rich man. That is yet another reason why we must clean up this horrible dingy muddle of life.") After all, the Jarrow marchers made the trip to London; it was London's duty to make the return journey. Again and again, Priestley challenges his readers with his travels: "I am always hearing middle-class women in London saying that they could do with a change. They should try being a miner's wife in East Durham."

None of this, of course, was new. It is the theme of Mrs Gaskell's *North and South*, of Disraeli's *Sybil*, or *The Two Nations*, of Dickens's *Hard Times*. Priestley's great strength lies in the way he manages to harness a whole tradition of writing about the industrial city and apply it to the immediately contemporary scene. Coketown, he showed, was not a fiction of the Victorian past, it was a grossly important constituent of the here-and-now.

What now seems strange and dated is the extraordinary confidence that Priestley was able to bring to his missionary expedition up England. The 39-year-old writer, the author of novels and successful West End plays, travelled like a visiting prince in a chauffeured Daimler when he was not riding on trams, trains, and buses; and throughout the book his tone makes it clear that a writer is the equal of any politician or industrial baron in the land. He can trespass across social barriers as no other dignitary could – can meet bosses, workers, aristos, and the out-of-work on candid terms. Yet his status as a lord of the language is as real, as unquestionable as any more orthodox peerage. When Priestley addresses the nation, he expects to be taken seriously.

And the book was taken seriously. It was not simply a literary success when it was first published; it pricked England's conscience. Priestley was seen to have taken the southern middle classes by the scruffs of their necks and dragged them off on a journey for the good of their souls and for the good of their country. No mere writer could ever do that now.

In 1983, when Beryl Bainbridge made her English journey, the number of people registered as being out of work was 3,104,700. (In the last year, that number has swollen by nearly a quarter of a million.) The figure is not to be found in Bainbridge's book, nor is it by any means the book's dominant fact. She has borrowed Priestley's title and Priestley's itinerary, but there the resemblance stops.

Bainbridge is not on a mission; she is on commission.

> Last year, in celebration of Mr Priestley's classic book, *English Journey*, B.B.C. Bristol sent a team of eight, which included me, to follow in his footsteps, recording on film the route he had taken and making a documentary series of what we saw and heard in the towns and villages of England during the summer of 1983.

Alas, how are the travelling writers fallen, from the proud and solitary iconoclasm of Priestley in his Daimler to "a team of eight, which included me". Tied to a shooting script, wired for sound, continually watched by the gleaming mauve eye of an Arriflex, Beryl Bainbridge travelled in tune with her time, as a component, like a coil or a resistor, in a high-tech electronic system. She was not so much a person as a part of "the media" – a singular noun for which at least half the British population now harbours a well-founded dislike and mistrust. Any striking miner would identify the television industry as a fat rich man intent on exploiting and misrepresenting him.

Bainbridge is, of course, far too good a writer not to spot such ironies for herself. Her book, or notebook, has a fugitive quality. Written up in the odd moments when she could escape from the other seven people in her crew, it often reads like a prison diary as it annotates the cigarettes gone up in smoke, the drinks knocked back, the conversations forgotten, the expensive, repetitive tedium of filming. Whereas Priestley confidently booms, Beryl Bainbridge squeaks from inside the cage.

Yet – because she is an accomplished novelist and because she is, thank God, one of the world's least likely television performers – her book manages to catch (often in an oblique and inadvertent way) a lot of the atmosphere of contemporary England. The "England" of her fiction is an infinitely unreliable place, chiefly inhabited by strays and fugitives, and Beryl Bainbridge's authorial manner has always been a touch elfin. So it is in her *English Journey*. She catches the spirit of 1983 best in the uncertainty of her own tone. The crispest enunciation of her attitude is set down in her preface:

> I have never been able to appreciate the present or look to the future. The very things that Mr Priestley deplored and which in part have been swept away, "the huddle of undignified little towns, the drift of smoke, the narrow streets that led from one dreariness to another," were the very things I lamented. Show me another motorway, I thought, another shopping precinct, another acre of improved environment and I shall pack up and go home.
> Some of the time I didn't know where home was . . .

To account for "England in the 1980s" it would be hard to improve on these sentences. For what Beryl Bainbridge is looking for, in the company of Mrs Thatcher, a large section of the British electorate, and the tourists who foregather round ruined villages in dried-up reservoirs, is an England she can recognize and put a name to as home. The England, in short, of Priestley's *English Journey* – the England of nasty bits of meat, fly-blown pastry, *Racing Specials*, and Rusty Lane, West Bromwich.

Whatever else was wrong with Priestley's England, it was recognizable. People had been taught to see it through the eyes of Dickens and Gustave Doré. The slums looked like authentic slums. The poor were dressed in what were obviously rags. The unemployed stood in the street, their pathos visible and affecting. The period photographs in the new edition of Priestley's journey bear this out brilliantly: for photographers like Bill Brandt, Humphrey Spender, and Edwin Smith, the Depression was eminently picturesque. The camera dwells on each familiar scene as if it were a famous beauty: the lines of washing, hung up to dry in a blackened street; the queues of men patiently waiting for work at dawn on a dockside; the back-to-back tenements, overhung with smoke; the slag heaps, outdoor privies, grubby children, dank canals. In the north of England at least, the Depression produced scene after scene that looked as if it had come out of a painting or a book. It was legible, symbolic; the unhappy present evoked the gloomy romantic past. It would have been hard to walk through this England of 1933 without wanting to recite Blake's "And was Jerusalem builded here,/Among these dark Satanic mills?"

It is not surprising that Priestley was able to write so well about it. Nor is it surprising that Beryl Bainbridge finds herself at a loss when she follows Priestley's route. For although the statistics have increased, the images have disappeared. She goes hopefully to Newcastle in search of the unemployed, and finds only a shopping precinct full of people spending money. Nothing to write about, or make a television film of, there. She goes to an "Action Centre" for the unemployed in Hanley:

> I talked to the dedicated young woman who runs the centre and asked her about the problems she deals with. She said the unemployment round here was higher than the national average and that the youth job employment scheme was a fiddle. It was exploitation, and besides it could only deal with about one per cent of the population. Things weren't just bad, they were hopeless. People came in on Wednesday asking for money to buy tea and bread for the rest of the week. "But I expect they smoke," I said severely. "And I bet they've all got televisions and even videos."

They *have* all got televisions, and even (rented by the week) videos. Therein lies the single most important distinction between Priestley's and Bainbridge's Englands.

For in 1933, most of English life took place out of doors. You even left your house to go to the lavatory. Out of a job, you stood in full view on the street. Because the slums were usually two storeys high at the most, their streets and backyards became communal living spaces, open to the gaze of visiting writers and photographers. It would have been possible for Priestley to see unemployment at first hand without stepping from his Daimler.

It is not so now. Since the 1950s we have moved, or been moved, indoors and upstairs. Unemployment, like so many other features of our social life, has gone private. It happens on the 20th floor, in a room full of plastic furniture, where a man in an ill-fitting but not ragged polyester shirt and jeans watches an old episode from *Dallas* on the video and listens simultaneously to a cassette on his Sony Walkman. As an image, it's not a patch on the lines of washing (now dried in a machine, probably in a public launderette) or the men in scarves and flat caps loitering under the rusty girders of a railway bridge filmed *contre jour*. It is an image that would make any television cameraman yawn. Considered not as an image but as a plight, it is surely just as shocking, pitiable, and arousing as anything described by Priestley. To convey it requires the right of access not just to the outside of the man's house, to his squalid and depressing plot of civic green space, but to the inside of his head.

This, one might have thought, was a classic job for a writer, to go into regions prohibited to the television camera and make the condition of unemployment legible – as it was legible in 1933. But Bainbridge is not that writer. She is the eighth member of her T.V. crew, looking for recognizable pictures that turn out to be in bafflingly short supply. Her best insights are fleetingly sad pictorial ones. On the top of a block of flats in Castlevale, outside Birmingham, she remarks, " I wouldn't fancy living in one of those top-floor flats. Not without wings." For a moment, as one is afforded a glimpse of angels dwelling at the tops of urban housing projects and drifting from high windows on their wings, one is reminded of just how good and odd a writer Bainbridge can be – and of how adrift she is in this England that she doesn't understand. It's true that she is attached to the Liverpool of her childhood, to bits and pieces of England remembered from her life as a young actress on tour during the 1960s, even to the England of her current London literary connections – but these ties only serve to underline Beryl Bainbridge's homelessness in the country at large.

Indeed, Bainbridge's incomprehension is her ticket of entry to the world she describes. Even by English standards, she comes across as curiously ill-travelled. Half the places she visits appear to be brand-new to her, and even now she seems to be under the innocent illusion that Skegness is in Scotland. Unlike Priestley, she is shy of advancing causes for what she sees, and even shyer of hazarding solutions to our unenviable problems. She is closer in spirit than she realizes to the manager of a crankshaft factory whom she meets in Lincoln:

> I asked him what he thought about the bomb. I kept thinking
> that here I was, almost at the end of my journey, and not
> once had we mentioned it. Ken looked taken aback for a

moment, and then, looking sideways at the camera, he said, "It's not for the likes of me to say."

It's not for the likes of me to say. There is a line that deserves to go on England's tombstone.

· Priestley in 1933 answered the optimistic national need for a sage; Bainbridge in 1984 caters to a peculiarly recent British taste for helpless irony. She claims no power over the world she charts. She finds it on the whole pretty alien. It would be nice if it were otherwise but it isn't, so she tries to make the best of it by taking a mild and mournful pleasure in its oddities. I'm afraid that in this glancing, quirky, breathless book, Beryl Bainbridge really does speak authentically for England.

1984

ON THE WATER MARGIN

It's wrong to say, as people almost always do, that London does not use its river. The Thames has never been the city's chief point of focus like the Seine in Paris or the Grand Canal in Venice. Yet London, no less than Venice or Paris, uses its river to define itself. The Thames marks the edge of things. It is what makes north London north and south London south. Like a twisty ruler, it measures out the intricate social and economic gradations between the east and west of the city. The Thames is what makes London articulate and knowable; but it is a boundary, not a thoroughfare, and like all boundaries it is there for people to turn back from. So London characteristically faces away from its river. It lives, even now, in a mental world where the Strand really is a strand – a border, edge, or coast. Modern attempts to break with this convention, like the South Bank complex, have an odd feel to them: we have been using our river for so long as a looping no-man's-land that it is difficult to adjust to a perspective which faces across the river rather than turning away from it.

It is not so much from neglect as from proper respect that we treat our river like this. More than any other city river, the Thames is associated with the mysterious margins of society. In Dickens, it is laden with corpses, as black and foreboding as the Styx. Nor was it any accident that the notorious Vauxhall Gardens of the 18th century were ranged on the far bank of the river, on the other side of no-man's-land. Boundaries are places where laws and social rules become uncertain, where licence thrives and anything can happen. They are also places to which people who feel themselves to be marginal, out on the far edge of society, naturally graduate.

In eight years of living in London, I've found myself tending again and again to the river for consolation. When things won't go, when depression, like a giant squid, gets one in its grip, the Thames is there to mooch by, mutter, clear one's head and think. It is the one part of London where gravity, sadness, a sense of loss always seem in place. Below Westminster, the river belongs to melodrama. At Dockside, just beneath Tower Bridge on the south bank, one can wander among empty warehouses that still smell of cinnamon, where tramp fires smoulder on the upper floors and Tooley Streeters sleep out the day on acrid sacks. It used to be called Saint Saviour's Dock, and was rechristened "Savoury Dock" because of the stench of "Folly Ditch", the open sewer that flowed into it. This was where the cholera epidemic of 1849 started – in the tiny houses that leaned together over the neck of the dock; and it was here that Dickens set the scene of Bill Sikes's death in *Oliver Twist*. It is still a shadowy, forbidding place; it's hard to look into the inert, scummy water of the dock inlet without expecting to see a body there.

Or there is the extraordinary wide sweep of the river past the Isle of Dogs. The Isle itself is one of the most desolate places I have ever seen: its docks deserted, windows smashed, walls spray-gunned. The Dogs now are lacklustre Alsatians with bad teeth, snarling in yards from behind chickenwire fences, guarding rusted heaps of chains, old cars and broken window-frames. The tower blocks are examples of the civic mind at its most brutish; the featureless green-space is a windy waste where only the dogs dare to venture. Yet this violent, uncared-for, desecrated place looks out on the longest, widest and most beautiful of all the reaches of the Thames. Nowhere is the idea of the river as a boundary more marked than here. The Isle of Dogs, with its heroic decrepitude, faces the stately, long, low wedding cake of Greenwich. One might be on the frontier between Korea and Switzerland.

To cross the river here is to make a real journey to foreign parts, and the lifts at either end of the foot tunnel seem to recognize this. They are splendid lifts: done up in polished teak, they are like old-fashioned ships' staterooms, and their attendants like captains.

They give the descent underground a due dignity; and after a half-mile walk through the dripping tunnel one rises, blinking, in Greenwich, like a real traveller, with all the rituals of departure, passage and arrival properly completed. And from Greenwich waterfront even the Isle of Dogs, softened by mist and distance, looks beautiful in return; its hideous flats (each block is called by a name out of Arthurian romance) taper and wobble in the light like columns of gas. The dogs are inaudible, the junk on the shore turns to a uniform burnt umber: like Hell, the Isle of Dogs is distinctly attractive from a distance.

But these stretches of the lower Thames are too oppressively loaded with associations; too steeped in urban literature and mythology. The boundaries they represent are old, and the reaches themselves have the air of haunted houses. One needs a corresponding melodrama in one's own life to fully appreciate and use them. Perhaps the bloody end of an affair justifies a walk around the edge of the Isle of Dogs, or the beginning of one a trip to Greenwich; but ordinary life demands less taxing and colourful frontiers. When I first came to London, hungry for extremity, I used to take myself off on bad days to the Pool of London, Bermondsey and Rotherhithe. Now I go to Putney and walk along the towpath to Kew and Richmond – a soft, suburban border country, more ambiguous and open to one's own impositions and interpretations. But it is a real fringe-place nevertheless; a strange, wandering community of solitaries and escapees who've come to the river to be for a while in no-man's-land, at once outside and inside the city. The names on the itinerary – Mortlake, Kew and Barnes – are like unfortunate synonyms for plump bourgeois solidity; but the bank of the Thames itself is mercifully unclassifiable. It belongs to temporary people – floaters, drifters, visitors, and refugees, whose passage along it is far too erratic and diverse to endow it with any sort of stable character. Putney to Kew is a seven-mile walk along the extreme margin of city life, as rich and comforting a stretch of nowhere as it's possible to imagine. Putney Riverside, bright with boats and boat-builders' yards, is like a chunk of a southern seaside town which got accidentally put down in the wrong place. Here middle-aged couples in well-preserved Vauxhalls come to snooze through the afternoon in their parked cars, with Sunday papers and thermos flasks of tea. On some evenings, there's even a seaside band playing in the illuminated stand in the park across the river. Last time I was there at dusk, the river was like black ice; the dinghy racers were hauling down their limp sails; and from the far shore there was the hugely amplified voice of a woman singing "Hot diggedy, pop diggedy, oh what you do to me!" coming over the darkened Thames. In its trip across the water, the song acquired a curious kind of melancholy. I suppose the woman on the bandstand must have had a visible audience in the park, but she seemed, as she punched her voice out in breathless gouts of simulated enthusiasm, to be trying to sing to Putney and not quite reaching. Putney is not a place that sensible people attempt to sing to: its sedate river-promenade is more Yarmouth, Isle of Wight than Yarmouth, Norfolk, at its most typical on a dull Sunday afternoon in a light drizzle. It's possible to sit for hours on a Borough of Wandsworth civic bench, just watching the tide widening and deepening the river to the level of the painted railings, and draining it again down to a sour channel through the mud-flats. And the tidewrack has a salty, ozoney smell. The flattened Fanta tins, fir cones, driftwood, twigs and the ubiquitous, rectangular lumps of polystyrene give off a faint whiff, at least, of ocean.

I wonder where all the condoms went. A few years ago, one couldn't go for a river walk without seeing them festooning the branches of overhanging trees like pale bulbous fruits. The long grass and bushes round the river banks afforded secret places for lovers to hide out, away from the eyes of parents and spouses. Perhaps it is simply because no one needs that secrecy now; the river, a natural resort for anyone up to anything clandestine, isn't necessary, and the condoms are gone. Now that Durex are allowed to sponsor racing cars and advertise on hoardings, who needs to escape to the river to make love? Or maybe everyone's just on the pill. At any rate, if fornication thrives in Putney, the river offers precious little evidence of it, and I'm sure that the members of Barclays Bank Rowing & Sailing Club don't gambol immodestly in the thickets of Barn Elms on summer nights.

Past a cottage called "Bleak House" and the tennis courts, and the Sea Scouts' hut and a muddy creek full of stoved-in-skeletons, the towpath starts. It's possible, according to the map at any rate, to walk from here to Lechlade along the riverside, which may explain the occasional presence of demented hikers with back-packs, looking as if they have wandered abstractedly out of the Kingsley Martin–C. E. M. Joad-and-Scrabble set of the mid '30s. It was here, last summer, that I met an oddly familiar looking man waving a butterfly net and carrying a killing-bottle. He wore khaki shorts that came down to his calves, thick N.H.S. spectacles, army boots; and his balding red hair was turning to the colour of white pepper. When I came across him, he was leaping around in some bushes of the sort that have names I don't know, pursuing what appeared to me to be a rather dog-eared Cabbage White.

His face bothered me, and it wasn't until past Barnes that I remembered, or thought I remembered, who he was. Eighteen years ago, the same man had loomed at me over the top of a treeless hill on the northernmost island in the Shetlands. His hair was thicker then, his glasses a good deal thinner. When he spoke, he boomed. "Any chance of a glass of water?" he'd bellowed down from the top of the hill to my uncle's cottage in the valley. And when he arrived at the gate, he asked: "Am I right for the Aurora Borealis?" He had disappeared, bow-legged, into the setting sun, trailing a butterfly net in which he was going to catch the northern lights. I had not expected him to show up twice in a lifetime, but the Thames is a place where loose ends have a habit of coming together.

You notice this the moment you round the first bend on the path and see what must be a mirage: upstream, flying a pair of union jacks from its twin gothic domes, is Harrods, or what appears to be Harrods. Its chocolate and faded-orange brickwork rises over the tilted green umbrellas of the anglers on Barn Elms Reservoirs. Framed by trees and a pumping station, Harrods-on-Thames turns the first mile into a bewildering puzzle. It refuses to budge back into its proper position; indeed, almost every step brings the curlicues of its whatnots and pilasters into harder definition. It is a small aurora borealis in its own right.

The external evidence is contradictory. On the one hand, a lady in a hacking jacket and headscarf is being taken for a walk by a pair of brushed borzois; on the other, there's a 'fifties ted in a suit of brand-new drapes. People rarely come in twos on the river bank, and each new passerby tends to cancel out the last one. If Harrods has its representative, so do Cecil Gee, Burtons, Oxfam and the dustbin. Harrods, though, is real. This building – a stubby twin to the one in Knightsbridge – is their furniture repository . . . or perhaps it just *was*, for Harrods Wharf is to let, and always has been since I've been walking here. Its windows are peppered with holes made by stones and airgun pellets; from some the glass has gone completely, leaving only bulging wire mesh. Behind them, a jumble of shadowy shapes – escritoires coupling with chaises longues, grandfather clocks with rolls of carpet. From the outside of the place, one might guess that half the stuff inside was put there fifty years ago and forgotten by its owners – time enough for junk to turn into antique, and ugly cast-offs into treasures.

But furniture is not the only thing which lands up, derelict, on the waterside. On Harrods' concrete wall, there's a neatly executed *graffito* in smart black paint: a symbol representing a stove and a flame, then the words METHYLATED SPIRITS 1977. The 7s in 1977 are done continental-fashion, with a curling stroke through the middle of the tail of each figure. Perhaps because people have more time here than in the street, these riverbank *graffiti* often have an elegance that suggests the work of some spraygun-perfectionist. The meths-slogan has a particular appropriateness: for just a few yards further on, in the lee of Hammersmith Bridge, there's a sort of open-air club of middle-aged men who sit about drinking their special poison out of a communal cider bottle. Unlike the ravaged wild men of Soho Square and Covent Garden, though, the Hammersmith Bridge winos have a precarious, clerkly gentility. They wear ties and frayed suits. They look as if it wasn't long since they were paying mortgages in East Sheen. They look like men who would take the trouble to add strokes to their 7s; and on my last walk, one of them had brought fresh supplies of booze in a bright Jubilee carrier bag. Their union jack put the shabby ones flying atop Harrods to shame; from their bowed heads and grave conversation, they might have been at a W.E.A. meeting.

From Chiswick on, the north bank of the river suddenly changes. Wharves, warehouses, gasometers and council flats give way to Georgian, neo-Georgian and pseudo-Georgian houses and riverside pubs cashing in on the real-ale craze. There are upturned boats on every barbered lawn, and Chinese willows trained to sweep in a waterfall of green down to the river's edge. At last, everything begins to look in on, rather than away from, the Thames. Or so it seems. Thackeray suggests otherwise. For Miss Pinkerton's Academy in *Vanity Fair* was at Chiswick, yet in the first chapter, which is called "Chiswick Mall", there is not one mention of the river. Even the coachmen look only in one direction – at the fronts of the houses. When Becky Sharp chucks Dr Johnson's dictionary out of the window, she could perfectly easily have thrown it into the Thames; perversely – or typically, perhaps – she lobs it back into the narrow front garden of the house.

From the towpath, though, the new chi-chi of Chiswick is comfortably distant. One walks through a muddy avenue of elders and wrecked seats, with the wind in the trees mixing with the deeper cardiac murmur of the traffic on the A4 across the river. This isn't country, nor town, nor park; and its oddity as a landscape is brought home by the way the people dress for it. Everyone looks out of place: the man in his featherweight denim holiday gear, the lady in tweed suit and brogues, the solitary slouchers in overalls, in fashion shoes with platform heels, in loud weekending checks, in rags and shawls. There is no way of looking right here, unless perhaps the joggers with tracksuits and pedometers, who treat the stretch as distance pure and simple, have got its measure. A year ago there used to be a gang of itinerant roadbuilders who camped out on the bank in tatty caravans and kept mongrels in chains; they gave the place a kind of recognizable tone, but they're gone now, and the mud-patch where they lived has been turned into a concrete boulevard.

I find myself reassured by this peculiar absence of identity; it's the most precious and important quality that the river has to offer, and it's something of a shock to reach Barnes, because Barnes is about nothing but identity. With its "village" shops and railway station, it shouts its spurious separateness from London at one. A man sits at an easel in the crook of the river wall, doing a tepid watercolour sketch of the main street; significantly, he keeps his back firmly turned on the river itself. Estate agents and colour supplements grind on about the pleasures of life in these cosy mock-villages. I find them dismal and pretentious: sooner Welwyn Garden City than Highgate, Barnes or Blackheath, with their pubs of the year and trellises of roses. I remember once going to a party of architects in Blackheath and finding everyone engaged in a curious competition which involved boasting about how *long* it took one to get to work in central London. The longer you took, the further "out of London" you were; and to be "out of London" is what places like Barnes and Blackheath crave. But it is a craving which flies in the face of the facts of their own existence: they are metropolitan quarters whose main *raison d'être* is their facile, if fashionable, contempt for the idea of the City – a contempt which has a great deal to answer for, since it is responsible for so much that is genuinely bad and deleterious in the life of contemporary London. The no-man's-land of the river is a metropolitan necessity: the pseudo-pastoral of Barnes is a corrupting urban fantasy.

The quarter-mile walk through Barnes always brings me out in a froth of bad temper, but fishing starts, for some obscure reason, on the far side of Barnes Bridge, and restores me to good humour again. There are eels here and little flaccid roach, and the odd bream – most of them about the same size and shape as a small sideplate. The worms used by the boys who crouch with rods over the warm-water outflow – brandlings and squirreltails, squirming in tins of wet moss – are as big as the fish they catch. Behind them, there's another *graffito* on the wall, sprayed on so meticulously that it looks like the work of a council sign-painter: SACK JOHN BROADSIDE THE P.M.G., then SUPPORT FREE RADIO, then LONG LIVE CAROLINE. The paint is only wearing a little with age; it will long outlast its message, whose three parts must already seem oddly unconnected to anyone now in their teens. Perhaps the council *should* hire its sign-painter to write footnotes for puzzled latterday scholars.

And then a sudden splash of broad farce. Just past Barnes (technically speaking, it must be in Barnes, but I don't imagine Barnes acknowledges it) there's a huddle of steep Victorian warehouses and factories. The biggest of these looks like a prison, with narrow barred windows, and at every window there's a tow-headed, oily-faced apprentice – a readymade chorus from a Peter Terson play. They're making a terrific row, shouting and catcalling from behind their bars.

"Give you five quid for it in half an hour!"

"Five pound fifty!"

"Six!"

"Seven!"

"Twenty-two!"

"Go on!"

"Why don't you *push*?"

"Oh, dear! oh dear, oh dear!"

"Yah!"

"Twenty-two quid fifty! and that's my last offer!"

"I think the tide's coming in, Cecil!"

"Watch your skirt!"

"He's got his feet wet!"

"One . . . two . . . three . . . Push!"

Pure delirium. Half an hour to go before lunch, and the apprentices are forty windows' full of unspoilt joy. Down on the slipway, some idiot has harnessed his boat trailer to his brand-new Triumph Toledo, now up to its rear-axle in soft Thames mud. He shouts incomprehensible instructions to his wife, who flounders around the back bumper, while his limp-looking teenage son rests one hand gracefully on the tailgate. Already the tide is licking at their feet. Every thirty seconds or so, Mr Triumph Toledo throws what's intended to be a withering look up at the factory windows, but it turns in transit into a stare of helpless pathos. With the apprentices on one side and the incoming tide on the other, he is King Canute in a double-bind.

"Oh, do shut up!" he yells, and gets a surge of applause worthy of a Chelsea home goal. I suppose someone must have got his car out for him in the end. I didn't stay to help: these river walks are like train journeys; one is oddly, satisfactorily, disconnected from the scenes one passes. They slide by – as vivid and remote as sketches in some rolling entertainment.

In fact, from here the action suddenly speeds up. The moment one passes under Mortlake Bridge, one moves into a quick-change world in which everything one sees is bizarrely out of kilter with everything else. First, Mortlake Crematorium goes by, like a displaced giant Californian bungalow done up in West Coast Moorish. Lines of graves stretch back until they're in the shadow of a sunken gasometer. Then comes a rubbish tip that looks like a jerrybuilt football stadium. Behind its high walls, something's going on: a mumbling, crunching, creaking sound – feeding time for the bottle-and-plastic-sack-eating hippopotami. A rowing club. A sewage plant (Mortlake seems to be one of those places where all our disposables end up, and where we ourselves finally turn to sprinkled ash). A brief stretch of hedge, ripe with haws and elderberries. And then the most puzzling no-man's-land institution of all.

It may be the back end of a factory. It could be a school. I have passed it on weekdays as well as at weekends, but have never seen a single person there. What never changes is the arrangement of white-painted steel pub tables and chairs, set out as if for a champagne party that has just ended. There are patches of bald ground, and other patches where the grass grows waist-high. When I was there two months ago, I realized what the place must be. For the entire back wall of the building was hidden behind stacks of old railway signs. The names of country and suburban stations, long ago axed by Beeching, were there, in the cream-on-coffee lettering of the old Southern Railway Company. There were signs for waiting rooms and lavatories and ticket offices, signs saying that one mustn't cross the line without a member of the company's permission, signs to the now demolished bridge, signs to the carpark that has since turned into somebody's garden.

Clearly it was British Rail's own dump. I walked there again two days ago, thinking that a few names of lost stations would fit my theme nicely. They had all gone. The tables and chairs were there – in exactly the same position as I had remembered them. But no railway signs. Instead, there were piles of doors. These doors were not, as one might have expected, the doors of railway carriages, stations or even B.R. transport trucks; they were just doors. One said "Private", but that was no great find for my notebook.

Now I would prefer never to discover what the place really is. I shall look the other way when I pass its frontage on the road to Kew Bridge. And I shall wait to see just what new curiosities arrive when the doors have gone the same way (wherever that is) as the railway signs.

I didn't mind about the disappearance of the signs too much, since there was an instant, and unasked for, consolation just round the corner where the path widens to a grassy nook among the elders: a picnic for cats. It had been organized by a distrait lady in a battered pink Ascot hat. Like the Chiswick winos, she looked as if she'd seen better days, and still had the clothes to prove it. She had spread an ancient travelling rug on the muddy grass, and set on it a wicker hamper, six willow pattern plates, two babies' bottles full of milk and a can of John West Tunafish. Around the rug sat three tortoise-shell and two black cats, each at their own appointed place. Before she noticed me approaching her, she was speaking to them – it sounded like bright picnic conversation. I hard the words "rather fatiguing" and "Ernest" before she took to silence and watched me frostily as I went by. I suppose Ernest mut have been one of the cats; or perhaps she was an actress who'd played Lady Bracknell in her heyday.

One does not expect to find cat picnics at Kew. Past a sunken terrace of cottages that look like accessories to a model railway layout and the Priory Park Club (BOWLS TENNIS SOCIAL: NEW MEMBERS WELCOMED), the towpath leads one into a fragment of an England that I thought had died with *John Bull* and the Festival of Britain. Hollyhocks stand in the gardens of pint-sized rural gothic houses; meticulously tended allotments glow with that improbably fertile green of illustrations by Beatrix Potter. Kew is a triumphant *trompe l'oeil*. If Barnes reveals the strain of pretending to be a village, Kew carries the thing off by sheer cheek; it looks, not so much pretentious, as absent-minded. With Kew's prim prettiness, the Thames suddenly stops being a city river.

For beyond Kew Bridge, to Richmond, Kingston and Hampton Court, walking the towpath is merely pleasant exercise. The landscape is mostly park; the river ceases to be a frontier territory of bits and pieces and loose ends. It has its moments – Eel Pie Island, where the 1960s burnt themselves out in a hotel fire; then, much further upstream, just south of Staines, the riverside shack-dwellers of Penton Hook who live under tarpaper and fish out of their bedroom windows. But something vital is gone: one feels that the river is no longer held in superstitious regard. It has become an "amenity", to be sported on and to add a few thousand pounds to the prices of houses that front it. On the towpath the solitary walkers give way to couples and families out on picnics. Marinas replace the warehouses and sewage disposal plants. The lower Thames is like the underside of a carpet: a colourful confusion of all the threads that go to make up the social pattern of the city. The upper Thames turns into a pattern in its own right. No longer a nowhere place, it stops being a refuge for escapees. Above Kew, the river sets a certain tone. From here on, winos are moved on by cops and park-keepers; Mr Toledo would find a dozen people to help him with his blessed boat; the cat-lady would shrink from the intrusive, amused stares of passers-by; and even the butterfly man might think twice before jumping in and out of bushes in his gig-lamp spectacles.

There is a special liberty associated with being on the margin of things; and the reaches of the Thames which I've described are free places, entirely hospitable to the lost, the vagrant, the eccentric, the cast out. I can think of no more important amenity for the life of a city as big as London than this long, broad, welcoming stretch of no-man's-land.

1977

FLORIDA

One classic American landscape haunts all of American literature. It is a picture of Eden, perceived at the instant of history when corruption has just begun to set in. The serpent has shown his scaly head in the undergrowth. The apple gleams on the tree. The old drama of the Fall is ready to start all over again.

I had thought that America had run out of Edens to ruin. The legend, and its literary landscapes, went hand in hand with the fact of the westward-moving frontier. After the Pacific coast, there seemed nowhere else to go. Then I read the thrillers of John D. MacDonald. With their bodice-ripper covers and titles like *Nightmare in Pink, A Deadly Shade of Gold* and *A Purple Place for Dying*, they didn't look or sound much like works of classic American fiction. Yet it seemed to me that MacDonald was doing something quite extraordinary in them. His plots were often banal. His private dick, Travis McGee, nailed the villain and bedded the lady with a regularity that struck me as both unlikely and depressing. The power of the books – and it mounted steadily as I read them in bulk – came from their indignant and passionate vision of the American landscape. At his best, Mac-Donald created a heartbreakingly vivid portrait of a jungly Eden, spoiled and besmirched by human vanity and greed. Travis McGee hunted down his thugs and shysters in a paradisal garden, a lovely wilderness that was being cut down to make room for shopping malls, condominium blocks, six-lane highways, giant billboards and pagoda-style Kingburger palaces. Taken together, the novels added up to a resounding "No! In Thunder!" They protested against this violation of the innocence of America with shocked and angry vigour.

The location of this raped Eden was Florida. Everyone knows that Florida is a ramshackle combination of a sunny old people's home and a refugee camp for exiled Cubans. MacDonald, though, made Florida sound like America's last frontier – the final, tragic battle-ground on which the war between civilization and the wilderness was being fought out. Tantalized and sceptical, enchanted by Mac-Donald's writing but in no mood for a package tour of Key West and Palm Beach, I booked a flight to Eden.

First, I wanted to meet the genius of the place. MacDonald himself lived out at Sarasota, on the western, Gulf shore of the state. The best way to reach him was by taking a back road from Miami through the Everglades; a 200-mile drive straight through the middle of the Garden. Beyond the last crappy Hispanic motel, the last taco house, the last Dodge dealership, the swamps opened out; a huge and empty flatland of puddled water, feathery cypresses, frizzled palmettos and mangroves squatting on knobbly knees. Even in December, the entire landscape steamed. Ahead, the highway glistened and wobbled in the heat. Fruit trucks, overtaking me, disappeared into what looked like a lake. They left behind a trail of smashed oranges and avocados and broken sticks of sugar-cane. Fresh from a mean London winter, I found it hard to credit such casual abundance – this immense acreage of sunlight, these horns of plenty roaring by.

I had only seen alligators in zoos. Here they littered the banks of the ditch by the side of the road. Sprawled any old how, on rotten logs and tummocks of spiky grass, they looked like tarnished pewter castings. Some slept with their jaws wide open in an expression of idiot optimism. Most were as inscrutably lumpish as garden slugs.

The birds, too, belonged to Genesis. Brown pelicans, like baggy tweed overcoats in flight, came tumbling through the cypress trees and made splashy landings in the water below. Chicken vultures went quartering the sky over the road, on the lookout for a meaty accident. A butterfly as big and gaudy as a Chinese kite pasted itself floppily across the windshield.

Everything looked as one expects the world to look when one is badly jet-shocked or hungover – improbable, violent, faintly obscene. I needed a drink to get in tune with it. Sixty miles into the swamp, there was a town marked on the map. It turned out to be a single shack with two gas pumps and a sign saying: MARRIAGES PERFORMED – $50.

The shack was a bar-café. The menu chalked on a blackboard over the counter announced that you could, if you cared to, have fried alligator tails for breakfast. I settled for a can of Schlitz and the soothing gloom of a corner-booth. A family was seated at the table across from me: a loose-limbed giant, his strapping wife and their baby – a dimpled giantling who was parked on the tabletop like a prizewinning vegetable marrow. Adam, Eve and Baby Cain.

The man wore a pair of stiff, snakeproof chaps. A cartridge-belt was slung loosely around the broad equator of his belly. The top of his face was hidden under the long brim of a gimme cap with its embroidered motto, IF GOD MADE MAN IN HIS IMAGE GOD MUST BE A REDNECK.

"Been out hunting?"

The brim of the cap wagged slowly, affirmatively, down.

"What for?"

"Deer. Didn't get none, though. Six shots. Missed every blame one of 'em."

Baby Cain howled. Eve gentled him against the bosom of her floral print shirt. Adam sucked at his beer. "Yesterday I got one. Killed a whole nest of rattlers, too." He listed the animals in the Garden. Behind the cypress-curtain on the roadside there were raccoons, bears, deer, snakes, rumours of panthers. Brought up as I was in the docile English landscape, I can never quite get used to the idea that a country stroll in the United States can easily be fatal.

"So it's no place to go for a walk in —"

"You don't want to go walking in there . . . 'cept you want to get bit. Or et. Or pisoned. Or caught in a trap."

Baby Cain's blue eyes were fixed solemnly on me. He looked as if he was squinting down the barrel of a gun. His mother, her hand cupping his bottom, rocked her infant hunter slowly back to sleep.

Outside in the sun, under a pair of circling vultures, I smelt the Everglades. It was a wild smell, of rotting timber, animal musk, ooze, warm grass, carrion. In England we have long lost what little wilderness we had. Beauty spots, safari parks and grouse moors make a dim substitute for real virgin land. We have good reason for forgetting that we were ever *not here*. In the Everglades, though, just an hour's drive from the Miami suburbs, the landscape was exactly as it would have been seen by De Soto and the 16th-century Spanish explorers. The highway and its jokey billboards were an insignificant scratch on the skin of the swamps; a very minor wound. If the real purpose of the Genesis story was to remind man that he's a temporary tenant of the world, that he came last in the order of creation and is by nature a moral weakling, then the Everglades were very close indeed to Eden.

The yellow lines on the road stretched dead ahead: a long thin arrowpoint aimed at the far coast. In the distance was a puzzling line of chalky cliffs, apparently facing inland. As I drove on, the cliffs gradually resolved into tall apartment blocks jammed end-to-end along the Mexican Gulf shore. Condominium country.

It's hard to convey the promise that the word *condominium* holds out in Florida. It's not a condom made of aluminium; it is a shared dominion, a way of buying your own small home in a great white concrete eggbox of identical apartments. There is a seductive whisper in the word. To the old and lonely it says: why don't *you* join our readymade community of folks just like yourself . . . Golden-agers, golfers, singles, fun-lovers . . . Come buy, come buy. A condo isn't just a two-bedroom flat: it's friendship, clubbability, creative leisure. It is as near as you'll ever get to a compact paradise on earth. In a condo, goes the whisper, you will die happy, suntanned and fulfilled.

As the road bent north by the sea, the condos thickened. Many were still just staked-out lots. Lopsided billboards stood in the middle of bulldozed patches of mangrove swamp:

ALOHA PLAZA
FLORIDA'S MOST PRESTIGIOUS ADULT COMMUNITY
SIESTA VILLAGE

96 CONDOMINIUM UNITS
COMING SOON!!

It was a goldrush landscape, torn to bits by the diggings of latterday prospectors. The skyline was jagged with unfinished condos, the roadside a bright mess of advertising hoardings that begged the passing motorist to invest in his own patch of heaven before it was too late. White Sands. Camelot. Suntide. Tivoli. Valhalla. Emerald. Jacaranda. The names varied, but the words with which they were tricked out were monotonously few: "club", "exclusive", "prestige", "luxury", "community", "lifestyle", "village".

At each stoplight little bands of elderly joggers in pastel romperwear stood running on the spot. They looked like toddlers until one saw their mottled, baked-potato skins. As the light flashed 'WALK!' the grandpas and grandmas of America went trotting nimbly to the beach. Others rode the links in rainbow golf buggies. They too wore clothes of an oddly infantile cut and colour. With their buggies parked on the lips of bunkers they were happily back in a world of tricycles and sandpits.

It was right that the old people should look so like children. All they wanted of Florida was sunshine, condos and playtime. Yet their pensions and savings supplied the gold in this goldrush. The retirees, pouring in by the planeload, were making Florida's population grow faster than that of any other state. While the rest of America was in gloomy recession, Florida was having a binge. These were flush times, and the place was in a high fever.

It was as if someone had discovered the Comstock Lode all over again. The prospectors had swarmed in. All you needed to make millions was an acre or two of swamp. Every tinpot speculator was trying to build himself a condo block, a shopping mall, a marina or a golf course. Like Nevada in the 1860s, Florida in the 1980s had the perfect climate for a life of racketeering, graft and thuggery.

"Money," wrote Mark Twain of the Nevada gold rush, "was wonderfully plenty. The trouble was, not how to get it – but how to spend it, how to lavish it, get rid of it, squander it." So it seemed to be here. Everywhere I looked, someone was trying to bribe me to inspect their condominium. The offers were extravagant, and odd. One prospector was dangling a plane ticket to Mexico City. Another promised a car. More modestly, I could have a Bar-B-Q grill, a dinner for two with wine, a stereo system, a cocktail shaker and bartender's handbook, putting irons, an electronic alarm clock, a portable colour

T.V. A man of reasonably adaptable tastes could live scot-free on the Gulf coast, just by looking at condominiums.

What I actually wanted at that moment was lunch. This was convenient, since squads of girls in bikinis were working the beach handing out free luncheon vouchers "in return for fifteen minutes of your precious time". Hoping to make myself more credible as a potential buyer, I decided to act as agent for an imaginary mother. I made Mother 82. She lived in New York. She was mean, rich and ferociously sociable. She played a powerful bridge hand and drank very dry vodka martinis with a twist. Anyone who would like to borrow her in future is welcome to do so: Mother comes fully tested and proven. In Florida she is an indispensable tool in the kit of the amateur gold-digger.

On Mother's behalf, I checked out a fourth-floor apartment in what I had better call The Orchid Bay Club – five gimcrack blocks arranged in a horseshoe plan around two swimming pools and facing out across the Mexican Gulf. "Welcome to the best of Florida Lifestyles," said the brochure. "You'll share active days and quiet evenings with people like yourself who desire a way of life that's as pleasing to the senses as it is comfortable and secure."

A saleslady called Marcia drove me round the site in an electrified surrey with a fringe on the top. Marcia had a splendid set of teeth and the shining eyes of an evangelist, and she was as wholesome as Doris Day. I was very lucky, she said. There was just one apartment still unsold in the block nearest to the sea. She was sure that it was exactly the thing for Mother. I hoped so, I said; but Mother was notoriously difficult and picky.

"I know what you mean," said Marcia, sparkling with sympathy.

It puzzled me that there were only half a dozen or so cars marooned in a parking lot designed for hundreds.

"Oh," Marcia said, "many of our members are out at present. Some are away on business . . . But if you came back next week, before Christmas, you'd see every space filled."

"Mother hates to be alone," I said.

"She'll make *so* many friends here —"

"I hope so."

"Look – there's the recreation centre." It was a brick shed, and there was no one in it.

"She's very keen on bridge."

"*Lots* of our members play bridge."

The block was resonantly empty. I noticed that there were no curtains in the windows of one supposedly tenanted apartment.

"Oh," said Marcia, "I expect they're away being cleaned." She unlocked a varnished pine door and let us in to an immaculate, unfurnished picture postcard. The whole flat was constructed round an epic window. Beyond the long verandah, palms and pines rose from lawns as virulently green as the artificial grass that undertakers use to spread over freshly-filled graves. Then there was a ragged fringe of blonde sea-oats, followed by a margin of white quartz sand as fine as baking powder, which shaded into the rime of breaking surf. Finally, there was the water of the Gulf, flecked, brilliant, the colour of milky Pernod. Even an irritable old bat like Mother would have been stirred by the view.

"A hundred and eighty thousand dollars," said Marcia tenderly.

"Oh, that's well within Mother's general range," I said. I peered knowingly into the laundry room, and looked at the bath to see if Mother would be likely to break her neck in it. I tapped a wall. It seemed to be made out of thin pasteboard and it sounded like a drumskin. I thought that Marcia was looking at me a bit over-seriously. She was studying my crumpled jeans, scuffed shoes and denim shirt with an interest that I didn't feel they merited.

"Just for this month, we have a special bonus," she said. "If your mother likes to close inside thirty days, we could offer you a $38,000 cash credit." The emphasis on the *you* was firm and confiding. It promised sealed lips.

I felt a shade queasy at the idea of cheating even an imaginary mother out of £25,000. "Wouldn't it be simpler," I said, "if you just offered the apartment at, say, $140,000 instead of $180,000?"

"Oh, we couldn't do that. It wouldn't be fair." Marcia sounded as if I'd made an immoral proposal. "It would lower the value of the property. Think of all the people who've already bought at the full price. We don't want to devalue *their* investment – do we?"

So I learned the peculiar Florida logic by which accepting a bribe can be nicely construed as an act of altruism.

"I'll have to talk to Mother."

"I do hope you'll enjoy your lunch," said Marcia. For a serpent, she was as sweet as pie.

Out of this mess of hasty development and eager dealing John D. MacDonald had created a metaphysical landscape. In his novels, the Florida coastline, with its butchered swamp and tacky concrete palaces, is a moral affront. But his villains are not evil men by nature. They are simply weak; easily dazzled by easy money. They are decent Rotarians, small-town politicians and businessmen, who can't resist a share of the takings when it is offered to them on a plate. They end up killing people to protect their stake. The irony at the heart of MacDonald's books is that these feeble, childish miscreants behave so wantonly in a setting that looks as if it really was designed to be a paradise – and could, even now, be rescued . . . just.

MacDonald himself keeps very well hidden, in a small unspoiled corner of the garden. It took a lot of telephone calls and wrong turnings to track him down to the green island off Sarasota where he lives with his wife. There were no condos on Ocean Boulevard; just a deep forest of cypress, pines and palmettos in which the only sign that anyone lived there was the occasional mailbox in the trees. A dark winding tunnel of foliage led to the MacDonald house. It was a lovely timber pagoda, raised on stilts and floating shiplike among waving fronds of cypress. Twenty yards away the Gulf began, and a brown pelican was diving for mullet from a wooden jetty. It was a perfect setting in which to seek a magus.

The magus was in trouble. He was trying to fit a catflap to his bathroom door. Surrounded by screws and screwdrivers of different sizes, he was pottering to no effect. He showed me the catflap. His hands were altogether too big to be practical; they looked like a pair of catcher's mitts.

"I'm astonished," I said. "Travis McGee fixes everything in a flash."

"I guess that's my compensatory fantasy," MacDonald said. "I was always useless at this sort of thing. You know my motto? If it ain't broke, don't fix it." He put the catflap away and dusted off his enormous hands.

MacDonald was a very big, very pink man. His pearl-grey suede jacket and saffron shirt looked as if they might belong to the vacation-ing vice-president of a bank; but his face seemed wrong for his clothes. His lips were chubby, his eyes mild and contemplative. He looked far gentler than his writing – a ruminant, not a carnivore.

I said that I had come to Florida because I'd read his books. For me, this landscape was all his invention. Yes, said MacDonald. But now I'd seen the real thing, were the books right? Did I recognize it?

"Absolutely," I said. "For the last few days I've been living in a Travis McGee story."

"Look —" He pointed out through the mosquito screen across

his own front yard. "The neighbours. Now the guy over there, beyond those trees, he's a minister of the church. Right now he's under indictment for selling eight million dollars' worth of phoney tax havens. Then there's another guy, just there; he's a qualified physician. He's never practised, so far as I know. He keeps a Rolls-Royce in his driveway – never cleans it. I don't know what he does. But every two weeks or so I hear his power boat going out to sea at three in the morning. Maybe an hour later, it comes back. That's what he does. I don't think I exaggerate too much in the books."

No. It was Florida itself that was almost too exaggerated for fiction. The only form the state could take was that of a thriller – with all the thriller's pace, improbability and spilled guts. MacDonald's violent parables were rooted in what passes, in Florida, for the ordinary. The writer and the state seemed made for each other.

He had arrived here by accident. In 1949, he had been living in New York State writing stories for the pulp magazines: thin, action-packed pieces that give no clue to MacDonald's genius for making a landscape come alive. He and his wife had set off to drive to Mexico, all their possessions piled into a camper.

"We got to Clearwater, Florida. Dorothy said 'what's wrong with here?' And that was it. The next week, the kids were in school. We were living in Florida."

He'd come at just the right time, before the Fall. There were few hustlers around then; the wild coastline was barely scarred. In the last 30 years the really big thriller – the story of Florida itself – had unfolded while MacDonald sat by. His own novels are basically incidents and chapters from that larger, even more ingenious work of fiction, the recent history of Florida. So the condo racket gave him *Condominium*; the drug trade, *The Dreadful Lemon Sky*; the Tampa biker gangs, *Free Fall in Scarlet*; the real estate business, *Pale Grey for Guilt*. There are seventy-something books altogether (he is still writing three a year); nearly every one deals head-on with a specific commercial area of life in Florida's corrupted garden.

The boom and its moral consequences supplied MacDonald with an obsessive – and inexhaustible – subject. It also helped in another way. "I've been able to hide behind it," he said. "It's a writer's duty to be an observer, not to show a high profile. Here, I've been able to keep hidden. The pace of things has been so fast, everyone's been so busy getting on with his own racket, they haven't had time to notice me watching them. In Florida, the crowd keeps on changing; I'm lost in the crowd."

He is a great noticer. His novels brim with intricate technical details. Even if he cannot instal a catflap, he can describe exactly how to lay a concrete foundation or strip a marine diesel. This love of know-how carries over into the way he writes his ravaged landscapes.

"I write from photographs now. In the mid '50s, I thought I'd lost my eye. I was trying to write a scene set in Laredo, Texas. There was nothing there. My imagination was a blank. I just couldn't see it. So I bought an Argus camera. I've been taking pictures ever since – it helps me to focus on what's there."

"Pictures of what?"

"Junk." He showed me some slides. As photographs, they were nothing much: full-face records of shacks awaiting demolition, the piles of a new bridge, a building site, hulks in a harbour, a pockmarked motel, a line of pylons. He had hundreds of thousands of them, filed in boxes. In bulk, they must have been the most complete dossier ever compiled of man's vandalism in the state of Florida.

We drove to lunch through Sarasota. MacDonald saw his city as a patchwork of real-estate deals. Along the way he jerked his thumb at building after building, naming dates, owners, prices. The first big Sarasota entrepreneur had been John Ringling the circus king, who'd come here in the 1920s when the place was a compact small town with its own archipelago of tangled islands. Since then it had been turned into a Monopoly board: every available square was choked with condominiums, parking lots, shopping centres and Ancient Greek mansions.

"There's almost nothing left now of Sarasota, even as I first remember it. Either it's all been built up, or it's all been pulled down."

At the end of another island, MacDonald stopped at a small dock where boats were moored under trees dripping with lianas. "This is one place that hasn't changed much." He pointed at the woody islet on the far side of the channel. It was busy with egrets and pelicans. "That was owned by the inventor of Airwick. He was a birdwatcher. You know the secret of Airwick? It's supposed to kill the stink; actually all it does is deaden your sense of smell. I guess he must have been kind of . . . conscience-stricken about that."

Over lunch we played a game of cat and mouse. MacDonald would not be caught as a literary man. I talked about writing; he talked about his new word processor. I said how vividly his best passages reminded me of the great American landscapists of the 19th century – Hawthorne, for instance . . .

"Hawthorne? Yes." MacDonald gazed over the top of his martini into the middle distance and kept his mouth buttoned.

Yet the epigraphs to the novels betray a man who lives deeply among books: they come from Santayana, Thoreau, Marcus Aurelius . . .

"A man's life is dyed the colour of his imagination," I said. MacDonald had attached that one to his latest Travis McGee story, *Cinnamon Skin*.

"Yes. Marcus Aurelius. I'm fond of that." He fingered a foil-wrapped after dinner mint. "You know the effect of mint on the digestion?" and he explained the chemistry of mint and the digestive system. It had no bearing on Marcus Aurelius.

"There's a joke they tell about Florida . . . Guy comes here to retire, arrives at Miami, meets a young guy in a bar. 'So how d'you like it here?' says the young guy. 'Oh, pretty much,' says the retiree. 'The sunshine's great, the beaches are great – everything's great. Only trouble is, I don't like to go out at night, with all the things you read in the papers.' The young guy says: 'What they print in the papers is horseshit. All that stuff about killings and muggings – it's a media fabrication. This town is the nicest, safest town in the whole United States. Nothing happens here. The only problem here is that life can get a little boring.' 'Thanks, fella,' says the retiree, 'I'm real indebted to you. I guess I just shouldn't believe what they say in the papers. And by the way, what's your job here?' 'Me?' says the young guy; 'Oh, I ride tailgun on a bread truck.'"

At Airwick Island one of the pelicans flapped off with a small silver fish in its beak.

Travis McGee lives on his houseboat at the Bahia Mar Marina, Fort Lauderdale. I drove east in search of him. The rural interior of Florida was a world and a half away from the manic hustle of the coast; an enormous placid sweep of farms and ranches. Nor were there any sensible limits on what people could raise here: brahma cattle cropped the grass under the palms; giraffes showed their heads over the treetops. Orange groves gave way to an elephant farm; a distant herd of cows turned out to be camels. After fifty miles of this kind of happy agricultural lunacy, I was quite prepared for unicorns and spaghetti trees.

I stopped at a town called Arcadia. No one was about on the wide streets. Its bleached clapboard houses, set deep in trees and flowers, had their shutters drawn against the Christmas sun. This must have been how the settlers of the 19th century had dreamed of Florida – as Arcady, a pastoral wonderland. I bought some postcards, for the pleasure of being able to write *Et in Arcadia ego* on them, and drove on.

It was late when I reached the Atlantic coast. The floodlights of the Fort Lauderdale marinas were shining on a solid mile of money; zillions and squillions of dollars' worth of white cruisers, lying hull to hull in watery streets and avenues. With their terraced decks, flying bridges and tuna towers, they looked like blocks of flats. Some of these private yachts were full-blown ships; even the smallest of them were around sixty feet long and had glassy saloons as big as an average London drawing room. Very few had any signs of life aboard. Those that did were floating advertisements for their owners' lives. Tall golden standing lamps were rooted in carpets that might have been made of dead Persian cats. There were plush leather bars with high stools, bulgy sofas, glass tables, gilt candlesticks, greenery in tubs and bowls of cut flowers. Everything, apparently, had been designed to go smash if the boat ever sailed into a real sea.

In a dark waterfront bar, I found the professional captains of these craft hunched in a line over their beers. They were a gloomy bunch. They'd run out of things to talk to one another about, and time hung heavy on their hands. The captain nearest me was an ex-cop from Cincinnati called Mike. His owner was from Cincinnati, too, but Mike hadn't seen him for over a year.

"When they first bought the boat, they flew down every weekend. Couldn't keep them off it. Then I guess the recession hit; he had to put more time into his business . . . I was expecting them this week-end, but I haven't heard nothing from them yet."

The boat – a modest 58-foot Hatteras – had cost its owner half a million bucks. The rent for its moorings at Pier 66 Marina came to $14,000 a year. The captain's salary was $25,000. Annual maintenance was about $20,000. It seemed a lot of money to spend to keep one man staring listlessly at a can of beer.

"What do you do all the time?"

"Fix the ice-maker. Fix the air-conditioner. Watch T.V."

He had given up his apartment in Fort Lauderdale and now slept in the fo'c's'le of the boat. His wife had gone back to Cincinnati.

"You must sometimes ache to just head out into the blue and hit the Bahamas . . ."

"Every day," said Mike.

"And these guys are all in much the same position?"

"There's some that's busy. But there's a lot like me."

He was marooned in Florida – just another component, like the ice-maker and the radar, in a rich businessman's abandoned toy. At least, that was what I thought then.

The next morning I was idling along a pontoon at the marina, inspecting the boats by daylight. I found it hard to rouse much affection for them. I love wooden boats of the kind that a man can sail by himself, but these moulded giants of ferroconcrete and fibreglass were just swagger for the sake of the thing. Their over-pointed, arching bows gave them the expression of supercilious sharks. Their immaculate saloons were as bland as deserted studio sets for *Dallas*. They were going nowhere: with their telephones, mains water and cable T.V. hookups, they were condominiums afloat and untenanted. To me they seemed pieces of heroic self-aggrandisement as useless as the pyramids, and much less beautiful.

At the far end of the pontoon I recognized Travis McGee's double: a rawboned figure in kneeboots and windcheater. Hunched and purposeful, he seemed out of place in this expensive fun-world. So, apparently, did I. He came striding down the pontoon. He looked short of sleep. The sockets of his eyes were the colour of emery paper.

"Are you off a boat here?"

"No – I was just looking. D'you work for the marina?"

"No." He handed me his card. It had the arms of the U.S. Treasury Department stamped on it. William De Gallio, Customs Patrol Officer. His job was to go racing round the ocean in a high-speed cruiser, hunting for narcotics smugglers; I persuaded him to join me for a drink.

De Gallio was from New York. At nineteen, he'd been drafted to Vietnam. As with so many vets that I've met, "Nam" had become his nightmare addiction. He had hated the war, but out in the Da Nang the adrenalin of action had got into his blood. When he came home, he couldn't settle. He'd drifted round the country telling his Nam stories like an ancient mariner as he shunted from casual job to casual job. Finally he'd landed in Florida and found an occupation in which he could go on fighting his private war. In the customs patrol vessel he was back to a life of shoot-outs, night ops and the chase.

"Every week I think I'm through with it," he said. "I don't much like myself. One day, I'll work it out and go back to New York." He was intelligent and funny, with an oddly dispassionate view of his own mental state.

In Vietnam, he had "messed about with everything": a lot of dope, acid, coke, speed; a little heroin. Now he had turned gamekeeper he was troubled by the moral contradiction of his position.

"It's the amateurs who bother me. The one-run guys . . . you know, the young couples with kids trying to make a down payment on a house . . . the guy whose business has been hit by the recession . . ."

"The John DeLoreans of the world —"

"Yeah – but it's little guys, mostly. They're the ones who stand there crying like little kids when you dig the stuff out of their boat. They're not criminals. Shit, it's only hash, anyway. We've all had hash . . ."

Harassing the professionals was different; a good clean fighting war. He watched the movements of their boats, had an eye for a millimetre's difference in the level of their waterlines. (With a hidden cargo of drugs, a light-displacement boat like a Hatteras or a Bertram will sink enough in the water to submerge the smear of algae along its usual waterline.) He had recovered hauls of magical substances from fake engine mountings, fake battery compartments, fake bilge-keels, fake bulkheads. He enjoyed demolishing other people's costly cruisers.

Only careless or unlucky smugglers got caught by De Gallio. The Florida coast is an intricate tesselation of reefs and islands. The peninsula itself dangles into a lawless sea, where a boat is never very far from the Bahamas, or Haiti, or Cuba, or Mexico. The suppliers of drugs are a short run away; the American shore is riddled with bolt-holes in the way of islands to hide behind and swampy inlets to escape into. De Gallio's patrol boat was like one dog trying to chase a field-full of rabbits at once; most of the time he ended up chasing his own tail.

I asked De Gallio to guess how many of the craft in the marina were involved in the drug trade.

"Forty per cent. At least. They'll try and make a run or two every year."

"What's the average profit on a run? – Not a heroin run, just marijuana."

"Around a hundred grand." The figure made rather precise sense of the list of maintenance costs that I'd been given by the captain the night before. One three-hour voyage would keep a 60-foot status symbol afloat for a year. The odds against running into trouble with the customs were very high. What businessman, pressed by recession but anxious to keep up appearances, could sensibly resist such a neat way of solving the problem? Florida was full of easy answers.

"You're a very curious guy," De Gallio said. "Don't get too curious, though, will you? Here in Florida, you get too curious, you can disappear. People disappear round here. It happens all the time."

I wanted to put Florida in perspective. Christmas was coming, and I dreaded Christmas; so I decided to swap the car for a rented boat and drift offshore until all the Yuletide hullaballoo had died down. In Lauderdale, the price of rental sailboats seemed to be based on the assumption that you would be packing their bilges with marijuana and making off with $100,000. I went in search of something cheaper down on the Keys.

The Keys are a long string of alluvial islands. They trail out for more than a hundred miles, from the swampy tip of Florida towards Havana; low hummocks of coral, mud and crushed seashells that are joined to each other by a chain of ingenious bridges. With the Atlantic on one side and the Gulf on the other, they form a continuous narrow strip of burger joints, trailer parks, bars, motels, washetarias and boatyards, with the surf breaking into the mangroves at both edges.

On Key Largo I found the man I wanted. He ran his yacht-broking business from a stool in a bar. A pathologist would probably have found him to have been in his early fifties; I judged him to be about fourteen and three-quarters – one of those Huck Finn boys who have always gravitated to whatever frontier has been going. Ron had run away from Southern California: it had been too grown-up for him. Florida suited him nicely.

It took a while to edge him round to the question of a boat. Ron wanted to play. We went for a ride in his ten-year-old black Cadillac. We had a drink with one of Ron's "girls" – a matronly lady in specs who looked as if she had a lot of trouble trying to keep Ron washed behind the ears. We looked at a motor cruiser that Ron had just bought "for a steal". Ron had buddies in every bar on the Key; balding boys with enviable tans who kept us stacked with Budweisers on the tab. Eventually Ron produced a boat – a neat 25-foot sloop that was only a fraction more expensive than the hire of a motel room.

"The trouble with this place," said Ron as we checked the boat's inventory, "is that it's getting all sewn up. Sometimes I reckon I'll have to take off again."

"Where to?"

"I don't know. South America, maybe. You ever been to Africa?"

I parked my bags in the cramped saloon and investigated the charts for the Gulfside coast. They showed a tricky, shallow sea full of sandbars, wrecks and atolls: it was a sea straight out of a schoolboy adventure story.

In colour it was like streaky jade, whipped up into sharp little houndstooth waves by a strong, warm westerly wind. I didn't bother to put the mainsail up: the boat shot away from the inlet under its jib alone. The day-glo clutter of the highway faded behind the screen of mangroves. A big dolphin rolled glossily over in the water on the beam. Three miles offshore, I could still see the ribbed and weedy bottom under the keel, and the long shadow of the boat printed as sharply as a photograph on the white sand.

At sea, a little drunk and very happy, I had Florida in focus as I tacked down the channel between coral spits and jungly islands. In a way, Ron was right. It was getting all sewn up. The state was rapidly being filled to bursting point. Old people and golddiggers pouring in from the top end . . . Cubans and Haitians and all manner of illegal aliens – and illegal substances – pouring in from the bottom . . . Not even Paradise could stand such unremitting pressure on its resources. And, at that moment, Florida really did look like a paradise. It was too rich, too improbably beautiful for ordinary human beings to cope with. So they were doing what they knew how to do best, and fouling it up.

Just before sunset, I let the anchor go in a bay off Lignum Vitae Key, an uninhabited island, posted against trespassers, where tall mahogany trees were banked above the shoreline of mangrove swamp. The chart showed the ruins of a house on the far side of the island, and I rowed round the edge of the beach in the dinghy. It was like being afloat in an aquarium. The water was brilliant, the rocky bottom studded with sea urchins, twists of pink coral, patterned crabs and sea anemones. A shoal of angelfish scattered at the sudden splash of my oar. A raccoon stood on the lip of the water, stared at me and bolted back to the underbrush.

I slept in the berth in the forecabin, and dreamed of emigration. When I woke, it was sometime after 2 a.m. and at first I couldn't think why I had tumbled out of sleep so suddenly. The boat lurched violently on a big, hard-muscled wave. Something crashed from a shelf in the saloon. There was a pause, then another wave hit it, this time a smaller one, on which the boat rocked and slammed. I put on the overhead light and groggily stumbled off up to the cockpit.

I couldn't see the motor boat which had caused the wake, but I could hear its engines. They cut out sharply, somewhere across the water, not much more, I guessed, than half a mile away. I searched the tangled shadows of the swamp and saw nothing. Whatever the boat was, it was showing no lights. As quietly as I could, I went below and clicked off my own light.

In Florida, you get too curious, you can disappear.

This is the way that Travis McGee stories begin. This is the way I'd prefer my own to end.

1983

II

The Dutch engineer had only been living on Key Largo for a month, and he was sweating badly in the steambath heat, his face a bunched fist as he struggled to repair the faulty depth-sounder on our rented boat.

"Corrosion!" he said, making it sound like lust or avarice, a celebrated deadly sin. He exposed the remains of a vital electric connexion. The wires were flaky-white with mold. "See? Dust in my fingers! That's the trouble with this climate. *Everything* – every *damn* thing – corrodes here."

I knew what he meant. I had come to the Keys to corrode a little myself. I liked the rusty morals of this scapegrace archipelago, its air of having seceded from the rest of the United States on the conscientious grounds that none of its inhabitants can bring themselves to believe in the Protestant Ethic. Five years before, I'd gone into temporary hiding in a run-down trailer park on Key Largo, and had been powerfully impressed by the genial loucheness of the place: its bars so dark that you couldn't identify the face of the man on the next stool; its clandestine economy, for which the New York street price of a line of coke was the Keys' own Dow Industrial Average; its ruffianly wildlife of chicken vultures, coral snakes and barracudas.

This time I had come with Caroline, my wife, and like most people who seek out the Keys, we were on the lam, evading the hard labor of an English Christmas. The idea was simply to go with the wind, drifting from island to island on a 32-foot sloop, to live grubbily in sawn-off jeans and gimme caps, to catch lunch over the stern, to see the roseate spoonbills and to fall in with as many disreputable characters as we could find.

You need a boat to see the Keys. Motorists, tailgating down US1 past the condo blocks and Burger Kings, never properly get the hang of the place. It is the ospreys, the fishermen, the delivery skippers on the dope passage from the Bahamas, who comprehend the Keys as they really are – an impossibly intricate tesselation of land and water, far wilder and more beautiful than you could ever guess at from the highway, and full of secrets, some of them unprintable.

Our boat was snug and foolproof. A mile and a half offshore, it was sailing itself sweetly down the Hawk Channel. The northeast wind was brisk enough to keep it slicing through the waves on the foresail alone. I tied a length of elasticated cord round the spokes of the wheel and looped it round the compass binnacle; it worked as a serviceable autopilot and left us free to lounge and stare like a pair of lazy passengers.

We were afloat on the Atlantic, but the Keys are sheltered by a barrier reef of coral heads that stops the ocean swell in its tracks and turns the sea into a milky-green lagoon. Despite the stiffish breeze, the waves broke harmlessly like spitting kittens, and the boat's motion was just a gentle lollop as it seated itself comfortably among these miniature breakers. We overtook a fleet of Portuguese-men-of-war running before the wind under their gelatinous, electric-blue sails and trawling for fish with sheaves of poisonous tentacles. A young porpoise broke the surface beside us and went squirming under our bows, then gave us up as too slow to be worth playing with.

Seen from the sea, the Keys lay as low on the water as rafts of floating weed. No motels, condos, shopping malls – the mangroves had swallowed them all whole and made the Keys miraculously green again. The only giveaway signs of civilisation were the high road bridges spanning the islands, with cars crawling across them in the sun like bugs with shiny wings.

I headed the boat for the narrow gap between Windley and Plantation Keys, and suddenly the mangroves declared what they'd been hiding, as strange things began to emerge shyly from the undergrowth - patches of cinderblock, glass, concrete and aluminium that slowly grew until the green was almost gone. As the Snake Creek lifting bridge tilted politely skyward to let us through, we sailed clean out of an idyll and into what passes, in these parts, for the real world.

Somewhere out of sight, a p.a. system was delivering a massed choral rendition of "Jingle Bells" at full blast. It's hard enough to match the joy of riding in a one-horse open sleigh with a temperature of 85° and a shoal of angelfish under one's keel; and harder still when, at the same time, you're navigating a tricky course between Swiss chalets, Mexican adobe ranches, Lincoln log cabins, Moorish temples, Chinese willow-pattern pagodas, collonnaded Doric villas, New England clapboard cottages and palm thatch pavilions that are a subtle mix of Tudor and Hawaiian. The untended boat slewed on the running tide, its loose sail thunderclapping in the wind. Drifting slowly backwards, we narrowly avoided a collision with a wooden Kentish oasthouse on concrete stilts.

Under way again, I took a second look at this eccentric village, and saw that at heart the place was as rigidly conventional as a respectable Boston suburb. An enterprising developer had gouged a grid of canals out of the mangrove swamp, and each custom-built dream house had been constructed around the same organizing principle – same mosquito-screened sundeck, same picture window, same private dock, same white, twin-screw cruiser with a dizzy tarpon bridge. Clad in palmetto, hibiscus, bougainvillea, with sprinklers playing on freshly-seeded lawns, the houses wore a suburbanly anxious look, as if each one was gazing at its neighbor and fearing that next door might be getting a fraction more fun, more fantasy, for its money.

Then, as quickly as they'd opened, the mangroves charitably closed round the houses like a curtain. Even at a sedate speed of around four knots, transitions on the Keys happen at a breakneck pace. Minutes before, we'd been on the Atlantic; now we were in the Mexican Gulf. We'd been in town, and now we were deep in a wilderness of floppy yellow butterflies, pelicans falling out of trees, egrets stalking prettily on fusewire legs and narrow black barracudas torpedoing away from the encroaching shadow of the boat.

This sea was very different to the one we'd left. It was disconcertingly shallow. We needed four feet of water to stay afloat, and the sea-floor, of silted coral, looked only inches-deep. It was like sailing in a tropical aquarium of the kind that dentists keep in their waiting rooms to soothe their patients' nerves. It didn't soothe mine. More than a mile out, and in the posted channel, the depth-sounder was still flickering between 4.6 and 5.8 feet, and I kept on waiting for the crash as the keel ground into an uncharted coral head. It failed to come, though I watched the stone crabs burying themselves hurriedly in the silt as we slipped past.

For as far as one could see, the mangroves were busy, adding more keys to the archipelago. The sea was riddled with shoals, where the rising mud showed purple, like a bruise, and wherever a shoal touched the surface of the water, a mangrove had seized on it. First an arch of root, then a sprig of green – and a fresh island was started. The NOAA charts couldn't keep up with this polyphiloprogenitive urge of the mangrove. There were dozens of small keys as yet undiscovered by the surveyors – tangled islets of virgin land, still waiting for names. I christened a few of them as we sailed past: Osprey Key, Cormorant Key, Michelob Can Key . . . Someone ought to honor the mangrove. As fast as the developers and realtors work down the main spine of the Florida Keys, so the mangroves are making up for their depredations by building more wild islands far out of reach of the highway and the men who think that every scrap of unspoiled green would be enhanced by a nice big condominium.

There were few other boats about. Far inshore, a pair of commercial crab- and lobster-fishermen were winching up their traps. The wind had dropped to a warm dog's-breath, and we ghosted along in a rapt silence, broken only by the riffle of the pages of Peterson's *Eastern Birds*, as we tried to resolve the Spoonbill/Ibis/Flamingo problem. Whatever it was, the handsome bird in question was certainly pink. Ahead of the boat, a submerging turtle left a momentary hole in the water the size of a large dinner-gong.

It was dusk when we closed with the shore again, to anchor in Lime Tree Bay and row the dinghy back into the United States. On the highway, things were hopping. Everyone was switching on their fairylights, and giant illuminated Santas were lurking behind the palm trees, their beards and nightcaps flashing. No-one round here seemed to have heard of zoning regulations: it was an improvised, ad hoc, happy sprawl of houses living cheek-by-jowl with the bar, the restaurant, the gas station, the Tom Thumb minimarket, the Bait 'n' Tackle shop, the R. V. park. Everything looked tinker-built, in the careless, hammer-and-nails Keys vernacular style of architecture, in which "pecky cypress", a wood consisting more of knots and holes than grain, plays a central part. With a pile of pecky cypress, you can knock a shop or a bar-restaurant together in a couple of minutes. It'll last till tomorrow, or the day after, or until the next hurricane, which is as far ahead as anyone on the Keys can bear of thinking. They're good-time buildings, and they don't give a damn.

In the restaurant, a ginger-bearded hulk was demolishing a small mountain of french fries while pursuing a conversation with a friend at the bar.

"You got new people moved in where you are, I hear. They *white*? They *Americans*?"

"Yeah. I ain't seen much of 'em, though. But they're *white* enough."

"Me, I had to move out. *Cubans*. I had Cuban kids wandering in my front yard, Cuban dogs shitting in my back yard . . . I got *sick*."

We rowed back to the boat. Even on the darkened water, I could hear the voice of the complaining hulk – gravelly, bullying, indignant. Escaping reality can be hard work. At dawn next morning, I jerked suddenly awake. I identified the noises that had woken me: surf on a nearby beach and crickets fiddling in the brush. During the night, the wind must have changed and the boat dragged its anchor. I was half out of my bunk when I listened again and heard the noises differently. The crashing surf was only the early traffic on US1; the crickets were the humming powerlines that march on high pylons down to Key West. It was a mistake that anyone could have made: on the Keys, Nature and Culture get hopelessly mixed up.

The guidebooks make far too much of the "Conchs" – the born-and-raised natives of the Keys. You might as well go in search of Golden Orioles as track the Conchs down in Monroe County. For the modern Keys are a creation of the North. It's in the hardworking, cold-winter states like Ohio, Michigan, New Jersey, that the essential character of the Keys has been forged, as a Northern dream of sunshine, easy living, easy money. So the founding fathers of the place came streaming over the bridge at Jewfish Creek, where Key Largo is lightly attached to the Florida mainland, in pursuit of a new kind of manifest destiny. Some merely wanted to put their feet up, to emulate the peaceful manatees and porpoises. Some saw a fruitful future in trapping tourists, peddling real estate or loading Broward cruisers with cargoes of white powder, taking their cue from the vultures and the sharks. What they shared was a common faith in the teaching St Matthew, Chapter 2, Verse 26: like lilies of the field, they saw no special reason to either toil or spin.

The closest Keys equivalent to the Puritan township of New England is the trailer park, where the Winnebagos lie hull to hull on rented plots, with shingles hanging over their doors saying "The Schmidts – Bill and Vera", and good-old-boys potter round the dock and grumble about the impeccable weather.

We tied up at the Jolly Roger Travel Park on Grassy Key, where a man of about my own age, but in far better physical trim, took our ropes. We talked for a few minutes and I asked him what he did. "Do?" – he looked puzzled; then his face cleared. "Oh, I ain't *worked* since 1969," he said with pride.

A barefoot boy of eleven or twelve was fishing from the end of the dock. He put his rod down to come over and inspect the boat. He was from Manchester, New Hampshire, he said, and he was here with his mother. I thought that, like me, he was on a Christmas vacation. "When did you come down here?" "Seven years ago," the boy said.

The trailer parks are friendly, improvised, close knit communities. On the Keys, people have time for each other. They borrow each other's bicycles to get to the store, and each other's boats to go out fishing. At the Jolly Roger, I saw the handicapped and the retarded being gentled along by their neighbors with a civility and concern long gone from the average American, and European, small town. It was thought unneighborly to lock your car, your front door, or your boat. The Christmas lights and strings of tinsel were looped from trailer-home to trailer-home in a shared celebration. For as long as we were docked, we had neighbors too: they dropped in to see how we were, drove us out to the local restaurant and the supermarket, and, after we'd left, they called us up on marine radio to ask where we were sailing and whether we were okay. They were all refugees from Northern cities; and in the trailer park they had managed to reconstruct that small, self-contained, intimate village life which is now usually confined only to nostalgic movies and period novels. It was a man in his seventies who, late in the afternoon, stared at the reddening sea and told me: "I'm dying here. I made up my mind. I ain't moving from where I am. I'm dying here."

I was sad to see the mangroves close in over the Jolly Roger. For the next few miles I was fantasising about my own Winnebago, its handkerchief-sized garden of bright flowers, its carpentered porch with a rocking chair facing the Gulf, its inviting shingle – The Rabans . . . But no. I concentrated on steering clear of the crab and lobster traps that dotted the water ahead. Their marker buoys showed as nodding dolls' heads, and there were hundreds, thousands, of them; many of them spaced barely a boat's width apart.

There are supposed to be six million traps set between Key Largo and Key West, and I reckon that I counted at least 1.5 million myself. By the lazy standards of the Keys, trapping crustacea counts as hard graft, but the sea is warm and calm, the pickings easy by comparison with the grim fishing grounds of Maine or Long Island. On the

Keys, two men in a boat will tend around 2000 traps, lifting maybe 300 traps in a working day. Stone crabs fetch $5.00 a pound, lobsters (though the Florida lobster is really a crayfish) about twice that price. On an average day, each boat will come in with at least 100lbs of stone crab – a comfortable living, as well as a good front for other, even more profitable activities.

The long city shore of Marathon sped past us like a cruise ship on the beam. The wind was getting up. With a cold front lying from Talahassee down to Yucatan, we were in for a "norther" – a modest gale that rakes the Keys in winter and turns the sea soapsud-white. Back to one sail, we scudded ahead of the wind, with the rope as rigid as an iron bar and the water hissing under the bilges of the boat. The chart, pegged down with binoculars, a winch handle and a 3lb sounding lead, was trying to take wing from the cockpit floor. We nipped under the central span of the Seven Mile Bridge, briefly out into the tame Atlantic, and headed back northeastwards to the shelter of Hog Key on the ocean side of Marathon. I had never sailed quite so fast with so little fright: within the comfortingly safe ambit of coral reefs and mangrove islands it was easy to play the windswept hero, and we entered Marathon like swaggering Athenians, with ten minutes to go before the end of Happy Hour at Bacchus By The Sea. Caroline threw a line from the bow; the bartender caught it, in a nice illustration of the special relationship that exists on the Keys between the land and the water. Tying a round-turn-and-two-half-hitches round a post, I ordered up a vodka martini and dislodged a brown pelican. It fell into the sea like a bundle of old clothes.

Robert Dustal had bought his restaurant and thatched "tiki bar" in May; now, in the wake of the October Crash, he was anxiously waiting for the "season". The tourists were late, and he was starting to fret. "Look at my sunset!" he said. It was a sunset worth looking at, too; as bloodily colorful as a major intestinal operation. "In the summer, it goes down on the Gulf side, but in the winter it plops down right there. *My* side. You come back next week, there'll be folks standing in line to see my sunset . . ." But there were no folks as yet. At the tiki bar, two professional fishermen and a travelling salesman were drinking beer, and drinking very slowly.

Dustal was from New Jersey; a lean, brown, soft-spoken man, with a few remaining traces of the fame he'd once enjoyed as pitcher for the Detroit Tigers. He still moved like an athlete, and sometimes one would see a shadowy stadium round him, as if he was lingering for a last moment in the applause of the crowd. He'd drifted down to the Keys, managed Key West's ailing baseball team for a while, and settled in Marathon. "Now ... well, take a look at me. I'm in paradise!"

He was nursing Bacchus By The Sea much as he must have managed his team. There were no profits yet, but he was building up a clientele of locals – fishermen, boat bums, the Marathon Rotarians and the men who dropped by to chew the fat over old ballgame records. Tracksuited, spry and smiling, he introduced everyone to everyone and ran his tiki bar as a private party to which we all had the luck to be invited.

I found myself wrangling contentedly over the respective merits of Churchill and Roosevelt with a man called Kevin, who'd been a keen Democrat in his time and was proud of having campaigned for Adlai Stevenson. But what about now? I asked him. Who was he rooting for?

"Oh, hell, the last guy I voted for must've been ... Hubert Humphrey, I guess. Since I came down to live in the Keys, I've sort of dropped out of the human race."

Dustal pointed out the "drug boat" moored alongside ours; a beautiful 50-foot wooden ketch. It had been impounded by the Coastguard, and sold off at auction up in Jacksonville, where its new owner had paid $7,000 for it – a fraction of what I guessed it must be worth. My interest in the ketch attracted the attention of a gimme-capped and parka'd "liveaboard", who said I could see his drug boat too. His boat, though, had made a successful run, landing 700lbs of cocaine somewhere in the mangrove-fringes of Marathon. After that, it had become valueless to its owners, who'd sold it for a nominal $5,000 to my parka'd friend. "Full electronics, solar panels – *everything*!" The only snag in the deal was that he'd had to rip out the secret compartments to make the boat legal. It had a false waterline, false cabin floor, false bulkheads, false fuel – and water-tanks. "It was damn hard *work*," he said, pronouncing the Keys' least favorite word. We couldn't visit the boat yet because he was waiting for his girlfriend to return from her job in the town; then we'd all go over in the dinghy, he promised.

"So *she* works," I said. "I've seen a lot of women round here working. Not many men, though."

"You got it. We have a club down here. The KYWW Club – you know about that? Keep Your Woman Working."

The drug trade distorts the prices of boats, just as it distorts the price of labor in the Keys. A deckhand on a run from the Bahamas, whose job it is to help hide the cargo, tend the ropes and watch the compass, earns, I am reliably told, $10,000 for the forty-eight-hour trip. At $284 an hour (with several of them spent asleep), it makes waiting on tables look a shade dull. Though Fat Albert, a barrage balloon loaded with surveillance devices ("They got things up there that can look right into your boat and tell what you're cooking for dinner"), keeps a baleful watch over the Keys, most drug boats still get through. The most common cause of drug arrests is not Fat Albert's vigilance but rewarded tip-offs by the coke-suppliers to the DEA. Around Marathon, where the DEA is known as "Bush's Racket", this is thought unsporting. "What kind of a government is it that puts money in the pockets of Cuban *drug* barons?" complained one injured boat bum.

Corrosion. It spreads in complicated ways down on the Keys. A few yards up the highway from Bacchus, I looked in on a vast and empty restaurant-bar called the South Seas Lounge, whose bartender was fresh from a suburban country club in Indiana. She was precise about figures. She was "almost 29½ years old" and had been living in Marathon for "just 3½ weeks". She couldn't contain the current big excitement in her life. Next Saturday she was off on "a *gambling* cruise" from Key West to Miami. I asked her what she was going to play. Blackjack? Craps? Roulette? "I don't know. All of them, I guess. I mean, they don't *have* nothing like that in Muncie, Indiana," and she named her home town with all the scorn that the truly-corroded have for the cold and proper life they've left behind them.

We were corroding nicely. With the norther still blowing, we'd set off to sail to Key West, but the boat had heeled over on its beam with the force of the wind, and the short, steep seas were difficult to ride. I listed all the things I couldn't face in Key West – historic markers, "Conch houses", gift shops, Hemingwayana – and turned the boat round to go back to Bacchus. Mrs Dustal helped us dock. "So you got the Keys disease already?" she said.

From then on, I stopped ruling long straight courses on the chart, with legends on them like "20.5 miles at 252°". Instead, we began to imitate the flight of the chicken vulture, circling and perching, circling and perching, without plan or destination. Days later, floating lightly through the Everglades after a long and voluble night at Alabama Jack's, I thought that my mind, like the mind of the man at the Jolly

Roger Travel Park, was almost made up to die here, too. I know a gap in the mangroves where . . . I know a man who . . . The rust was eating into my head. With what little resolution was still left, I got the ruler out and plotted a course that would eventually lead back to the cold, northern city where I'm afraid that I belong. We work hard here. Our afternoons are dark. My chief distraction lately has been a poorly-printed color magazine called *The Real Estate Book of the Florida Keys*. I think the corrosion is malignant, for I have spent the last half hour staring at an indecipherable photo involving palm trees and pink cinderblock, and reading the caption as if it was poetry.

> TROPICAL PARADISE – 2 BR, 1.5 BA. 60' concrete dock on clean wide canal. Strg shed, scrnd Fla rm. Very well kept mobile w/unusual trees and flowers. $25,000 dn long term mort. $99,000 . . .

1989

III

Joan Didion's Miami is at once an aggressively real city and a legendary domain to which Swift might well have posted Gulliver, or Voltaire Candide. At a time when the American empire is sustained on a rhetoric of "deniable" abstraction and temporization, Miami is the ominous place where "words tend to have consequences, and stories endings". In the index to *Miami*, some of the longest entries appear under the headings, "assassinations", "betrayals" and "bomb-ings" – and these register only the endings of a few minor sub-plots in the main, and continuing, story of a city where loose talk, bad writing, calculated economies with the truth are swiftly and inevitably translated into bloody action. In Didion's exact, rational and appalled portrayal, Miami is the price that America is paying for the corrupted language in which it conducts its political business.

In this book Didion the novelist and Didion the moralist work hand in hand to create a work that combines intense imaginative vision with extraordinary argumentative force. It is the novelist who seizes on water as Miami's defining element, who finds herself afloat in a floating city, the least corporeal metropolis in the United States, bounded by a coral reef on one side and a liquid mangrove swamp on the other. It is the moralist who teases out the logic of that image, who finds that Miami is a city in which truth dissolves, in which it is impossible to touch bottom. Every story she is told has to be "sounded", but the lead keeps on going down, and down. She pursues what she calls – beautifully – the "underwater narrative" of Miami; a resourceful scuba diver, flippering cautiously, knife at the ready, in the territory of the moray eel and the barracuda.

The knife is out before she dives, to cut away the tangle of protective illusions with which Miami has surrounded itself. It is not the last great American melting pot in which the Cubans supply (in the words of the *Miami Herald*) the city's "Hispanic flavor". The Anglos form a "beleaguered raj", unable to speak Spanish, which is now the first language of the city, pathetically ignorant about Cuban attitudes, ostrichlike in their determination to go on believing that the Cubans are "immigrants" whose chief desire is to emulate the Anglos and become "good Americans" in the classic immigrant mould. The *Miami Herald* line is that the chief Cuban contribution to Miami has been their cute ethnic music and cute ethnic food, and that Little Havana is a marketable tourist draw. Demolishing Miami's own bad language of patronage and self-delusion, Didion prepares for her descent into that foggy, subacquaeous world where all sentences are inherently untrustworthy and where words are mainly used for telling lies.

El exilio, the communal exile, is the name the Cubans give to their own condition in Miami – a term with the idea of return built into it. Castro, like Machado, Prio, Batista, will be overthrown, just as the Contras will destroy the Sandinistas. *NICARAGUA HOY, CUBA MAÑANA!* go the slogans, saying only what successive presidents, from Kennedy to Reagan, have said when it suited them. More zealously "anti-communist" than even Reagan himself, the Miami Cubans have armed the Contras while plotting coups on their own account. CIA money has been one of several peculiar fluid and powdery substances on which the city of Miami has stayed afloat: the people of *el exilio* have grown used to being funded by one government agency and investigated for illegal arms-possession by another. It is the first lesson in basic Administration English to be hailed as a "freedom fighter" in the morning by the CIA and arrested as a "terrorist" in the afternoon by the FBI.

In Miami, the meaning of meaning itself is now all but lost. No-one speaks anyone else's language. The word *diálogo* is synonymous with treason: people who advocate talking to the Castro regime have been assassinated in the streets. The heroes of *el exilio* are the Rambo-style "men of action", while the "men of words" are vilified as cowards and traitors.

In Didion's book, two kinds of talk predominate, and both are rendered brilliantly on the page. One is furious and Cuban; declamatory, indignant, bewildered, punctuated by the stubbing-out of unlit cigarettes and terminating in bristling silence, personal recrimination or the slap of an open palm on a tabletop. The other is the bland cloud-cuckoo-speak of the Washington administration. "It wasn't looking good, so we kind of moved it back," says a White House spokesman of Reagan's Central American policy, as if he was an account executive discussing an advertising campaign. Or Reagan himself, in one of his notorious "thinking aloud" moments, talking of Nicaragua: "Tómas Borge, the communist interior minister, is engaging in a brutal struggle to bring the freedom fighters into discredit. You see, Borge's communist operatives dress in freedom fighter uniforms, go into the countryside and murder and mutilate ordinary Nicaraguans . . ."

The second kind of talk fuels the first and is the driving force behind Miami's "underwater narrative", in which all stories are by nature "unverifiable", in which fact and fiction have become so interwoven that their blend now constitutes a world in which people live their daily lives. Jesus Garcia, for instance, jailed for illegal possession of a MAC-10, tells a typical Miami story of how he was involved in a plot "to assassinate the new American ambassador to Costa Rica, blow up the American embassy there, and blame it on the Sandinistas":

> The idea, Jesus Garcia said, had been to give the United States the opportunity it needed to invade Nicaragua, and also to collect on a million-dollar contract the Columbian cocaine cartel was said to have out on the new American ambassador to Costa Rica . . .

Another example, among hundreds in the same genre, comes from Marita Lorenz, who testified before the House Select Committee on Assassinations in 1978. In November 1963, she said, she was in a group of Cubans who drove Lee Harvey Oswald from Miami to a motel room in Dallas where they were met by Jack Ruby. She remembered seeing rifles and scopes in the room . . . But "the committee found no evidence to support Lorenz's allegation".

Of course not. "Evidence" is not a negotiable commodity in a city that lives on government-inspired fantasy and where the chief usefulness of language lies in its capacity to launder facts. "Words tend to have consequences . . .", but the syntax of Miami, its serpentine progress from subject to object, has gone beyond the comprehension of the sane grammarian. In Miami, at least in Joan Didion's Miami, the paranoiac emerges as the most likely guide to the truth of the place, which bears an uncanny resemblance to that famous building described in Genesis XI. *Therefore is the name of it called Babel; because the Lord did there confound the language of all the earth.*

1988

CAPE VERDE ISLANDS

This, perhaps, is how things will be after the bomb. Seen from a distance, the Cape Verde Islands show as jagged piles of brickdust stacked up in the sea; an archipelago of scorched rubble. The only signs of life are painted words, for every mountainside has its slogan laid on to the red shale in giant white letters. VIVA! VIVA! LONG LIVE SOCIAL JUSTICE! LONG LIVE REVOLUTIONARY SOCIAL DEMOCRACY! LONG LIVE AMILCAR CABRAL!

The legible mountains face the sky, and their messages have the air of distress signals from a wreck. Who are they addressed to – God? overflying 747 captains? me? Are there survivors down there? LONG LIVE AGRARIAN REFORM! LONG LIVE ARISTIDE PEREIRA!

My plane banked, leaving a Viva-this to starboard and a Viva-that to port. The slogans zapped past, too fast for the eye to follow. I was sorry to miss them, since there's a notable shortage of literature on the Cape Verdes and I was hungry to read everything about the place that I could find. So far I hadn't found much except for a handful of scathing travellers' remarks. Sir Richard Hawkins sailed here in the *Dainty* in 1593 and didn't take to the islands at all. "It is wisedome to shunne the sight of them," he wrote. They earn an unkind reference in Robert Burton's *Anatomy of Melancholy*, where he says that they're famous for "fluxes", "fevers" and "frenzies". Charles Darwin, in the *Beagle*, stopped off at the Cape Verdes just long enough to meditate on "the novel aspect of an utterly sterile land".

Down on the tarmac I collected my bag and junked my complimentary pair of blue nylon slippers and airline slumbershade.

"You're not leaving the flight *here?*" asked my South African neighbour, for whom the islands were a tiresome refuelling stop. "I've been on this flight a dozen times, and I haven't seen a *white* get off here yet." He looked out of the window at a landscape of grit and cinders. "It's *nowhere*."

In my book, Nowhere is a better address than Cape Town. Glad to escape from my neighbour's tales of peddling cosmetics in the suburbs, I quit the plane and took stock of a world as reduced to bare essentials as a first-grader's crayon picture.

Item: one spindle-shanked black goat cropping the dust.

Item: one dwarf hunchback acacia tree, bent double by the North East Tradewinds. Its brittle foliage points south and west as accurately as a compass bearing, towards the Amazon basin 1800 miles across the Atlantic.

Item: one yellow dog, its ribs showing through its pelt, with sores.

Item: one cheerful militiaman, in sweat-stained fatigues, larking with a submachine-gun.

Item: one woman walking away along a sandy cobbled road, balancing on her head a five-gallon kerosene drum filled with water from the airport tap. The road is dead straight, with no sign of a hut or a house beside it. The woman will, apparently, be walking away for ever, until the laws of perspective reduce her to a microdot in the red dust.

Item: the words VIVA O IIa CONGRESSO DO PAIGC painted with careful artistry on a cracked concrete wall.

The first-grader would have more difficulty in capturing the quality of the light. It was like bright steam, and made everything in it swim and wobble. If you looked hard at the sentry, you could see right through him and his indiarubber gun. The hot wind, blowing off the Sahara, carried a great deal of Africa with it. Its journey here, across four hundred miles of open sea, hadn't robbed it of its pungency: it tasted of sand, rust, flies, rotten fruit, perspiration and dead dog. It had real substance to it – it was the kind of air that you could dine off, at a pinch. The goat was chewing contentedly on the stuff. I tried it out on my own tongue and throat, and reckoned that Cape Verde air must be an acquired taste like escargots or sheep's eyes.

Only the air was rich. Everything else in sight was arid and tindery. The name of the islands seemed like a joke in poor taste: it would be hard to find an inhabited place on earth that was more spectacularly unverdant than the Cape Verdes. Watching the woman wearing her can of precious water like an opera hat, I wondered if anyone in their right mind, given this bald volcanic upthrust of ash and lava, could learn to love it and think of it as home.

The islands have a shabby history. In 1462 they were settled by Portuguese slave traders. The surrounding sea turned them into a convenient prison, and boatloads of captive West Africans were disembarked here before being sold abroad. Escaping slaves ran away into the mountains, where they grubbed a living from whatever damp crevices in the rock they could find. The Portuguese took black mistresses, and soon the characteristic skin colour of the Cape Verdian was a sort of muddy khaki. He was an unperson; neither an African nor a European – and he spoke an unlanguage. Cape Verdian Creole emerged, a mishmash of bits of Portuguese, bits of tribal African dialect, with words filched from English, Dutch, French, Italian and Arabic.

When the slave trade ended, the American press-gang began. Whaling ships from New Bedford and Nantucket, bound for the South Atlantic, sailed short-handed from Massachusetts and took on their full complement of crew at the Cape Verdes. For the Captain Ahabs of the 19th century, the Cape Verdians were a godsend: they were good sailors, they were tractable and their services could be bought dirt-cheap.

The two main ports, Praia and Mindelo, became luridly cosmopolitan. Ships from every country in Europe stopped by for fuel and R. & R. The Cape Verdians, pathetically poor in natural resources, had nothing to sell except their labour and their bodies. They learned to talk a little of almost everybody's language. The girls were obliging. The faces of the babies were distinctly odd, with Afro hair over Roman noses and fat lips set in Nordic complexions. In Cape Verde, everyone's genes got mixed up with everyone else's.

This process, of endless addition and dilution, defined what it meant to be a Cape Verdian; and language kept the score. Creole, with its sloppy habit of picking up anything that was going, was a sensitive register of the mongrel experience of the islanders.

At the first bar I visited, I asked for a measure of the local hard stuff. The bar was a one-room building made of rocks, with unglazed windows and a palm-thatch roof. The drink was distilled from sugar-cane, and had a sickly kick to it.

"What's the word for this?" I asked, in atrocious Portuguese learned on the plane.

"Grog," said the albino woman who was tending bar.

Grog? It was a word that had come a long way since Admiral Vernon had ordered that the British rum ration on naval ships be diluted with water in 1740. The admiral was famous for wearing a grogram cloak, and the watered rum had been named after this peculiar garment.

So I drank grog, and made six friends with the help of a pocket dictionary. When I left the bar, everyone carolled "Ciaou!", "Ciaou!" like people saying goodbye at the worst sort of Soho loft party.

Ciaou? I wondered what horny *marinaio* had been responsible for that one.

"Ciaou!" I called back, speaking in good Creole.

In 1975, the Portuguese abandoned the islands to their own devices. No departing colonial power has left a stranger or more confused legacy. Linguistically, genetically and economically, the place was a mess. The Cape Verdians, with their Portuguese grandfathers and American grandmothers, along with sundry other ancestors distributed round the globe, didn't know who they were. Every time they opened their mouths and spoke in Creole, they rode from boxcar to boxcar on other men's languages. For ten years, there had been a drought (it has continued ever since); and thousands of people had died of starvation. They were penniless, and the Portuguese left them a pile of fancy, pastel-coloured architecture, with handsome piazzas, balconies, shutters, verandahs and stucco work. They were overpopulated, and the Portuguese left them with schoolfuls of swarthy, half-European children. It was some legacy. No wonder that the slogans on the hills looked like desperate cries for help.

LONG LIVE PAIGC! LONG LIVE AMILCAR CABRAL! But Cabral was dead – assassinated in 1973. He had been a clever man, with a pale Cape Verdian father and a black mother from Guinea-Bissau on the African mainland. He had dreamed of reuniting his own mixed parentage and creating a new, African identity for the two Portuguese colonies. He led the African Party of Independence for Guinea-Bissau and Cape Verde in a series of guerrilla actions against the Portuguese. Chubby-faced and bespectacled, looking like a renegade professor, Cabral had stood for Roots and Negritude in a country chronically rootless and off-white. When Guinea-Bissau went its own way after Independence, PAIGC had to be repainted (on some of the hills) as PAICV. It was the only party on the Cape Verdes, but its brand of Marxism-Leninism was essentially Creole and easygoing. It takes a funny sort of communist state to boast an airport largely funded by

South African Airways – the sort of state where people say "ciaou" and drink grog.

On an atlas the islands appear as a tight cluster of heatspots; in fact they are separated from each other by many miles of disturbed sea. They keep in touch by means of a fleet of disreputable tramp coasters, an old sailing schooner and a handful of Twin Otter aircraft in the red and white livery of the state. My companion on the flight to Praia on the island of São Tiago was a middle-aged Cape Verdian who was studying English, teaching himself from a book designed for schoolchildren. He wanted help with his pronunciation.

"Thee seize John's pain—" he said. Four thousand feet below, the sea broke around the rocky edge of Boa Vista. It was first turquoise, then boiling milk.

"This . . . is . . . John's . . . pen," I said. Why is it that new languages always start with the word for *pen*? I remembered my own infantile agonies over *la plume de ma tante*. Nowadays, I always begin on the word *ashtray*. In Portuguese, it is *cinzeiro*.

"Pain," said my companion.

"Pen," I said.

"*Pen*," he echoed.

"Absolutely."

"Absohlootly!" he said, giving my own voice back to me. It sounded unpleasantly like the voice of a bird-brained Wodehouse toff.

We circled over a city of tangerine-tiled roofs, passed a lighthouse built like a Catholic church, and touched down on an airstrip barely longer than an English cricket pitch. I was a little disconcerted by the way that everyone on the plane clapped the pilot's performance as he brought us to a stop.

Praia was still haunted by the Portuguese. You could pick out their faded names in the stucco over the shopfronts. Their fountains were dry, their civic statuary was birdlimed. Their wide streets and ceremonial squares looked altogether too pompous for the people who were walking on them now. Their ornate hanging galleries were coming dangerously adrift from the walls, and their pink paint needed retouching. Praia only really came to life in its back streets, where I walked down low terraces of one-room houses, and was pointed out by mothers to their children as an interesting object-lesson in pallor.

"Branco! Branco!" said the women, pointing. Indeed, I felt conspicuously white: these Praia people were as black as Nigerians. They sat out in the dust in front of their houses listening to antique transistor radios playing soggy Portuguese dance music. The interior of each house was decorated with coloured pictures torn from Brazilian magazines. As far as I could see, the only thing here that was native to the Cape Verdes was the curiously scrubbed and tidy style of poverty. The dogs were tame and friendly; the beggars who were exhibiting their stumps had the good manners of desk-clerks fallen on hard times. I put some money into a hand that projected from a pile of rags.

"Thank you very much, sir," said the pile of rags. "Good day!" I felt that, had my Portuguese allowed it, we might have entered into an amiable discussion about the weather and the state of the stock market.

On the outskirts of the city, Praia had spawned what looked at first like the usual kind of Third World suburb: a hillside littered with tiny shelters made of rocks, sacks, cardboard boxes and scraps of corrugated iron. Smoke from cooking fires fogged the air. Underfed pigs, goats and chickens wandered in and out of people's bedsitting rooms, and potbellied infants trailed uphill with watercans. That was a saddening but familiar sight. What was strange was the way that almost every human kennel had its own flower-garden planted out in rusty oildrums. The flowers, in velvety bloom, glowed yellow, mauve and scarlet in the darkening light. Against the cracked dirt of the hillside, they looked as unlikely as a good miracle.

Jesus entered my life. Jesus owned a well-sprung Peugeot taxi; he was rich. Two possessions can give a Cape Verdian his economic liberty: one is a taxi, the other a tuna boat. Neither can be bought for the kind of money one can earn on the islands, so the Cape Verdian becomes an *emigrante*. He works abroad, sends money home, and saves against the day when he'll come back to his own transportation or fishing business. The pattern was established in the time of the New Bedford whalers, and it has hardly changed since.

The modern *emigrante*'s route takes him to the "Rotterdam Pool", the international labour exchange for seamen. There are still a lot of seagoing jobs to be had for the taking – especially at the shady end of the shipping business where flags of convenience fly. By European standards, these jobs are often cruelly underpaid, but by Cape Verdian ones they carry lordly salaries.

Jesus had spent five years as a deckhand on tankers and cargo ships, saving for his taxi. Now he and his brother were saving for a tuna boat. He spoke rough-and-ready English, as well as Dutch, French, German and Italian. He wore the standard uniform of the *emigrante* – a gimme cap, to boast of where he'd been. Jesus's said: RODEO – AMERICA'S #1 SPORT.

On Sunday we drove out into the mountains at the back of Praia. It was a dizzying landscape, like something out of an allegory: each bend in the road opened out a new succession of precipices and ravines. The dominant texture and colour were those of ground cayenne pepper. There were kites and vultures in the sky, but it looked as if they must be on short rations, for precious little lived or grew here. A few stalks of Indian corn had been planted on the bald skull of the hillside; they weren't flourishing. From isolated stone cottages, perched on outcrops of red dust, people were somehow managing to keep their few scrawny livestock from starvation.

All around, there were mocking reminders of water. The hills were printed with the fern-patterns of dried-up rivers that hadn't flowed for years. Overhead, the tradewind filled the sky with goosedown clouds. In England, banks of cumulus like this would mean certain rain. Here they wouldn't leak a drop; they grazed the mountaintops and kept on going to Brazil.

Then, round the corner of another Empire State-shaped mountain, there was a sudden fissure of green like a vein of emerald in the rock. The zig-zag crevice was a plantation, packed solid with banana-palms, mango, papaya, maize and sugar-cane. It was watered by a stony little river that looked as if it might have its source in a leaky faucet in someone's bathroom further up the valley.

A group of men with long banana knives came out from the dense shadow of the palms. They were kitted out in the sort of clothes the *emigrantes* sent home – levis, Hawaiian shirts, broken training shoes and gimme caps. HOUSTON INTERNATIONAL SEAMEN'S MISSION stood side by side with NEWPORT R.I. – HOME OF THE AMERICA'S CUP.

I was rudely curious about them. Jesus braked, raising a tree-high swirl of peppery dust. How much did they earn on this state-owned plantation? Eighty escudos a day, said Newport, R.I. It was about a dollar and five cents.

Did they have wives? children? Yes, said Houston. A wife and five little ones. I divided seven people into one dollar. It didn't go. Only the ghostly presence of the *emigrantes* could fill in the shortfall between the men's wages and their air of genial Sunday-morning wellbeing.

The taxi scaled the next bare mountainside. Jesus said that the last Englishman he'd met had been a real screwball. The man had visited the Cape Verdes in search of sparrows. *Sparrows?* Yes, said Jesus: brown birds, very small, not interesting. The man went all over the world, looking for sparrows. He was writing a book.

"Weird."

"Some people think it mad. Not me. The way I see it, a diesel car can go on . . . what is it? the smoke? . . . of the petrol car in front."

"The exhaust fumes."

"Right. That is like the people of Cabo Verde with the sparrow-guy. A big number of people can live off the . . . exhaust . . . of such a man, I think."

There was another rift of green. São Giorgio.

"You are very happy here – yes?" Jesus said.

It was the colour of wet moss. Deep down in the valley there was the steeple of a whitewashed church; the churchgoers, leaving Mass, formed a ribbon a mile long. The men were dressed in stiff best clothes, the women, in hats and floral prints, twirled black London umbrellas over their heads. The ribbon of people spilled on to the road through a tunnel of eucalyptus and bougainvillaea. It seemed a world away from the dust a thousand feet or so below.

We drove on, up and up, and the island grew greener all the time. It is part of the general topsy-turvydom of Cape Verde life that the valleys are nearly all barren but the mountaintops are thick with vegetation wherever they are brushed by passing banks of cloud. The Arab navigators who called the islands *el ras elkhader* – "the green top" – got them right; they wear their verdure so high up that it can't be seen from the ground. Nor is it of much practical use. You cannot farm a precipice, however green. Shale-falls cascaded in broad fans through curtains of leaves; there were invisible small monkeys, floppy butterflies and birds I couldn't name but thought I'd seen in zoos. It was all beautiful but useless. To the islanders, this vertical jungle must have struck them as their crowning irony.

They had tried to do with it what they could! Every temporary flattening of the terrain was a field, and every pinnacle of rock had a lean-to farmhouse clinging to it like a beetle on a stalk.

I was a great disappointment in the mountains. When a taxi is spotted, working its way round the bumpy hairpin bends a mile below, the shout goes up in the hill villages – *Emigrantes! Emigrantes!*

For the returning migrants bring new dresses for the women, Sony Walkman cassette players for their brothers, food for the larder and money for all the family. The homecoming of a migrant turns the day into a local festival. But they looked inside the taxi and saw me. "Portugo," called the women to each other, and went back to humping stones and carrying water. I was just another damned Portuguese.

Each cavelike village store was waiting for the *emigrantes*. Beside the fly-specked bananas and tins of Carnation milk, there were bottles of Chivas Regal, stick-packs of Marlboro cigarettes, unopened boxes of Coca Cola. A single can of Coke cost 60 escudos, or about six hours' worth of agricultural labour.

This business of emigration had affected the life of the islands in a thousand small and significant ways. It accounted for the beachside lobster restaurants in the poorest fishing villages. It gave photographs and photography a peculiar importance. Every house I saw had one framed picture on the wall. It usually showed a ship – a Dutch tanker or Panamanian coaster – and, set around it, the fading faces of absent fathers, sons and husbands. Whenever I produced my Nikkormat, people posed themselves like professional models, putting on Karsh-of-Ottawa faces, as if they were deliberately creating an image of themselves that was designed to be hung over a lonely bunk three thousand miles away at sea.

Jesus's metaphor made more sense of all this than anything else I'd seen or heard so far. The Cape Verdes *were* living on other people's exhaust fumes. The *emigrantes* provided much of the gas on which the islands ran. International aid organizations like the World Bank were busy enriching the mixture. U.N.-financed wells were being sunk into the mountainsides; dams were being built to hold what little soil there was and catch whatever rain might come; the country was alive with projects for new roads, docks, cold stores, schools, hospitals, desalinization plants. The Cape Verdians were both astoundingly poor and astoundingly rich all at once; they earned a dollar a day and drank Chivas Regal.

At sea between islands a few days later, I stood on deck with Johnny, aka Jose Luis, an *emigrante* returning to his ship. We were joined by a girl barely out of her teens who was feeding two babies at once and had four more toddlers in tow.

"It is the 'eat," Johnny said, pointing at the children. "In the sun, the prick rises. In Cabo Verde we have much sun, so . . ." he laughed. "Too many babies."

The 150 miles of sea that separate Praia from Mindelo on the island of São Vicente might as well divide Africa and Europe. For Praia is a dark city, Mindelo a light one. Praia is closed, political and inward; Mindelo open, lax and intellectual. Mindelo has bookshops, fountains that really work, street cafés, silver dance bands. It even has the best slogans. NO TO SLOTH! NO TO OPPORTUNISM! YES TO LABOUR! YES TO STUDY! One could almost rumba to that one, and it sounds pacier in Portuguese. The colonial architecture here goes more happily with the way people actually live in the city than it does in Praia: at night, Mindelo is lamplit and sexy, with tender scuffles behind the shutters and shadowy girls calling from the balconies.

Praia is the administrative capital of the islands, but Mindelo feels like a metropolis: its long history as an international port and bunkering centre has given it a worldly cynicism and whorish charm. It might claim a certain distant cousinship to Naples and New Orleans.

It is the headquarters of the Cape Verdian tuna fleet, and I was there to go fishing. On all the islands that I'd visited, I'd watched the fishermen push out 14-foot home-built skiffs through the surf and come back with tuna as big as aero engines, looking comparably silvery and riveted. That enterprise struck me as dangerous: at sea, the boats were no bigger than walnut shells and everywhere I looked I saw sharks. I wanted to ride on an altogether more substantial craft.

The *Conceição III* was . . . substantial. Its engine stank. Its deckworks were slippery with fish-slime. Its flat-bottomed spadelike stern made it roll and roll in the breaking swell. The crew of ten lived aboard all day and all night during the tuna season, and the boat managed to combine all the most unpleasant features of a see-saw, an abattoir and a dosshouse within its 18-metre span.

Yet the *Conceição III* was, in its way, the flagship of the Cape Verdes' only thriving industry. There are a lot of fish in the sea around the islands, and their presence goes a long way towards compensating for the brutal aridity of the land. As Jesus had told me back in Praia, a big tuna boat will make its owner a rich man.

All night we lurched towards the fishing grounds, fifty miles out from Mindelo. Flying fish arrowed away from our bows like overcharged clockwork toys. It was impossible for me to politely decline to share Capitano João's itchy bunk in the wheelhouse; and we slept turn and turn about, too close to Ishmael and Queequeg for my squeamish sense of comfort. At dawn, the look-out boy climbed on to the pitching roof, where he clung to a stay and scanned the surface of the water for signs of a tuna school.

"Atum! Atum!" shouted the look-out.

"Feesh! Feesh!" said the late companion of my bed. It was his one word of English. He swung the boat round, shouting to his crew. Everyone was milling around the stern, grabbing at bamboo poles, while the look-out stood by the big saltwater tank amidships, chucking live sardines into the sea.

First, there was an isolated swirl, like a rising salmon. Then the entire sea on the port side of the boat went on the boil. There were tuna everywhere – "skipjack" of seven and eight pounds apiece – winking dark blue underwater, splashing, jumping, threshing, diving. Capitano João flipped a switch in the wheelhouse, and began to spray the sea with fish-gutty water from the hold. The tuna were in an advanced state of ecstasy.

Now the rodsmen went to work. Six of them, in oilskins, stood in a long wooden trough in the stern. They locked their poles into canvas pouches worn at the groin like codpieces, baited-up with sardines, and let their lines swing out over the sea. Within moments, they were going like a line of pumps, with tuna flying over their heads and crashing to the deck and into the hold. As soon as the bait touched water, it was grabbed, and the fish was describing an arc of raw silver in the sky. The swell broke around the rodsmen's waists and they went on, shouting and pumping. It was like watching a Sunday afternoon angling contest that has got insanely out of hand, as the fish piled up in heaps and the frantic drumming of their tails on the deck began to drown the sound of the boat's engine.

"Feesh! Feesh!"

The yellow oilskins were running with tuna-blood, and the dead and dying fish wore a common expression of open-mouthed astonishment at their fate.

The water suddenly went dead. Capitano João grabbed my sleeve and pointed to the long blunt shadow of a shark under the boat.

"Não Feesh!" The captain put the engine Ahead. The rodsmen hosed each other down. The look-out climbed back on to the roof to search for another distant ripple in the water, like the sudden crease made by a cat's-paw of wind.

"Atum! Atum!"

We raided half a dozen schools of tuna during the morning. It seemed to me that we must be decimating the whole tuna educational system as the hold filled and the decks were stacked with bodies. Each strike was like a parable of amazing plenty, as exciting as finding gold. Off the Cape Verdes, where nothing came easy, it was no wonder that the rodsmen yelled in pure joy at a fantastic catch.

It was a sad-faced accountant, recently returned from six years at college in the United States, who put the predicament of the Cape Verdians as bluntly as it can decently be stated. "It was only here in Cape Verde," he said, "that the Portuguese deliberately bred with the black women. It was intentional. It was not an accident. They wanted 'second whites' to run their colonies, to help them in places like Angola and Mozambique. And so they created us. They said to the people, 'Now, you are not African, you are not black.' And the people liked it. They wanted to be white . . . like Portuguese. And the Portuguese used them. We came in useful for all the jobs in Africa that the Portuguese did not like to do themselves. We weren't black, and we weren't white. We were *conveniences*. And the Portuguese invented us."

It was inevitable, then, that after Independence the Cape Verdians tried to redefine their identity in terms of wistful, would-be Marxism and a wistful, would-be negritude. The Cape Verde literary magazine is called *Raizes*, or "Roots", and the handful of modern Cape Verde poets (of whom Amilcar Cabral himself was one) are wedded to a vision of themselves as Blacks, as Africans. The word "black" is used like a talisman in their poems, as if by saying it sufficiently often it would make the vision come true and return Cape Verde to the mainland of Africa.

> Get up and go forward, black son of Africa,
> Get up and listen to the people's cry,
> Africa! Justice! Liberty!

– writes Kaoberdiano Dambara. But the Cape Verdian has never been simply a "black son of Africa". His identity is as difficult and paradoxical as the physical conditions in which he lives. He inhabits a sort of crack between the continents, and to be a Cape Verdian is to inherit a very complex fate.

It is a hard fate to confront. One writer from the islands has made it his obsessive subject: Baltasar Lopes da Silva, a retired schoolteacher whose stories are known and read by almost every literate Cape

Verdian. I was conducted to da Silva's house on a Mindelo back street as if I was being taken to a national shrine.

His study was dark and dusty – a cultural rag-and-bone shop. His books, in antique Penguin paperback and broken-spined Tauchnitz editions, were a library of unlikely marriages: Hemingway to Camões, Tolstoy to Somerset Maugham, Eric Linklater to Cervantes, Shakespeare to H. E. Bates, Victor Hugo to Frank Swinnerton. There were blotchy prints of Titian and Van Dyck on the walls, old 78s of Haydn on the floor beside a tower of yellowing copies of *John O'London's Weekly* from the 1950s.

"Do you read *John O'London's*? It has kept me in contact with new developments in English literature." Da Silva's face was of a piece with his library. His black skin was stretched over the precise features of an equatorial Bernard Malamud, while his cropped grey hair made him look oddly vice-presidential, like the manager of a Portuguese bank.

"Please excuse my English; I fear it has grown rusty with lack of use."

In fact it was an exquisite fossil. Learned from books, it had preserved the dry formality and the rhetorical flourish of a dead class of Edwardians. Da Silva spoke exactly like a character from his favourite British author, Somerset Maugham.

"I find myself in the desert here," he said. "This is a bad milieu in which to become a self-taught intellectual." The yellow dogs were making a rumpus on the street outside Da Silva's door and he had to raise his voice to make himself heard over the noise of the Third World a few feet from his desk.

"In London, you have a circle where you discuss your ideas? A café, perhaps, where you gather to drink cocktails?"

"Well – sort of . . ."

"It is not so in Cape Verde. It is a disease, I'm afraid, this . . . isolation, this lack of taste for conversation."

Da Silva talked with the eloquence of a man indulging himself in a treat.Now he had retired from teaching, he saw his literary career as "just beginning". He had started a novel; it was the most ambitious thing he'd ever tried. Set on the islands, it was about fathers and daughters and it dealt with the collision between old colonial ideas and new republican ones.

"It is about Love and Independence. The personal and the political. You see, what I am now struggling to create is a picture of this new society which is coming into being in Cape Verde. It is difficult.

Very difficult. We need perspective. The society here is transforming itself, and for a writer it is like a miner who finds something in the rock . . . you know?"

"A vein? a seam?"

"A seam. This new society is a seam full of possibilities for the Novel."

Over da Silva's head there was an ivory statuette of Christ, and a withered Easter palm. His hands moved over the surface of his desk, as fidgety as a pair of rabbits in a field.

"Colonialism here was such delicate work, you understand. The harmony between the colonizers and the colonized was always fragile. The Portuguese were never hated but they were not loved. It was not simple, as it was in Angola. In Cape Verde, what happened was a sexual exchange, an exchange of sensibilities. The Portuguese were, in a way, assimilated into Cape Verde society . . ."

"You mean, you colonized them almost as much as they colonized you —"

"*Almost*," said da Silva carefully, as if acknowledging that his own study told a rather different story. Everything in it came from Europe or the United States. Only the smell of the air and the noise of the street outside were African. Its very isolation from the rest of Mindelo gave it the air of a remote colonial outpost, as the black novelist spent his mornings trying to rival the "fluency" and "polish" he admired in Somerset Maugham.

"It is so hard to write about this society. It is a very, very complicated object."

At dinner that night, the first item on the hotel menu was billed as Knorr Soup. It was a tasteless chicken bouillon with a pile of alphabetti-spaghetti lying inert in the bottom of the bowl. They looked like a collection of collapsed slogans. I stirred them with my spoon, and the letters reassembled into a new, Creole jumble of meanings. Every time you looked into the bowl, there was another damaged and inchoate message there. I reckoned that Cape Verde ought to declare this its national dish – a crossword-puzzle-island, in the soup.

1983

CYCLONE

It had been raining for weeks. People had forgotten the last morning when the sky was not draped low over the roof-tops of England like a giant wash-cloth. The days were so dark that the only sign of nightfall was the slow brightening of lights in people's windows.

Rain turned the flat farm land of East Anglia into corrugated paddy fields, with standing water in every furrow. In London, people who lived in basements came home to find that their carpets had turned black with damp as the water-table rose.

Travel agents liked it. Their carousels of brouchures showing places in the sun were stripped bare by customers in Barbour coats and green Wellington boots. Everyone who could find an excuse to be abroad on business was leaving the country, with the weathermen saying that they could see no change in the foreseeable future. Tomorrow, there would be more rain, with more rain moving in at the weekend. On television, there were pictures of punts afloat in village streets and men in oilskins carrying pensioners to safety. Going anywhere on the Underground was an unpredictable adventure because of flooding in the tunnels.

Then the storm came. It began as a vacuum in the atmosphere, far out over the Atlantic. Trying to fill itself, it set up a spinning mass of air, like a plug-hole sucking water from a bath; but the faster the winds blew, the more the vacuum deepened. It was an insatiable emptiness. It sucked and sucked; the air spiralled around it; the hole got bigger.

It did its best to flatten a corner of north-western France, then raced across the Channel, from the Cherbourg peninsula to the Dorset coast. Its edge was a jet stream of southerly air, weighted and thickened with moisture from the ocean. When it hit, it had the impact of a runaway truck. It made walls ballon and totter, then threw the bricks about like confetti. It lifted roofs off schools, ripped power-lines away from their pylons and let them blow free, lighting the night with flashes of St Elmo's Fire. Along the edge of the sea, it rained boats and caravans; sixty miles inland, the wind pasted windows with a grey rime of salt from the Atlantic.

The trees were still in leaf. After the many days of rain they were rooted in soft mud that released even full-grown oaks as if they were seedlings in a gardener's tray. On south-facing hillsides, whole woods were plucked out of the soil by the wind and strewn in heaps, ready for the chain-saw.

The cyclone worked its way towards the Home Counties. By two in the morning it was on the outskirts of London, where its first victim was a goat in Woking. The goat lived in a kennel, lovingly disguised by its builder as a miniature Tudor cottage, complete with half-timbering and painted thatch. The wind seized this piece of fond make-believe and tossed it skywards. No one knew for how long the goat and its cottage had been in flight, but both were found the next morning, five gardens away, with the dead goat hanged by its chain. There were several human deaths in the storm, including a tramp who was killed by a falling wall in Lincoln's Inn Fields, but the story of the flying goat gained most coverage in the popular papers.

Some people slept through the storm, mistaking the commotion for a turmoil inside themselves. They dreamed violent dreams. Others sat up through the night in dressing-gowns, making cups of tea and listening to the falling slates, the windows shaking in their frames, the oboe- and bassoon-noises of the wind as it blew down narrow streets and funnelled through the gaps between houses. Older people heard the falling trees as bombs. They huddled downstairs, waiting mutely for the first soft crump, then the flying glass, the shaking walls, the sudden entry of the open sky – but there were no wardens, no sirens; it was lonelier, more eerie than the Blitz.

No one dared go outside. You couldn't open the door against that wind, and who in his right mind would want to face the skirl of tiles, dustbins, garden furniture and plant pots? So people sat tight. In the suburbs, telephones went dead in the middle of a comforting chat with the neighbours. Electric lights dickered and snuffed out. Old candles were discovered in tool-drawers. People who cooked by electricity remembered primus stoves at the back of cupboards. *Just so long as you can boil a kettle*, people said, *that's the main thing, isn't it?* Camping out in their houses, brewing tea, talking in low voices and listening to the wind, they surprised themselves with the cosiness of it all. At three and four in the morning, husbands and wives who'd grown as used to each other as they were to their curtains and carpets found themselves reaching for each other's nakedness.

Soon after dawn, the storm quit London, leaving a high wind blowing under a sky of bad milk. Light-headed from lack of sleep, people stared through their salt-caked windows to see cars crushed by trees and craters of muddy water in the pavements where the trees had been. Roads were strewn with tiles and broken bricks, bits of picket fencing, garden shrubs, up-ended tricycles, glass, tarpaper, fish bones, carboard boxes. During what the radio news now called The Hurricane, everyone's rubbish had mated with everyone else's, and white stucco house fronts were curiously decorated with dribbles of gravy, tomato ketchup and raspberry yogurt.

On the Saturday morning, a day after the passage of the cyclone, Hyde Park was closed to traffic. The Carriage Road and The Ring were blocked by dozens of crashed trees, and the police had put up Danger signs on trestles to warn people away from the open craters and the trees that were still falling, slowly, their enormous roots half-in, half-out of the ground. The park was as noisy as a logging camp, and its resiny smell of sawn timber drifted deep into the city, to shoppers on Oxford Street and motorists caught in the jam on Brompton Road. There was allure in the smell alone. People felt themselves drawn to the park without quite knowing why; they ignored the warning signs; they stepped easily over the barriers of red tape that the police had strung between the trestles, and each one felt a surge of private exultation at the sight of what the storm had done.

It's so sad! people said, trying to quench their smiles – for they didn't feel sad at all. They were thrilled by the magnificent destruction of the wind: it was as if the world itself had come tumbling down, and even the shyest, most pacific people in the crowd felt some answering chord of violence in their own natures respond to this tremendous and unlooked-for act of violence in nature itself.

The sky had lifted. A meagre ration of diffused sunlight – the first for many days – lit the scene of an anarchic picnic. Children in coloured blousons swarmed in the branches of the humbled trees. Muddy dogs, tongues lolling, scrambled out of the craters. A black-and-white striped Parks Police van patrolled the bank of the Serpentine, its twin loud-hailers yawping about *risk, responsible,* and *in your own best interests*; but its presence only added to the air of carnival.

Whoever you were, the wrecked landscape had something in it for you personally. For some people, it was simply an enjoyable reminder of their grace – they'd got away with it; they were survivors. They strode across the skyline of the park like generals on a battlefield after a famous victory. Others stood still, gazing, hands in pockets. Exiles, from Beirut, Kampala, Prague, Budapest, felt a proud glow of kinship with the uprooted trees. Saturday fathers, borrowing children from their one-time wives, dwelled, with a pleasure they couldn't explain to themselves, on the ragged pits in the earth, the torn turf, the canopies of exposed roots; while their children saw the park as a territory at last made fit for all-out war, and zapped their fathers with death-ray guns from behind safe jungle cover. Everyone was irrationally happier that Saturday, even the people who'd lost their roofs, who saw themselves as heroes of the hurricane and came to the park to enjoy disaster on a scale grand enough to match their own. *Isn't it sad?* they said, their voices drowned by shrilling gulls circling trees that still survived.

1988

SEA ROOM

Whenever I find myself growing grim about the mouth; whenever it is damp, drizzly November in my soul; whenever I find myself involuntarily pausing before coffin warehouses, and bringing up the rear of every funeral I meet; and especially whenever my hypos get such an upper hand of me, that it requires a strong moral principle to prevent me from deliberately stepping into the street, and methodically knocking people's hats off – then, I account it high time to get to sea as soon as I can. This is my substitute for pistol and ball. With a philosophical flourish Cato throws himself upon his sword; I quietly take to the ship.

HERMAN MELVILLE, *Moby Dick*

It was the classic last resort. I wanted to run away to sea.

It started as a nervous itch, like an attack of eczema. All spring and summer I scratched at it, and the more I scratched the more the affliction spread. There was no getting rid of the thing. Lodged in my head was an image, in suspiciously heightened colour, of a very small ship at sea.

It was more ark than boat. It contained the entire life of one man, and it floated serenely offshore: half in, half out of the world. The face of its solitary navigator was as dark as demerara. He wasn't flying a flag. His boat was a private empire, a sovereign state in miniature, a tight little, right little liberal regime. He was a world away from where I stood. Lucky man. He'd slung his hook, and upped and gone. Afloat, abroad, following his compass-needle as it trembled in its dish of paraffin, he was a figure of pure liberty. He had the world just where he wanted it. When he looked back at the land from which he'd sailed, it was arranged for him in brilliant perspective, its outlines clean, like the cut-out scenery of a toy theatre.

I was plagued by this character. Each time I gave him notice to quit my private territorial waters, he sailed mockingly past. Smoke from his pipe rose in a fine column of question marks over my horizon. His laughter was loud and derisive. He wouldn't go away.

I was landlocked and fidgety. I paced the deck of an urban flat and dreamed of sea-room, with the uncomfortable feeling that I'd picked up a dream which didn't belong to me, as if I'd tuned in my mental radio to the wrong station.

Lots of people would claim the dream as their own. The idea of taking ship and heading off into the blue is, after all, a central part of the mythology of being English. Elias Canetti writes that the "famous individualism" of the Englishman stems directly from his habit of thinking of himself as a lone mariner; a perception endorsed by whole libraries of bad Victorian novels.

In the books, the English are always running away to sea. The ocean is the natural refuge of every bankrupt, every young man crossed in love, every compromised second son. The Peregrines and Septimuses of the world behave like lemmings: their authors seem powerless to stop them from racing for the nearest quayside at the first sign of trouble.

They do it with such stylish finality too. The bag is secretly packed in the small hours, the farewell letter left like a suicide note beside the ormolu clock on the hall table. Goodbye, family! Goodbye, friends! Goodbye, England!

They close the front door behind them as gently as if they were dismantling a bomb. They tiptoe across the drive, careful not to wake the dogs, their faces grave at the audacity of what they've done. They pass the misty church, the doctor's house behind its cliff of pines, the bulky shadows of Home Farm. By sunrise, they're on the open road, their past already out of sight.

When next heard of, they are up on deck with a full gale blowing out of the Sou'west. The ship is falling away from under their feet in a mountainous swell. They cling to the shrouds, their hands bloody from hauling on ropes and scrubbing decks with holystone. They are changed men.

The sea voyage is more than an adventure; it is a rite of passage, as decisive as a wedding. It marks the end of the old self and the birth of the new. It is a great purifying ordeal. Storms and salt-water cleanse the ne'er-do-well and turn him into a hero. In the last chapter he will get the girl, the vicar's blessing and the family fortune.

I knew that I was pushing my luck, and running against the clock. Peregrine and Septimus aren't usually men of forty with dental problems and mortgages to pay. I wasn't a scapegrace young tough. I wasn't made for the outdoors. My experience of the sea was confined to paddling in it with the bottoms of my trousers rolled up, collecting coloured pebbles, and lolling on the edge of the ocean in a stripey deckchair until the peeling skin on my nose made me head back to the more manageable world of the hotel bar.

My kinship with the runaways was of a different kind. What I envied in them was the writing of their letters of farewell.

Dear Father,

By the time you read this, I shall be . . .

Magic words. I was excited by their gunpowdery whiff of action and decision. Both were in pretty short supply where I was sitting. Moping at my worktable, I decided to change a comma to a semi-colon. Framed in the window under a bleary sky, the huge grey tub of the Kensal Green gasometer sank lugubriously downwards as West London cooked its Sunday lunch.

. . . far away on the high seas. Please tell Mother . . .

Well, I had fallen out with the family, too. I couldn't put a date on the quarrel: there'd been no firelit showdown in the library, no sign of the riding whip, not even any duns at the front door. It had been a long, unloving wrangle, full of edgy silences, niggling resentments and strained efforts at politeness. One day I woke to realize that there was nowhere I felt less at home than home.

Perhaps it was simply that I'd turned into an old fogey a bit earlier in life than most people. At any rate, my own country suddenly seemed foreign – with all the power that a foreign land has to make the lonely visitor sweat with fury at his inability to understand the obvious. *Je ne comprends pas! Min fadlak! Non parlo Italiano! Sprechen Sie English – please!*

I'd started to forget things, as the senile do. Wanting a small brown loaf, I strolled down to the bakery on the corner. I should have remembered. It didn't sell bread any more. It sold battery-powered vibrators, blow-up rubber dolls and videotapes of naked men and women doing ingenious things to each other's bodies. The African

Asian who now rented this flesh shop was noisily barricading his windows with sheets of corrugated iron.

He seemed calm enough; a man competently at home on his own patch. He expected a race riot at the weekend.

"The police come and tell us to do it. Saturday, we have trouble here. Too many Rastas —" he waved, in a vague easterly direction, at the dark continent of Portobello, and placidly banged in another nail.

He made me feel like a tourist; and like a tourist I goggled obediently at the local colour of this odd world at my doorstep. Four doors down from the bakery there'd been an ailing chemist's full of stoppered bottles and painted drawers with Latin names. Someone had pulled it out of the block like a rotten wisdom tooth and left a winking cave of galactic war machines. All day long they chattered, bleeped and yodelled, as the local kids zapped hell out of the Aliens. The kids themselves looked pretty alien to me: angry boys, bald as turnips, in army boots and grandfathers' braces; dozy punks with erect quiffs of rainbow hair, like a troupe of Apaches.

Our only patch of civic green space had been taken over by joggers in tracksuits. They wore yellow latex earmuffs clamped round their skulls with coronas of silver wire. They were filling their heads with something: Vivaldi? The Sex Pistols? No. Both would be equally old hat. They quartered the oily turf, blank faced, as exclusive and remote as astronauts.

The streets themselves looked as they'd always done; imperially snug and solid. On a sunny morning, you could easily believe that nothing essential had changed among these avenues of plane trees and tall, white stucco mansions. Even now, there were nannies to be seen – solemn Filipino women, who pushed their pramloads as if they were guarding a reliquary of holy bones in a religious procession. Vans from Harrods still stopped at brass-plated tradesmen's entrances. From a high open window there still came the sound of a child practising scales on the family piano. *Doh, reh, me, fa, ploink. Fa, fa, soh, lah, tee, ploink, doh.*

But there were misplaced notes on the streets, too. At every hour there were too many men about, men of my own age with the truant look of schoolboys out bird-nesting. They huddled outside the betting shops. Alone, they studied the handful of cards in the window of the government Job Centre. The vacancies were for Girl Fridays, linotype operators, book-keepers – nothing for them.

Nor for me, it seemed. I felt supernumerary here. Letting myself in to the whitewashed, partitioned box where I lived, I was met by the wifely grumble of the heating system. It wasn't much of a welcome, and I returned it with a stare of husbandly rancour at the litter of unread books, unwashed dishes and unwritten pages that told me I was home.

I wasn't proud of the way I lived, lodged here contingently like a piece of grit in a crevice. There was something shameful in being so lightly attached to the surrounding world. I wasn't married. I was childless. I didn't even have a proper job.

When I had to give the name of my employer on official forms, I wrote: "SELF". This Self, though, was a strange and temperamental boss. He would make me redundant for weeks on end. He sent me on sick leave and sabbaticals, summoned me back for a few days' worth of overtime, then handed me my papers again.

"What am I supposed to do now?"

"Get on your bike," said Self, not bothering to look up from the crossword in *The Times*.

I'd grown tired of my dealings with Self. He struck me as a textbook example of what was wrong with British industry. He was bad management personified: lazy, indifferent, smugly wedded to his old-fashioned vices. Self loved the two-bottle business lunch. He collected invitations to drinks at six-to-eight. His telephone bills were huge. He poisoned the air with tobacco smoke. It was a miracle that under Self's directorship the company hadn't yet gone bust.

I told him about the Right to Work.

"We'd better lunch on that," said Self.

By the brandy stage, Self and I were reconciled. We merged back into each other.

I was fogbound and drifting. One morning I breathed on the windowpane and played noughts and crosses against myself. I waited for the telephone to peal. It didn't. In the afternoon I went to the public library and looked up my name in the catalogue to check that I existed. At night I listened to the breaking surf of traffic in the streets, and the city seemed as cold and strange as Murmansk.

An hour or so before the house began to shudder to the cannonball passage of the underground trains, before the early-morning rattle of milk bottles on steps, I was woken by the bell of the convent down the road. It was ringing for Prime and sounded thin and squeaky like a wheezing lung. The sun never rises on North Kensington with any marked enthusiasm, and the light that had begun to smear the walls of the room looked dingy and secondhand. I didn't much care for the appearance of this new day, and took flight into a deep sea-dream.

In novels, when the black sheep of the family takes ship, his running away is really a means of coming home. His voyage restores him to his relations and to society. I had the same end in view. I wanted to go home; and the most direct, most exhilarating route back there lay by sea. Afloat with charts and compass, I'd find my bearings again. I saw myself inching along the coast, navigating my way around my own country and my own past, taking sights and soundings until I had the place's measure. It was to be an escape, an apprenticeship and a homecoming.

It was a consoling fantasy. I sustained it by going off at weekends and looking at real boats. As a minor consequence of the recession, every harbour in England was crowded with boats for sale: hulks under tarpaulins, rich men's toy motor cruisers, abandoned racing yachts, converted lifeboats and ships' tenders. Their prices were drifting steadily downwards, like the pound; and their brokers had the air of distressed gentlefolk eking out the last of the family capital. They made a feeble play of busyness and spotted me at once as another optimist trying to rid himself of his unaffordable boat. *No dice*, their eyes said, as they shuffled the paper on their desks.

"I'm looking for a boat to sail round Britain in," I said, trying the words out on the air to see if they had the ring of true idiocy.

"Ah. *Are* you now —" The broker's face was rearranging itself fast, but it looked as if he'd forgotten the expression of avuncular confidence that he was now trying to achieve. All his features stopped in mid-shift: they registered simple disbelief.

He showed me a wreck with a sprung plank. "She's just the job, old boy. It's what she was built for."

A sheet of flapping polythene had been pinned down over the foredeck to stop leaks. The glass was missing from a wheelhouse window. It was easy to see oneself going down to the bottom in a boat like that. It had the strong aura of emergency flares. Mayday calls and strings of big bubbles.

"Know what she was up for when she first came in? Ten grand. And that was over four years ago – think what inflation must have done to that by now." The broker consulted the sky piously, as if the heavens were in the charge of a white-bearded wrathful old economist. "At two-five, old boy . . . two-five . . . she's a steal."

Lowering myself down slippery dockside ladders to inspect these unloved and unlovable craft, I felt safe enough. The voyage stayed securely in the realm of daydream. I liked the pretence involved in my seaside shopping expeditions, and from each broker I learned a new trick or two. I copied the way they dug their thumbnails into baulks of timber and the knowledgeable sniff with which they tasted the trapped air of the saloon. I picked up enough snippets of shoptalk to be able to speak menacingly of rubbing-strakes and keel-bolts; and soon the daydream itself began to be fleshed out in glibly realistic detail.

As I came to put names to all its parts, the boat in my head grew more substantial and particular by the day. Built to sail out of the confused seas of Ladbroke Grove and Notting Hill, it had to be tubby and trawler-like. It would be broad in the beam, high in the bow, and framed in oak. It would ride out dirty weather with the buoyancy of a puffin; inside, it would be as snug as a low-ceilinged tudor cottage. It was perfectly designed to go on imaginary voyages and make dream-landfalls.

Then I bought a sextant, and the whole business suddenly stopped being a fantasy.

The sextant was old. I found it stacked up with a collection of gramophones and ladies' workboxes in a junkshop. Its brass frame was mottled green-and-black, the silvering on its mirrors had started to blister and peel off. It came in a wooden casket full of accessory telescopes and lenses bedded down in compartments of soft baize.

It had been made for J. H. C. Minter R.N., whose name was engraved in scrolled letters on the arc by J. H. Steward, 457 West Strand, London. A certificate vouching for its accuracy had been issued by the National Physical Observatory, Richmond, in July 1907. Its pedigree made it irresistible. I had no very sure idea as to how a sextant actually worked, but this tarnished instrument looked like a prize and an omen.

For the first few days of ownership, I contented myself with rubbing away at it with Brasso until a few of its more exposed parts gleamed misty gold out of the surrounding verdigris. I loosened its hinged horizon- and sun-glasses with sewing-machine oil. I brushed the dust out of the baize and polished the oak case. Midshipman Minter's (*was* he a midshipman?) sextant was restored to a pretty and intricate ornament for a drawing-room.

Next I went to a shop in the Minories and came away with a chart of the Thames estuary, a pair of compasses, a protractor, a nautical almanac and a book on celestial navigation. At last I was in business again with a real vocation to follow. For months I had stumbled along at my old journeywork of writing reviews of other people's books and giving voice to strong opinions that I didn't altogether feel. Now I was returned to being a freshman student, with the art of finding one's own way round the globe as my major subject. I holed up with the sextant and the book on navigation, ready to stay awake all night if that was what was needed to master the basic principles of the discipline.

I read on page one:

> We navigate by means of the Sun, the Moon, the planets and the stars. Forget the Earth spinning round the Sun with the motionless stars infinite distances away, and imagine that the Earth is the centre of the universe and that all the heavenly bodies circle slowly round us, the stars keeping their relative positions while the Sun, Moon and planets change their positions in relation to each other and to the stars. This pre-Copernican outlook comes easily as we watch the heavenly bodies rise and set, and is a help in practical navigation.

Obediently I saw the earth as the still centre of things, with the sun and the stars as its satellites. I was happy to forget Copernicus: my own private cosmology had always been closet-Ptolemaic. This geocentric, egocentric view of the world was infinitely preferable to the icy abstractions and gigantic mileages of the physicists. Of course the sun revolved around the earth, rising in the east and setting in the west; of course we were the focus of creation, the pivot around which the universe turns. To have one's gut-instincts so squarely confirmed by a book with a title like *Celestial Navigation* was more than I could possibly have bargained for. I became an instant convert. I saw Sirius and Arcturus tracking slowly round us like protective outriders; I watched Polaris wobbling, a little insecurely, high over the North Pole.

For the essence of celestial navigation turned out, as I read, to consist in a sort of universal egoism. The heavenly bodies had been pinned up in the sky to provide an enormous web of convenient lines and triangles. Wherever he was, the navigator was always the crux of the arrangement, measuring the solar system to discover himself on his ship, bang at the heart of the matter.

Here is how you find out where you are. You are standing

somewhere on the curved surface of a globe in space. Imagine a line extending from the dead-centre of the earth, through your body, and going on up into the distant sky. The spot where it joins the heavens over your head is your zenith, and it is as uniquely personal to you as your thumbprint.

Now: your latitude is the angle formed at the earth's centre between the equator and your zenith-line. You are a precise number of degrees and minutes north or south of the equator. Check it out in an atlas. The latitude of my North Kensington flat is 51°31′ North.

The sun, remember, revolves around the earth. Imagine now that it is noon on one of those rare days – at the time of the spring or autumn equinox – when the sun is exactly over the equator. Get your sextant ready.

Focus the telescope, twiddle the knobs and set the mirrors to work. Excellent. You have now measured the angle formed between your horizon and the sun over the equator. If you happen to be standing in my flat, I can tell you that the figure you have just read off from your sextant is 38°29′.

And what use, pray, is that? inquires Poor Yorick.

It is a great deal of use. Take it away from 90° and what do you get?

51°31′. Our latitude.

Precisely.

I don't understand why.

Think. Your zenith-line cuts your horizon at right-angles. If the sun is over the equator, then the angle formed on the earth's surface between the sun and your zenith-line is the same as the angle formed at the earth's centre between your zenith-line and the equator.

I never did understand spherical geometry.

Nor did I, but the calculation works, and you can play exactly the same game with the Pole Star as you can with the sun. Find the angle between it and your horizon, and you can quickly work out your latitude in degrees north or south.

51°31′ North is not a position: it is a line several thousand miles long encircling the earth. To find North Kensington on that line, you must time the sun with a chronometer and so discover your longitude.

Longitude – your personal angle east or west of the zero meridian – is measured from Greenwich. "Noon" is not a time on the clock: it is the instant when the sun is highest overhead above your particular meridian. In North Kensington, which is West of Greenwich, noon comes later than it does to the Royal Observatory, for the sun goes round the earth from east to west at a reliable speed of fifteen degrees of longitude in an hour, or 360° in a day.

Pick up the sextant again and clock the angles of the sun around noon. It rises . . . rises, and now it starts to dip. What was the exact moment when it peaked? Just forty-eight seconds after noon by Greenwich Mean Time? Please don't argue. Let's agree that it was forty-eight and not a second more or less.

Forty-eight seconds, at a minute of longitude for every four seconds of time, is twelve minutes of longitude. You are precisely twelve minutes West of Greenwich, or 0°12′W.

So there is home: 51°31′N, 0°12′W. St Quintin Avenue, London W10, England, the World, the Celestial Sphere. How easily is the lost sheep found, at least at noon on the vernal equinox, with the aid of Midshipman Minter's sextant. No matter how twisty the lane, or how many back alleys must be broached to reach him, the navigator dwells in the intersection between two angles. His position is absolute and verified in heaven. It all makes a great deal more sense than house numbers and postal codes.

That is the theory. But nautical astronomy is founded on a nice conceit, a useful lie about the way the universe works. It's muddied by the unruly behaviour of the sun and stars as they whizz round us on the celestial sphere. The sun, unfortunately, is a vagrant and unpunctual bird. Only twice in the year is it actually over the equator at noon. Between March and September it strays north, lying at a slightly different angle every day; between September and March it goes south. Solar noon never quite corresponds with noon by Greenwich Mean Time. It can be late or early, according to the clock, by as much as twenty minutes.

It would have been pleasant to go abroad, Crusoe-fashion, with just a sextant and a good clock. In practice, apparently, both were useless without a book of tables called an *Ephemeris* – tables that are meant to keep one posted on what all the heavenly bodies are up to at any particular moment.

It was time to take my first noon sight. I unfolded the sextant from its wrapping of dusters, feeling that I was handling an instrument of natural magic. From the *Ephemeris*, I'd found that today, because the sun was now down south over Africa, nineteen degrees beyond the equator, it was running three minutes late.

I stood at the kitchen window and squinted through the telescope at the jam of cars and trucks moving slowly past on the elevated motorway like targets in a shooting-gallery, and made my first significant and disconcerting discovery: London has no horizon.

This was serious. Without a horizon, you don't know where you are. Unless you can measure the angle between yourself, the sun and the plane surface of the earth, you might as well be underground. London presented an impenetrable face of concrete, clotted stucco-work, bare trees, billboards, glass, steel, tarmac and no horizon anywhere. No wonder it was famous for getting lost in.

I had to guess at where the city's notional horizon might be, and found a window-full of typists four floors up in a nearby office block. I focused the eyepiece on the girls and gently lowered the reflected image of the sun to join them in their typing pool. It was three minutes past noon. The girls had a peaky, distracted, time-for-lunch look; the sun, clarified through blue smoked glass, was rubicund and warty. The girls worked on, oblivious to the presence of this uninvited guest, as I twiddled the micrometer-screw with my thumb and laid the sun neatly between the filing cabinet and the Pirelli calendar.

With the swivelling magnifier on the arm of the sextant I read the sun's altitude on the inlaid-silver scale, took away the nineteen-degree declination of the sun, subtracted the total from ninety, and found my latitude – 45°30′N.

Had I only been in Milan or Portland, Oregon, it would have been spot-on. As it was, it did at least put a precise figure on the complaint from which I'd been suffering for the last few months: I was just six degrees and one minute out of kilter with where I was supposed to be.

The details were wonky but the exercise opened a shutter on a tantalizing chink of air and space. It seemed to me that the navigator with his sextant had a unique and privileged view of the world and his place in it. He stood happily outside its social and political arrangements, conducting himself in strict relation to the tides, the moon, the sun and stars. He was an exemplary symbol of solitude and independence. His access to a body of arcane and priestly knowledge made him a Magus in a world where Magi were in deplorably short supply; and I was bitten by pangs of romantic envy every time I thought of him. The fact that he was probably also soaked to the skin, parking his breakfast over the rail, with his circulation failing in fingers and toes, didn't then strike me as being either likely or relevant. This was North Kensington, after all, where

the sea-beyond-the-city was always unruffled, bright and cobalt-blue.
I tacked up a quotation from *Purchas His Pilgrims* over my desk:

> The services of the Sea, they are innumerable: it yields
> . . . to studious and religious minds a Map of Knowledge,
> Mystery of Temperance, Exercise of Continence, Schoole of
> Prayer, Meditation, Devotion and Sobrietie . . . It hath on
> it Tempests and Calmes to chastise the Sinnes, to exercise
> the faith of Sea-men; manifold affections in it self, to affect
> and stupefie the subtilest Philosopher . . . The Sea yeelds
> Action to the bodie, Meditation to the Minde, the World
> to the World, all parts thereof to each part, by this Art of
> Arts, Navigation.

In the 17th century the navigator really had been the hero of the
moment: John Donne, for instance, could define passionate love in
terms of the movement of a pair of navigator's compasses on a chart,
and Purchas's seductive litany had in it all the intellectual excitement
of seagoing in the English Renaissance. There was something worthwhile to aim at. It would, I thought, be wonderful to be able to
salvage just a small fraction of that sense of the philosophical bounty
of the sea.

Leaning out of the window to shoot the sun, the sextant clamped
to my eye, I attracted the attention of a good many upturned faces
in the street below. Even in North Kensington it's rare to see such
an unabashed voyeur in action in the middle of the day, and I came
in for a fine selection of sniggers, jeers and whistles. The passers-by
were quite correct in their assessment of my case: I was a peeping-
Tom. I felt aroused and elated by what I was watching through the
telescope – the teasing prospect of another life, a new way of being
in the world, coming slowly into sharp focus.

As soon as I saw it, I recognized the boat as the same craft that I'd
been designing in my head for weeks. The tide had left it stranded
on a gleaming mudbank up a Cornish estuary. It stood alone, in
ungainly silhouette the official residence of the old woman who lived
in a shoe.

The local boatyard had given me the keys and a warrant to view.
I slithered across the mud in city clothes, past knots of bait-diggers
forking worms into buckets. There wasn't much romance in the
discovery of the boat. Each new footstep released another bubble of

bad-egg air. The trees on the foreshore, speckled a dirty white with china clay dust from the docks across the river, looked as if they had dandruff. The surface of the mud itself was webbed and veined with tiny rivulets of black oil.

The boat had been lying here untenanted for three years. It was trussed with ropes and chains on which had grown eccentric vegetable beards of dried weed and slime. Its masts and rigging were gone, its blue paintwork bleached and cracked. My shadow scared a sunbathing family of fiddler-crabs in the muddy pool that the boat had dug for itself as it grounded with the tide. They shuffled away across the pool-floor and hid in the dark under the bilges.

No one would have said the thing was beautiful. What it had was a quality of friendly bulk, as solid and reassuring as an old coat. I liked its name: *Gosfield Maid* sounded like a description of some frumpish, dog-breeding country aunt. I've always had a superstitious belief in anagrams. Rearranged, the letters came out as *Die, dismal fog*. Not bad, under the circumstances.

I found a boarding ladder under a dusty tree, climbed nine feet up on to the deck and became a temporary captain lording it over a small and smelly ocean of mud. I inspected my ship with ignorant approval. The deck was littered with pieces of substantial ironmongery that I didn't know the names of or uses for, but I trusted the look of their weathered brass and cast steel. Up front, two anchors lashed down in wooden cradles were big enough to hold a freighter. There was nothing toylike or sportive about this boat: it was the real thing – a working Scottish trawler refurbished for foul-weather cruising.

The wheelhouse stuck up at the back like a sentry box. It was snug and sunny inside, a good eyrie to study the world from. Leaning on the brassbound wheel, I followed the sweeping upward curve of the deck as it rose ahead to the bows. From here, the boat looked suddenly as graceful and efficient as a porpoise. It had been built to take steep seas bang on the nose, and its whole character was governed by its massive front end. Given pugnacious bows like that, you could go slamming into the waves and ride the tallest breakers, with the rest of the boat tagging quietly along behind.

The compass above the wheel was sturdy and shiplike, too. It showed our heading as East-North-East, on course across the wooded hills for Devon, Somerset and Wiltshire. I rocked the bowl in its hinged frame and watched the card settle back into position as the lodestone homed in on the pole; a small satisfying piece of magic

. . . one more bit of the marvellous jigsaw of ideas and inventions by which captains find their way around the world.

Four steps down from the wheelhouse the boat turned into a warren of little panelled rooms: a kitchen just about big enough to boil an egg in, a lavatory in a cupboard, an oak-beamed parlour, a triangular attic bedroom in the bows. The scale of the place was elfin, but its mahogany walls and hanging oil-lamps suggested a rather grand Victorian bachelor elf. Its atmosphere was at once cosy and spartan, like an old-fashioned men's club.

I opened a porthole to freshen the pickled air in the saloon. It was possible now to make out a fine seam down on the far edge of the flats where shining mud was joined to shining water as the tide inched upriver from the sea. I sprawled on the settee, lit a pipe, and generally wallowed in my captaincy. This wasn't just a boat that was on offer; it was a whole estate. Whoever bought it would have a house to live in, a verandah to sit out on, a fine teak deck to pace, acres of water to survey, and a suit of sails and a diesel engine to keep him on the move through life. Who could ask for more of Home?

ACKNOWLEDGEMENTS

"A Senior Lectureship" and "Living in London" were first published in *London Magazine*. The two pieces on Byron were published in the *New Statesman* and the *Sunday Times*. The review of John Carey's book on Thackeray was published by the *Sunday Times*, the essay on Henry Mayhew by *Encounter*. Of the three pieces on Trollope, the first comes from the *New Statesman*, the second from *Radio Times* and the third from the *Sunday Times*. "Charles Kingsley" was published by the *New Statesman*, the essay on *Innocents Abroad* as an introduction to the Century edition of the book, the *Huckleberry Finn* piece by *TV Guide*, 'Rudyard Kipling" by the *Observer*, "Max Beerbohm and William Rothenstein" by the *New Statesman*, "V. S. Pritchett" by the *New York Review of Books*. The three pieces on Evelyn Waugh were published, respectively, by the *New Review*, the *New Statesman* and the *Sunday Times*. "Anthony Powell and Peter Quennell" is from the *New Statesman*, "Eudora Welty" and "Saul Bellow" are from the *Sunday Times*. The first Robert Lowell piece came out in the *New Statesman*, the second in the *Observer*; the first Tom Wolfe piece in the *Sunday Times*, the second in the *Observer*. "John Updike" was a *Sunday Times* review.

"Living on Capital", and "Living With Loose Ends" were published by the *New Review*. "Freya Stark on the Euphrates" was an article for *Radio Times*. "Fishing" was run by the *Sunday Times* in their "Pleasures of Life" series.

"The Journey and the Book" was first published, in an abbreviated form, by the *New York Times Book Review*, then, without cuts, by *Quarto*. "Kinglake in the Middle East" was written to introduce the Century edition of *Eothen*. "Stevenson: Sailing Towards Marriage" was an introduction to the Hogarth Press reissue of *The Amateur Emigrant*. "Belloc at Sea" introduced *The Cruise of the Nona* for Century Books, and "Wilson in Europe" introduced *Europe Without Baedeker* for the Hogarth Press. "Young's Slow Boats" and "Priestley and Bainbridge in England" were both reviews for the *New York Review of Books*. "On the Water Margin" was published in *Vole*, "Florida" (i) in the *Sunday Times*, "Florida" (ii) in *Condé Nast Traveler*, "Florida" (iii) in the *Observer*. "Cape Verde Islands" was commissioned – and rejected – by *Geo*, and later published by *City & Country Home* (Canada) and *London Magazine*. Both "Cyclone" and "Sea Room" appeared in *Granta*.